FINAL
DAY

FINAL DAY

10 CHARACTERISTICS OF THE SECOND COMING OF JESUS CHRIST

RICHARD D. WILES

Published in the United States of America by
Great Company Publishing LLC
www.GreatCompanyPublishingLLC.com

ISBN Hardback: 978-164764649-3

The information presented in this book represents the views of the author at the date of publication. This book is presented for informational purposes. The author reserves the right to alter or update his opinions based on new information obtained after the publication of this book. While every effort has been made to verify the information in this book, neither the author or publisher or any distributor assume responsibility for any errors, inaccuracies, or omissions.

The Authorized King James Version of the Holy Bible is the source for all scriptures quoted in this book. Italics added for emphasis.

This book is dedicated to my Savior, the redeemer of my soul. His name is Jesus Christ. He is God in human flesh. As an adopted son in the family of God, I revere and admire Jesus as my older brother, role model, hero, and dearest friend. I'm always bragging about Him because He is the best bro imaginable. My sincerest desire is for you to know Him too. Turn your heart toward home and be reunited with your Heavenly Father. He loves you and desires your presence at the big family reunion He is planning to call together someday. Don't let anything in this world prevent you from attending.

TABLE OF CONTENTS

ACKNOWLEDGMENT

NO WORTHWHILE PROJECT IS accomplished alone. The contributions of many people come together to produce something new that impacts multitudes of people who will never know about the work, sacrifice, time, effort, struggle, and investment that was necessary to make the project a success.

First, I must thank my wife Susan for surrendering 40 weekends in 2019 so that I could devote my time to writing *Final Day*. I must also thank my son Jeremy who, more than any other person in my life, has consistently encouraged me to pursue my passion to write. Because of Jeremy, I was motivated to make a radical change in my daily schedule for nine months in 2019 to write this book and prepare it for publication in January 2020.

Our daughter Karissa and son-in-law Marshall, and our daughter-in-law Tiana and son Jeremy must be thanked too for giving Susan and me 10 awesome grandchildren who are my motivation to take a firm stand for Jesus Christ and His kingdom. I desire them to remember their grandfather as a righteous man who loved God with all his heart, mind, and soul, and refused to compromise the integrity of the Word of God in an age of spiritual rebellion and apostasy. I hope my example emboldens them as adults someday to fearlessly stand upright for God and never bend or back down.

Lastly, I extend my sincere appreciation to all our wonderful team members who performed their duties during my extended absence from our office much of each day throughout 2019. In particular, I especially thank Raymond "Doc" Burkhart for stepping up and managing the day-to-day operations while I was writing; Jody Schlabach and my wife Susan for proving to me that our administrative affairs would not fall apart without my daily presence; and Paul Benson for ably assisting me in building the website and other digital tools for *Final Day*.

One more "thank you" goes to Gator, my 11-year-old Golden Retriever buddy who tirelessly forced himself to sleep next to my feet for nine months as I wrote this book. Most of my time writing was spent in the back yard of our Florida home. Gator and I moved like sundials from one shady spot to another throughout each day. Now that the book is finished, Gator and I can swap places so I can get some rest and he can finally write his very revealing and up-close autobiography *They Treat Me Like a Dog*.

PROLOGUE

THERE ARE TWO ITEMS I desire you, the reader, to know about this book before you turn the page to begin reading.

First, the title *Final Day* is not my attempt to invent and introduce into the Holy Bible a new proper pronoun. It is a two-word literary phrase that encompasses the sign of the Son of man, the last trumpet, the Second Coming of Jesus Christ, the day of the Lord, the darkening of the sun and moon, the extinguishing of the stars, the rolling up of the universe, the shout, the opening of all graves, the taking away of the wicked to be bundled and burned in the lake of fire, the catching up of the dead in Christ, the catching up of those who are alive and remain, the gathering of all humans according to their respective nations, the separation of goats and sheep, the day of judgment, the testing of our works by fire, the creation of a new earth and heavens, the restitution of all things, the arrival of New Jerusalem, and God's relocation from Heaven to New Jerusalem. The Final Day is going to be spectacular! I am so excited and eager for that day to arrive.

Second, Chapter 3 is *His Second Coming Shall be Singular.* The theme is that Jesus Christ shall return to earth once, not twice. Simple enough, right? The truth of His second advent is so obvious that Chapter 3 should be the shortest chapter in this book. My challenge as an author was to write a short chapter that explained why I felt compelled to dispel a pervasive misconception about our Lord's second advent. The misconception is "The Rapture," a mythical event concocted in the mid-1800s by a cultist. Sadly, tens of millions of Christians have been indoctrinated to believe that the return of Jesus Christ will be a two-stage event over seven years.

How do you explain a simple truth to people who believe a complex lie? It's akin to saying the sky is blue and the crowd responds, "It's pink!" How do you explain in a few pages that the sky is blue when your readers have been indoctrinated to suspend reality and believe the sky is pink? It's not easy. Their eyes clearly see that the sky is blue, but their minds have been programmed to believe it is pink.

Furthermore, "The Rapture" is intricately tied, like cancerous tentacles wrapped around vital organs, to numerous other false doctrines propagated by the folks who defend and spread this damnable heresy. These cancerous tentacles include the belief that the Jews must rebuild Solomon's temple before Jesus returns, and the crazy idea that babies will be born on earth after the Lord returns.

Final Day could have been published six months earlier had I not struggled so much with the chapter *His Second Coming Shall be Singular.* I wrote and rewrote the chapter numerous times. I probably have enough discarded material to publish one or two more books on the topic! Finally, under pressure to get the manuscript to the printing company, I wrote Chapters 1 and 2 to briefly explain the origin of "The Rapture" doctrine. God willing, I will produce a documentary film on the topic because the truth must be told. The lie has been permitted to exist too long and expand its domain. It must be confronted, exposed, and shipped back to Hell.

If you are a big fan of "The Rapture" and you idolize the State of Israel, reading Chapters 1 and 2 will be like swallowing horse pills. Have plenty of water on hand and gulp a lot. Eventually, it will go down. Should you find it impossible to digest Chapters 1 and 2, don't quit reading the book. Move on to Chapter 3, finish the book, return to Chapters 1 and 2 and give it another try. Truth is always shocking when you realize you've been fed lies. I know. God took me through a religious deprogramming process years ago and showed me that much of what I had been taught in American Evangelical churches is not Biblical. Those years were painful and unsettling, but I am deeply grateful that God opened my eyes.

I promise that your present understanding of the Second Coming of Jesus Christ will not be the same by the time you finish reading this book. There are some amazing revelations in it. I hope these revelations bless you as much as I was blessed writing the book because the Holy Spirit enlarged my understanding of the Parousia during the writing process. Enjoy!

INTRODUCTION
The True Story Behind The Writing of This Book

DO YOU BELIEVE THE universe had a first day? Do you believe the universe has a final day?

Anything that has a beginning must have an end. This book is about the final day of the cosmos, the earth, and the age of mankind. It is about the last day before the first day of eternity.

I was physically born on August 20, 1953. My body came out of my mother's womb alive, but my spirit arrived DOA - dead on arrival. Nearly 25 years later, my spirit was reborn on June 11, 1978. I was baptized by immersion in a nearby creek on the same day. In my early years as a young Christian, I heard many inspiring sermons about the Second Coming of Jesus Christ. Christians were excited in the 1970s and 1980s about Jesus returning to earth. They were also motivated to finance foreign missionary projects to evangelize lost souls on every continent.

As the years passed by, I detected a cooling of the religious zeal of American evangelical churches. Saving souls was no longer their passion. Evangelists proclaiming the coming of the Lord were replaced by life coaches teaching personal motivation, self-improvement, empowerment, and financial success. Additionally, Zionism crept into many American evangelical churches and introduced idolatry of the State of Israel, and even Kabbalah mysticism. The occult-inspired Star of David replaced the Cross in many churches. Charismatic churches gradually became infested with New Age gurus, pagans, witches, and warlocks serving as self-appointed apostles and prophets. What a mess! The cooling off that started in Evangelical churches in the 1990s eventually became a spiritual ice age in the 21st century.

Meanwhile, the mass popularity of *The Late Great Planet Earth* bible prophecy book and the *Left Behind* novels and films subtly seduced Christians not to yearn for the glorious appearing of our blessed hope Jesus Christ and our resurrection from the grave, but instead, to become obsessed with escaping persecution and tribulation, and transferring our faith in Jesus Christ and His finished work on the Cross to faith in the Zionist State of Israel to save and bless us.

By the 1990s, selling "The Rapture" had become a thriving multibillion-dollar religious business. Pastors, prophecy teachers, and television celebrity evangelists assured Evangelical Christians they would not experience trouble, persecution, or tribulation. The "rapture" would take them away and everybody else will be "left behind." Some rapture enthusiasts even purchased "rapture insurance" policies for their dogs and cats. Such policies guarantee that an atheist or pagan (somebody who will not be raptured away) will take care of the policy owner's beloved pet during the Great Tribulation.

For the reader's benefit, I freely acknowledge that I do not believe in a secret, invisible rapture of Christians seven years before the Second Coming of Jesus; nor do I endorse Christian Zionism. Furthermore, I do not believe a Jewish kingdom in Jerusalem will rule the world for 1,000 years after the Lord returns. If you insist, although I resist, on placing me in a religious box, I am a traditional, orthodox Christian who rejects chiliasm and embraces amillennialism. An amillennialist is a Christian who believes Revelation 20 refers to Jesus Christ ruling and reigning in and through His holy church now in the span of time between His ascension to Heaven and His second coming to earth. Revelation 20's one thousand years refers to an unlimited number of years in the same way that Psalm 50's "cattle on a thousand hills" means God owns all creatures worldwide.

I was saved in an old-time Pentecostal church in 1978. For 20 years, our family attended church congregations affiliated with Church of God (Cleveland, TN), Assemblies of God, the Southern Baptist Convention, and several non-denominational churches along the way. For many years, I identified as an all-American, flag-waving, red-white-and blue patriotic Protestant Evangelical Christian. In other words, I was a proud member of American Babylonian Churchianity. Today, I am no longer associated with it. I left the evangelical plantation decades ago to pursue primitive Christianity. At best, today's American evangelical churches are lukewarm. At worst, they are apostate.

What am I today?

I am a follower of The Way, a disciple of Jesus Christ! I affirm the three ancient creeds of the true apostolic church: The Apostles' Creed, the Nicene-Constantinopolitan Creed, and the Athanasian

Creed. I affirm the seven sacraments of the universal church. I believe confession of faith in Jesus Christ and Trinitarian baptism in water are required for salvation. I also believe in the real presence of Jesus Christ in the Lord's Supper (Holy Communion, the Eucharist, Thanksgiving Feast). I do not believe in transubstantiation and a bloodless sacrifice on a church altar. I agree with my eastern Orthodox brothers and sisters who say that the Lord's real presence in the Holy Communion meal is a "holy mystery" that cannot be understood by human minds. By faith, we simply believe that our Savior is present in the Lord's Supper nourishing our soul with his pure flesh and blood. In this regard, I lean toward traditional, conservative Anglican, Presbyterian, Lutheran, Reformed, and Methodist theology.

I study church history, particularly the ante-Nicene age and the Reformation age. I also collect and read very old Christian books. I see good things in almost all Christian denominations. Most of them began with a holy fire to truly proclaim the gospel of the kingdom and to defend the ancient faith. Along the way, however, doctrinal error crept in, and lukewarm spirituality became the norm. Some became apostate and now ordain homosexual clergy, perform same-sex marriages, promote abortions, deny the divinity of Jesus, and invite witches, warlocks, and pagans to preach and teach in their churches. Such denominations and churches have departed the faith and can no longer be called Christian.

I would readily join a new denomination that cultivates the best statements of faith, traditions, and characteristics of great religious movements in Christian church history. Perhaps they could name it the United Traditional Reformed Anglican, Presbyterian, Wesleyan Methodist, Lutheran, Primitive Freewill Baptist, Holiness Pente-costal, Eastern Orthodox, Holy Apostolic Old Catholic, African

Methodist Episcopal, Evangelical Moravian, Messianic Disciples of Christ Assemblies of God! Forget it. That name won't work. The outdoor church sign would be massive. City governments will never issue permits for church signs that big. The point I'm making is that I find good things in almost all Christian denominations. I can fellowship with members of most denominations and respect our differences.

Regardless, my soul yearns to know, and practice, primitive Christianity as found in the Acts of the Apostles and the writings of the ante-Nicene church fathers. The closer I get to original Christianity, however, the more alien and strange Babylonian Evangelical Churchianity looks to me.

At the time of this book's publication, I have been a born-again Christian for 41 years. The Word of God is a lamp unto my feet. The Bible is my supreme source for God's guidance of my life's affairs. Along the way, God has given me dreams and visions that also gave me direction and/or insight into matters in my life. Indeed, the Lord gave me a dream about the Final Day before I was saved! It motivated me to go to church in 1978 where I heard the Gospel and eventually surrendered my life to Jesus Christ. Someday I will share it in another book.

Twenty years later - 1998 - the Lord gave me another dream about the Final Day.

I was employed as director of marketing for Trinity Broadcasting Network. My office was in Irving, Texas. I loved my job. I loved Texas, barbeque brisket, rodeos, pickup trucks, and Texas sunsets. I was happy! (Did I tell you that I love Texas?) I was traveling around the United States of America meeting with cable television executives persuading them to sign affiliate agreements to carry TBN on their cable systems, overseeing national advertising campaigns, attending national and regional trade shows, and encouraging prestigious trade publications to publish positive articles about TBN. Life could not have been better for me at age 44 as corporate recruiters offered me lucrative marketing management positions with other cable television networks. I was a cocky corporate marketing hotshot and I knew it.

Little did I know that my life would abruptly change.

For weeks in March 1998, the Holy Spirit nudged me to begin a fast. I put it off by telling myself that my business schedule was too full for fasting. Airline travel, meetings, conferences, trade show expos, breakfast meetings, luncheons, dinners with clients filled my calendar. How could I fast meals and do business at the same time? Couldn't the Lord see how busy I was working for Him?

By April 1998, the promptings intensified. I finally succumbed to the Holy Spirit and started fasting in the third week of April. On the third or fourth day of the fast, the Holy Spirit interrupted my business schedule by nudging me to meet Him in TBN's chapel. It was approximately 2PM. I told the office secretary I would be away from my office for 15 minutes. Little did I know how long I'd be in the chapel.

As I walked to the chapel inside TBN's International Production Center in Irving, Texas, an ominous foreboding came upon me. I became aware that my appointment with God would be more than having "a little talk with Jesus." I felt a spiritual heaviness descend upon me. I remember thinking that perhaps God would tell me I had only a few months to live, and I must get my life's affairs in order. By the time I reached the chapel door, I was nervous. I felt like a bad schoolboy on his way to the principal's office to be reprimanded.

The chapel was empty. Let me clarify my statement: There were no humans in the chapel. The room, however, was saturated with the holiness of Almighty God. Immediately, I thought about Isaiah when he was given a vision of God upon his throne.

"Woe is me! For I am lost; for I am a man of unclean lips, and I dwell in the midst of a people of unclean lips; for my eyes have seen the King, the Lord of hosts!" (Isaiah 6:5)

Unlike Isaiah, I did not see God in the chapel. It was his holiness that was present. I felt like Adam: naked, hiding behind a tree, and God asking, "Who told you that you were naked?"

Yes, I was spiritually naked in front of my Maker. I was very aware of my carnal humanity as the Holy Spirit's presence saturated the room. I wasn't gleeful that the Holy Spirit was manifested so strongly in the chapel. Just the opposite! I was trembling that I was a mortal human suddenly in the presence of the Spirit of the eternal living God who formed me in my mother's womb, gave me a soul, breathed life into my nostrils, and keeps my heart beating.

Often, I have heard Christians exclaim how much they wish Jesus would appear and speak to them. Typically, they say, "Oh my, I would shout and jump up and down and dance before the Lord!" Truthfully, that's not what you would do if Jesus walked into a room! Get real! You would fall on your face, shake, and tremble in the presence of Almighty God. Most Christians have little comprehension of the overwhelming holiness of God. They will fully see it on the Final Day.

There I was that day in April 1998: a 44-year-old guy in his prime who was marketing the world's largest religious television network. Suddenly my life flashed before my eyes and it wasn't pretty. I was sadly aware that my life fell woefully short of the glory of God and the heavenly calling in Jesus Christ.

What if it was *my* final day? Was I satisfied with my life? I knew I was saved, but would my works survive the test of fire on the Final Day?

I did a lot of repenting, crying, and pleading for forgiveness. I promised God I would change my ways. I don't recall how much time passed, but I still remember the moment when God forgave me. I truly felt his love restore my relationship with him. All was well again between the Lord and me.

That's when the vision started! It was like a movie screen suddenly appeared in front of me. I was standing there, eyes wide open. I literally saw the heavenly movie screen supernaturally suspended in the air in the chapel!

What movie was showing that day? It was a day of judgment.

The scene was a modern city on fire! Black billowing smoke rose from the city and filled the sky. Skyscrapers were ablaze. Chaos filled the streets. Terrified citizens frantically fled the destruction.

I was never told what happened to the city. I perceived it was terrible and only a remnant of the city's millions of inhabitants survived to tell the story. All of them looked shell-shocked like they had passed through a battlefield and were amazed they were still living. I saw survivors walking through farm fields outside the urban center. They were disheveled. Their clothing was torn and tattered. Their faces were covered with ashes and soot. Many were bleeding. I saw frightened mothers carrying infants in their arms. I saw fathers pulling children in wagons. I saw a man pushing his elderly mother in a wheelbarrow.

The vision ended as quickly as it started.

With tears streaming down my cheeks, I asked God to reveal what I saw in the vision. In my spirit, I heard the quiet, still voice of the Holy Spirit whisper, "This is the future of your sinful nation. Tell the people to repent."

I fell to my knees and wept. I asked God for a Bible scripture verse to confirm the vision was from Him. I opened my Bible and looked down. I was staring at Isaiah 24. Still on my knees, I read the entire chapter.

Behold, the Lord will empty the earth and make it desolate, and he will twist its surface and scatter its inhabitants. (Isaiah 24:1)

Isaiah's prophecy (verses 1-23) is one of the Bible's dual-fulfillment prophecies, meaning it was fulfilled once in the land of Israel, and will be fulfilled again in the last days. It foretells of God's judgment upon mankind's wickedness and rebellion. The "Lord will empty the earth and make it desolate." The stark meaning is God will depopulate the planet. He will remove its inhabitants and take away its bountiful wealth. God will also twist its surface through cataclysmic calamities that disfigure the planet. So great will be the firestorm of judgment that nobody will recognize the planet. Earth will rewind to revert to its original state of darkness without form and void.

But wait! God isn't finished in Isaiah's vision. There's more destruction on the way. First, however, Isaiah told us the cause of the divine judgment. The planet is defiled by the sins of its inhabitants. The people transgressed God's commandments, violated his statutes, and broke His everlasting covenant with them. He is no longer bound to honor it among those who sinned against him. A curse will devour the earth, and the people will suffer for their guilt. They will be scorched. Few will survive the judgment.

The earth mourns and withers; the world languishes and withers; the highest people of the earth languish. The earth lies defiled under its inhabitants; for they have transgressed the laws, violated the statutes, broken the everlasting covenant. Therefore a curse devours the earth, and its inhabitants suffer for their guilt; therefore the inhabitants of the earth are scorched, and few men are left. (Isaiah 24:4-6)

Many bible scholars interpret Isaiah 24 as judgment upon ancient Israel. Some Arabic Christian scholars, however, interpret the "emptying" as the removal of the inhabitants of the whole world by incomprehensible calamities that befall humanity when the seven bowls of God's wrath will be poured upon the wicked.

Then I heard a loud voice from the temple telling the seven angels, "Go and pour out on the earth the seven bowls of the wrath of God." (Revelation 16:1)

Isaiah's vision is in harmony with St. John's vision in the Apocalypse. Isaiah saw the city's commerce disappear in the darkness of judgment. There was no wine, no food, no parties, no music, no singing in the streets. Only sorrow, wailing, and mourning resounded through the desolate city.

St. John saw the sudden destruction of Babylon.

The merchants of these wares, who gained wealth from her, will stand far off, in fear of her torment, weeping and mourning aloud, "Alas, alas, for the great city that was clothed in fine linen, in purple and scarlet, adorned with gold, with jewels, and with pearls! For in a single hour all this wealth has been laid waste." And all shipmasters and seafaring men, sailors and all whose trade is on the sea, stood far off and cried out as they saw the smoke of her burning, "What city was like the great city?" (Revelation 18:15-18)

Still crying, I asked God why He showed these things to me. Again, I heard the gentle voice of the Holy Spirit. He said, "I am calling you today to tell the people to repent."

I reminded the Lord that minutes earlier He chastised me for sinning against Him. I said, "I'm not holy like you. I'm the wrong man for this task. There are other men who are holy whom you can send to tell the people to repent."

The response I heard in my spirit was, "I did not call you because you are holy. I called you because you are a good repenter. When I convict you of your sins, you repent quickly. Go tell the people to repent of their sins. I will forgive them."

I returned to my office and never mentioned the chapel experience to anybody at TBN. I remained quiet throughout the day. My soul was troubled by my encounter with God in the chapel. I did not tell my wife, son, and daughter when I went home that evening.

The next morning our daughter said to me, "Dad, Jesus spoke to me last night." Karissa was nearly 22 years old when this happened in 1998. Surprised by her remark, I asked, "Did you see Jesus last night?" Karissa replied, "No, I was asleep. He came into my room and stood next to my bed and spoke to me in my sleep. I knew it was Jesus standing next to me."

"What did he say?" I asked. Karissa replied, "Daughter, beginning tonight I will speak to you about the last days through dreams and visions."

"Dad, He gave me a dream," Karissa continued with her amazing story. "You, Mom, Jeremy (our son), and I were huddled together as a family. We were surrounded by thousands of people. They were rotating around us like they were standing on a giant moving carousel. Dad, there's something else I must tell you. The people were skeletons! I remember seeing their skulls and peering into their eyeball sockets. They had long bony arms and fingers. They were pointing their bony fingers at you and crying in a loud voice, 'If you knew this was going to happen, why didn't you tell us?' Dad, I don't know what God is telling you to do with your life, but you better do it!"

Stunned by my daughter's dream, I told her what happened in the TBN chapel. I also vowed to God that I would devote the rest of my life to telling people to repent of their sins, believe on the name of Jesus Christ, and get ready for divine judgment to strike the planet. My life was never the same since that day in April 1998.

Over the next months, I privately shared the vision with Dr. Paul F. Crouch in his office. The founder and president of TBN listened intently and respectfully but said little about it. I reasoned that God gave me the vision because Dr. Crouch was too busy building and managing TBN's global affairs, and I was supposed to relay it to him. I foolishly hoped Dr. Crouch would go on his international television program and tell the world to repent, and I could quietly go back to work as a marketing director. After all, I was a business marketing hotshot, not a seminary-trained preacher.

It didn't work out my way. God had a different plan. Eventually, I reluctantly submitted to it.

Once again, the Holy Spirit spoke to me in June 1998. "Write a book titled *Judgment Day*," is what I heard the Lord say.

If you are a parent, have you ever given an instruction to your child and he or she immediately ran off to start the task while you were still describing the instruction? Well, that's what I did to God. I didn't wait for God to finish telling me His instruction. I just galloped off to write the book. I assumed He was pleased with how fast I jumped in to start the assignment. In hindsight, I should have waited upon the Lord in prayer and Bible study before commencing the task. The business world loves self-motivated, aggressive men who don't need supervision. Things get done differently in God's kingdom. Success requires a careful balance between patiently waiting on God and your dogged determination to complete His assignment. Such wisdom comes over time as we age and mature.

In the days after the stunning spiritual experience in TBN's chapel, I pondered in my human, carnal mind what could be a logical explanation for the things I saw in the vision. Cities on fire! Burning skyscrapers! Fleeing refugees! It had to mean that a catastrophic event was on the horizon.

What was the scariest item in the news in 1998? Y2K! Computers were going to crash worldwide at midnight on December 31, 1999 when the calendar turned over to 2000. "Certainly," I reasoned, "this must be the explanation of the vision. God wants me to warn people to prepare for Y2K! The chaos will be judgment."

I immediately went to work researching the dire and ominous Y2K projections and warnings issued by reputable computer IT experts, scientists, government officials, corporate executives, bankers, and military commanders. Newspapers, magazines, and online news websites were warning that "doomsday" was coming to the world on December 31, 1999, when computers rolled over to the new millennium.

The experts warned that computers around the world would crash because they were not programmed to recognize double zeros as a date. They said global havoc would be unleashed. Banking systems would crash. Utilities would cease functioning and cities would be plunged into darkness. Air traffic control systems would go haywire and airliners will crash. Nuclear-armed ICBMs would accidentally launch from silos and kill tens of millions! Such warnings were not imagined and propagated by "conspiracy theorists." These dire doomsday predictions came from many of the world's most educated experts, IT professionals, government officials, military generals, bankers, and economists. They deliberately spread frightening information throughout the world.

What was their motivation? We may never know the answer. Perhaps it was a massive psychological warfare operation to motivate millions of people, corporations, businesses, hospitals, colleges, schools, hospitals, and research centers to download a CIA-approved Y2K patch or upgrade to new NSA-designed computers with pre-installed backdoors that allowed intelligence agencies to snoop on the owners over the next decade. Regardless of the real story behind Y2K, over $300 billion was spent worldwide on remediation efforts to avoid a meltdown. If Y2K was only a conspiracy theory, it was a very expensive hoax.

Regardless, I wrongly concluded that the vision God gave me in April 1998 was a glimpse of the chaos that supposedly was coming on December 31, 1999. Immediately, I galloped off to write the book *Judgment Day* as instructed by the Lord, but I added something to the title. I called the book *Judgment Day 2000*. That was my idea, not the Lord's instruction. I did it all by myself with no help from anybody else. Like many Christians, I did not wait on God for the full instruction, and I added something to it. Whenever we do it, we produce an Ishmael. Giving birth to an Ishmael means making child support payments for years.

14

In August 1998, the Holy Spirit told me that my time at TBN was over. I submitted my resignation letter to Paul Crouch. My last day as TBN's director of marketing was September 8, 1998. I said goodbye to my friends and coworkers. I walked out the door and went to my vehicle in the parking lot. I took a final gaze at the majestic TBN headquarters, drove away and never looked back.

Judgment Day 2000 was published in October 1998. It briefly shot up to the Top 10 best-selling Christian books in America. Something unusual happened one night in October 1998. Earlier that day, my daughter Karissa called to suggest that I attend a town hall meeting about Y2K in Garland, Texas. We were living in Colleyville at the time. I told her I was too busy to drive to Garland for a meeting about a topic I already knew. After all, I wrote a book about it! I was a Y2K expert. Karissa persisted and I relented. I went to Garland and sat near the back entrance of the hotel conference room. Several hundred people were there too.

To my surprise, the moderator had read *Judgment Day 2000* and recognized me. He asked me to stand up and tell the audience about the book. When I sat down, I felt a tap on my shoulder. It was a woman seated behind me who whispered that she had to speak to me immediately. We both went to the hotel hallway. Her name is Leah. (Susan and I are still friends with Leah today.) The well-dressed woman appeared rattled. She nervously said, "I've been praying for you for two years!" I replied, "How could that be so? We are meeting for the first time now." Leah answered, "Two years ago I had a vision of a man sitting at a desk typing a book manuscript on a computer. The title of the book was Judgment Day. You are that man in the vision! I've prayed for two years for you to write the book."

Okay, that was weird too, but it really happened.

Throughout the remainder of 1998 and the first five months of 1999, I crisscrossed America speaking to audiences in hotels, meeting halls, and churches, including a tour for Stan Johnson's Prophecy Club which was flourishing in the 1990s. I told them about the vision and pleaded with them to repent of their sins. I paid my way by draining down the $52,000 in our savings account that Susan and I had accumulated to purchase a house in Texas.

Besides my public speaking engagements, many radio talk show hosts interviewed me in late 1998 and early 1999. One day in April 1999, the manager of a popular religious radio station in Dallas-Ft. Worth called me while I was in a hotel room during a speaking engagement in another city. He asked if I ever thought about hosting a radio show. I told him the thought never occurred to me and I wasn't interested. He politely insisted that we should meet when I returned to DFW.

We eventually met and he offered me an hourly weekday slot at 7:30AM. As a marketing professional, I knew that 7:30AM was drivetime when millions of people were in their cars and trucks commuting to work. Ah, but there was a catch! It was paid programming time. I had to buy the airtime. It was nearly $7000 per month. And the station's terms required cash up front each month! In 1998, seven thousand dollars per month was a lot of money to a guy who was no longer employed in business! I also had a problem. The $52,000 in our personal savings account was nearly depleted. I had lived on it since resigning from TBN nine months previously. I self-published the book too. I financed my travel expenses, including a trip to London, with profits from book sales, thus I kept nothing for myself. There was no way I could sign a legally binding 12-month contract and tap the last remaining dollars to pay the first installment of $7,000 for the radio show.

God, however, had a plan. The man who hosted the Y2K meeting in Garland the previous year invited me to lunch. We met at a barbeque restaurant along TX-183 somewhere between Euless and Haltom City. My friend invited one of his friends to join us. Near the end of the lunch, my friend asked me to share with his friend the opportunity to host a radio program. I did, and he asked me what I would say on the radio show. I told him I would tell people to repent of their sins and believe on the name of Jesus Christ. He asked me if I planned to accept the radio station's offer. I replied that I did not have the personal finances to pay for a weekday show. The businessman also asked me how much I needed to get started. The luncheon ended. We exchanged business cards and went our separate ways.

The next day the businessman who joined our lunch meeting called and asked me to visit his office in Fort Worth. He said he would not be there, but his secretary had something for me. I drove to his office that afternoon and introduced myself to his secretary. She smiled and handed me an envelope. I thanked her and went to my vehicle. I opened the envelope and found a check for $7,000 and a note from the man that said, "Start the radio show."

Amazed by the miraculous appearance of the money, I promptly called the radio station manager and agreed to start the weekday radio show. The first broadcast was May 24, 1999. The broadcast was called *America's Hope*. My daily message was "Jesus Christ is America's only hope."

Weeks before the launch of the radio show, our son and daughter each entered a British Airways contest. They both won!

Jeremy and Karissa each received two free roundtrip tickets to Europe. God generously gave us a memorable 2-week family vacation in Great Britain, France, and Switzerland before starting a new adventure as a radio talk show host. We returned from Europe on May 22, 1998. I vividly remember saying to God, "I am not afraid of work. Work me hard for Your kingdom." Be careful what you say to the Lord. He took me up on the offer. I have never stopped working hard for Him. He's taken me to Africa, Europe, Asia, Central America, Latin America, and the Caribbean representing His kingdom. What an adventure! And what a privilege!

To my utter surprise, the show was an immediate success. People responded to the message of repentance. The audience size soared throughout the summer of 1999.

In early June 1999, the Holy Spirit instructed me to say on the radio program for 90 days, "Judgment starts in America on September 11." I did not know the meaning, but I obeyed and said it many times over the next three months. Because Y2K was on its way, many radio listeners assumed it meant September 11, 1999. But the Lord never said the year - only the month and day. "Judgment starts in America on September 11."

By September, the radio station manager was transferred to another station in Denver. An acting manager assumed management of the Dallas radio station. Because I did not own a production studio, hosting the show required me to drive each morning in heavy rush hour traffic to Dallas to produce it live from the radio station's studio. One morning in September 1999, the acting manager was waiting for me to exit the studio. She wanted to talk privately with me. I followed her to an empty office where she hesitantly gave me the bad news. The station's wealthy owner had decided to change the station's format and, therefore, was cancelling all religious programming in 30 days despite having legally binding contracts. My world collapsed. Two weeks prior to the cancelation notice, I confidently signed real estate agreements to purchase a house under construction and a small older office building. I used a "creative financing" idea on both sellers and it worked. Both contracts were 90-day leases starting on October 1 with the closing date on December 28, 1999.

I knew the radio cancellation was not a surprise to God. He inspired me to purchase both properties, told me what to offer, and gave me favor with the sellers. Surely God had a plan. Once again, my inner man heard God's voice gently speak: "I will stretch your faith. I will build a studio for you. I will take your ministry nationwide."

Thirty days later, *America's Hope* signed off the Dallas radio station. I earnestly sought God for direction. The Holy Spirit gave me another instruction: "Go on international shortwave radio and the Internet." The instruction did not make sense to me as a media professional. Shortwave radio broadcasting was a World War II technology that was losing its aging audience and Internet audio streaming had few users. Certainly, I reasoned, this plan would not work.

I had no choice. I was off the air and quickly going broke. It was sink or swim. I decided to swim by faith.

We moved into the small office building that we purchased on a 90-day lease-to-buy deal. I had three months to find the money to pay for it! The same thing for the house I acquired. The office building was an old house that had been converted to a daycare center. The carpets reeked with pungent odors of urine and vomit. To me, it was a palace! We were excited to have a headquarters for the ministry. My son Jeremy and I ripped out and replaced the old stained carpet, painted all the rooms, and made other upgrades. Within weeks, we had a nice facility.

Jeremy and I also constructed a studio in a small room approximately the size of a walk-in closet. We used leftover new carpet to soundproof the walls. Mike, a friend, donated a vintage 1960s-era AM radio studio audio control board from a station he previously owned. There was enough money in our account to purchase a high-quality broadcast microphone for $500. We were in business again! America's Hope was streamed "live" during the day on the Internet, and we posted MP3 audio files on our website for audio-on-demand listening. I was podcasting before there were pods! (The iPod was invented in 2001 and the term "podcasting" wasn't coined until 2004.) We also covered North America and Western Europe every night via our international shortwave radio broadcast.

Remarkably, our radio program found an audience on shortwave radio and the Internet in late 1999. We benefited from the sizeable audience in North America that was still listening to world news programs on the BBC's shortwave transmissions. Sufficient donations arrived each week to keep the lights on, but not much more.

Y2K fizzled and life went on. The remaining inventory of *Judgment Day 2000* books went to the landfill. The last five chapters of *Judgment Day 2000* were the only chapters worth reading. They were prophetic warnings of impending judgment on America because of rampant sin. In hindsight, I should have published a five-chapter book. Decades later, a five-chapter version would still be relevant.

Regardless, I put on my big boy pants and carried on despite the post-Y2K ridicule directed at me. Nobody blamed the "experts" who said doomsday would happen on December 31, 1999. The public only mocked the people who believed the experts and reported what they said. Life is not fair.

Twenty years after writing Judgment Day 2000, the Holy Spirit inspired me to write another book. I drafted the chapter outline in 2018. I started writing this book in February 2019. The original working title was "10 Characteristics of the Second Coming of Jesus Christ." I knew the working title was too long, but the core of my focus was the Lord's return. What will happen on that day?

The official title came to me on Monday March 25, 2019. I taught from this book's unfinished manuscript the previous Sunday evening at the church where I am a presbyter and teaching elder. (For the record, I am a Bible teacher, not a preacher.) In my sermon, I told the congregation that there have been many "day of the Lord" events in history. For example, the day of the Lord arrived suddenly and unexpectedly for the inhabitants of Sodom and Gomorrah. In a similar way, the day of the Lord arrived in 70AD when the Romans captured Jerusalem and destroyed the Jewish temple. You could say Pompey had a "day of the Lord" experience too.

The day of the Lord is a sudden and unexpected visitation by God to strike a city or nation with divine judgment after repeated prophetic warnings failed to change the hearts of the inhabitants. The population is always forewarned that a day of the Lord will spring upon them if they refuse to repent of their sins. God patiently pleads with inhabitants of a city or nation to change their ways. He repeatedly sends prophets and watchmen to warn them. Eventually, God's patience runs out and he visits them with sudden destruction. Although God often declared his intentions to judge their sins, his visitation was unexpected because the people did not believe God would do what he threatened.

At the conclusion of my sermon on March 24, 2019, a member of our ministry team made a comment to me. Edward Szall is currently a co-host of Trunews, the weekday Christian newscast that started in Dallas/Ft. Worth in 1999 as *America's Hope*. Edward said something that changed this book. He said, "As you were teaching, I was thinking that the book you are writing is about the last day of the Lord." His words resonated with my spirit. I thought about them that night. The next morning, I heard the Holy Spirit say to me, "The book's title is Final Day."

Four weeks later, which was the third week of April 2019, another revelation came to me. That week was the 21st. anniversary of the vision in TBN's chapel. I'm referring to the vision of a burning city, God's call to me to preach repentance, and my daughter's dream about the skeletons asking me why I did not warn them. The vision is what inspired me to write a book in 1998. As I explained earlier in this Introduction, the Lord told me to call it Judgment Day. I foolishly added the year 2000 to the title. I also erroneously focused on Y2K as the logical explanation of the vision I saw in TBN's chapel. I was wrong. God desired me to write a book about the one and only Judgment Day for the entire world, but I messed up the instruction.

In the third week of April 2019, I heard the Holy Spirit speak inwardly to me, "You are now writing the book you were meant to write in 1998."

This book is about the Final Day. It is the last "day of the Lord." I've done my very best to get it right this time. I hope my Heavenly Father is pleased with this book. I love him very much.

Maranatha! O Lord, come!

CHAPTER 1

ARE YOU A MEMBER OF A RELIGIOUS CULT?

WOULD YOU JOIN a religious cult? Most people would emphatically reply, "No!"

Yet, tens of millions of Evangelical Christians, primarily in the United States of America, have been unknowingly indoctrinated with the false doctrines of a 19th century religious cult. The cult is as deceiving as Mormonism and Jehovah's Witnesses, two other religious cults that were also founded by Kabbalistic Freemasons in the 19th century.

What is this cult?

Let's call it "The Rapture" cult. Its father created a proper pronoun – "The Rapture" – and brazenly convinced Christians that the proper pronoun is in the Holy Bible even though nobody can see the words! The doctrine teaches that Jesus will tiptoe secretly from Heaven to Earth and instantly snatch away millions of Evangelical Christians without the other seven billion humans seeing Him do it! He will come back seven years later and whack everybody who was "left behind" except for the people who changed their ways when they realized their mama was right about "The Rapture."

Perhaps you are a member of a church that teaches "The Rapture," but privately you can't find it in the Holy Bible. Relax! There's nothing wrong with you. "The Rapture" is not in the Bible. That's why you cannot see it. Magical glasses are necessary to make the invisible ink appear on the pages of your Bible!

Most likely, you are reluctant to admit to your pastor that you can't find "The Rapture" in the Bible because he'll make you feel like a spiritual dwarf. The reason he'll belittle you is because inwardly he fears you're going to pull back the curtain and discover the biggest hoax in the history of Christianity. The Great Rapture Oz is a big phony! If you will allow this book to pull back the curtain in your mind, you'll see that The Great Rapture Oz is nothing more than Kabbalah Freemasons scheming to rebuild Solomon's Temple so that they can acquire Babylonian hidden knowledge and openly worship Lucifer, the one whom they believe is the source of their illumination.

"The Rapture" cult emerged in the 1830s in Great Britain and grew slowly throughout the 19th century. It developed a foothold in America in the late 1800s and early 1900s. The Rapture cult took off like a rocket in the 1970s when Hal Lindsey co-authored and published *The Late Great Planet Earth*. A second booster rocket propelled The Rapture cult into orbit in the 1990s with the wildly successful *Left Behind* series of fictional novels and films coauthored by Tim LaHaye and Jerry Jenkins. The cult's doctrines are now settled law in tens of thousands of churches in the 21st century. Few clergy and members dare to question the origin of "The Rapture" doctrine. They simply assume that all Christians in every nation have always believed it.

Is Your Brain Infected with The Rapture Cult's STD Virus?

Have you ever attended an Evangelical Zionist church service? What about religious media? Have you watched religious television shows or videos? Have you listened to religious radio shows or podcasts? Have you attended an End Time prophecy conference? What about prophecy books? Have you read any about the Last Days? Does your church have a Star of David flag on the stage? Does your pastor wear a Star of David neck chain or lapel pin? Does your pastor invite Israel Defense Forces military representatives to speak in your church about the necessity of supporting the State of Israel? Did you visit Theodor Herzl's grave during a tour of Israel? Do you wear a Jewish prayer shawl when praying to God?

Most likely you have a STD virus lodged deep in your brain. That's a Spiritually Transmitted Doctrine. You can easily be exposed to one or more STDs by attending Evangelical Zionist church services, accessing Evangelical Zionist religious media content, and reading Evangelical Zionist books. The cult's deceptive messages are everywhere in the Christian world, particularly the United States of America. "The Rapture" is spiritual syphilis. Left untreated, syphilis can inflict serious damage to a victim's heart, brain, and eyes. Likewise, "The Rapture" syphilis will damage your spiritual eyesight, heart, and mind. The uncompromised Word of God is the penicillin needed to cleanse your mind, body, and soul of the virus. Make an appointment with Doctor Jesus. Ask Him to vaccinate you with truth. It's your protection from "The Rapture" virus circulating in the religious environment around you.

One indicator that a cult has taken over a church is when no other views about the Second Coming of Jesus are permitted to be studied or even discussed. Church members who question the cult's doctrines are typically ostracized and oftentimes asked to leave the congregation. Pastors who stray from the cult's doctrines can quickly find their ministerial credentials revoked by the cult's pharisees. The cult is not nice. It will aggressively defend its turf, especially its lucrative business of selling books, films, and conferences that promote the cult's doctrines. "The Rapture" is a multi-billion-dollar industry. Thou shall not touch "The Rapture" golden goose, nor its golden eggs.

This book has a name for the cult's convoluted menagerie of heresies, lies, deceptions, and kooky beliefs. Their theology is DPPZism (dip-zee-ism). Cult fanatics are DPPZites (dip-zee-ites).

DPPZ (dip-zee) is an acronym for Dispensational, Pre-Millennial, Pre-Tribulational, Zionism. It would take one or more additional books to delve deeply into the fallacies of the cult's eschatology, but it isn't necessary. Why scuba dive to the bottom of a septic tank to analyze what's in it? The septic tank and DPPZism are both full of rancid fecal matter.

Why are we talking about a religious cult? What does this have to do with the topic of this book? Everything! The minds of millions of Evangelicals have been captured by a wicked force that is diabolically opposed to Jesus Christ and His kingdom. The cult's Freemason ringleaders, masquerading as Evangelical prophecy teachers and mega-church celebrity pastors, are devoted to a future Masonic Kabbalah Zionist Kingdom.

"The Rapture" cult is a Masonic Kabbalah sect that captured control of Evangelical churches in the 20th century and fundamentally altered the core tenets of the ancient Christian faith. DPPZism is not simply another point of view about the End Time. The once-great Evangelical churches were gradually infiltrated by a foreign agent that changed the way Evangelicals think, speak, and perceive the Christian faith. For over a century, the cult has been injecting a deadly poison into the Body of Christ that must be eradicated with the penicillin of truth.

Are you shocked that Satan purposefully infiltrated Evangelical churches to change the Gospel? The churches are still evangelizing, but it's not the Gospel of the kingdom of God that they are spreading. Instead, they are evangelizing the world with a Jewish Kabbalah Freemason gospel that seeks to build a temple in Jerusalem for their god Lucifer so that he can rule the world as he did before Noah's Great Flood. The wickedness of that culture is what finally compelled God to flood the planet with water and kill every human and animal except Noah, his family, and the animals onboard the ark. Jesus said His second coming shall be as the days of Noah. Behind-the-scenes, the Freemason-Kabbalah cult is excited that their god Lucifer will be released from his chains to roam the earth again to deceive the nations before Jesus returns to establish His kingdom that shall have no end.

This does not mean every pastor and member of churches controlled by the cult are Freemasons. It means that their minds have been captured by Freemason deceivers hiding behind church pulpits, hosting prophecy shows on religious media outlets, writing prophecy books, and speaking at prophecy conferences. Sadly, there are many good, honorable, conscientious men serving God as pastors of churches who do not know that they too were indoctrinated by Freemasons in Bible colleges, seminaries, and denominational training centers. Such pastors are regurgitating Masonic doctrines that were deceptively taught to them as the true Gospel. Thank God that your eyesight can be restored once you identify the hidden hand behind the propaganda and deception. Thereafter, you will speedily discern lies and recognize truth. The spiritual syphilis can be expelled from your mind and spirit and transform you into a mighty warrior for the kingdom of God.

"The Rapture" cult is not Christian. It functions and expands through mimicry. The cult is a clever imposter that lures people into its lair because it mimics Christianity. It acts like ransomware on computers by encrypting important files and slyly renaming them without the owner noticing the changes. If left undetected, the ransomware will eventually seize control of the entire computer. Likewise, "The Rapture" cult has been slyly encrypting Biblical doctrines for over 100 years and renaming them as they seek to take control of the worldwide Church in anticipation of the return of their god Lucifer.

The father of the cult was John Nelson Darby. More about this skillful deceiver will be revealed later in the next chapter. He was the leader of the Plymouth Brethren sect in Great Britain. His flock never amounted to much in size, but Darby won the top prize in Hell's "Best Deceiver" contest in the 19th century. Satan found a winner when he latched on to John Nelson Darby, a man whose deception did immeasurable damage to Evangelical churches.

Darby excelled at gathering assorted heresies and false doctrines and assembling them into a coherent systematic theology that could be taught to others. His claim to fame was the invention of

Dispensationalism. He came up with that whopper all by himself. He stitched it to Pre-Millennialism, a variation of another heresy formerly known for centuries as chiliasm (pronounced kilee-azam). Darby sewed Dispensationalism and Premillennialism to Pre-Tribulationism, a new heresy among some 19th century Pentecostals that caught his attention. Finally, he glued all three heresies to Zionism, a political movement of radical Marxist Communist Jews to establish a Zionist political state in Palestine. Shazam! Darby conjured up a new religion. It shrewdly supplanted the Apostles' Doctrine and the Nicene Creed in Evangelical churches.

Here is a brief description of the four pillars this religious monstrosity stands upon.

- DISPENSATIONAL: Darby audaciously invented Dispensationalism in the 19th century whereby he arbitrarily divided world history into seven "dispensations" of time. DPPZites teach that God interacted differently with mankind in each dispensation (age) as compared to other dispensations. Each dispensation is administered in a separate way, and humans in each age are held responsible by God as stewards of their dispensation. The seven dispensations are Innocence, Conscience, Human Government (or Noahide Laws), Promise, Law, Grace, and Millennial Kingdom. DPPZites teach that mankind is presently in the Dispensation of Grace, also called "the Church age" and the "time of the Gentiles." Darby's last dispensation on his prophetic timeline is a Jewish-controlled "Millennial Kingdom," which is the sole purpose of DPPZism.

- PREMILLENNIAL: DPPZites retrieved from the ecclesiastical trash bin an old and rejected heresy called chiliasm (kilo – meaning one thousand). Using chiliasm as their base, they constructed an elaborate, complex eschatological edifice entirely upon a literal interpretation of the 20th chapter of the Revelation of Jesus Christ, and a thoroughly mangled misinterpretation of Daniel 9:24. Pre-Millennialism is the doctrine that says the Second Coming of Jesus Christ will precede the establishment of a Jewish kingdom on earth that will rule the world for 1,000 years.

- PRE-TRIBULATIONAL: For Kabbalah-Masonic Jews to be in control of the world, DPPZites had to find a way to get Gentile Christians off the planet. They conveniently invented a new proper pronoun and arbitrarily inserted it in the Bible: "The Rapture." In the same manner that he invented Dispensationalism, the father of DPPZism proposed a radical new concept never heard previously in the history of Christianity. The devilish deceiver taught his disciples that the return of Jesus Christ will be a two-stage event spread out over seven years. First, "The Rapture" (the removal of Gentile Christians), followed by the Second Advent of Jesus (the establishment of a Jewish kingdom) which will occur after seven years of Great Tribulation. No apostle, bishop, presbyter, or theologian in the history of the glorious Church of Christ taught that Jesus Christ will return twice at the end of the age.

- ZIONISM: This is the Mega-Lottery Jackpot in DPPZland. The winner takes all. The grand prize is total control of the world for a thousand years with millions of goyim worker bees serving the Freemason-Kabbalah-Zionist empire. Darby argued that Israel and the Church were two separate religious entities. DPPZism teaches that the Jews are God's true covenant people who will inherit all the promises God made to Abraham, and the Church is a temporary stop-gap entity that God had to create to fill in the time between the Jews' rejection of Jesus at His first advent and their acceptance of Jesus at His second advent. In Darbyland, Christians go to Heaven and the Masonic Jews go to the bank to get the deed to the entire world.

Who Are the DPPZ Virus Carriers?

"The Rapture" cult is a very American Evangelical thing. Presently, approximately 228 million Americans identify themselves as Christians. Among them, approximately 35% - roughly 90 million Americans – identify as Protestant Evangelicals. That's a sizeable portion of the American population. It is miniscule, however, compared to the 2.2 billion Christians in the world. Despite their vocal and visible presence in American society, U.S. Evangelicals represent less than four percent of the worldwide population of Christians! "The Rapture" is popular in the USA, but almost unknown around the world except in cities where American Evangelical missionaries have planted churches to spread the doctrine and where U.S. religious media ministries have penetrated other nations to spread the Kabbalah-Masonic propaganda.

Darby's DPPZism is now the dominant theology in most Evangelical denominations, churches, and ministries. Many Evangelical denominations that started in the late 19th century or early 20th centuries were originally led by great soul-winning pastors, evangelists, and Bible teachers. As is too often the story, they lost their way over time and strayed into doctrinal error or outright apostasy. Gradually over decades they morphed into Evangelical Zionist denominations, churches, and ministries. Today they worship a two-headed goat god: "The Rapture" and the Zionist State of Israel. You cannot separate the two heads. They are attached together at the idol's neck like Siamese twins. If you eliminate "The Rapture," you no longer need Zionism. If you detach the Zionist head, there's no useful purpose for "The Rapture" head. Both heads nourish the idol with deceived souls.

Who are these two-headed goat god idol worshippers? The Who's Who of America's Religious Right, the most famous faces or voices on religious television and radio presently living or deceased, are now or were priests in the Masonic Temple of the Two-Headed Goat God. Where can they be found? Evangelical Zionists are found mostly in Southern Baptist, independent fundamentalist Baptist, Pentecostal, Charismatic, Hebrew Roots, Messianic Judaism, and non-denominational churches primarily in the United States of America and in other countries where Evangelical Zionist zealots have planted churches.

Prominent and influential Evangelical Zionist denominations that worship the two-headed goat god idol ("The Rapture" and Zionist Israel) include the Southern Baptist Convention, the Assemblies of God, the Church of God (Cleveland, TN), Calvary Chapel, the Church of God in Prophecy, and the International Pentecostal Holiness Church. Most of the biggest non-denominational churches in the USA also bow to the two-headed goat god. Many influential seminaries and Bible colleges enthusiastically teach "The Rapture" and Zionist Israel including the Dallas Theological Seminary, Moody Bible Institute, Bob Jones University, Liberty University, and The Master's Seminary. Furthermore, most religious media ministries in the United States of America, such as TBN, Daystar

Television, God TV, CBN, The Word Network, Moody Radio, and AFA Radio are staunch defenders of "The Rapture" and the Zionist State of Israel.

Are there Christian denominations and churches that do not worship the two-headed goat god? Yes, most churches in the world do not bow down to it! Conservative Lutheran, Anglican, Presbyterian, Methodist, Reformed, Orthodox (Greek, Russian, Syrian, Eastern, Assyrian, etc.) and Catholic (Roman, Melkite, Maronite, Armenian, Malabar, Ethiopian, Syriac, Coptic, Ethiopian) affirm the traditional doctrine that Jesus Christ will return to the earth one time. That does not mean, however, that Freemasons have not infiltrated those denominations too. If the truth would ever be revealed, the Church of England probably is tied with the Southern Baptist Convention for the number of Freemasons among their ranks as clergy and members. Likewise, Jesuit Freemasons clandestinely walk the streets of Vatican City as Cardinals and Archbishops worming their way deeper into the Roman Catholic Church even though the RCC forbids Catholics from joining Masonic lodges.

Take the DPPZ Quiz!

"The Rapture" cult's ludicrous claims are crazier than an out-of-control Mr. Toad's Wild Ride at Disneyland. You may be shocked to discover what your church and favorite Bible prophecy teachers truly believe about the End Time. How many cult doctrines are embedded in your mind? Are you ready to take the quiz?

Comedian Jeff Foxworthy hilariously entertained audiences in the 1990s with a country comedy routine titled *You Might be a Redneck*. His *You Might be a Redneck If* album sold more than three million copies. Mr. Foxworthy's comedy routine was outrageously funny. Some of his memorable quotes are:

- If you've ever made change in the church offering plate, you might be a redneck.
- If you ever mowed your lawn and found a car, you might be a redneck.
- If your dad walks you to school because you're in the same grade, you might be a redneck.
- If you ever got too drunk to fish, you might be a redneck.
- If you've ever financed a tattoo, you might be a redneck.

What if there was a *"You Might be a DPPZite If"* quiz? What questions would be asked to discern whether a person is a DPPZite? Let's find out how much DPPZism is stuck in your brain.

You might be a DPPZite if…

- You believe God divided human history into seven dispensations (ages).
- You believe Jesus Christ failed in His mission to give the kingdom to the Jews.
- You believe God called "time-out" when Jesus failed, and He switched His attention to a plan to save Gentiles while He waited on the Jews.
- You believe the Church is a parenthesis (time out or gap) on God's prophetic calendar.
- You believe God's prophetic timeclock stopped in the 69th week of the fulfillment of Daniel's prophecy when the Jews surprised God by rejecting Jesus as their king.
- You believe that the Church and Israel are two separate entities.
- You believe the Jews are still God's chosen people despite their rejection of Jesus Christ.

34

- You believe Jews represent all 12 tribes of Israel.
- You believe Lord Balfour was led by the Holy Spirit in 1917 to issue the Balfour Declaration.
- You believe the United Nations' establishment of the State of Israel in 1948 was a prophetic act of Almighty God.
- You believe Jews have a legal right to reclaim all the land that the Israelites possessed over 3,000 years ago in King David's kingdom.
- You believe there was never a place called Palestine.
- You believe most Palestinians are Muslim terrorists who want to kill Jews and destroy Israel.
- You believe Palestinians are obligated to abandon their homes, farms, and lands and surrender their properties to Jews because the land rightfully belongs to Jews today.
- You believe Jews have the right to use military force to compel Palestinians out of their homes and off their land.
- You believe Palestinians who are injured, wounded, or killed while refusing to voluntarily surrender their homes and lands to Jews must accept responsibility and blame for whatever injuries they suffered because the Jews have a right to take their properties by whatever means necessary.
- You believe the Star of David is an authentic Biblical symbol used by King David.
- You believe the Hebrew language spoken today is the same language spoken by ancient Hebrews thousands of years ago.
- You believe the Jews must return to Israel before Jesus can take Christians away in "The Rapture."
- You believe the State of Israel is a vital indicator on God's prophetic timeclock, and that Christians should watch what

is happening in Israel to know God's plans for the end of the age.

- You believe Christians are obligated to bless Jews and the State of Israel.
- You believe people who criticize Jews and the State of Israel will be cursed by God.
- You believe there is a Bible scripture that says, "whoever blesses Israel is blessed by God and whoever curses Israel is cursed by God."
- You believe the United States of America has suffered calamities and disasters because political officials sometimes made decisions that were not in the best interests of the State of Israel.
- You believe in The Rapture.
- You believe Jesus will come first for the Church in the Rapture and return seven years later in the Second Coming.
- You believe non-Christians will be left behind on the earth after the Rapture.
- You believe there will mass chaos on the earth after the Rapture (meaning panic caused by the instantaneous disappearance of millions of Christians).
- You believe God's prophetic timeclock will be restarted when the Rapture happens.
- You believe there will be a powerful ruler on the earth called The Antichrist.
- You believe The Antichrist will be assassinated by a wound to his head but will come back to life.
- You believe there will be a time known as The Great Tribulation.

- You believe The Great Tribulation begins immediately after the Rapture of Christians.
- You believe the duration of The Great Tribulation will be seven years.
- You believe The Rapture marks the beginning of the fulfillment of Daniel's 70th Week.
- You believe Daniel's 70th Week and The Great Tribulation are synonymous
- You believe The Antichrist will impose a one-world government, a one-world religion, and a one-world currency.
- You believe the Roman empire will be revived.
- You believe the European Union is the revived Roman empire.
- You believe there is a massive super-computer hidden in Brussels that is storing data on every Christian in the world.
- You believe that the Roman Catholic Pope will be the false prophet during The Great Tribulation.
- You believe a big, tall golden statue known as the Image of the Beast will instantly start talking and walking when The Antichrist supernaturally imparts life into it.
- You believe that Christians are God's "heavenly people."
- You believe that Jews are God's "earthly people."
- You believe the Holy Spirit will be taken from the earth during or after the Rapture.
- You believe exactly 144,000 Jewish male virgins will start preaching throughout the world immediately after the Rapture.
- You believe many people "left behind" after the Rapture will be saved through the preaching of the 144,000 Jewish male virgins.

- You believe the Christians (heavenly people) who go up in the Rapture will wait in Heaven for seven years during The Great Tribulation.
- You believe the Islamic mosque currently on the Temple Mount must be destroyed to make room for the Tribulation Temple.
- You believe that a Tribulation Temple must be constructed on Jerusalem's Temple Mount before Jesus can return to the earth.
- You believe a spotless red heifer will appear as a divine sign that the time has arrived to offer animal sacrifices in the new Tribulation Temple.
- You believe The Antichrist will enter the Tribulation Temple three and a half years after the Rapture, declare himself as God, and thus fulfill the role as the abomination of desolation.
- You believe two humans will be special witnesses for God, they will be killed, their bodies will lie on a street in Jerusalem, and suddenly, on live worldwide television, the two men will come back to life and ascend to Heaven.
- You believe The Antichrist will trick the State of Israel into signing a peace treaty that he intends to violate.
- You believe The Antichrist will surround the State of Israel with a vast army to destroy it and kill all the Jews.
- You believe there will be a War of Armageddon fought at Megiddo.
- You believe Jesus will return at the last minute in the War of Armageddon to save the Jews and the State of Israel from being destroyed.

- You believe Jesus will establish in old Jerusalem a kingdom that will rule the world for 1,000 years.
- You believe Jews will manage the kingdom government for Jesus.
- You believe the altar in the temple in Jerusalem will be the center of mankind's worship during the Millennial Kingdom.
- You believe the Levitical order of the sons of Zadok will be reinstituted to provide a priestly ministry in the temple.
- You believe that Jews must reinstate the system of sacrificing animals in the temple.
- You believe prescribed rituals will be required for the cleansing of the altar.
- You believe morning sacrifices will be offered daily in the temple.
- You believe observances of new moon and sabbath days will be required during the Millennial Kingdom.
- You believe the Jewish Feast of Tabernacles will be observed during the Millennial Kingdom.
- You believe Passover will be observed during the Millennial Kingdom.
- You believe the Year of Jubilee will be observed.
- You believe Jewish priests shall issue regulations that will govern the manner of dress and lifestyles during the Millennial Kingdom.
- You believe the priests shall enforce the Noahide Laws during the messianic Millennial kingdom.
- You believe the city of New Jerusalem will hover in the atmosphere above old Jerusalem for 1,000 years.
- You believe God's heavenly people (Christians) will live

in New Jerusalem above the earth during the Millennial Kingdom.

- You believe the people saved during The Great Tribulation are called Tribulation Saints.
- You believe the Tribulation Saints will not receive glorified bodies when Jesus returns.
- You believe Tribulation Saints will live in their mortal physical bodies in the Millennial Kingdom.
- You believe Tribulation Saints will continue to sin in the Millennial Kingdom because they will still dwell in mortal bodies.
- You believe many Tribulation Saints and their offspring will have to be restrained by Jesus' rod of iron.
- You believe Tribulation Saints will marry and have children during the Millennial Kingdom.
- You believe Millennial Kingdom children and their offspring will be born with Adam's fallen nature; thus, they too will sin during their lives in the Millennial Kingdom.
- You believe Tribulation Saints and their offspring will physically die during the Millennial Kingdom.
- You believe there will be funerals and cemeteries on the earth during the Millennial Kingdom.
- You believe Tribulation Saints and their offspring who die during the Millennial Kingdom will be resurrected at the end of the thousand years.
- You believe Tribulation Saints and their offspring born during the Millennial Kingdom will receive their glorified bodies at the end of the Millennial Kingdom.

- You believe Satan will be released from the bottomless pit near the end of the Millennial Kingdom to deceive the nations again.
- You believe many Tribulation Saints' offspring will join Satan in a final rebellion against God.
- You believe the Gog and Magog War will be a final battle between God and Satan near the end of the Millennial Kingdom.
- You believe all unsaved sinners who died from the beginning of time to the Second Coming will not be judged until the end of the thousand years.
- You believe God will not destroy the earth by fire but will refurbish the old earth.
- You believe New Jerusalem will descend to the refurbished earth at the end of the Millennial Kingdom.
- You believe "heavenly people" (Christians) and "earthly people" (Jews) will live in New Jerusalem for eternity.

Escape "The Rapture" Cult

Congratulations if you answered "no" to all or most of the DPPZ Quiz statements. It means you have little DPPZ virus lurking in your brain. If, however, you answered "yes" to most of these statements, it means "The Rapture" cult has sunk its talons deep inside your head. You need deliverance from deception. There is hope for you. Your Heavenly Father desires to set you free from the cult. Somehow the Holy Spirit got this book into your hands. It will explode in your head like a truth bomb.

This book was written to help you escape "The Rapture" cult. This book's message is the Final Day is coming! The cult's message is "The Rapture" is coming. Forget "The Rapture." It isn't real. It's a hoax. Do you see the subtle deception? Jesus desires you to focus on His second coming, but the Evangelical Zionists want you to focus on an imaginary event. There's only one main attraction on God's calendar of events. It is the glorious appearing of the King of Kings and Lord of Lords.

If you swallowed the cult's magical potion, your spirit, mind, and body have been lulled into a false security that prevents you from preparing your soul for the Final Day. Consequently, many people foolishly anticipating "The Rapture" may lack the extra oil needed for their lamps when the midnight cry is heard that the bridegroom is on His way. Consequently, they will stumble in the darkness, arrive late, discover the door closed, and read a sign that says, "Go away!" Only those who endure to the end shall be saved.

On the surface, the cult is full of smiley faces welcoming you to fellowship with them. Their lodges have friendly pastors, comfortable foyers with fresh coffee and sugary donuts, wonderful programs for children, captivating teachers, talented musicians and singers, and the best fried chicken dinners in town. And the pastors even cancel worship services one Sunday night per year so men can watch the Super Bowl on the lodges' big digital screens! Once inside, the cult will infect your mind and soul. Eventually, "The Rapture" deception will rob you of your identity in Christ as the true Israel of God, the elect, a chosen generation, a royal priesthood, a holy nation, a peculiar people saved by God to praise Him for calling you out of spiritual darkness into His marvelous light.

As you read this book, your mind and soul will be refreshed with an exciting revelation of the magnificent simplicity of the Lord's return. The Second Coming of Jesus Christ is not a mystery that requires religious oracles to decipher hidden mysteries and secret codes in the Bible. There are no mysteries in the Bible. God desires you to understand the Bible for your personal spiritual growth so that you will be ready for the Resurrection and Judgment Day. Your Heavenly Father desires you to escape the clutches of "The Rapture" cult and live an enjoyable, peaceful, productive life as a Christian eagerly waiting for the Second Coming of Jesus Christ and the Resurrection, never fearing you will miss "The Rapture" and be "left behind."

CHAPTER 2

THE RAPTURE'S OCCULT ORIGIN

WHO CONJURED UP THIS crazy cult? You're going to be stunned when you discover the dark, occult history of "The Rapture" cult. Although there were many men and women, such Reverend Dwight L. Moody, who were involved in the formation of the cult along the way, this chapter will focus on the two men who were vitally instrumental in making the cult what it is today. Without them, "The Rapture" would not be known today. Those men were John Nelson Darby, an Irish Anglican priest, and Cyrus Ingerson Scofield, a man who missed his calling in life to be a snake oil salesman in an Old West traveling medicine show.

Darby began introducing his strange doctrines into some churches in Great Britain in the early 1830s. He dominated Great Britain's Plymouth Brethren movement. Darby's bizarre doctrines, however, remained quarantined in Great Britain for decades even though Darby made trips to America looking for new fields to sow his tares.

Two men who gladly received his tares were Dwight L. Moody and Cyrus I. Scofield. Moody built a Bible college to teach Darbyism. Scofield went ever farther! He inserted Darbyism in the Holy Bible.

Scofield was a flimflam man who always seemed to be outrunning Kansas and Missouri law enforcement officers to escape jailtime. Always scouting for his next hustle, he re-invented himself by becoming a Bible prophecy expert. After Darby's death in 1882, Scofield eagerly plagiarized Darby's weird teachings and brazenly inserted them in an annotated Holy Bible as his prophecy notes in what he called the Scofield Reference Bible. Backed by the money and prestige of Oxford University Press, the publishing arm of a university infested with Freemasons, Scofield mass marketed Darby's heresies to Evangelical churches throughout America. More than any other single man or woman, Scofield transformed them into Evangelical Zionist churches.

Origin of Darby's Plymouth Brethren Cult

If you desire to pinpoint the place and time "The Rapture Cult" was conceived and born, your quest will take you to Plymouth, England in the 1830s. Prior to Plymouth, however, an earlier group met in homes in Dublin, Ireland, in the 1820s to pray, receive Holy Communion, and study Bible prophecy without the spiritual oversight of Church of Ireland priests. There was nothing wrong with studying the Bible, praying, and receiving Holy Communion. The error was they did it in rebellion to their church overseers without their approval and spiritual covering, thereby they acted as seditious schismatics. Like so many private Bible studies in homes without pastoral oversight, the Dublin group quickly went awry. The culprit was John Nelson Darby, a disgruntled Church of

Ireland priest who quickly seized control of the Dublin group to make them his flock.

In December 1831, a similar group of dissatisfied Anglicans left the Church of England to start a nonconformist assembly known as Providence Chapel in the city of Plymouth. They were known to local citizens as the "Providence People." They later became known as the Plymouth Brethren. One of the participants was Benjamin Newton. He heard about John Nelson Darby's nonconformist meetings in Dublin. In 1832, Mr. Newton and Mr. Darby resigned their priestly positions in their respective Anglican churches. Mr. Newton viewed Mr. Darby as his mentor, and Mr. Darby viewed Mr. Newton as his disciple.

Originally, the Plymouth Brethren were united by four common beliefs:

- They rejected all clergy. The "true church" had no deacons, presbyters, and bishops. (Darby and his disciples were schismatics because they rejected all ecclesiastical authority. Darby, of course, demanded obedience from his followers!)
- They believed local churches should be governed by unpaid elders.
- The Lord's Supper should be received weekly.
- Brethren must separate from the world. Therefore, the Brethren could not be members of denominational churches, nor participate in any armed forces.

The Plymouth Brethren tightly limited the group's membership to whom they considered as true "brethren." According to William Blair Neatby, author of the 1901 book *A History of the Plymouth Brethren*, "A circle was to be drawn just wide enough to include 'all the children of God,' and to exclude all who did not come under that category." It didn't take long for the sect to split. The circle was drawn even tighter. In Mr. Darby's eyes, not all Brethren were created equal. Some were more illuminated than others. By 1848, there were two competing groups: The "Open Brethren" and the "Exclusive Brethren." The Exclusive Brethren faction was led by argumentative John Nelson Darby. His fanatical "exclusive" disciples were known as Darbyites. It was Darby's way or the highway. Members who disagreed with him were told to hit the road and not come back. Mr. Darby accepted no other views about the Bible and prophecies other than his own. Darby-the-schismatic who rejected all church authority was also Darby-the-autocrat who demanded total allegiance to his views. Darby's divisive and argumentative DNA was passed on to the cult's gene pool and is deeply embedded in today's Evangelical Zionist churches and clergy. If you want to see Darby's ugly spirit come out, tell a Southern Baptist or Charismatic that "The Rapture" is a hoax and the Church is true Israel. Be prepared for the fireworks!

How fanatical was Darby? When his longtime disciple and friend Benjamin Newton dared to publicly disagree with Darby's End Time doctrines, the teacher scorched his pupil with public humiliation. A major point of disagreement was Darby's insistence that Christians would be removed from the earth in a secret "rapture" before the start of tribulation. Newton taught the Plymouth Brethren that the Bible does not mention anything remotely close to a secret, pre-tribulation rapture of Believers. Darby was furious. For his crime of "heresy," Newton was excommunicated from the Plymouth Brethren. Today's Christian Zionist pastors and prophecy teachers behave like Darby. Church clergy and members must accept "The Rapture" or leave their churches.

Darby prohibited Newton from receiving Holy Communion until he publicly repented of the sin of disagreeing with Darby about "The Rapture." When the Plymouth Brethren refused to bow to Darby's demand, he split the movement into "Open" and "Exclusive' groups. Darby was the undisputed grand poohbah of the "Exclusive Brethren." Thereafter, Darby would only fellowship with "Exclusive" Brethren who strictly adhered to his fanatical views about the Last Days.

John Nelson Darby and his Darbyites arrogantly proclaimed that they were recipients of divinely inspired "recovered knowledge" and new revelations about the Last Days and the Second Coming of Jesus Christ. They foolishly and arrogantly believed God chose Darby and the Exclusive Plymouth Brethren to reveal truths about the Second Coming of Jesus that the Creator kept hidden from His church for over 1800 years.

A Man is Known by His Enemies

There's truth in the adage that you can know a lot about a person by the enemies he or she makes in life. John Nelson Darby had enemies. His most fearsome critic was Reverend Charles Spurgeon, the legendary 19th century Reformed Baptist pastor whose eloquent sermons thundered from the pulpit of London's Metropolitan Tabernacle.

For the record, Pastor Spurgeon was a classic Millennialist. He believed there would be a literal 1,000-year Christian kingdom on earth after the Second Coming of Jesus. He vehemently opposed Darby's Jewish-centric Millennial Kingdom eschatology. Rev. Spurgeon believed the kingdom was meant for Christians only, and to be ruled by Jesus Christ for His glory. He did not believe

Darby's nonsense about Tribulation Saints, Millennial Kingdom babies, a Tribulation Temple, and animal sacrifices. Such talk was blasphemy in the ears of the fiery soul winner.

The great Reformed Baptist preacher used his powerful pulpit and influential *The Sword and the Trowel* magazine to denounce Darby and his gang as a mean-spirited religious cult. Ironically, today many Evangelical Zionists speak glowingly about Charles Spurgeon's ministry, yet are unaware or deliberately conceal Spurgeon's vehement repudiation of Darby's heretical doctrines.

Darby and his disciples developed a reputation for being rude, unreasonable, obnoxious, and confrontational. Reverend Spurgeon viewed Darby and his disciples as mean-spirited cultish heretics. One day in 1867, a Plymouth Brethren cultist left a small tract at the door of Pastor Spurgeon's Tabernacle. The London preacher said the tract was "so devoid of all sense, Scripture, and reason, that it needs no reply." Rev. Spurgeon also sarcastically wrote that his church had long ago learned the unpleasant lesson that "the unpardonable sin is declared to be speaking against the Darbyites."

Pastor Spurgeon denounced the Darbyite rapture cult as cruel, heartless, without feelings, and selfish. He blistered Darby and the Plymouth Brethren in his *Sword* and *Trowel* magazine published in June 1869:

"Plymouth Brethren have no feeling wherever their principles are concerned. I know indeed of no sect or denomination so utterly devoid of kindness of heart. It is the most selfish religious system with which I am acquainted. It is entirely wrapped up in itself. It recognizes no other denomination, whether the Church of England, or either of the Nonconformist denominations, as a church of Christ. Mr. Darby has again and again said in print, as

well as written in private, that those who belong to his party in the metropolis, constitute the only church of Christ in London..."

Spurgeon also blasted Darby's "unbearable" arrogance. He called Darby the "Protestant Pope" who claimed infallibility in all matters of sound doctrine:

"The Brethren look upon all other denominations, however evangelical in sentiment, and however high their standard of personal religion, as so largely infected with error in doctrine, as well as wrong in relation to church government, that they believe it would be sinful to associate with them for the promotion of religious ends. And this conviction, which is never absent from their minds, naturally has the effect of puffing them up with spiritual pride. Believing that they alone of all religious bodies have attained to the knowledge of the truth, it could hardly be otherwise than that they should look down on every other Christian sect with supreme pity, mingled, even according to the admission of some of their own number, with contempt....." (*Sword and Trowel*, June 1869)

If Charles Spurgeon were alive today on the earth, he would not qualify for ministerial ordination in most Evangelical Zionist church denominations - including the Southern Baptist Convention, the Assemblies of God, the Church of God (Cleveland), and Calvary Chapel. Furthermore, Rev. Spurgeon would not be permitted to preach in most Evangelical Zionist churches, nor would he be allowed to host a television or radio program on religious media outlets. Why? Charles Spurgeon's voice would thunder from his pulpit and pen that the Darby Deception introduced strange, new doctrines: "The Rapture" and the separation of the Church and Israel. Rev. Spurgeon correctly taught his Reformed Baptist church members that Jesus Christ will return once, not twice. Unlike Darby, Spurgeon could count.

The Rapture's Connection to Occultism

John Nelson Darby was born in his father's house in London on November 18, 1800. He was the youngest son of John and Ann (Vaughan) Darby. Young John's middle name Nelson was given in recognition of Vice Admiral Horatio Nelson, a close family friend. John Nelson Darby's uncle was Admiral Henry D'Esterre Darby.

The Darby family owned a castle in Leap, Ireland that was built by the O'Bannon clan sometime around the year 1250. Touted as the most haunted castle in Ireland, its chapel is known as "Bloody Chapel" because Mulrooney O'Carroll, a Catholic priest, was murdered in the chapel at the altar in 1532 by his brother while the priest was conducting the Catholic mass.

The first Darby to own the castle was Jonathon Darby II, a Cromwellian soldier who acquired the property in 1649 in lieu of payment for his military service. When he was 15 years old, John Nelson Darby's family moved into the Darby ancestral castle in 1815 which was owned at the time by his uncle Henry D'Esterre Darby. Seances were held in the Darby family castle, and an elemental demon known as "It" often made appearances. Mildred Darby, John Nelson Darby's sister-in-law, told the Occult Review journal in 1909 that "It" was the size of a sheep, thin, gaunt, and shadowy. She described it as repulsive and devilish. The frightening demon had an "inhuman" face, partially decomposed eyeballs in black cavities, blueish-gray hands, loose slobbery lips, a thick saliva-dripping jaw, dark coarse hair, claw-like fingers, and a sickening odor like a nauseous decomposing corpse.

"It" was not the only demon who lived in the Darby castle. The Red Lady ghost, described as a tall, menacing woman dressed in scarlet, walked the castle's halls carrying a sharp dagger.

Using the pen name of Andrew Merry, Mildred Darby authored the book *The House of Horrors*. It was her first-hand account of living in the Darby castle. For the sake of protecting family members, she used pseudonyms for relatives and changed the castle's name from Leap to Kilman. Her dramatic narrative described the hideous foul-smelling elemental demon, a shrieking banshee, ghosts, and sounds of phantom battles on the castle grounds. According to Mildred, the Darby Castle was occupied by more than Darby family members. She described a thing that slept on beds and snored, a burly man dressed in rough clothing like a peasant who pushed a heavy barrel up the stairs near the servants' bedroom and then rolled it back down the steps, and a monk with a tonsure who walked in and out of windows in the Priest's House.

Darby family members were necromancers. John Nelson Darby's sister-in-law Mildred dabbled in the occult, conducted seances, and channeled automatic writings from spirits.

There shall not be found among you anyone who makes his son or his daughter pass through the fire, or one who practices witchcraft, or a soothsayer, or one who interprets omens, or a sorcerer, or one who conjures spells, or a medium, or a spiritist, or one who calls up the dead. For all who do these things are an abomination to the Lord, and because of these abominations the Lord your God drives them out from before you. (Deuteronomy 18:10-12)

Workers discovered a dungeon during renovations of the Darby castle in the early 1900s. It was hidden behind a wall in Bloody

Chapel. At the bottom of the dungeon's shaft were piles of human skeletons amassed on wooden spikes. It took three cartloads to remove the human bones. It is believed that victims fell through a trap door to be impaled on the spikes eight feet below. A pocket watch dated to the mid-1800s was found in the dungeon among the skeletons, thereby indicating the Darby family's death dungeon was still in use in the mid-19th century when John Nelson Darby was traveling and speaking as a prophecy expert. No need to worry, folks. Every family has some skeletons in their closet, right?

With a family history rich in dark occultism, it is not surprising that John Nelson Darby – the father of "The Rapture" doctrine – peppered his religious writings with esoteric, Masonic, occultic words and phrases. There is ample evidence to accuse Darby of syncretism, the merging of conflicting religious beliefs to form a new religious philosophy. Darby's writings are liberally sprinkled with words and phrases that have strong theosophical, occultic, Kabbalistic, and/or Masonic connotations. These words and phrases in Darby's writings include:

- Heavenly Architect
- The Absolute
- The Coming One
- The Divine Mind
- Divine Intelligence
- Vital Force
- Divine Energy
- Divine Essence
- Master of the Masters
- Divine principle
- Divine doctrine

- Energy of faith
- Energy of love
- Lord of love
- Secret wisdom of God
- Unintelligent energy

John Nelson Darby's Connections to Freemasonry and British Intelligence

Some Darby critics suspect he was a British intelligence operative used to promote in churches the Crown's Masonic agenda to establish a Zionist Jewish state in Palestine. Indeed, one of Darby's closest friends and disciples was a spy for the Crown. Robert Anderson was a British intelligence officer, Assistant Commissioner of the London Metropolitan Police (Scotland Yard), and a high-ranking Freemason. Anderson's brother Samuel was also an intelligence officer for the Crown. Robert Anderson, Darby's close friend and fellow Dispensationalist, was the top Scotland Yard investigator in the notorious Jack the Ripper murder mystery.

In the book *Jack the Ripper: The Final Solution*, published in 1976, investigative author Stephen Knight postulated that the five murders were an elaborate conspiracy involving the British royal family and Freemasons. It was suspected that Darby's disciple Robert Anderson, a Freemason and intelligence agent, deliberately botched the Scotland Yard investigation of the Jack the Ripper murders on orders from the Crown and Britain's aristocracy. Other Freemasons involved in the alleged cover-up included Sir William Gull, the Royal physician, and Prince Albert Victor, the Duke of Clarence.

Anderson's boss at Scotland Yard was Sir Charles Warren, also a high-level Freemason. Approximately 20 years prior to the

Jack the Ripper murders, Warren led the Palestine Exploration Fund's expedition in 1869 to Palestine to acquire the Moabite Stone and take it to England. Moab was Lot's son and Abraham's nephew. King David's great-grandmother Ruth was a Moabite. The Moabites' religion, language, and culture closely mimicked the true Hebrews. Their god, however, was Chemosh, not Yahweh. Solomon populated his harem with Moabite concubines, and he erected a shrine to Chemosh on the outskirts of Jerusalem. Dibon was the ancient capital of Moab. Reverend F.A. Klein, an Anglican medical missionary in Palestine, was led by Bedouin nomads in the summer of 1868 to the Moabite Stone in Dibon, now known as Dhībān in west-central Jordan approximately 20 miles east of the Dead Sea. The stone bears a 34-line inscription of Mesha, king of Moab, that commemorates his victory over the Israelites that reestablished the independence of Moab. Also known as the Mesha Stele, the ancient stone is presently on display in the Louvre Museum in Paris, France.

Sir Charles Warren, Scotland Yard supervisor of Darbyite Robert Anderson, was initiated into Freemasonry in 1859 and was involved in numerous lodges in various regions of the British empire including Gibraltar. An earnest seeker of Babylonian hidden knowledge, Warren excavated underneath Jerusalem's Temple Mount and surveyed Herod's Temple (1867 to 1870). A Royal Engineers' lieutenant-colonel, Warren authored a Masonic research paper that he read to his fellow Masons in March 1887 titled *The Orientation of Temples*. His archeological excavations in Jerusalem and research at the Dome of the Rock earned Warren recognition as an expert on the ancient Jewish temple. He wrote numerous books including *Underground Jerusalem, The Temple or the Tomb*, and *The Survey of Palestine: Jerusalem*. Warren served as president of the Palestine Exploration Fund. The archeological research organization's funding came from the British Crown, the Rothschild family, the Church of England, and the United Grand Lodge of England. The United Grand Lodge is the mother lodge of worldwide Freemasonry.

Warren's driving motivation was to discover archeological evidence to prove that Freemasons participated in the construction of Solomon's Temple, hence, to establish the existence of Freemasonry in Biblical times. Such evidence would also bolster efforts by radical Zionists to destroy the Islamic mosque on the Temple Mount and replace it with a third Jewish temple. Nicknamed "The Mole," Warren excavated and explored many tunnels and chambers below the Temple Mount as he searched for Masonic and Knights Templar artifacts and engravings.

Warren convened a Masonic ritual in a cavern deep underneath Jerusalem known as King Solomon's Quarry. It is also known as Solomon's Cave, Zedekiah's Cave, Korah's Cave, and the Haunted Cave. The cave's entrance is beneath the Old City wall between the Damascus and Herod Gates. It is part of the largest underground quarry in Jerusalem. In ancient times, it stretched from the Garden Tomb (Jesus' burial tomb) to the walls of the Old City. Except for the cave's mouth, the quarry was chiseled by men. Beyond the cave's entrance is a massive 300-foot wide auditorium. Droplets of spring water trickling through the ceiling are called "Zedekiah's tears" because King Zedekiah used the quarry as his escape route when he attempted to flee from Babylonian King Nebuchadnezzar's invaders who eventually captured him as he exited the cave.

It was discovered in 1854 by Dr. James Barclay when his dog, chasing a fox's scent, vigorously dug the dirt with his paws and disappeared into a hole near Damascus Gate. Dr. Barclay and his two sons returned that night dressed in Arab clothing and carrying candles to explore the cave. Immediately the three men came upon a very deep pit which contained a human skeleton with a fractured skull. They also startled a large colony of bats.

Charles Warren, the Freemason archeologist and Royal Engineer, was excited when he saw the underground chambers were the product of human quarrying, thus evidence that stone masons had chiseled out huge blocks of rocks to form the walls of the cavern. For Warren, the unusual symmetrical patterns and chisel marks were proof that Solomon's workers were Freemasons.

Freemasons believe King Solomon used the quarry as the source for white Melekeh (royal) limestone for the temple. In 1873, French archeologist Charles Clermont-Ganneau discovered in Solomon's Quarry a carving of a Biblical cherub with long wings, a curled tail, and bearded human head wearing a headdress.

Dr. Robert Morris, former Grand Master of the Grand Lodge of Kentucky, visited Jerusalem in May 1868 and met with Warren. The British archeologist proposed that they convene a Masonic meeting deep underground as close as possible to the Temple Mount, known to Muslims as the Haram esh-Sharif (the Noble Sanctuary).

The consensus among Freemasons is that Warren held the Masonic ritual in Zedekiah's Cave and used a stone pillar that protruded out of the ground as their ritualistic altar. According to Masonic records, a British naval vessel had arrived earlier in Jaffa. The captain and several officers were Freemasons. Dr. Morris invited them to attend the Masonic ritual in the degree of Secret Monitor in Zedekiah's Cave on May 13, 1868. Other prominent Freemasons who attended included Noureddin Effendi, Governor of Jaffa, a 28th degree member of a lodge in Paris; Harry Petermann, the Consul of Prussia in Jerusalem; R. Beardsley, the American Vice-Consul from Elkhart, Indiana. The impromptu Masonic ritual led to the eventual formation of the Royal Solomon Mother Lodge No. 293 on February 17, 1873.

Starting in the days of the British Mandate in the 1920s after the Balfour Declaration, Zedekiah's Cave was used for convocations to advance Masons to the Mark Master degree. Jews were blocked by the Arab Legion in 1948 from conducting Masonic rituals in the cave when war broke out after the European Ashkenazi Jews declared the establishment of the State of Israel in Palestine. Nineteen years later, Freemason rituals resumed in the cave in 1967 when the Zionist Jews captured East Jerusalem. Two years after seizing control of Jerusalem, Jewish Freemasons conducted the Consecration of the Supreme Royal Arch chapter of the State of Israel on July 2, 1969. The Grand Lodge of Israel continues to hold Masonic rituals in Hebrew and English several times each year in Solomon's Quarry, also known as Zedekiah's Cave.

Warren, who later was appointed as Scotland Yard commissioner, also co-founded and served as the first Worshipful Master of the Quatuor Coronati Lodge Number 2076 (The Four Crowns Lodge), a London lodge dedicated to Masonic research endeavors. The lodge's other co-founder was Albert Edward, Prince of Wales, later King Edward VII, who was also the Grand Master of the powerful United Grand Lodge of England. Officially chartered in 1886, the lodge's inaugurating speech was titled, *Freemasonry as Seen in the Light of the Cabala*" (Kabbalah). The lodge's purpose was to establish a Jewish state in Palestine and to rebuild Solomon's temple. Sir Walter Besant was also a founding member of the lodge and treasurer of the Palestine Exploration Fund. His sister-in-law was Annie Besant, the successor to Helena Blavatsky, the queen of 19th century occultism, as president of the Theosophical Society.

Warren's deputy Robert Anderson retired as Scotland Yard deputy commissioner in 1901 and was appointed Knight Commander of the Order of the Bath. British intelligence agent and Freemason Anderson had a close friendship with Darby and was a member of Darby's Plymouth Brethren congregation. Anderson authored over 20 religious books that promoted John Nelson Darby's heresies. *The Coming Prince* is hailed by modern-day Darby DPPZites as the all-time classic defense of Darby's heretical teaching that Old Testament prophet Daniel's 70th week has been held in suspended animation for several thousand years and will not be fulfilled until after "The Rapture." Another highly esteemed Anderson book among DPPZites is *The Gospel and Its Ministry*. Yes, religious books written in the 19th century by a high-level Freemason, British intelligence agent, and close associate of occultist John Nelson Darby are still read today by Evangelical Zionists who promote "The Rapture" and adoration of the State of Israel.

Intelligence agent Anderson was closely associated with other prominent early advocates of Darby's heresies, including Cyrus Scofield, Moody Bible Institute president John Martin Gray, and E.W. Bullinger, an Anglican ultra-dispensational theologian. Bullinger, who rejected as necessary the sacraments of water baptism and the Lord's Supper, was a close friend of socialist Theodor Herzl, the founder of modern Zionism. Bullinger's views were so extreme that fellow Darby DPPZite Reverend Harry A. Ironside branded Bullinger's theology as an "absolutely Satanic perversion of the truth." Bullinger was a member of the Universal Zetetic Society, a 19th century precursor to the Flat Earth Society.

Evangelical Zionist hero Lord Balfour was a Necromancer

The Anderson brothers' careers as British spies and their membership in Freemasonry, along with the possibility that Darby was also an intelligence agent and Freemason, is relevant because Britain controlled Palestine and Transjordan in the early 20th century under the Mandate for Palestine adopted by the League of Nations in the aftermath of World War I. Zionist Jews and Evangelical Zionists revere the Balfour Declaration that was issued on November 2, 1917, by the British government that announced support for a Zionist state in Palestine.

The Balfour Declaration was a letter from U.K. Foreign Secretary Lord Arthur Balfour addressed to Lord Walter Rothschild to be distributed to the Zionist Federation of Great Britain and Ireland. Walter Rothschild, whose family has deep roots in Freemasonry, was a friend of socialist Theodor Herzl, who is revered as the founder of the Zionism. Balfour served as prime minister of the United Kingdom from 1902 to 1905, and as foreign minister from 1916 to 1922. Evangelical Zionist pilgrims typically pay homage to Herzl by visiting his grave during tourist trips to the Holy Land. Ask any Evangelical Zionist who has been to Israel whether he or she visited socialist Herzl's grave. It's a "must stop" on the itineraries of most Evangelical Zionist tours of Israel.

Lord Balfour, the man who wrote the infamous Balfour Declaration, was the president of the Society for Psychical Research while he was a member of Parliament. The Society was founded to investigate paranormal, supernatural, psychic, and parapsychological phenomena. Balfour, the hero of modern Zionists, participated in ghoulish seances that attempted to communicate with the spirits of dead people. The Bible calls it necromancy. For the record, it is a big sin.

His obsession with necromancy was inspired by the death of a woman he deeply loved. Balfour intended to propose marriage to Mary Catherine Lyttleton, but she fell ill and died suddenly on Palm Sunday, March 21, 1875, before Balfour could ask her to marry him. Grief stricken, the author of the famous Balfour Declaration idolized by today's Evangelical Zionists, never married and spent the next 55 years until his death in 1930 attempting to communicate with deceased Mary's spirit in the afterworld. Thousands of fragmentary messages acquired by mediums through automatic writings were gathered and analyzed over decades. Balfour went to his grave heartbroken that he never communicated with his beloved Mary. Among occultists, it is known as the Palm Sunday Case.

Arthur Balfour was not alone in his family practicing necromancy. Numerous members of the prominent Scottish family shared his morbid obsession with ghosts and talking to dead spirits. Eleanor Mildred Balfour was a leading figure in the Society for Psychical Research. Her husband Henry Sidgwick was a founding member and the first president of the Society. Sidgwick started a committee in the Society to research the mediumistic claims of Madame Helen Blavatsky, founder of the Theosophical Society. Sidgwick was a member of the committee and funded a trip by Richard Hodgson to India to investigate Blavatsky's occult activities in the Asian country. Henry and Eleanor (Balfour) Sidgwick also led a Society committee that studied ghosts and apparitions. The committee surveyed 17,000 people, of which 1,684 claimed to have experienced encounters with paranormal apparitions. Their work was published in 1886 in the journal *Phantasms of the Living* by Edmund Gurney, F.W.H. Myers, and Frank Podmore.

Henry and Eleanor (Balfour) Sidgwick were also fascinated and impressed by the paranormal activities of Eusapia Palladino, an Italian medium. Palladino practiced seances, materialization, levitation, and rapping (knocking noises used by demons to announce their presence). In 1894, the Sidgwicks were members of a Society team that observed Palladino practicing her witchcraft. The Italian medium claimed that her "controller" was the spirit of John King, a deceased pirate. The demonic spirit first identified himself to her when she sat at a séance table. The spirit remained in control of Palladino's life until her death in 1918. Henry Sidgwick was also fascinated by the supernatural powers of Leonora Evelina Simonds Piper. Born in New Hampshire in 1859, Piper communicated with dead spirits and practiced automated writings.

Other Balfour family members involved in paranormal activities included Gerald William Balfour, the second earl of Balfour. He too was a member of the U.K. parliament (1885-1906). He joined the Society for Psychical Research in 1893 and served as the Society's president in 1906 and 1907. His focus was on studying cross-correspondences. Correspondences are associations between symbols, names, objects, and forces that are used in magic rituals. Correspondences are prominent in Jewish Kabbalah in which every letter of the Hebrew alphabet corresponds to spirits, colors, ideas, perfumes, and gems. For example, a Jewish Kabbalah wizard can translate the name of a spirit into a formula to make a perfume that can be used in magic rituals that will entice the spirit to communicate with the wizard. Gerald Balfour's sister, Evelyn Balfour Strutt, was married to Lord Rayleigh, 3rd Baron Rayleigh of Terling Place. His full name was John William Strutt. He was a Nobel-Prize winning physicist and an active member of the Society. Francis Balfour, Arthur's younger brother, was a respected biologist who conducted paranormal research, participated as a medium in attempting to communicate with Arthur Balfour's deceased girlfriend, and participated in cross-correspondences with spirits.

The Darby PK Who Went to Hell

Almost all church members have heard stories about PKs – preacher kids – who strayed away from their father's church and the Christian faith. Often, those stories have a happy ending when the pastor's wayward son or daughter spiritually returns home to a solid walk with Jesus Christ. There wasn't a happy ending, however, for the son of a Darbyite preacher who, as a child, heard Darby preach about "The Rapture", Daniel's 70th Week, the Great Tribulation, a Tribulation Temple, the Antichrist, and Israel. After Darby's death, the boy's father continued Darby's legacy by preaching Darby's Dispensational, Pre-Millennial, Pre-Tribulation, Zionism heresies. The ending to this PK story, however, is downright wicked. One of the rotted fruits of John Nelson Darby's ministry turned out to be the most notorious Satanist in modern times. This is the true story of the preacher's kid who literally went to Hell.

Edward Crowley, a former Quaker, was a traveling Plymouth Brethren preacher in Great Britain in the late 1800s. His wife was Emily Bertha Bishop. She gave birth to a son in 1875. His name was Aleister. Mother Crowley nicknamed her son "the Beast." Little

Aleister grew up in a strict Exclusive Brethren household where he was taught the rigid tenets of Darby's Evangelical Zionism.

Aleister "the Beast" Crowley later renounced his parents' Plymouth Brethren cult and devoted his life to the darkest of all cults - Satanism. Crowley, who called himself "The Great Beast," was a Freemason and practitioner of Jewish Kabbalah, and was known as "the wickedest man in the world." His first and second wives went insane, and five of his mistresses committed suicide. Crowley's picture appeared on the cover of the Beatles' *Sergeant Pepper's Lonely Hearts Club Band* album, and Crowley's haunted Scottish estate – the Boleskine House – on the southeast side of Loch Ness, was owned by Led Zeppelin guitarist Jimmy Page from 1970 to 1992. Page developed a fascination with the occult at age 15 when he read Crowley's *Magick in Theory and Practice*. Page credits Crowley as the inspiration for Led Zeppelin's music, especially its Led Zeppelin IV album that featured the hit song *Stairway to Heaven*.

Crowley's personal secretary and protege was Israel Regardie, a fellow practitioner of the occult. Francis Israel Regardie was born to Jewish parents who immigrated from Ukraine to London. At age 16, his sister introduced him to the writings of Helena Blavatsky, the Russian-born occultist who founded theosophy. Blavatsky was the queen of 19th century occultism. She believed all modern-day religions originated from an ancient global religion that possessed secret knowledge of ancient wisdom. Blavatsky's Theosophical Society's emblem was a six-pointed star like Zionism's occult-inspired "Star of David" symbol.

In 1921 the Regardie family moved from London to Washington, D.C. Young Israel read books in the Library of Congress about Hinduism, theosophy, and Kabbalah. Approximately six years later, he read *The Book of the Law* by Aleister Crowley, the Satanist whose father was a preacher for John Nelson Darby's Plymouth Brethren cult. Regardie wrote to Crowley, the Master of Darkness. Crowley, also an alleged British spy, invited Regardie to join him in Paris and serve as his personal secretary. Regardie spent the next four years as Crowley's underling. During this time, the young Jewish occultist co-authored *The Legend of Aleister Crowley*, and joined Stella Matutina, the successor to the Hermetic Order of the Golden Dawn. Crowley had been a member of the Order of the Golden Dawn, a secret society devoted to the practice of the occult, mysticism, and necromancy, and the inspiration for 20th century Wicca. The magical order was founded by wicked Freemasons William Woodman, William Westcott, and Samuel Mathers. The secret society was structured like Freemasonry and had three orders. Members of the first order were introduced to Jewish Kabbalah. Members in the second order practiced astral travel, alchemy, and scrying (psychic seeing, peeping, prophesying). Men in the highest order directed members of the two lower orders through spirit communication.

Aleister Crowley's protégé Regardie retired in 1974 and lived out his final years in Sedona, Arizona. Just before his death in 1985, Regardie prophesied by the secret ways of the Golden Dawn that Western Civilization would be destroyed in the Northern Hemisphere in the coming decades.

Every Christian who believes in "The Rapture" and supports the ministries of prominent Evangelical Zionists must recognize that "The Rapture" doctrine, Zionism, support for the State of Israel, and support for the building of a third temple in Jerusalem are deeply rooted in occultism, Jewish Kabbalah, and Freemasonry. Millions of Evangelicals have been hoodwinked by Satan and his loyal deceivers. Once you know the truth about Darby, Scofield, Balfour, Zionism, and the State of Israel, a Christian truly committed to Jesus Christ cannot continue to believe and teach the Made-in-Hell eschatology. Do you sincerely believe that Almighty God used occultists, necromancers, swindlers, liars, deceivers, Kabbalah wizards, wicked rabbis, and Freemasons to do His will?

Rapture STD Virus Transported Across Atlantic

Using the proven tricks of his trade, Satan, the crafty deceiver, used cultist John Nelson Darby to plant false doctrines in American Evangelical churches that had never been preached or taught in North America.

James Inglis (1813-1872), publisher of *Waymarks in the Wilderness* magazine, was one of the first American preachers to popularize "The Rapture" concept promoted by Darby. Following Inglis' death, Saint Louis Presbyterian pastor Rev. James H. Brookes (1830-1898) picked up Darby's baton in America. In 1876, he organized the first Niagara Bible Conference, also known as the Believers' Meeting for Bible Study.

The Niagara conference was the forerunner of today's plethora of bible prophecy conferences throughout the USA extolling the tenets of Darbyism. Pastor Brooks' conference was also supported by William E. Blackstone (1841-1935) and Cyrus Scofield (1843-1921). Rev. Blackstone was a popular evangelist in America who wrote one of the first end-time prophecy books published in the United States of America. His *Jesus is Coming* book sold millions of copies and was translated into 48 languages. Scofield was the publisher of the wildly popular *Scofield Reference Bible* published by Oxford University Press.

Another influential peddler of Darbyism was Chicago-based evangelist Dwight L. Moody (1837-1899) who was introduced to Darby during his numerous trips to London. Rev. Moody founded the Moody Bible Institute which continues today teaching Darby's deception to its seminary students.

Other prominent and influential Darbyites were Reuben A. Torrey, Harry Ironside, F.W. Grant, C.H. MacKintosh, William Trotter, *Scofield Reference Bible* editor A.C. Gaebelein, and Lewis Sperry Chafer, founder of the Dallas Theological Seminary. Mr. Chafer served in the 1920s as pastor of Scofield Church in Dallas, Texas. Prominent and influential Dallas Theological Seminary graduates include J. Dwight Pentecost, J. Vernon McGee, Hall Lindsey, Chuck Swindoll, Tony Evans, Charles Ryrie, and John Walvoord.

"The Rapture" Peddled to American Churches by a Snake Oil Salesman

Whereas Darby excelled at collecting a hodgepodge of heresies crafted by others and assembling them into a systematic theology, he lacked the personal charisma necessary to sell and market his unholy hokum. He wasn't a likeable guy. Darby's aberrant beliefs remained trapped primarily in Great Britain among the small Plymouth Brethren cult despite growing acceptance of Darby's warped doctrines among a select group of American preachers such as D.L. Moody and William E. Blackstone.

What Darbyism lacked was a traveling medicine show huckster who could sell cases of his evangelical elixir to gullible, Biblically illiterate American Evangelicals. The carnival huckster was Cyrus

Scofield. The crafty con-artist saw flashing dollar signs in Darby's theology. Scofield shamelessly plagiarized Darby's doctrines by brazenly inserting them in an annotated Holy Bible as his "notes," thus tricking Evangelicals into believing that Scofield's notes must be inspired by God "because they are in the Bible." Without the *Scofield Reference Bible*, it is doubtful that Darbyism would have survived beyond the 19th century. Darby died in 1882, but his deception lives on today thanks to a legion of cultists who perpetuated DPPZism into the 21st century.

The Scofield Reference Bible was the primary marketing tool used to infiltrate American Evangelical churches and homes with Masonic Darbyism. "Doctor" Scofield was a slick flimflam man who was prosecuted in his younger days in Kansas for fraudulently robbing investors whom he duped into trusting him with their money. Scofield routinely used aliases to throw the police off his scent. Sometimes he was Cyrus Scofield, other times he was Cyrus Ingerson, and somedays he was Charles Ingerson. Scofield posed as "Charles Ingerson" while pretending to be a wealthy cotton plantation owner from Mobile, Alabama. The owner of the Metropolitan Hotel in Milwaukee, Wisconsin, had the phony cotton plantation owner evicted on charges of vagrancy when he could not pay for his lodging.

In 1878 he was arrested in Wisconsin on criminal charges filed by the St. Louis Chief of Police. Scofield spent six months in the county jail for forgery. Criminal charges were dropped in 1879 when his sister Emmaline paid off her brother's debts that got him locked up.

In addition to charges of fraud and forgery, Scofield was previously accused in 1873 of political corruption by accepting bribes and was forced to resign "under a cloud of scandal" as a U.S. District Attorney in Kansas after only serving six months in the job. Some of the allegations that swirled around Scofield's abrupt resignation included stealing political contributions intended for U.S. Senator John J. Ingalls, the politician responsible for Scofield obtaining the political plum as a U.S. district attorney. Other accusations included accepting bribes from railroad lobbyists and securing bank promissory notes by forging signatures.

Senator John Ingalls, Scofield's political mentor, was a lawyer from Massachusetts who relocated to Kansas in 1860 to launch his political career in the Midwest farm state. He was a direct descendent of two New England Puritan families. Senator Ingalls pulled political strings to get young Scofield admitted to the Kansas Bar despite Scofield's lack of any law school education. Ingalls was a second cousin of Charles Ingalls, the father of Laura Ingalls Wilder, author of the Little House series of books. Charles Ingalls was portrayed by Michael Landon, a Hollywood actor and producer, as "Pa" in Landon's popular television series Little House on the Prairie. Charles Ingalls was a Freemason. Charles Ingalls' paternal grandmother was Margaret Delano, ancestor of President Franklin Delano Roosevelt.

Scofield found religion shortly after his release from jail in Wisconsin in 1879. Details of his religious conversion are sketchy. Scofield said he was introduced to evangelical Christianity by a lawyer friend. Months after his release from jail, Scofield was assisting in the St. Louis evangelistic campaign led by Dwight L. Moody. Immediately, the 36-year-old Scofield attracted the attention of James H. Brookes, pastor of Walnut Street Presbyterian Church in St. Louis. Reverend Brookes was an ardent devotee of Darbyism.

THE RAPTURE'S OCCULT ORIGIN

Scofield's criminal career experienced an amazing turnaround. The scoundrel who was standing behind bars in a county jail cell in 1879 suddenly was standing behind a preacher's pulpit in 1881, the same year lonely Leontene, his devoted wife and mother of their children, filed for a divorce on grounds of abandonment. Scofield served as the pastor of Hyde Park Congregational Church in St. Louis, MO, from 1881 to 1883. Obviously, the Hyde Park congregation ignored Apostle Paul's advice to Timothy not to rush to ordain men to ministry.

Lay hands suddenly on no man, neither be partaker of other men's sins: keep thyself pure. (I Timothy 5:22)

In the summer of 1881, some Kansas newspapers reported that the infamous and incredulous Cyrus Scofield had resurfaced as a "Campbellite preacher." Campbellites were followers of Thomas and Alexander Campbell, leaders in the Stone-Campbell Restoration Movement in the 19th century.

The Topeka Daily Journal published a blistering gossip update on the latest whereabouts of Cyrus Scofield. The newspaper's August 27, 1881 edition said:

"Cyrus I. Scofield, formerly of Kansas, late lawyer, politician and shyster generally, has come to the surface again, and promises once more to gather around himself that halo of notoriety that has made him so prominent in the past. The last personal knowledge that Kansans have had of this peer among scalawags, was when about four years ago, after a series of forgeries and confidence games he left the state and a destitute family and took refuge in Canada. For a time he kept undercover, nothing being heard of him until with the past two years when he turned up in St. Louis, where he had a wealthy widowed sister living who has generally

come to the front and squared up Cyrus' little follies and foibles by paying good round sums of money. Within the past year, however, Cyrus committed a series of St. Louis forgeries that could not be settled so easily, and the erratic young gentleman was compelled to linger in the St. Louis jail for a period of six months."

Scofield moved to Texas in 1883 to become the pastor of First Congregational Church in Dallas. Reverend Scofield, however, neglected to inform the clergy selection committee about his financially struggling wife and children whom he abandoned many years earlier and neglected to support. Leontene Scofield was finally granted a divorce from her wayward husband Cyrus on December 8, 1883, on grounds of "willful abandonment."

Shortly thereafter, Reverend Scofield married Hettie Hall Wartz in 1884, a woman who was a member of his Dallas congregation. Scofield left Dallas in 1895 to become the pastor of D.L. Moody's Trinitarian Congregational Church in East Northfield, Massachusetts. He returned to his former church in Dallas, however, in 1903 but was often absent from the pulpit because of his commitment to Oxford University Press to prepare his notes for a soon-to-be published annotated Bible.

Scofield also embellished his Civil War military record as a Confederate soldier, made a perjurious oath of office when he became a U.S. District Attorney, and dishonestly used the title "doctor" with no proof he attended nor obtained a degree from any college or seminary. He went to his grave still lying about his educational credentials and Civil War military record. The first edition of the Scofield Reference Bible, published in 1909, falsely identified him on the title page as C.I. Scofield, D.D. It was an outright lie. Scofield had never been awarded a Doctor of Divinity degree by any reputable educational institution or seminary. His modern-day admirers continue to cover up his dishonesty. If a man is willing and able to print a big lie on the title page of the Holy Bible, would he hesitate to print more lies on every page of the Bible? Such a scoundrel has no fear of God.

Despite his checkered past, "Dr. Scofield" is still revered today by Evangelical Zionist leaders in many denominations, churches, and seminaries. Scofield's protégé, Lewis Sperry Chafer, founded the Dallas Theological Seminary in Texas which has indoctrinated thousands of seminary students with the Darby Deception and "Doctor" Scofield's religious quackery.

Scofield Received Boost from Rothschild Lawyer

With Darby in the grave, there was nobody to legally challenge Scofield's ownership claim of Darbyism. Thus, there would be no copyright royalties owed to Darby. The hustler had a wide-open opportunity to make a fortune selling the Darby Deception in America.

Scofield privately shared with his friend Arno Gaebelein in 1901 his idea to publish Darby's theology in an annotated Bible. Gaebelein was a prominent Bible teacher, popular conference speaker, and early champion of Darby's Dispensationalism. Scofield and Gaebelein were speakers at the Niagara Bible Conference and the Sea Cliff Bible Conference. Gaebelein fluently spoke Yiddish in his outreach to Jews. He published *Our Hope*, a magazine dedicated to educating Evangelicals about Zionism and Jewish affairs. It was said that he immersed himself so much in Jewish culture that Jews often thought Gaebelein was a Jew. Gaebelein was also a proponent of the "gap theory" that claims there is a gap of time between two distinct acts of God's creation in the first two verses of the first chapter of the Book of Genesis. The gap theory of Creation is like "The Rapture" doctrine. You need magical glasses to see the invisible words printed on the pages of the Bible.

Initially, Scofield went nowhere with his scheme to enter the prophecy business. Always ambitious but financially-challenged, the resourceful snake oil salesman needed an influential benefactor to open doors for him. Lucifer provided the Magical Money Man that Scofield requested. His name was Samuel Untermeyer, an influential Wall Street lawyer for the Rothschild banking cartel who drafted the U.S. Senate bill that established the Federal Reserve System. Untermeyer, who was Jewish, was a fanatical Zionist who chaired the American Jewish Committee. He sponsored Scofield, the pastor of D.L. Moody's Trinitarian Congregational Church, East Northfield, Massachusetts, to join the Lotos Club, a prestigious upscale gentlemen's club in New York City that catered to literary artists.

Untermeyer served as a member of the club's literary committee. Samuel Clemmons, alias Mark Twain, was a member of the Lotos Club when Scofield was admitted into the inner circle in 1901, the same year that Scofield confided to Yiddish-speaking Arno Gaebelein his idea to place Darby's notes in the Holy Bible. Wall Street tycoon Andrew Carnegie and automobile manufacturer Walter Chrysler were Lotos Club members too. It remains a mystery why Zionist zealot Untermeyer sponsored Scofield's membership in the Lotos Club. What did he see in Scofield? What useful purpose did Scofield serve to advance Untermeyer's Zionist agenda? Once again, an influential lawyer, a man who worked for the Rothschild banking dynasty, gave moneyless Scofield a huge career boost much like when Senator

Ingalls pushed through Scofield's appointment as a U.S. district attorney in Kansas despite Scofield's lack of law school training. Some guys have all the luck!

Untermeyer's influence as a Rothschild agent opened doors of opportunity for moneyless Scofield and gave instant credibility to the bamboozler with a checkered past peppered with allegations of fraud, bribery, and lying. Scofield had previously met Robert Scott at Dwight Moody's ministry campus in Illinois. Scott was a principal in Morgan & Scott, a British publishing house. Scott took Scofield to his home near Dorking in the United Kingdom. During the visit, Scott introduced Scofield to McHenry Frowde, Publisher of London's prestigious Oxford University Press.

Oxford's association with Freemasonry is well-known. Thousands of Oxford undergraduates have been initiated into Freemasonry and joined the University of Oxford's Apollo Lodge, including Oscar Wilde, Cecil Rhodes, and Edward, Prince of Wales. Frowde had a longtime close relationship with Darby's "Exclusive Brethren." The willingness of Oxford University Press officials to meet with an unknown pastor of a small American church who had never written a book was highly unusual, but Frowde was a closet "Exclusive Brethren" Darbyite, therefore "the fix" was in: British Freemasons and Jewish Zionists had tapped Scofield to place Darby's heretical notes in the Holy Bible to hoodwink Evangelical Christians into supporting their secret agenda to rebuild Solomon's temple in Jerusalem to exalt Lucifer and advance the understanding of ancient Babylonian secret knowledge.

After consulting with executives employed by Oxford's branch in the United States, Oxford University Press signed a publishing deal in 1907 to print and distribute the Scofield

Reference Bible. Although Scofield had no working capital, Yiddish-speaking Arno Gaebelein was hired as Scofield's assistant editor to assist Scofield in assembling Darby's notes to be published in the Holy Bible. Some critics suspect that Gaebelein was the true author of the annotated Bible's extensive notes that promoted Darbyism. The first edition of the blasphemous Scofield Reference Bible rolled off Oxford's printing presses in 1909. Over 10 million copies have been sold over the years. Interestingly, Scofield did not hold the copyright to his Scofield Reference Bible. It was owned, and remains owned today, by Oxford University Press, American Branch.

Amazed by Scofield's success, Gaebelein published in 1921 his own annotated Bible. His son Frank Gaebelein served as one of the editors of the translation committee that published the New International Version (NIV) Bible. Together, Scofield and Arno Gabelein were twin dynamos for two decades promoting Darbyism to American Evangelicals. The rest is history. Darby's DPPZism was successfully planted in American Evangelical denominations, churches, seminaries, and ministries. Today it dominates the thinking of tens of millions of Evangelicals who know nothing of its diabolical origin.

Truth Left Behind on the Late Great Planet Earth

Sixty-one years passed by before a Dispensational author outperformed Cyrus Scofield in selling books that promoted Darby's DPPZism. The author was Hal Lindsey, a former Mississippi River tugboat captain. Lindsey was indoctrinated with Darby's DPPZism while studying at Dallas Theological Seminary, the institution founded by Scofield's protégé Lewis Sperry Chafer, the mentor of DPPZism heavyweights J. Dwight Pentecost, Charles Ryrie, J. Vernon McGee, and John Walvoord.

Lindsey's book was *The Late Great Planet Earth*. Published in 1970, it was the top selling non-fiction book in America for over a decade. An estimated 40 million copies have been sold worldwide in multiple languages. No other prophecy book matched its impact on American Evangelical churches than Lindsey's *The Late Great Planet Earth* book.

Twenty-five years later, Tim LaHaye and Jerry Jenkins co-authored *Left Behind*, a fictional novel about "The Rapture." *Left Behind* became a runaway best-selling series of 16 novels and four films to date (1995-2007). *The Late Great Planet Earth* and the *Left Behind* series were enormously successful in mass marketing Darby-Scofield DPPZism to millions of Evangelicals who assumed the books and films were based on sound Biblical doctrine. The *Left Behind* novels and films are classic DPPZism that warned people not to be "left behind" when "The Rapture" occurs before "The Great Tribulation" when "The Antichrist" takes over the world. The not-so-subtle inference was that really bad things happen to everybody who will be left behind.

The Hidden Hand in Evangelical Churches

Darby's family history with occultism and Scofield's shady history of dishonesty should be enough to make all upright Evangelicals reconsider their endorsement and advocacy of Darby's theology. How can good fruit grow on bad trees?

The hidden hand that stealthily captured Evangelical Christianity is Kabbalah-driven Masonic Zionism. During his twenties, Darby was employed by Nathan Rothschild as a tutor for his sons Lionel and Anthony. Nathan Rothschild was a wealthy and influential Jewish banker and third son of Mayer Amschel Bauer who changed his name to Rothschild, which means "red sign." It represented the red hexagram that his German father, a money lender, placed over the door of his bank. Mayer Rothschild was founder of the sinister Rothschild banking dynasty. His son Nathan Rothschild was a member of the Emulation Lodge, No. 12, of the Premier Grand Lodge of England, originally formed as the Grand Lodge of London and Westminster, and later called the Grand Lodge of England.

It isn't surprising that Darby was employed by Nathan Rothschild. The two men shared a kindred spirit. Darby must have felt at home in the presence of Rothschild. The banker was deeply involved with Kabbalah mysticism, the Talmud, and Freemasonry's international network of illuminated ones who were the keepers of Lucifer's "light." Darby came from an Irish family with a disturbing history of involvement in occultism. Hideous demons manifested in the Darby castle, ghosts roamed the castle halls, a priest was butchered on the altar during Holy Communion in the castle's chapel, and numerous skeletons were discovered impaled on wooden spikes in a secret dungeon behind the castle chapel's wall. Satanist Aleister Crowley's father was a Darby protégé in the cult.

Things were not much better for Cyrus Scofield. What were his credentials? Swindler, liar, forger, perjurer, embellisher, and bribe-taking crook! He abandoned his wife and children in Kansas, eventually moved to Dallas to accept a pastoral position in a church but forgot to inform the clergy selection committee that he had a wife and children back in Kansas whom he abandoned and failed to financially support, and married another woman in the Dallas church months after his divorce was quietly finalized. He went to his grave lying about his educational credentials and Civil War military record. Scofield was such a colossal liar and exaggerator that he printed on the title page of the Scofield Reference Bible that he had a Doctor of Divinity degree.

Scofield was a close friend of Arno Gabelein. Scofield privately confided to Yiddish-speaking Gaebelein his scheme to publish Darby's notes in the Holy Bible. Amazingly, a powerful Jewish lawyer on Wall Street, who just happened to be one of the top executives and financiers of an influential Jewish organization that promoted Zionism, contacted unknown Scofield in Massachusetts and offered to make him a member of the prestigious Lotos Club in New York City where Scofield could mingle with famous authors and wealthy bankers and manufacturers. Coincidentally, Samuel Untermeyer was also the Wall Street lawyer who wrote the Congressional law that established that monstrous Federal Reserve Banking system, which dovetailed with the underhanded shenanigans to amend the U.S. Constitution to permit the taxation of American citizens' income through the newly established Internal Revenue Service.

Shortly after joining the Lotos Club, Scofield-the-swindler was whisked off to London to meet the top executives of Oxford University Press, the publishing arm of the University of Oxford, home of the Apollo Lodge of influential Freemasons in the United Kingdom. Suddenly, Scofield had a publishing contract with Oxford University Press! It was a stupendous accomplishment for an unknown preacher from a small church in America who had never written a single word of the notes for the annotated Bible he proposed to publish. To help poor Cyrus collect and assemble

Darby's notes, Yiddish-speaking Gabelein was hired as Scofield's assistant and paid by somebody because flat-broke Scofield barely had enough income to pay his own expenses. The mighty Oxford University Press put his stamp of approval on Scofield's project and the rest is history. Millions of *Scofield Reference Bibles*, tainted with Darby's blasphemous and wicked Kabbalah-Masonic ideas, have been sold to unsuspecting Evangelical Christians. This was how Evangelicals morphed into Deceived-vangelicals without knowing they had been snookered by the Devil.

In the same decade that Scofield was tapped to defile God's Holy Bible with Kabbalah-Masonic ideas, communist Jews also overthrew the Czar of Russia, killed millions of Russian Christians, ransacked and defiled Russian Orthodox churches and cathedrals, declared atheism as Russia's state religion, and established the world's first communist regime. Immediately after the Bolshevik Revolution, which received secret funding from Wall Street tycoons and the New York Federal Reserve Bank, communist Zionists from Europe and America began infiltrating Palestine to form New Yishuv communist terror cells such as Haganah and Irgun to sabotage Britain's Mandatory Palestine and overthrow Arab towns and villages where Old Yishuv Jews, Christians, and Muslims lived together peacefully for centuries.

Yes, it looks suspicious, but let's not jump to conspiratorial conclusions! If you take this line of reasoning too far, you'll conclude that America's Evangelical Christians were hoodwinked by clever Zionist Freemasons to alter the Word of God, accept Kabbalah-Masonic ideas about the Last Days, promote their objectives to rebuild Solomon's temple, recover ancient Babylonian knowledge, worship Lucifer, and establish a worldwide Masonic-Zionist empire for 1,000 years. Hopefully, this book will be used by Almighty God to awaken the Church to perceive and discern Satan's tactics and strategies he used to takeover Evangelical Christianity.

Only God knows how many deceased pastors, Bible prophecy teachers, authors, theologians, and seminary professors in Evangelical denominations, churches, seminaries, and ministries were closet Freemasons. Likewise, only the Lord knows how many secret Freemasons presently occupy lofty and influential positions of power inside Evangelical Zionist religious organizations today, especially religious media organizations, seminaries, and publishing houses. The truth will be revealed on the Final Day.

The Rapture Cult would not be the first religious cult started by Freemasons. Joseph Smith, founder of Mormonism, was a Freemason. Charles Taze Russell, founder of the Jehovah's Witnesses cult, denied he was a Freemason like his father, but the cult's historic literature is peppered with Masonic emblems such as pyramids and the Egyptian sun god Ra. Russell was buried in 1916 in the Rosemont United Cemetery in Pittsburgh, PA. John Rutherford, the second president of the Watch Tower Bible and Tract Society, authorized the construction of a large pyramid tomb on a plot of land in the Rosemont United Cemetery where Charles Taze Russell and other members of the Society were buried.

The Egyptian-like pyramid that honors Russell's burial site contains numerous engravings including the cross and crown. The cross and crown symbol is associated with the Knight Templar degree of the York Rite of Freemasonry. In Freemasonry, the symbol is known as "Knight Templar Blood-Red Passion Cross and Crown." The Masonic symbol appeared on numerous early publications of the Watch Tower cult.

Left Behind co-author Tim LaHaye's book *The Power of the Cross* (1998) also featured the cross and the crown symbol on the front cover. The same symbol that adorns Tim LaHaye's book is also the key emblem of the Royal Black Institution, a Masonic order of Protestants in Great Britain.

Some modern editions of Oxford University Press' *Scofield Study Bible III* published in the first two decades of the 21st century feature a Masonic emblem on the front cover. The letter "O" in Scofield has a dot in the center. It is eerily like the Masonic circle and point. The Masonic emblem originated in ancient Egypt and has a close connection with ancient sun worship.

Why did Charles Taze Russell, the Jehovah Witnesses, Tim LaHaye, and Oxford University Press include Masonic emblems in their publications? Why did John Nelson Darby frequently use Masonic or occult words and phrases in his writings and sermons? Why is the Southern Baptist Convention top heavy with Freemasons in key positions? A mere coincidence or by intentional design?

Devilish Darby's Counterfeit Christianity

John Nelson Darby excelled in inventing new doctrines and plagiarizing old heresies started by other deceivers. He fastened together a mishmash of strange doctrines that only a handful of unknown fringe preachers espoused in the 18th and 19th centuries and sprinkled them with some old heresies such as chiliasm that periodically resurfaced in some churches over many centuries. His real skill was the ability to assemble a cafeteria-style assortment of heresies and false doctrines and mold them together to form a new systematic theology that could be taught to others through indoctrination. The result was a radical remaking of Evangelical thinking. Today's Evangelical churches and ministries are no longer Christian. They espouse a different religion that tells its followers that their salvation and blessings are found in their adoration of the State of Israel, not the Lord Jesus Christ.

The spiritual vigilance of men such as Reverend Charles Spurgeon kept Darby's hodgepodge of heresies contained, like a deadly virus, in pockets of Great Britain in the 19th century. Eventually, the STD virus was carried to America by Darby and Dwight L. Moody, the famous Chicago evangelist who befriended Darby during his trips to London. Moody mingled with London's leaders of Evangelical Restorationism, a legitimate Anglican movement to evangelize Jews. Although Dwight L. Moody eventually parted company with Darby for unknown reasons, Rev. Moody retained Darby's DPPZ theology and taught it to American Christians. Cyrus Scofield also worked for Moody for a short time writing a Bible correspondence course that Moody sold to his supporters. Today, the Moody Bible Institute is one of the most influential religious educational institutions in the world that indoctrinates seminary students with DPPZism.

Darby crossed the Atlantic Ocean approximately seven times to sow his tares in North America. In addition to Dwight Moody, Darby befriended American preachers William E. Blackstone, James H. Brookes, and Scofield. These four men embraced Darbyism and introduced it to some Evangelical churches in America. DPPZism had little support in America at the time of Darby's death in 1882. It was the publication of the revolutionary *Scofield Reference Bible* in 1909 that pushed Darby's poisons into the veins of American Evangelical churches.

Satan pulled off a masterful stroke of deception by orchestrating over many decades the confluence of people, events, and unbiblical teachings in the 19th century that culminated in the publication of the *Scofield Reference Bible* in the early 20th century. Satan used Darby, Scofield, and Gabelein to insert a vile mixture of deception and lies into the pure Word of God, thus audaciously printing the corrupted words of flawed humans on the same pages with infallible scriptures inspired by the Holy Spirit.

Scofield's blasphemous publication formed the foundation of a radical new systematic theology that eventually spread like leaven throughout Evangelical and fundamentalist denominations, churches, and ministries primarily in the United States of America, thereby giving the daughter of Babylon her own Babylonian religion of modern Evangelical Masonic-Zionism in a similar fashion as Jewish rabbis discovered Babylonian secret knowledge while held captive in the city-state, thus giving birth to Kabbalah-driven Judaism. Modern Israel has Jewish Kabbalah Zionism and America has Evangelical Kabbalah Zionism. Both religions worship the same god. They share "Judeo-Christian" values.

Eventually the Rothschild-orchestrated Darby-Scofield deception produced a profound paradigm shift within American Evangelical churches, ministries, and educational institutions. By the 20th century, conservative Evangelical denominations were teaching strange doctrines unknown to the worldwide Church since the Book of the Acts of the Apostles.

Tens of thousands of Evangelical churches have sunk so deep into the mire of Darby's deception that they can no longer be recognized as Christian. They slowly morphed into another religion, and their pastors and congregations do not discern it. Today, they constitute a new religious entity: American Babylonian Churchianity. It has no resemblance to first-century Christianity, and little resemblance to 19th century Christianity. They teach Replacement Theology: Jesus Christ is no longer the focus of their worship and adoration. The King of the Jews has been replaced by the State of the Jews. The old rugged cross has been replaced by the occult Star of David. The Resurrection has been replaced by The Rapture. The promise of eternal life in New Jerusalem has been replaced by idolizing old Jerusalem as the eternal capital of Israel.

The *Scofield Reference Bible* was the syringe that Satan used to inject his toxic lies into the Body of Christ in the United States of America. The poisons spread quickly throughout America in the 20th century as Evangelicals read, absorbed, expanded, and fanatically promoted the heretical theology presented in the *Scofield Reference Bible*. In doing so, America's Evangelicals tossed into the trash bin traditional orthodox Christian theology that was the bedrock of the worldwide Christian church since the days of the apostles. In other words, American Evangelicals rewrote and redefined Christianity. The blasphemous heresies promoted by Darby, Scofield, and their legions of disciples directly contradict and repudiate the Holy Bible, the Apostles' Doctrine, the Nicene Creed, and the Reformation's confessions of faith.

In an Alice-in-Wonderland-type of reality, DPPZ theology is so deeply embedded in Evangelical Zionist churches today that traditional orthodox Christians are now branded as heretics for defending the ancient Christian faith. Most Evangelical Zionists assume that their church's theology is Christian. They have no awareness that they are attending churches that openly repudiate the apostles, the church fathers, the early orthodox catholic churches in the first centuries of the New Covenant, the creeds, and the Protestant Reformation. DPPZism was not taught by Jesus

Christ, Apostle Paul, Apostle Peter, Apostle John, Polycarp, Clement of Rome, Ignatius, Barnabas, Irenaeus, Justin Martyr, Clement of Alexandria, Tertullian, Hippolytus, Cyprian, nor Martin Luther and John Calvin. Yet, John Nelson Darby and Cyrus Scofield claimed, as do the modern pharisees of Moody Bible Institute and Dallas Theological Seminary, to possess superior knowledge about God's marvelous plan to redeem mankind and bring forth His eternal kingdom of righteousness.

Bluntly spoken, Evangelicalism is no longer Christian. It is another religion: Evangelical Zionism. Its disciples should be identified as "EZs" and not as Christians. Jewish Zionism and Evangelical Zionism share a common heritage: Kabbalistic Freemasonry. The blasphemous heresies promoted by Darby, Scofield, and their legions of disciples directly contradict and repudiate the Holy Bible, the Apostles' Doctrine, the Nicene Creed, and the Reformation's confessions of faith. It must be eradicated from God's holy universal church.

CHAPTER 3

HIS SECOND COMING SHALL BE SINGULAR

H OW MANY TIMES DOES Jesus Christ return to Earth? Once or twice? Will there be one "Second Coming" of Jesus or two?

The question sounds silly. If Jesus returns twice the second "Second Coming" would have to be called the Third Coming of Jesus Christ. The obvious answer is: There is only one Second Coming of Jesus Christ.

Why must such a ridiculous question be asked?

Despite the absurdity of the question, tens of millions of sincere Christians have been taught that Jesus will return twice. Adding to their confusion, they've also been taught that the first Second Coming of Jesus doesn't count!

Evangelical Zionists count differently than the rest of us. John Nelson Darby invented EZ New Math. In traditional churches, one plus one always equals two. Math is different in Evangelical Zionist churches. For them, one plus one always equals one because the first one does not count. Are you following along? If you are going to see "The Rapture" in the Holy Bible, you must learn how to add and subtract using EZ New Math.

If you ask Evangelical Zionists how many times Jesus will return, most likely they will reply, "Once!" Yet, if you asked them, "Do you believe in 'The Rapture?" they will also respond "yes!" Here's the crux of their dilemma: You can't believe Jesus Christ returns to earth only once if you also believe in "The Rapture" as taught by the doctrine's zealots. If Jesus Christ comes first in "The Rapture" and again in the "Second Coming" it means He will return to earth twice. One plus one always equals two in real math regardless of how Evangelical Zionists count.

Doesn't the Bible say that Christians shall meet the Lord in the air? Absolutely yes! Isn't "The Rapture" and the Second Coming the same event? Absolutely not! The former is an imaginary man-made event and the latter is an authentic Biblical event. Evangelical Zionist denominations, seminaries, Bible colleges, churches and ministries teach John Nelson Darby's bizarre doctrine that says Jesus Christ's return will be a two-stage re-entry spread over seven years.

According to the cultish teaching, Jesus will sneak into the earth's atmosphere unseen by the entire human population except "saved Christians" - meaning Southern Baptists, Pentecostals, Charismatics, Hebrew Roots, Messianic Jews, non-denominational church members, and everybody else who watches or listens to religious television or radio shows. Although many Evangelical Zionists are reluctant to publicly say it, privately they doubt that members of Lutheran, Anglican, Presbyterian, Methodist, Reformed, Orthodox, and Catholic churches arc truly saved. They smugly think the traditional Christians will be "left behind" and get a second chance to be really saved after "The Rapture" evacuates the Evangelical Zionists away from Planet Earth and transports them to Heaven. The Evangelical Zionists are supremely confident that they will, as they rapturously boast, "leave on the first load."

Do You Believe In the Rapture Pooka?

This chapter poses three important questions to the reader:

- Does Jesus Christ return to earth once or twice?
- Are the Rapture and Second Coming the same or different events?
- If the Rapture and Second Coming are different events, doesn't that mean Jesus returns twice?

This is the core of the confusion that clouds the minds of many Evangelical Zionists who love the Lord and believe in His promised return. They attend churches, however, that acquired their eschatology from a 19th century cult, but they don't know it. Most pastors, Bible teachers, and theologians who believe and teach "The Rapture" doctrine do not know that it originated with a cult leader whose family owned a haunted castle in Ireland where seances were held and apparitions appeared, who worked for Nathan Rothschild, was the spiritual father of Aleister Crowley's biological father, and who was a close friend of a British intelligence agent and high-level Freemason.

They also don't know that the most influential Evangelical Zionist marketer of "The Rapture" was a flimflam man who abandoned his wife and children, swindled money from people he duped into trusting him, perjured himself by swearing falsely in an oath of office, resigned from a federal law enforcement position over accusations of bribery, lied about his Civil War record as a Confederate soldier, embellished his resume by pretending to possess a Doctor of Divinity degree, and was befriended and elevated by a powerful Rothschild-connected Wall Street lawyer who was a prominent leader in the Zionist movement. That's quite a legacy for the early fathers of Evangelical Zionism! Good fruit cannot grow on bad trees.

Tens of millions of Evangelical Zionists have been taught that the Lord's return is a two-stage re-entry: "The Rapture" will secretly happen first, followed seven years later by a visible Second Coming. According to Evangelical Zionist theologians, "The Rapture" is secretive because only Evangelical Christians will see Jesus in "The Rapture," but everybody else will see Him seven years later in the Second Coming.

How do you persuade people who believe in an invisible secret event that it isn't real? It would be akin to convincing Elwood P. Dowd, portrayed by Hollywood legend Jimmy Stewart, that his Celtic mythical pooka rabbit friend Harvey wasn't real. In the 1950 movie *Harvey*, only Elwood could see Harvey, the 6-foot 3-inch-tall rabbit.

Evangelical Zionists have an invisible pooka pal too. His name is Rapture. You cannot see the Rapture bunny in the Bible, but his devotees passionately swear it is there. They become irate and angry if you challenge their religious delusion. Its best to smile and say you see their pooka pal too if you want the conversation to remain civil. Keep peace in the family. You never know when you'll need your Evangelical Zionist brother-in-law to repair your air conditioner.

Millions of sincere Evangelical Zionists have been told they too must confess belief in their denomination's invisible pooka pal.

Privately, they admit they don't see it, but refrain from saying it in their local church because they fear a confrontation with their pastor who is obligated to defend the honor of his denomination's cherished pooka, "The Rapture." Often pastors do not believe in the pooka either, but they too are afraid to say it for fear their denomination's pharisees will revoke their ministerial credentials. Its time for pastors to bravely say in public, "I don't believe in your Rapture pooka!"

Tens of millions of Evangelical Zionists who attend churches that espouse any version of this aberrant doctrine have been told by their religious elders that there really is a Rapture pooka, yet few ever question where the Rapture pooka myth originated. It's the same as moms and dads deceiving their children about Santa Claus, the Easter Bunny, and the Tooth Fairy. Santa Claus isn't coming someday, and neither is "The Rapture." The odds are higher that Santa Claus will come down your chimney and leave toys under your Christmas tree than for the Rapture pooka to appear. Jesus Christ is returning for His holy nation of true Israel, but He's only making one trip. You better be waiting at the bus stop when He pulls up to the intersection of Believe Avenue and Baptism Boulevard. The Salvation Bus is coming one time, and its arrival will be sudden and unexpected. We must always be ready and waiting for it to arrive.

Sadly, this unbiblical doctrine has infected millions of minds and contributed to much confusion and division in the Body of Christ over the subject that should give all Christians the greatest hope and joy: the resurrection of the dead when our blessed hope Jesus Christ gloriously appears! By peddling the Rapture pooka, Satan craftily tricked Evangelicals to turn their eyes away from the magnificence of Jesus Christ and, instead, become fixated with a mythical event that promises to evacuate them from the inconvenience of persecution, suffering, and tribulation. Our hope must be fixed on the promise of the physical presence (Parousia) of our Savior Jesus Christ and the Resurrection, not the return of Greater Israel and a temple.

Besides, Jesus doesn't need to make two trips from Heaven to Earth. He'll get it all done in one trip. Jesus is amazingly capable of doing far more than we can imagine. Therefore, wrapping up the age of mankind on one day – the Final Day – will not cause the Lord to overexert Himself and profusely sweat. His Heavenly Father will not say, "Son, you tried to accomplish too much in one day. Flying from Heaven to Earth, flashing your sign in the sky, turning off electricity to the sun and moon and stars, resurrecting the dead, meeting the saints in the clouds, sitting on your Judgment Seat, organizing all humans by their respective nations, separating them into groups of goats and sheep, judging all of mankind, bundling and burning the wicked in the lake of fire, judging the works of humans, apprehending the Devil and tossing him in the fire, setting the Earth and heavens on fire, rolling up the universe like a scroll, creating a new Earth and heavens, transporting New Jerusalem to the new Earth, and moving all your stuff from your palace here in Heaven to your new home in New Jerusalem. Wow! What were you thinking? You should have stretched it out over a thousand years. Now your back hurts because you overexerted yourself. Please make an appointment with Heaven's chiropractor and have your spine adjusted in the morning." No, my friend, Jesus will not sprain his back getting it done in one day. He's been waiting a long time to get the job done. He will move, act, and complete His to-do list speedier than any of us can humanly imagine is possible.

Darby's Reason for Inventing "The Rapture"

Millions of church members don't know it because their idolized celebrity pastors and Bible prophecy gurus will never admit it, but Evangelical Zionism's endgame is a worldwide Freemason-Kabbalah-Zionist empire that will reign for a thousand years. It is the capstone of Freemasonry: Babylon's conquest of God and His Son, and the arrival of a utopian Babylonian society centered around Lucifer, Solomon's Temple, and the ancient Babylonian secret knowledge that Solomon allegedly stored in the temple's library. It is why Freemasons revere Nimrod, the founder of Babylon and the father of Freemasonry. Nimrod and Babylon epitomize the post-Great Flood rebellion against Jesus Christ and New Jerusalem.

To arrive at their desired goal, Darby and his minions worked their way backward by radically redesigning Western Christian thinking about the Holy Bible, Jesus Christ, the identity of true Israel, the Church, Jerusalem, and the Kingdom of God. Along the way, Darby's Evangelical Zionists arbitrarily invented proper pronouns that they pompously declared as Biblical in origin. It takes a lot of chutzpah to pull it off, but they did it anyway. Their fake, unbiblical proper pronouns include:
- Heavenly People (Christians)
- Earthly People (Jews)
- God's Prophetic Timeclock (restarted by "The Rapture")
- The Rapture (invisible secret snatching away of the Heavenly People)

- The Great Tribulation (a seven-year time of horrible persecution)
- Daniel's 70th Week (seven years congruent with time of tribulation)
- The Antichrist (world dictator)
- Antichrist Peace Treaty
- Revived Roman Empire (the European Union)
- One World Government
- One World Religion
- One World Money
- Spotless Red Heifer
- Tribulation Temple (also called the Third Temple)
- Tribulation Saints (people who will be saved during The Great Tribulation)
- The War of Armageddon (world war to destroy Israel)
- Millennial Kingdom (1,000-year Jewish empire)

None of the above proper pronouns are inside the Holy Bible. Go ahead and spend the rest of your day searching for them in the Bible. You won't find them. All were invented by DPPZites to dupe Christians into believing things that the Holy Bible does not say. So far, its been working marvelously.

Furthermore, not only have they created proper pronouns that are not in the Holy Bible, they brazenly elevated these fake religious terms to the level of authentic Biblical pronouns such as the Sabbath, the Exodus, the Passover, and the Resurrection. Evangelical Zionists cleverly talk about "The Rapture" with such pompous authority that most people who hear them assume that "The Rapture" is in the Holy Bible along with the Garden of

Eden, the Exodus, Moses, Abraham, and Apostle Peter. DPPZites want you to believe that Jesus and His disciples talked about "The Rapture" every day during their lunchbreak at the Caesarea Café while dining on salted fish, dried figs, and sipping Hibiscus tea.

For I testify unto every man that heareth the words of the prophecy of this book, If any man shall add unto these things, God shall add unto him the plagues that are written in this book: and if any man shall take away from the words of the book of this prophecy, God shall take away his part out of the book of life, and out of the holy city, and from the things which are written in this book. (Revelation 22:18-19)

By far, the most crucial proper pronoun invented by Darby is "The Rapture." It is the vital lynchpin that holds together all the moving parts in Evangelical Zionism's Rube Goldberg contraption. Without it, their flimsy house of cards would collapse. Darby's obsession was not the true Kingdom of God. His quest was for a mystical Kabbalah Kingdom. For Darby to make it work, he had to find a way to get those pesky Bible-quoting Christians off the planet so that Protestant Freemasons and Jewish Freemasons could get down to business rebuilding Solomon's temple and restoring Nimrod's lost Babylonian knowledge. "The Rapture" is a fake exodus of Christians from Planet Earth. Its purpose is to clear the planet of people who represent Jesus Christ so that His enemies can finally have the entire world to themselves to accomplish their dream of restoring Babylon to a position of global supremacy for 1,000 years. Thus, this is why God called Jerusalem "Sodom and Egypt," the great city, the mother of harlots. John the Revelator identified the city that is Sodom and Egypt. He said it where "our Lord was crucified."

And their dead bodies shall lie in the street of the great city, which spiritually is called Sodom and Egypt, where also our Lord was crucified. (Revelation 11:8)

Fast-talking Evangelical Zionists glibly tell their enraptured audiences that "The Rapture" truly is in the Bible even though they can't point to the verse that says, "The Rapture." They insist that it is mentioned in the 17th verse of 1 Thessalonians 4 which says, *"then we which are alive and remain shall be caught up together with them in the clouds, to meet the Lord in the air: and so shall we ever be with the Lord."* Let's read the words of Apostle Paul:

But I would not have you to be ignorant, brethren, concerning them which are asleep, that ye sorrow not, even as others which have no hope. For if we believe that Jesus died and rose again, even so them also which sleep in Jesus will God bring with him. For this we say unto you by the word of the Lord, that we which are alive and remain unto the coming of the Lord shall not prevent them which are asleep. For the Lord himself shall descend from heaven with a shout, with the voice of the archangel, and with the trump of God: and the dead in Christ shall rise first: *then we which are alive and remain shall be caught up together with them in the clouds, to meet the Lord in the air: and so shall we ever be with the Lord. Wherefore comfort one another with these words.* (I Thessalonians 4:13-18)

Did you read the phrase "The Rapture" in Apostle Paul's words? Evangelical Zionists can insist that "The Rapture" is in I Thessalonians 4:17 until their faces turn blue, but it doesn't change the truth. Only delusional people would argue that "The Rapture" is there when people in their right minds clearly know it isn't there.

Is there any doubt that the dead in Christ shall rise first and those who are alive at the time of His coming shall be caught up together with them in the clouds to meet the Lord? That's not the issue. Apostle Paul was referring to the one and only Second Coming of Jesus Christ, not a mystical, invisible, secret mass intervention to relocate Christians from earth to Heaven.

Will Christians be Snatched or Raped?

Words matter. Evangelical Zionists are from Venus. Traditional Christians are from Mars. They don't speak the same language.

Why do Evangelical Zionists insist "The Rapture" is in the Bible? Their emphasis is on the words "caught up." According to them, "caught" comes from the Latin words rapiemur, rapere and raptus. The problem with that argument is that the original New Testament manuscripts were not written in Latin. They were written in Greek. Furthermore, "up" is not in the Greek manuscripts.

The etymology of the Latin word rapere denotes "to abduct, the action of forcibly and violently dragging or plucking off." The Latin word raptus means "seized." Thus, rapere means "to seize" and raptus means something has been "seized." In Roman law, raptus referred to crimes of property such as robbery and confiscation. It was also used for crimes of kidnapping and rape. The English word rape is derived from rapere. Is Jesus Christ coming to violently rape the Christian Church? Why do Evangelical Zionists insist on using a Latin word that denotes a violent criminal act of rape?

What is the English dictionary definition of rapture? It is a mystical religious experience! The Merriam-Webster Dictionary defines rapture as a noun that means: "an expression or manifestation of ecstasy or passion; a state or experience of being carried away by overwhelming emotion; a mystical experience in which the spirit is exalted to a knowledge of divine things." Thus, Evangelical Zionists are claiming that there is a special religious event coming someday – identified by the proper pronoun "The Rapture" – that will be both a violent raping and an expression or manifestation of ecstasy or passion, a state of being carried away by overwhelming emotion, a mystical experience in which their spirits are exalted to a knowledge of divine things. That sounds very New Age!

Let's stick with the facts: Rapere, raptus, and rapture are not in the original Greek manuscripts of the New Testament Bible. The Greek word used by Apostle Paul in his first epistle to the ecclesia (the assembly of called out ones) in Thessalonica is harpazo. Harpazo is a verb that means "to pluck, snatch and take." It conveys the sudden exercise of physical force. When used properly as a verb, harpazo refers to the act of forcefully snatching somebody or something.

The Authorized King James Bible translated harpazo as "caught up." The translators inserted the English word "up." The direction an object or person goes after it has been plucked or snatched is not relevant to the use of the word harpazo. It makes no difference whether an object or person that has been plucked or snatched goes up, down, over, or sideways. Harpazo is a verb, not a noun. It is an action, not an event. It is the "how" something happens, not the "what" that happens. It is used multiple times in the Bible, always as a verb, never as a noun. Never is harpazo used in the Bible as a proper pronoun to denote a special event called "The Plucking" or "The Snatching." Whenever harpazo is used in the Bible it refers to the forceful manner that a person was transported. Here are scriptures that use harpazo:

And from the days of John the Baptist until now the kingdom of heaven suffereth violence, and the violent *take it by force*. (Matthew 11:12)

Or else how can one enter into a strong man's house, and *spoil his goods*, except he first bind the strong man? and then he will *spoil his house*. (Matthew 12:29)

When any one heareth the word of the kingdom, and understandeth it not, then cometh the wicked one, and *catcheth* away that which was sown in his heart. This is he which received seed by the way side. (Matthew 13:19)

When Jesus therefore perceived that they would come and *take him by force*, to make him a king, he departed again into a mountain himself alone. (John 6:15)

But he that is an hireling, and not the shepherd, whose own the sheep are not, seeth the wolf coming, and leaveth the sheep, and fleeth: and the wolf *catcheth* them, and scattereth the sheep. (John 10:12)

...and I give unto them eternal life; and they shall never perish, neither shall any man *pluc*k them out of my hand. My Father, which gave them me, is greater than all; and no man is able to *pluck* them out of my Father's hand. (John 10:28-29)

And when they were come up out of the water, the Spirit of the Lord *caught away* Philip, that the eunuch saw him no more: and he went on his way rejoicing. (Acts 8:39)

And when there arose a great dissension, the chief captain, fearing lest Paul should have been pulled in pieces of them, commanded the soldiers to go down, and to *take him by force* from among them, and to bring him into the castle. (Acts 23:10)

And I knew such a man, (whether in the body, or out of the body, I cannot tell: God knoweth;) how that he was *caught up* into paradise, and heard unspeakable words, which it is not lawful for a man to utter. (2 Corinthians 12:3-4)

And of some have compassion, making a difference: and others save with fear, *pulling them out* of the fire; hating even the garment spotted by the flesh. (Jude 22-23)

The debate is not whether Christians will be caught up in the clouds to meet King Jesus. Clearly, the Bible tells us that the saints will meet Jesus in the clouds. That event is the Parousia, the glorious physical arrival of the King of Kings and Lord of Lords.

"Parousia" is a Greek word used 24 times in the New Testament Bible that denotes the arrival of a very important person. In ancient times, it was customary for a town to send an official delegation to greet a visiting monarch or nobleman. The special arrival of the VIP was called the "Parousia." Most of the New Testament verses that include Parousia refer to the Second Coming of Jesus Christ. The Latin word "advent" corresponds to the Greek word Parousia. Thus, traditional orthodox Christians interchangeably use the terms Second Coming, Second Advent, glorious appearing, and Parousia to refer to the glorious physical arrival of King Jesus on the Day of the Lord when the Church will meet King Jesus in the air to escort our triumphant monarch. That event is the Second Coming of Jesus Christ, not a mystical secret event called "The Rapture" that Evangelical Zionists claim will occur seven years before the Second Coming of our Lord and Savior.

There is no polite way to say it that won't offend Evangelical Zionists. The hard, cold truth is "The Rapture" is a colossal religious hoax perpetrated by Kaballah-entralled Freemasons dreaming of a third temple and a Masonic-Zionist empire. It is a fake proper pronoun that was deceitfully slipped into the lexicon of Christian churches. It is freely spoken with pompous authority in tens of thousands of churches, seminaries, and religious media programs, yet few hearers know the origin of "The Rapture" deception.

Eve-vangelicals Ate the Wrong Fruit

Most Evangelical Zionists mistakenly think that "The Rapture" and the Second Coming of Jesus are the same event. They glibly hear pastors, Bible prophecy teachers, and religious media celebrities extol "The Rapture" and assume they are talking about the Second Coming of the Lord. The pastors, prophecy teachers, and media celebrities know the difference, but intentionally don't fully explain it to their followers. That would be like a magician showing his audience how he made the tiger disappear on stage.

Only when a serious Bible student investigates the origin of "The Rapture" doctrine and delves deeply into the foundational tenets of its full theology does he or she come to the shocking realization that "The Rapture" and its interrelated teachings are not just another valid viewpoint worthy of consideration. The deeper you go into it, the more obvious it becomes that "The Rapture" industry is selling blasphemous heresies that directly contradict and repudiate the very foundation of Christianity. It is a demonic stronghold that grips the minds of millions of sincere Christians. Evangelical Zionist denominations, churches, ministries, and clergy should be placed on a cult watch list.

The Second Coming of Jesus Christ, the resurrection of the dead, and the arrival of New Jerusalem should be the source of hope and joy for all Christians, not confusion, fear, anxiety, division and strife. Millions of sincere Christians are confused because of one thing: "The Rapture." Evangelical Zionists insist the Second Coming of Jesus Christ is split into two parts: a secret removal of Christians followed seven years later by a public arrival of Jesus to establish a Jewish-controlled dynasty that last 1,000 years.

Aha! The sneaky serpent persuaded Christians to change God's spoken words. Its Satan's oldest trick in his worn bag of deception. He entices people to doubt and/or misquote the Word of God. Satan is amazed the trick still works on humans after all these years since the Garden of Eden, but he knows that human nature has not changed. We can only be changed by a genuine born again experience by placing our faith in Jesus Christ and His finished work on the Cross.

Satan tempted Eve to eat the fruit of the tree of knowledge of good and evil by asking her a question: Did God say you shall not eat of every tree of the garden? Satan knew precisely what God said about the trees in the Garden of Eden. Satan slyly twisted God's words, however, to interject confusion in Eve's mind. Eve herself misquoted God in her reply to Satan. She told the devil that God said *"Ye shall not eat of it, neither shall ye touch it, lest ye die."* God did not tell Adam he could not touch the fruit. He told him not to eat it.

God gave the instruction to Adam before Eve was made. Adam's responsibility as Eve's husband was to accurately teach his wife the word of God. One of three things happened: (1) Adam taught God's words incorrectly to his wife Eve; or, (2) Eve did not listen closely to what her husband correctly said; thus, she misunderstood his words; or, (3) Adam correctly taught Eve, but she consciously chose to change her husband's instructions.

Regardless, Eve misquoted God and Satan took advantage of her inaccuracy. He deceived her through her unwillingness to stick with the exact words God said. The lesson to us is this: do not tinker with the Word of God. We must always quote it accurately.

Now the serpent was more subtle than any beast of the field which the Lord God had made. And he said unto the woman, Yea, hath God said, Ye shall not eat of every tree of the garden? *And the woman said unto the serpent, We may eat of the fruit of the trees of the garden: but of the fruit of the tree which is in the midst of the garden, God hath said, Ye shall not eat of it, neither shall ye touch it, lest ye die.* **And the serpent said unto the woman, Ye shall not surely die: for God doth know that in the day ye eat thereof, then your eyes shall be opened, and ye shall be as gods, knowing good and evil. And when the woman saw that the tree was good for food, and that it was pleasant to the eyes, and a tree to be desired to make one wise, she took of the fruit thereof, and did eat, and gave also unto her husband with her; and he did eat. And the eyes of them both were opened, and they knew that they were naked; and they sewed fig leaves together, and made themselves aprons. (Genesis 3:1-7)**

This example shows us how easily we can be deceived and not know it. Eve thought God said she couldn't touch the fruit, but God said they couldn't eat it. It was a slight variation of God's word, but the damage was significant. We must vigilantly guard our minds and lips from believing and speaking things not in the New Testament Bible. Jesus Christ fulfilled all of God's promises to Israel. The Old Covenant is old! It was replaced by the New Covenant which is new! Yet, Evangelical Zionists teach that the Jews must return to the land of Palestine, rebuild the temple that

God destroyed, and once again sacrifice bulls and goats because the blood of Jesus isn't good enough to atone for the sins of Jews.

Eve opened her heart to be deceived by Satan because she misquoted God's words. She paid a steep price for not precisely knowing or by altering what God said to Adam. Mankind's first couple were booted out of the Garden of Eden for not obeying God's instructions. Let their punishment be a stark reminder to all of us to not misquote God's word, and neither add nor take away anything in the Holy Bible. Do you still believe in "The Rapture" when you now know it isn't in the Bible? Will you continue to defend "The Rapture" now that you know its spiritual fathers were tainted with Freemasonry, necromancy, occultism, lying, and fraud?

Evangelical Zionists act like Eve. She sincerely believed that God said she could not touch the fruit of the tree of knowledge of good and evil, or she consciously changed God's instructions. Like Eve, Evangelical Zionists either sincerely believe the Bible says there will be a secret rapture of Christians, or they consciously deceive others to make them believe there will be a secret "Rapture" of saints. Eve was sincerely wrong, and so are Evangelical Zionists. Eve lost her place in the Garden of Eden. Evangelical Zionists may lose their place in the Kingdom of God. They are dangerously pushing lies inside the Church of God. Apostle Peter said false prophets and teachers who bring in damnable heresies bring upon themselves swift destruction. A similar warning was issued by Apostle Paul who included heresies in a list of "works of the flesh" that will prevent practitioners of such sins from inheriting the kingdom of God.

But there were false prophets also among the people, even as there shall be false teachers among you, who privily shall bring in

damnable heresies, even denying the Lord that bought them, and bring upon themselves swift destruction. (2 Peter 2:1)

Now the works of the flesh are manifest, which are these; Adultery, fornication, uncleanness, lasciviousness, idolatry, witchcraft, hatred, variance, emulations, wrath, strife, seditions, heresies, envyings, murders, drunkenness, revellings, and such like: of the which I tell you before, as I have also told you in time past, that they which do such things shall not inherit the kingdom of God. (Galatians 5:19-21)

Indoctrinated by that master seducer and deceiver John Nelson Darby and his snake oil hustler sidekick "Doctor" Cyrus Scofield, Evangelical Zionists arrogantly and frivolously toss around proper pronouns that they arbitrarily inserted in the Holy Bible without asking God's permission: The Rapture, Heavenly People, Earthly People, The Antichrist, The Great Tribulation, Tribulation Saints, Tribulation Temple, The War of Armageddon, Daniel's 70th Week, Revived Roman Empire, God's Prophetic Time Clock, Antichrist Peace Treaty with Israel, Star of David, One World Religion, One World Government, One World Money, Millennial Kingdom. And let's not forget the wonderful Spotless Red Heifer that Evangelical Zionists eagerly anticipate its appearance much like tribal people waiting for the Great White Buffalo.

Eve was deceived and so are today's Evangelical Zionists. Perhaps they should be renamed "Eve-vangelicals" or "Deceived-vangelicals." They foolishly believe their silly Rapture pooka is real. Deceived themselves, they go about deceiving others too. Evangelical Zionist teachers and disciples fit Apostle Paul's warning to Timothy that evil men and seducers will grow worse as years go by. Those who seduce and lead astray others, deceive themselves and ruin their own souls as they depart farther from God's truth. They also persecute men and women who defend and adhere to the Apostles' Doctrine.

Yea, and all that will live godly in Christ Jesus shall suffer persecution. But evil men and seducers shall wax worse and worse, deceiving, and being deceived. (2 Timothy 3:12-13)

Using the proven tricks of his trade, Satan, the crafty deceiver, used John Nelson Darby to start a cult (Plymouth Brethren) that claimed God exclusively gave them "recovered knowledge" lost to the church over 1800 years. Satan later used a crafty Zionist lawyer for the Rothschild banking dynasty to assist Cyrus Scofield, a lying swindler, to insert Darby's deception in the Holy Bible and peddle it to tens of thousands of churches, thereby cunningly and quietly changing the Gospel. Consequently, the Evangelical churches morphed into the Deceived-vangelical churches by enthusiastically promoting big lies they readily ate that were dangling from Scofield's Tree of Babylonian Knowledge in Darby's Garden of Deception.

Is the Blessed Hope a Who or What?

What does the Bible say about our Lord's Second Coming? Let's start with Apostle Paul's admonition to live soberly in this world while awaiting the arrival of Jesus Christ. In his Second Epistle to Titus, the beloved apostle wrote:

For the grace of God that bringeth salvation hath appeared to all men, teaching us that, denying ungodliness and worldly lusts, we should live soberly, righteously, and godly, in this present world; *looking for that blessed hope, and the glorious appearing of the great God and our Savior Jesus Christ;* **who gave himself for us, that he might redeem us from all iniquity, and purify unto himself**

a peculiar people, zealous of good works. These things speak, and exhort, and rebuke with all authority. Let no man despise thee. (Titus 2:11-15)

The phrase "blessed hope" requires our attention. Evangelical Zionists say it means one thing, and traditional orthodox Christians say it means something else. Words matter. Evangelical Zionists are from Venus. Traditional orthodox believers are from Mars. The two groups do not speak the same language. Both, however, must accurately quote the Bible or they will be guilty of committing Eve's sin.

What is the "blessed hope"? Evangelical Zionists teach that the "blessed hope" is their mythical Rapture pooka - the great evacuation of God's "Heavenly People" to safety in Heaven during a time of great tribulation that they claim will last seven years.

Instead of asking *what* is the blessed hope, we should ask *who* is our blessed hope?

Our blessed hope is a person, not an event. St. Paul the Apostle encouraged us to anticipate the arrival of our blessed hope. He did not say we should hope for a great escape from persecution. The blessed hope is not the "Rapture" as taught by Evangelical Zionists.

...looking for that blessed hope, and the glorious appearing of the great God and our Savior Jesus Christ... (Titus 2:13)

Jesus is our blessed hope. Men and women of faith in the Old Testament and New Testament held onto their hope of the promised arrival of the Messiah. Old Testament patriarchs were not looking for land. They were yearning for the promised Messiah to deliver them from the curse of death brought upon mankind by Adam and Eve's sin. New Testament apostles never spoke a word about the Jews returning to Israel someday to reclaim their land. Instead, they told both Jews and Gentiles to look for that city whose builder and maker is God. The glorious appearing is the Second Coming of Jesus. Therefore, the saints are waiting for the glorious appearing of our blessed hope who is Jesus Christ.

For centuries, traditional orthodox Christians always focused on the glorious appearing of our blessed hope - Jesus Christ - and everything His appearing will bring: the opening of all graves, the resurrection of the dead, the Church caught up into the air to meet the Lord, the judgement of all mankind, the testing of our works, the destruction of the old Earth, the creation of new heavens and a new Earth, the arrival of New Jerusalem, and the restoration of all things. Traditional orthodox Christianity is focused on Jesus Christ and His eternal Kingdom that shall have no end.

Cultish Evangelical Zionists, however, are obsessed with things: their escape from persecution, the State of Israel, politically supporting Zionists to militarily seize more land from Palestinians, and a future global Zionist kingdom. The former ("The Rapture") makes a way for the latter ("The Millennial Kingdom"), meaning the removal of non-Jewish Christians from the Earth makes it possible for Masonic Greater Israel to reappear and dominate the entire planet for 1,000 years.

The Parable of the Weeds and the Second Coming of Jesus Christ

The Bible does not say anything about a secret Rapture, but the New Testament Bible says much about the Final Day - which is the Day of the Lord, the Second Coming, Judgment Day, and the restitution of all things all rolled together into one mega-cosmic event. First, Jesus told us that all wicked and unrepentant sinners will be gathered first by the angelic reapers. They will be bundled and burned like weeds tossed into a fire. You can find His words in the Parable of the Weeds:

Another parable put he forth unto them, saying, The kingdom of heaven is likened unto a man which sowed good seed in his field: but while men slept, his enemy came and sowed tares among the wheat, and went his way. But when the blade was sprung up, and brought forth fruit, then appeared the tares also. So the servants of the householder came and said unto him, Sir, didst not thou sow good seed in thy field? from whence then hath it tares? He said unto them, An enemy hath done this. The servants said unto him, Wilt thou then that we go and gather them up? But he said, Nay; lest while ye gather up the tares, ye root up also the wheat with them. *Let both grow together until the harvest: and in the time of harvest I will say to the reapers, Gather ye together first the tares, and bind them in bundles to burn them: but gather the wheat into my barn.* **(Matthew 13:24-30)**

There are no mysteries about the parable. In Matthew 13, Jesus gave us the key in Matthew 13:36-43 to unlock the code. Using the key to this parable we know that:

- The Sower of good seed is Jesus Christ.
- The field is the world.
- The good seed are the children of the kingdom (Christians from all nations, races, and tribes).
- The tares (weeds) are the children (unrepentant sinners/the wicked) of the wicked one (Satan).
- The enemy who sowed the tares (unrepentant sinners/the wicked) is Satan.
- The harvest is the end of the world.

- The reapers are the angels.
- Jesus shall dispatch His reapers (angels).
- The reapers (angels) shall gather out of His kingdom all things that offend Him (unrepentant sinners), and those who do iniquity (the wicked).
- The tares (unrepentant sinners/the wicked) shall be tossed by the reapers (angels) into a furnace of fire (the lake of fire).
- There shall be wailing and gnashing of teeth among the tares (unrepentant sinners/the wicked) in the furnace of fire.
- Then (notice that Jesus told us when the saints will be gathered) shall the righteous shine forth as the sun in the kingdom of their Father.

Then Jesus sent the multitude away, and went into the house: and his disciples came unto him, saying, Declare unto us the parable of the tares of the field. He answered and said unto them, He that soweth the good seed is the Son of man; the field is the world; the good seed are the children of the kingdom; but the tares are the children of the wicked one; the enemy that sowed them is the devil; the harvest is the end of the world; and the reapers are the angels. As therefore the tares are gathered and burned in the fire; so shall it be in the end of this world. *The Son of man shall send forth his angels, and they shall gather out of his kingdom all things that offend, and them which do iniquity; and shall cast them into a furnace of fire: there shall be wailing and gnashing of teeth. Then shall the righteous shine forth as the sun in the kingdom of their Father. Who hath ears to hear, let him hear.* (Matthew 13:36-43)

Who gets plucked up first by the angels on the Final Day? The righteous or the wicked? Clearly, Jesus said His angels will first gather the wicked and unrepentant sinners.

Let both grow together until the harvest: *and in the time of harvest I will say to the reapers, Gather ye together first the tares, and bind them in bundles to burn them: but gather the wheat into my barn.* (Matthew 13:30)

When are Christians caught up to meet the Lord? Jesus said it will happen after the wicked are gathered by the angels, tied up in bundles, and tossed into the fire like weeds.

"Then shall the righteous shine forth as the sun in the kingdom of their Father. Who hath ears to hear, let him hear." (Matthew 13:43)

The "when" is "then." The "then" comes after that which is first. Therefore, "then" (when the righteous shine forth) comes after the wicked have been bundled and burned.

Evangelical Zionism brazenly contradicts the words of Jesus Christ. Why can't Evangelical Zionists accept Jesus' words without tinkering with them? How could millions of Evangelical Zionists be duped into believing that Christians will be "raptured away" and transported to Heaven seven years before the Lord's Second Coming? Can they not see that their man-made doctrines contradict the words of Jesus?

Only the lying Devil is crafty enough to pull off such a feat in Christ' church. The Bible tells us the proper sequence of events. Jesus said the wicked are gathered first, followed by the saints. Do Evangelical Zionists know more than Jesus? Or have they changed His words? Whom do you believe? Evangelical Zionists or Jesus? Always believe Jesus. He cannot lie. John Nelson Darby, a man from an Irish family that practiced occultism, was a deceiver in the 19th century. His lies are still deceiving people in the 21st century. Cyrus Scofield was a liar and deceiver. His deception is still at work in many churches through the Scofield Reference Bible. There was a plan. It worked.

The Parable of the Wedding Banquet and the Second Coming of Jesus Christ

Jesus gave us another parable about the wicked being bundled and burned first on the Final Day.

And Jesus answered and spake unto them again by parables, and said, The kingdom of heaven is like unto a certain king, which made a marriage for his son, and sent forth his servants to call them that were bidden to the wedding: and they would not come. Again, he sent forth other servants, saying, Tell them which are bidden, Behold, I have prepared my dinner: my oxen and my fatlings are killed, and all things are ready: come unto the marriage. But they made light of it, and went their ways, one to his farm, another to his merchandise: and the remnant took his servants, and entreated them spitefully, and slew them. But when the king heard thereof, he was wroth: and he sent forth his armies, and destroyed those murderers, and burned up their city.

Then saith he to his servants, The wedding is ready, but they which were bidden were not worthy. Go ye therefore into the highways, and as many as ye shall find, bid to the marriage. So those servants went out into the highways, and gathered together all as many as they found, both bad and good: and the wedding was furnished with guests. And when the king came in to see the guests, he saw there a man which had not on a wedding garment: and he saith unto him, Friend, how camest thou in hither not having a wedding garment? And he was speechless. Then said the king to the servants, Bind him hand and foot, and take him

away, and cast him into outer darkness; there shall be weeping and gnashing of teeth. For many are called, but few are chosen. (Matthew 22: 1-14)

Let's breakdown the sequence of events in this parable:

- The King (God the Father) called a wedding for his Son (Jesus Christ).
- He sent forth His servants (the Church) to call those who were invited to the wedding (the Jews).
- The Jews would not come.
- He sent forth more servants (the Church) to announce a great wedding feast for the invited guests.
- The invited (Jews) made fun of the wedding invitation and went about their daily affairs.
- The invited (Jews) spitefully mistreated the servants (Christians) who proclaimed the Gospel and killed them.
- When the King heard what the Jews did to his servants (Christians), he was wroth with anger.
- He sent forth his army and burned up their city - Jerusalem and the Temple. (This happened in 70AD when the Romans destroyed the Temple.)
- When the invited guests (Jews) spurned the king's (God's) invitation, he sent his servants (Christians) out into the highways and gathered anybody who would come to the wedding: gang members, homosexuals, prostitutes, drunkards, drug addicts, the poor, the lame, the blind...all were welcomed!
- The wedding party was full of guests.
- The king, however, noticed one man in the wedding party who was not properly attired for the event. The king asked

how he managed to slip pass the security guards to get into the wedding party.

- The man was speechless.
- The king ordered his servants to bind his hands and feet, take him away into outer darkness, and there shall be weeping and gnashing of teeth.
- Many are called to the wedding, but few are chosen. (The Holy Spirit invites people to be among the elect, but many disqualify themselves by refusing to submit to the king's ways.)

This parable utterly refutes Evangelical Zionism. Originally, the Jews were the only people on the wedding invitation list. They not only rejected God's royal invitation to attend the wedding of His Son Jesus Christ to New Jerusalem, they mocked the invitation, and persecuted and killed both the Old Testament prophets and the New Testament apostles who delivered the invitation. The Jews ignored the wedding invitation so that they could tend to their business affairs. Insulted and furious by the Jews' snub to attend His Son's wedding, God sent His messengers out into the world to invite anybody who would accept the invitation.

For God so loved the world, that he gave his only begotten Son, that whosoever believeth in him should not perish, but have everlasting life. (John 3:16)

But go ye and learn what that meaneth, I will have mercy, and not sacrifice: for I am not come to call the righteous, but sinners to repentance. (Matthew 9:13)

For whosoever shall call upon the name of the Lord shall be saved. (Romans 10:13)

The king's servants (Christians who share the gospel with sinners) filled up the wedding hall with guests from every nation wherever they could find people who would listen and respond to the invitation (evangelization of the world). When the place was full (the time of the end when no more would be invited) it was time for the wedding to begin. The grand and glorious wedding party is scheduled to be held on the Final Day. The Final Day is the Second Coming of Jesus, the Day of the Lord, Judgment Day, the day that the universe goes dark, the day when the cosmos is rolled up like a scroll, the day that all humans who ever lived will be separated into groups of goats and sheep, the day that our works are judged, the day that the wicked are cast into the lake of fire, the day that earth will disappear in flames, the day that a new earth is created, the day that New Jerusalem comes down from Heaven, the day that God moves from Heaven to New Jerusalem! Will you attend the wedding? Please RSVP the king!

In the parable, the king noticed a man who sneaked into the wedding hall. What gave him away as an imposter? It was his clothing. He was improperly dressed for such a grand celebration. Would you wear blue jeans, an old sweater, and boots to attend a state dinner at the White House or Buckingham Palace? Even if you succeeded getting pass the guards, you still would be the odd little duck in the banquet room if all the other guests were dressed in tuxedos and gowns. You would be noticed.

What will make you conspicuous to the reaper angels on the Final Day? What will cause you to stand out in the masses of mankind as somebody unfit to attend the grand and glorious wedding of Jesus Christ and His bride New Jerusalem? It will your spiritual clothing. When the Final Day suddenly arrives, we must be clothed with garments of salvation, covered with the robe of righteousness, and adorned with jewels. If you are not wearing them, the reaper angels will bind your feet and hands and toss you into outer darkness where you will wail and gnash your teeth forever.

I will greatly rejoice in the Lord, my soul shall be joyful in my God; for he hath clothed me with the garments of salvation, he hath covered me with the robe of righteousness, as a bridegroom decketh himself with ornaments, and as a bride adorneth herself with her jewels. (Isaiah 61:10)

And I John saw the holy city, new Jerusalem, coming down from God out of heaven, prepared as a bride adorned for her husband. (Revelation 21:2)

When will this happen? Those unworthy to attend the glorious wedding celebration will be "cuffed and stuffed" by Heaven's cops immediately before the start of the wedding ceremony on the Final Day. Once again, we see the same pattern: The unsaved shall be bundled and burned first before the spotless Church enters the wedding party.

Yet, the Evangelical Zionists insist that Jesus will first secretly rapture away the saints and whisked them to Heaven while the wicked Antichrist rules the world for seven years, 144,000 Jewish male virgins will preach that God will soon end His postponement of the kingdom, the ancient Davidic empire will soon be restored, the Holy Spirit will be removed, and the Antichrist will persecute and behead people who manage to get saved without the Holy Spirit calling them to Calvary's cross and presbyters baptizing them into the Church. It is astounding that millions of men and women have fallen for this unholy hooey. John Nelson Darby, the master deceiver, cleverly added his leaven into Evangelical churches in the 19th century. Cyrus Scofield kneaded the yeast into tens of thousands of Evangelical churches with his blasphemous

Scofield Reference Bible. Sadly, the damage has been done. Darby and Scofield created an ecclesiastical toxic waste dump that has polluted the Body of Christ with its poisons. Nobody should enter an Evangelical Zionist church without wearing a HAZMAT suit, boots, and gloves to handle the church's hazardous materials.

In His Own Words: Jesus Speaks About His Second Coming

Jesus clearly warned that His return to earth would be sudden and unexpected, and that His disciples must always be ready. Jesus never promised Christians an easy exit from earth during a time of war, violence, upheaval, famine, calamities, and persecution. He did promise, however, to never leave nor forsake us. Furthermore, Jesus never mentioned a two-stage return to earth - meaning a secret evacuation of believers before the start of tribulation, followed seven years later by a full-scale Second Advent. Unfortunately, millions of Evangelical Zionists have more of Darby's DPPZism stockpiled in their brains than the Word of God stored in their hearts.

Be strong and of a good courage, fear not, nor be afraid of them: for the Lord thy God, he it is that doth go with thee; he will not fail thee, nor forsake thee. (Deuteronomy 31:6)

I pray not that thou shouldest take them out of the world, but that thou shouldest keep them from the evil. (John 17:15)

Jesus Christ said:

- Diseased trees that produce bad fruit shall be burned.
  Every tree that bringeth not forth good fruit is hewn down, and cast into the fire. Wherefore by their fruits ye shall know them. (Matthew 7:19-20)

- Spiritual imposters shall be cast away from His presence.

  Not everyone that saith unto me, Lord, Lord, shall enter into the kingdom of heaven; but he that doeth the will of my Father which is in heaven. Many will say to me in that day, Lord, Lord, have we not prophesied in thy name? and in thy name have cast out devils? and in thy name done many wonderful works? And then will I profess unto them, I never knew you: depart from me, ye that work iniquity. (Matthew 7:21-23)

- People who build their lives on shifting sand shall be washed away.

  And every one that heareth these sayings of mine, and doeth them not, shall be likened unto a foolish man, which built his house upon the sand: and the rain descended, and the floods came, and the winds blew, and beat upon that house; and it fell: and great was the fall of it. (Matthew 7:26-27)

- We must fear God who can cast our soul and body in Hell, not men who can only murder our physical body.

  And fear not them which kill the body, but are not able to kill the soul: but rather fear him which is able to destroy both soul and body in hell. (Matthew 10:28)

- People who witness the mighty works of God on earth and reject Him will burn hotter in the lake of fire than the people who lived in Sodom and Gomorrah.

  But I say unto you, It shall be more tolerable for Tyre and Sidon at the day of judgment, than for you. And thou, Capernaum, which art exalted unto heaven, shalt be brought down to hell: for if the mighty works, which have been done in thee, had been done in Sodom, it would have remained until this day. But I say unto you, That it shall be more tolerable for the land of Sodom in the day of judgment, than for thee. (Matthew 11:22-24)

- The evil fish caught in the net will be separated and burned in a fiery furnace.

  Again, the kingdom of heaven is like unto a net, that was cast into the sea, and gathered of every kind: which, when it was full, they drew to shore, and sat down, and gathered the good into vessels, but cast the bad away. So shall it be at the end of the world: the angels shall come forth, and sever the wicked from among the just, and shall cast them into the furnace of fire: there shall be wailing and gnashing of teeth. (Matthew 13:47-50)

- Jews who stubbornly reject their Messiah Jesus Christ shall perish. The vineyard tenants who beat the master's servants and plotted to kill his son to seize his inheritance shall be cast away. Their punishment occurs when the lord of the vineyard comes to his vineyard.

  But when the husbandmen saw the son, they said among themselves, This is the heir; come, let us kill him, and let us seize on his inheritance. And they caught him, and cast him out of the vineyard, and slew him. When the lord therefore of the vineyard cometh, what will he do unto those husbandmen? They say unto him, He will miserably destroy those wicked men, and will let out his vineyard unto other husbandmen, which shall render him the fruits in their seasons. (Matthew 21:38-41)

- Christians shall suffer affliction, be killed, and hated for the name of Jesus, but many spiritually weak Christians will fall away and betray the true Christians.

Then shall they deliver you up to be afflicted, and shall kill you: and ye shall be hated of all nations for my name's sake. And then shall many be offended, and shall betray one another, and shall hate one another. (Matthew 24:9-10)

- Christians who endure unto the end shall be saved.

  But he that shall endure unto the end, the same shall be saved. (Matthew 24:13)

- Christians will preach the Gospel globally to the end of the age (meaning that the Holy Spirit will not be removed during the time of great tribulation). The end (the Final Day) shall come when the gospel of the kingdom (not the gospel of wealth, the gospel of personal motivation, the gospel of social justice, nor the gospel of Zionism) is preached in the entire world for a witness to all nations as evidence to be presented when the nations are judged.

  And this gospel of the kingdom shall be preached in all the world for a witness unto all nations; and then shall the end come. (Matthew 24:14)

- Sinners will be swept away when the Lord returns in the same manner that sinners were swept away when the Great Flood came during the days of Noah. The people who are "taken" are not the Christians. The Christians are those who are left behind. That totally contradicts the fictional Left Behind novels co-written by Tim LaHaye and Jerry Jenkins. Jesus said sinners will be "swept away" when He returns, not "left behind." The Bible is truth. The *Left Behind* novels and films are fiction. Believe the Bible!

  But of that day and hour knoweth no man, no, not the angels of heaven, but my Father only. But as the days of Noah were, so shall also the coming of the Son of man be. For as in the days that were before the flood they were eating and drinking, marrying and giving in marriage, until the day that Noah entered into the ark, and knew not until the flood came, and took them all away; so shall also the coming of the Son of man be. Then shall two be in the field; the one shall be taken, and the other left. Two women shall be grinding at the mill; the one shall be taken, and the other left. Watch therefore: for ye know not what hour your Lord doth come. But know this, that if the goodman of the house had known in what watch the thief would come, he would have watched, and would not have suffered his house to be broken up. Therefore be ye also ready: for in such an hour as ye think not the Son of man cometh. (Matthew 24:36-44)

- Foolish religious people whose lives are empty of the Word of God will be denied entrance into the Kingdom of God when Jesus suddenly and unexpectedly returns.

Then all those virgins arose, and trimmed their lamps. And the foolish said unto the wise, Give us of your oil; for our lamps are gone out. But the wise answered, saying, *Not so;* lest there be not enough for us and you: but go ye rather to them that sell, and buy for yourselves. And while they went to buy, the bridegroom came; and they that were ready went in with him to the marriage: and the door was shut. Afterward came also the other virgins, saying, Lord, Lord, open to us. But he answered and said, Verily I say unto you, I know you not. Watch therefore, for ye know neither the day nor the hour wherein the Son of man cometh. (Matthew 25:7-13)

- Slothful servants who do nothing with their talents and resources for the kingdom of God shall perish.

  His lord answered and said unto him, *Thou* wicked and slothful servant, thou knewest that I reap where I sowed not, and gather where I have not strawed: thou oughtest therefore to have put my money to the exchangers, and *then* at my coming I should have received mine own with usury. Take therefore the talent from him, and give *it* unto him which hath ten talents. For unto every one that hath shall be given, and he shall have abundance: but from him that hath not shall be taken away even that which he hath. And cast ye the unprofitable servant into outer darkness: there shall be weeping and gnashing of teeth. (Matthew 25:26-30)

- People who have no compassion for the poor, hungry, naked, imprisoned, and sick shall burn in Hell.

  Then shall he say also unto them on the left hand, Depart from me, ye cursed, into everlasting fire, prepared for the devil and his angels: for I was an hungred, and ye gave me no meat: I was thirsty, and ye gave me no drink: I was a stranger, and ye took me not in: naked, and ye clothed me not: sick, and in prison, and ye visited me not. Then shall they also answer him, saying, Lord, when saw we thee an hungred, or athirst, or a stranger, or naked, or sick, or in prison, and did not minister unto thee? Then shall he answer them, saying, Verily I say unto you, Inasmuch as ye did it not to one of the least of these, ye did it not to me. And these shall go away into everlasting punishment: but the righteous into life eternal. (Matthew 25:41-46)

- Church members who are embarrassed to be known as disciples of Jesus Christ shall be rejected.

  Or what shall a man give in exchange for his soul? *Whosoever therefore shall be ashamed of me and of my words* **in this adulterous and sinful generation; of him also shall the Son of man be ashamed, when he cometh in the glory of his Father with the holy angels.** (Mark 8:37-38)

- Christians shall be present on earth during the time of great tribulation.

  For in those days shall be affliction, such as was not from the beginning of the creation which God created unto this time, neither shall be. And except that the Lord had shortened those days, no flesh should be saved: *but for the elect's sake, whom he hath chosen, he hath shortened the days.* **(Mark 13:19-20)**

- Angels will gather God's elect after the tribulation when Christians see Jesus coming in the clouds.

  But in those days, after that tribulation, **the sun shall be darkened, and the moon shall not give her light, and the stars of heaven shall fall, and the powers that are in heaven shall be shaken. And then shall they see the Son of man coming in the clouds with great power and glory.** *And then shall he send his angels, and shall gather together his elect from the four winds, from the uttermost part of the earth to the uttermost part of heaven.* **(Mark 13:24-27)**

- Believers are admonished to stay awake and watch for Jesus' return.

  But of that day and that hour knoweth no man, no, not the angels which are in heaven, neither the Son, but the

Father. *Take ye heed, watch and pray: for ye know not when the time is.* For the Son of man is as a man taking a far journey, who left his house, and gave authority to his servants, and to every man his work, and commanded the porter to watch. *Watch ye therefore: for ye know not when the master of the house cometh,* at even, or at midnight, or at the cockcrowing, or in the morning: lest coming suddenly he find you sleeping. *And what I say unto you I say unto all, Watch.* (Mark 13:32-37)

Where o where is "The Rapture" of God's "Heavenly People" before the time of tribulation? Did Jesus forget to mention it to His disciples? Did the Holy Spirit not inspire the apostles to include it in the Gospels? Did Matthew, Mark, Luke and John omit it because they didn't think it was important enough to be in the Holy Bible? No, my friend. The reason "The Rapture" is not in the Bible is because it isn't from God. And if it isn't from God why do so many foolish, deceived Evangelical Zionists vehemently insist it is in the Bible? They willingly choose to believe a lie. They believe in a mythical pooka conjured up by a man whose family practiced occultism. Their pooka pal was sold to them by a conman who went to jail for duping trusting souls.

Evangelical Zionists who fanatically cling to Darby's Deception have Bibles to study, yet willfully believe and propagate spiritual lies to deceive people and take away knowledge of the truth. They own the consequences. Woe to them if Jesus says to John Nelson Darby and his disciples in seminaries, Bible colleges, religious publishing houses, religious media outlets, and church denominations that teach his deception:

Woe unto you, lawyers! for ye have taken away the key of knowledge: ye entered not in yourselves, and them that were entering in ye hindered. (Luke 11:52)

Jesus Christ was offered once to bear the sins of many. He shall appear the second time for those who are looking for Him. There's no mention anywhere in the Holy Bible of a third time or a secret time. The Book of Hebrews says:

"...so Christ was *once offered to bear the sins of many*; and unto them that look for him shall *he appear the second time without sin unto salvation.*" (Hebrews 9:28)

Apostle Paul gave Christians some good advice: Don't be ignorant.

But I would not have you to be ignorant, brethren, concerning them which are asleep, that ye sorrow not, even as others which have no hope. For if we believe that Jesus died and rose again, even so them also which sleep in Jesus will God bring with him. For this we say unto you by the word of the Lord, that we which are alive and remain unto the coming of the Lord shall not prevent them which are asleep. For the Lord himself shall descend from heaven with a shout, with the voice of the archangel, and with the trump of God: and the dead in Christ shall rise first: then we which are alive and remain shall be caught up together with them in the clouds, to meet the Lord in the air: and so shall we ever be with the Lord. Wherefore comfort one another with these words. (1 Thessalonians 4:13-18)

Is Apostle Paul referring to "The Rapture" or to the glorious Second Coming of Jesus Christ? Brazenly, Evangelical Zionists quote this scripture as evidence for both "The Rapture" and the

Second Coming! Which is it? You can't use the same Bible verses for two different events. It's no wonder so many Christians are confused.

Fortunately, Apostle Paul was not confused. He received revelation about the Parousia directly from Jesus Christ. John Nelson Darby was a cultist whose "revelations" came from demons. He told his Plymouth Brethren cultists that he possessed "recovered knowledge" about Biblical truth that had been lost to the world-wide Church since the Book of Acts. Who imparted this "recovered knowledge" to Darby? Was it the Holy Spirit or demons? Were the revelations channeled to Darby in seances? Apostle Paul said he received the gospel by the revelation of Jesus Christ. Darby's family held seances in their castle. Whom do you believe? Apostle Paul or Darby?

But I certify you, brethren, that the gospel which was preached of me is not after man. For I neither received it of man, neither was I taught it, but by the revelation of Jesus Christ. (Galatians 1:11-12)

Jesus revealed to Apostle Paul what will happen when our Savior returns for His saints. He saw the glorious appearing of our blessed hope. Paul said Jesus shall descend with a shout, with the voice of the archangel, and with the trump of God. What happens next? All graves are opened! All the dead from the beginning of time – wicked and righteous – shall come out of their graves and tombs. Angels will grab the wicked, bundled them, and take them away to be burned in the lake of fire. And then what happens? The saved saints who will come out of their graves will rise first into the air. Then we which are alive and remain (all the Christians alive on that glorious day) shall be caught up together with the righteous saints who were in the graves to meet Jesus in the air. We shall be the royal welcoming party that greets our King Jesus!

Will Jesus whisk us away to Heaven? No, my friend. We are not going to Heaven after the Second Coming of Jesus! We shall ever be with the Lord in New Jerusalem on the new Earth. Humans were not made to live in Heaven. We have legs and feet. We were made by God to walk on terra firma. Our Heavenly Father will make a new Earth for His saved elect, and He will pack up all His stuff in Heaven and relocate to New Jerusalem so that He can move in with His children. Stop trying to get into Heaven. Set your eyes upon New Jerusalem, the royal city which has foundations, whose builder and maker is God.

"...then we which are alive and remain shall be caught up together with them in the clouds, to meet the Lord in the air: and so shall we ever be with the Lord." (1 Thessalonians 4:17)

The Second Coming of Jesus on the Final Day shall be:

- Singular

CHAPTER 4

HIS SECOND COMING SHALL BE SUDDEN AND UNEXPECTED

H AVE YOU EVER TAKEN a long journey on a highway across several states or provinces?

You drive endless hours knowing that many more miles are ahead. You chat with fellow travelers in the vehicle, listen to music or an informative talk program, or just look at the interesting scenery as the miles pass by your window.

Prior to satellite-based radio navigation systems (GPS), travelers relied on paper highway maps to show them the way to their destination. Today drivers listen to an automated voice that instructs them where to go and prompts them to turn onto another road or street. The voice even tells them when they have arrived at their destination. (At the time of the publication of this book, society is quickly moving toward autonomous-driven vehicles that will not need humans to do anything other than to get in and out of the vehicle.)

Currently, how would you travel from one place to another if global positioning satellites failed because of an electromagnetic storm or attack? Do you know how to read a map? Do you even own a highway map? Do you have a compass? Can you read a compass?

Back in the day, drivers without GPS also relied on highway signs. There was no need to be super-alert when your destination was a hundred miles or kilometers away. As you got closer, however, it was necessary to sit up in your seat and pay close attention to the highway signs.

A succession of signs alerted you to the distance to your destination. 100 miles (kilometers). 50 miles (kilometers). 25 miles (kilometers). 15 miles (kilometers). 10 miles (kilometers). 5 miles (kilometers). 1 mile (kilometer). Next exit!

Notice that the closer you get to the exit more signs appear to alert you to get ready for the exit. At the 100-miles (kilometers) marker, the next sign is 50 miles (kilometers) away. By the time you reach the 10-mile (kilometers) marker, the next sign is only five miles (kilometers) away. It is shouting, "The exit is very close. Prepare to exit!" Shorter space between signs means you are quickly approaching the end of the journey. Failure to pay attention to the highway signs or the GPS navigation voice could result in bypassing the exit.

So too will be the coming of our Lord Jesus Christ. We must watch for the signs of His glorious appearing. The closer we approach our exit from this world, the faster the signs will appear along the way. Devout Christians walking closely with God, fellowshipping with the Holy Spirit, studying the Holy Bible, and closely monitoring world events and trends will not be surprised by Jesus' arrival. Indeed, they will be eagerly anticipating Him! For alert Christians, the Lord's return will be sudden, but not unexpected. It's like a friend who calls to say he is coming to your house soon. Suddenly, your doorbell rings and there stands your friend waiting to enter your house. You knew he was coming soon, but amazed at how quickly he arrived! Your friend's arrival is sudden, but not unexpected. He told you he was coming to your house.

It will be a different story for the unsaved and spiritually dull church members. Jesus' arrival will be sudden and unexpected. He will come quickly when they least expect it.

One of the highway signs Jesus told us to anticipate is the world returning to its wicked, rebellious state as in the days of Noah before the Great Flood. Raunchy sexual behavior, lewdness, homosexuality, sorcery, thievery, lying, violence, and wanton bloodshed had become the norm in human society. Adam's fall in the Garden of Eden produced a harvest of wickedness, sin, rebellion, and bloodshed. Almighty God was so grieved by mankind's obsession with sin that he lamented the day he made Adam.

And God saw that the wickedness of man was great in the earth, and that every imagination of the thoughts of his heart was only evil continually. And it repented the Lord that he had made man on the earth, and it grieved him at his heart. And the Lord said, I will destroy man whom I have created from the face of the earth; both man, and beast, and the creeping thing, and the fowls of the air; for it repenteth me that I have made them. But Noah found grace in the eyes of the Lord. (Genesis 6:5-8)

Unbeknownst to the lustful, violent inhabitants of Planet Earth, a verdict was rendered in Heaven's Court by the Judge of the

Universe. His gavel came down, a guilty verdict was declared, and the sentence was execution by drowning.

The earth also was corrupt before God, and the earth was filled with violence. And God looked upon the earth, and, behold, it was corrupt; for all flesh had corrupted his way upon the earth. And God said unto Noah, The end of all flesh is come before me; for the earth is filled with violence through them; and, behold, I will destroy them with the earth. (Genesis 6:11-13)

Jesus, who was an eyewitness to all of it, recounted to His disciples what went down that day more than 2,300 years earlier. He said people were partying, getting drunk, feasting, and getting married right up to the day Noah entered the ark. It was just another day in Sin City. Humans lived in an unrestrained state of rampant sinfulness for over a thousand years after Adam's fall in the Garden. Rebellion against God became a way of life. The "garden story" was old news. People had moved on. Humans no longer feared the God who evicted their ancestors Adam and Eve from the Garden of Eden. Indeed, humans no longer thought about God. He was irrelevant to their daily lives. They were living their best lives now.

Then it happened! They didn't see it coming. Bam! God re-entered humanity's dimension of time, space, and matter. He made a big statement to humans who arrogantly rebelled against their Divine Maker. This event is not a parable. It is not a fable. It is history. The Bible tells us the exact day it happened. Heaven's Court found mankind guilty of rebellion. A verdict was rendered and the Judge of the Universe pronounced a death sentence. Unbeknownst to sinful humans on earth, Heaven's great Judge had set the date for the guilty parties' swift execution. In God's sovereign kingdom, the guilty have no rights and are not entitled to know the date of their execution. Only the Judge knows the day and hour.

Moses, the human author of the Book of Genesis, told us the "when, what, who and where" details of the story.

In the six hundredth year of Noah's life, in the second month, the seventeenth day of the month, the same day were all the fountains of the great deep broken up, and the windows of heaven were opened. And the rain was upon the earth forty days and forty nights. In the selfsame day entered Noah, and Shem, and Ham, and Japheth, the sons of Noah, and Noah's wife, and the three wives of his sons with them, into the ark; they, and every beast after his kind, and all the cattle after their kind, and every creeping thing that creepeth upon the earth after his kind, and every fowl after his kind, every bird of every sort. And they went in unto Noah into the ark, two and two of all flesh, wherein is the breath of life. And they that went in, went in male and female of all flesh, as God had commanded him: and the Lord shut him in. (Genesis 7:11-16)

Take note of the last six words above: "And the Lord shut him in." Noah and his family were safely sealed inside the Ark. Divine judgement swept over the planet, but Noah and his family were kept from it even while they were in the midst of it. They were not removed from the place of the judgment, but safely sealed and preserved while the judgment was executed on everybody else. God's wrath was not meant for them. They found refuge and safety in the ark that God provided for them to ride out the flood.

What happened for 40 days is incomprehensible. A worldwide flood of water was a one-time event. It will never happen again. Every rainbow is a reminder of God's promise to never flood the world again with water.

And the flood was forty days upon the earth; and the waters increased, and bare up the ark, and it was lift up above the earth. And the waters prevailed, and were increased greatly upon the earth; and the ark went upon the face of the waters. And the waters prevailed exceedingly upon the earth; and all the high hills, that were under the whole heaven, were covered. Fifteen cubits upward did the waters prevail; and the mountains were covered. And all flesh died that moved upon the earth, both of fowl, and of cattle, and of beast, and of every creeping thing that creepeth upon the earth, and every man: all in whose nostrils was the breath of life, of all that was in the dry land, died. And every living substance was destroyed which was upon the face of the ground, both man, and cattle, and the creeping things, and the fowl of the heaven; and they were destroyed from the earth: and Noah only remained alive, and they that were with him in the ark. And the waters prevailed upon the earth an hundred and fifty days. (Genesis 7:17-24)

Another flood, however, is coming. Jesus told His disciples that when He returns to earth people will be gleefully sinning and rebelling against God just as they did in the days of Noah.

But as the days of Noah were, so shall also the coming of the Son of man be. For as in the days that were before the flood they were eating and drinking, marrying and giving in marriage, until the day that Noah entered into the ark, and knew not until the flood came, and took them all away; so shall also the coming of the Son of man be. (Matthew 24:37-39)

Noah entered the ark. The flood came. All sinners were swept away. They didn't see it coming. Their gross carnality blinded their eyes. The second coming of Jesus will be the same as the Great

Flood in Noah's age: Sudden and unexpected judgment upon the wicked and unprepared!

Beware the Three Snares

The next Great Flood will not be a worldwide deluge of water. It will be a global flood of fire! Jesus Christ will torch this old world with a consuming fire. Everybody not securely dwelling in the New Testament ark of baptism (1 Peter 3:18-20) will perish in the global furnace.

One thing is certain: The flames will appear suddenly and unexpectedly. No fire alarms will ring to warn sinners to flee to safety in Jesus' arms. No stairwells will appear to safely exit the planet. No firefighters will respond to extinguish the raging inferno. All unsaved sinners will be quickly bundled and burned with no prior warning of the impending global combustion.

The truth is they have been warned. And they are still being warned today by righteous men and women preaching repentance of sins, and salvation by believing on the name of Jesus Christ and water baptism. The world, however, is stepping up its efforts to censor and silence the voices who are warning that judgment is coming.

Warnings to repent, to believe on the name of Jesus Christ, and be baptized into the one, holy, catholic and apostolic church will continue to go forth throughout the world until the reapers suddenly appear to separate the wheat and tares, the sheep and the goats. The harvest of souls will be sudden, swift, and final.

Billions of unsaved souls will not be granted an opportunity to state their defense before the Great Throne of Judgement. Their arrival will be classified as "GOA." Guilty on arrival. And because they are already guilty, they are also condemned. They won't go before the Great Judge of the Universe to plead their case and make excuses for their behavior on earth. They will arrive shackled and escorted by angelic bailiffs into Heaven's courthouse with "Guilty!" stamped on their foreheads. The purpose of their brief appearance before God will be to receive their just punishment: eternal damnation in the Lake of Fire. They were found guilty while living on earth in defiance of God's commandments and by their rejection of His free gift of salvation made possible by the sacrifice of his dear son on Calvary's cross. A large sign in Heaven's Court will warn, "No repenting allowed." The time for repenting is now. Your tears will not move God's heart on the Final Day. Now is the time for remorse and weeping over your sins. There are no hankies in Heaven.

And take heed to yourselves, lest at any time your hearts be overcharged with surfeiting, and drunkenness, and cares of this life, and so that day come upon you unawares. For as a snare shall it come on all them that dwell on the face of the whole earth. Watch ye therefore, and pray always, that ye may be accounted worthy to escape all these things that shall come to pass, and to stand before the Son of man. (Luke 21:34-36)

These words were spoken by Jesus during his discourse about the end of the age and His second coming to earth. He talked about signs in the sun, and in the moon, and in the stars; the distress of nations, the powers of heaven shaken. Then He tossed in gluttony, excessive drinking, and the cares of this world. Where did that come from? What does our eating and drinking habits have to do with the second coming?

Referring to His return, Jesus told the crowd "And take heed to yourselves..." What does that mean?

Jesus told His disciples (and is telling us today!) to live chaste and holy lives before the all-seeing God of the Universe. "Take heed" means to "be on guard." It also means "make sure you don't let this happen." In today's parlance, Jesus would say to us, "Heads up! This is a warning. Pay attention to what I'm saying to you. I'm telling you three traps that can destroy you." His "heads up" alert was directed at specific traps that must be avoided at all costs in the lives of Believers:

- Surfeiting
- Drunkenness
- Cares of this life

Let's start with surfeiting. The Authorized King James Version used the old English word "surfeiting" which simply means "excessiveness." Primarily, it refers to gluttony in food and drink. A person who is prone to surfeiting is a man or woman who overindulges in food and drink. He or she eats far too much food and drinks far too many beverages than is necessary. The physical desires of their bodies overrule their minds and souls. They excessively eat and drink to satisfy an emotional emptiness, pain, weakness, need, craving, or lust. Jesus said it is a sin that must be conquered by Christians before they die or His second coming. Hopefully there isn't a weight limit for Christians to be caught up to meet the Lord in the air!

Next is drunkenness. It is the twin sin of surfeiting. Both originate from little or no self-discipline over physical and/or emotional cravings and lusts for satisfaction. Devout Christians may sincerely differ whether Christians are permitted to drink beer and wine, but there can be no toleration of drunkenness among disciples of Jesus Christ. Drunkenness is forbidden. There is nothing to debate.

Obviously, the admonition against intoxication also applies to marijuana and all mind-altering drugs. What about antidepressants and pain medications? How many Christians are stumbling through life addicted to pills to combat depression? How many Christians are addicted to pain medications? Do they know that pharmacia is witchcraft? The minds of disciples of Christ should not be blurred by alcohol or drugs. The Lord is coming back! We must be sober and ready for His return. If you are addicted to anything now, there is good news. The blood and name of Jesus can and will set you free if you truly desire to be liberated from any addiction. You cannot be vigilant if you are not sober. The Lord expects us to be sober when we exit this life or He returns.

But the end of all things is at hand: be ye therefore sober, and watch unto prayer. (I Peter 4:7)

The third trap is the cares of life. This is a familiar theme in Jesus' words. His famous Sermon on the Mount told us not to worry about food, clothing, and housing. His parable of the sower said the seed falling among the thorns refers to people who hear God's word, but the cares of this world and the deceitfulness of riches choke out the word and make it unfruitful. As Mary sat next to Jesus' feet listening to Him teach about the kingdom, her sister Martha fretted in the kitchen as she scurried to prepare a meal for a full house of unexpected guests. Jesus lovingly admonished her, "Martha, Martha, thou art careful and troubled about many things…" Martha was blessed with what few people on earth ever experience: A divine visitation of God in her home. The Son of God was in Martha's house personally teaching the principles of the kingdom, and the only thing on Martha's mind was mashed potatoes!

Christians can unknowingly be ensnared by one or more of the three traps: surfeiting (gluttony), drunkenness (booze and drugs), and the cares of life. How do they hinder our spiritual preparations for the Final Day? They make us inebriated with the world. Therefore, our senses are dulled. We become stupefied with carbohydrates, sugar, wine, entertainment, social media, politics, sports, business, investing, and a host of other attractive distractions. A life devoid of Bible study, church attendance, prayer, fasting, and fellowship among other Christians will inevitably become insensitive and unaware of spiritual things happening in the world, signs of the times, and the condition of our soul. Consequently, complacency in this present world will replace passion for the next world.

Jesus said we must "take heed" so that our hearts are not "overcharged" (burdened) with gluttony, liquor, drugs, pharmaceuticals, making a living, entertainment, and day-to-day living. Why? Because "that day" will come upon you suddenly like a trap.

"That day" is the Final Day when we shall see the glorious appearing of our blessed hope!

He said it will arrive suddenly and unexpectedly. "That day" will capture billions of lost souls like animals in traps. They will not see it coming and, thus, will blindly step into the snare.

For as a snare shall it come on all them that dwell on the face of the whole earth. (Luke 21:35)

Therefore, we also must always be watchful and prayerful in our daily lives so that we may be accounted worthy to escape what's coming to this world, and to stand before Jesus at the end of the age.

Watch ye therefore, and pray always, that ye may be accounted worthy to escape all these things that shall come to pass, and to stand before the Son of man. (Luke 21:36)

Does that mean there will be church members who will not be accounted worthy to escape all these things? Apparently so! That is a sobering thought for all of us to contemplate. Apostle Paul told the church in Philippi to "work out your salvation with fear and trembling." Salvation is a free gift, but it must be cherished, valued, and zealously guarded throughout our lifetime as precious beyond measure. We must never lose our awareness and unending appreciation that our sins are forgiven and we were rescued from living eternally in the Lake of Fire.

And that, knowing the time, that now it is high time to awake out of sleep: for now is our salvation nearer than when we believed. The night is far spent, the day is at hand: let us therefore cast off the works of darkness, and let us put on the armor of light. Let us walk honestly, as in the day; not in rioting and drunkenness, not in chambering and wantonness, not in strife and envying. (Romans 13: 11-13)

The command is given to all disciples of Jesus Christ: Take heed to yourselves. Do not become addicted to the pleasures of this world. Always be ready for that day when all the calamities prophesied in the Bible shall come upon rebellious mankind. And always be ready for the hour your soul separates from your body. We must live each day in a state of humility, obedience, expectancy, and hope. Nobody can be eternally secure if he or she is carnally minded throughout life. Our thoughts must always be upon our wonderful Heavenly Father throughout each day as we go about the necessities of daily life in this world. Neither death nor His second coming should catch us in acts of sin, drunkenness, gluttony, sexual sin, and pursuing the carnal pleasures of this world with no thoughts about God, judgement, and the eternal destination of our soul. King Solomon said a wise man thinks much of death, while the fool thinks only of having a good time now. He also said the day of death is better than the day of birth.

A good name is better than precious ointment; and the day of death than the day of one's birth. (Ecclesiastes 7:1)

You must be ready! The Final Day is coming. Jesus will come unexpectedly and suddenly. Billions of souls will be caught off-guard and unprepared for the Final Day - a day of instantaneous universal calamity, destruction, judgment, and the beginning of eternal punishment.

Therefore be ye also ready: for in such an hour as ye think not the Son of man cometh. (Matthew 24:44)

Are You Prepared for the Final Day?

The entire New Testament Bible is about being ready for the Final Day. If you asked Christians to describe the primary mission of John the Baptist, most would reply, "To baptize people." Yes, John the Baptist baptized multitudes in the Jordan river. His purpose, however, was:

"...to make ready a people prepared for the Lord" (Luke 1:17).

John's mission was not to make everybody prepared for the Lord. His assignment was to "make ready a people." And what was this specific group of people made ready for? They were to be "prepared for the Lord." And how did John make them ready? He preached repentance, baptism, and straight living!

In those days came John the Baptist, preaching in the wilderness of Judaea, and saying, Repent ye: for the kingdom of heaven is at hand. For this is he that was spoken of by the prophet Esaias, saying, The voice of one crying in the wilderness, Prepare ye the way of the Lord, make his paths straight. (Matthew 3:1-3)

Early Christian were originally known as "people of The Way." What was the way? Whose way? Early Christians followed "the way of Jesus." He instructed the Apostles to teach the people to walk the straight and narrow path through life in this sinful, wicked, lustful, carnal, vile, greedy, violent, bloody, and selfish world. Only by walking his way can his disciples keep their souls unstained by contact with this filthy world.

Repentance is necessary daily. Indeed, it is needed hourly. This is why hundreds of millions of orthodox, traditional Christians around the world pray the Jesus Prayer throughout each day: "Lord Jesus Christ, Son of God, have mercy on me, a sinner."

Unbeknownst to most members of Baptist, Charismatic, and non-denominational churches, millions of orthodox, traditional Christians sing each Sunday morning the Kyrie Eleison: *"Lord have mercy."* Eleison is the Greek word for *"have mercy"* that is used in many church liturgies. It shares the same Greek root word which means the oil from an oil tree. In the Book of Genesis, Noah released birds from the ark to seek land. A dove brought Noah a twig from an olive tree. Thousands of years later, the image of a dove holding an olive tree twig in its beak is a symbol of mercy, forgiveness, peace, and love.

The way of the Lord is mercy, forgiveness, peace, love, and holiness.

John the Baptist was sent "to make ready a people prepared for the Lord." He made them ready for the Lord by showing them "the way." After the resurrection of Jesus Christ, His disciples were called people of "the way." His way has not changed. It is the same today. If we are to be ready for His second appearance on earth, we must first prepare His way. The true church on earth shall be in a perpetual state of repentance, mercy, forgiveness, peace, love, and holiness.

Be ready! "That day" will come suddenly when you least expect it.

For yourselves know perfectly that the day of the Lord so cometh as a thief in the night. For when they shall say, Peace and safety; then sudden destruction cometh upon them, as travail upon a woman with child; and they shall not escape. But ye, brethren, are not in darkness, that that day should overtake you as a thief. (I Thessalonians 5:2-4)

That day - the day of the Lord - will come suddenly and unexpectedly like a violent intruder bursting through the door at 3AM startling the unsaved and wicked from a deep sleep of sinful living. Shocked and groggy, they will stumble in the darkness, unable to match the aggressive speed and actions of the thief in the night. Sudden destruction shall pounce upon them like a fierce roaring lion, and they shall not escape the fire.

But the day of the Lord will come like a thief. The heavens will disappear with a roar; the elements will be destroyed by fire, and the earth and everything done in it will be laid bare. (2 Peter 3:10)

What must we do to be ready?

We must make every effort to be found spotless, blameless, and at peace with Jesus Christ before He bursts into our dimension of time, space, and matter like an intergalactic space invader coming to wage war with a rebellious human civilization.

Wherefore, beloved, seeing that ye look for such things, be diligent that ye may be found of him in peace, without spot, and blameless. (2 Peter 3:14)

We Must Keep the Commandments

It is our personal responsibility - not the Holy Spirit's job - to be diligent so that we can be found in peace, without blemish, and blameless. How do we do it?

We must keep the commandments. Saint Luke said that Zacharias and Elizabeth, the parents of John the Baptist, were righteous in the eyes of God. They walked blamelessly in all the commandments and ordinances of God.

And they were both righteous before God, walking in all the commandments and ordinances of the Lord blameless. (Luke 1:6)

Isn't keeping the commandments an Old Testament religious thing? Why are New Testament Christians required to keep the commandments? The answer is simple: Jesus is returning for those who keep His commandments! Christians keeping the commandments are mentioned three times in the Apocalypse.

And the dragon was wroth with the woman, and went to make war with the remnant of her seed, which keep the commandments of God, and have the testimony of Jesus Christ. (Revelation 12:17)

Here is the patience of the saints: here are they that keep the commandments of God, and the faith of Jesus. (Revelation 14:12)

Blessed are they that do his commandments, that they may have the right to the tree of life, and may enter in through the gates into the city. (Revelation 22:14)

These three scriptures in the Apocalypse tell us:

- Satan (the dragon) makes war with the Church which keeps the commandments of God and have the testimony of Jesus Christ.
- Christians who remain faithful to Jesus while facing tribulation and persecution, and patiently awaiting His glorious

appearing, will be known to the Dragon and the world as those who keep God's commandments despite the extreme cost of such obedience. For them, there is no magical, pre-tribulation, secret rapture of Believers to Heaven before persecution and tribulation grip the worldwide church.

- Christians who keep the commandments shall be blessed, permitted to eat the fruit of the Tree of Life, and invited to enter through the gates into the New Jerusalem.

Furthermore, Jesus said that if you love Him, you'll keep the commandments. Thus, the opposite is true. Those who do not keep His commandments do not love Him.

If you love me, keep my commandments. (John 14:15)

He that hath my commandments, and keepeth them, he it is that loveth me: and he that loveth me shall be loved of my Father, and I will love him, and will manifest myself to him. (John 14:21)

If ye keep my commandments, ye shall abide in my love; even as I have kept my Father's commandments, and abide in his love. (John 15:10)

What are the key points of these three verses?

- Prove you truly love Jesus by keeping His commandments. Talk is cheap. Actions speak louder than words.
- Christians who keep the commandments shall be loved by God the Father, and God the Son will love them and manifest himself to them.
- Christians who keep the commandments shall dwell in Jesus' love just as he kept the commandments while on earth and abided in his Heavenly Father's love.

Diligence in keeping the commandments is our obligation if we are to be found by Jesus on the Final Day to be at peace with Him, without spot, and blameless. The day of the Lord will come like a thief in the night. The second advent of Jesus Christ shall be sudden and unexpected. His dramatic reentry into the affairs of mankind on earth will terrorize the planet's population of rebellious lawbreakers caught in their acts of sin, unbelief, and defiant disobedience to his commandments. The Lion of Judah shall roar! The heavens shall roar too as they disappear forever. The universe's elements will instantly melt. A massive ball of fire shall engulf the earth and devour it. And everything done by humans from the Garden of Eden until the last second of time will be exposed and fried.

But the day of the Lord will come as a thief in the night; in the which the heavens shall pass away with a great noise, and the elements shall melt with fervent heat, the earth also and the works that are therein shall be burned up. (2 Peter 3:10)

Wherefore, beloved, seeing that ye look for such things, be diligent that ye may be found of him in peace, without spot, and blameless. (2 Peter 3:14)

Each of us must be found blameless by God in the day our Lord returns. We must diligently make every effort in this present life to be found spotless, blameless, and at peace with Christ. Do not despair at the thought of being rejected by God on that day of wrath. There is hope! Saint Paul told the church in Corinth that Jesus shall confirm you unto the end so that you may be blameless in the day of the Lord. Christians who diligently keep his commandments shall be kept by Him. He will keep them until the end from the sensual temptations and corruption of this world.

I thank my God always on your behalf, for the grace of God which is given you by Jesus Christ; That in everything ye are enriched by him, in all utterance, and in all knowledge; Even as

the testimony of Christ was confirmed in you: So that ye come behind in no gift; waiting for the coming of our Lord Jesus Christ: Who shall also confirm you unto the end, that ye may be blameless in the day of our Lord Jesus Christ. God is faithful, by whom ye were called unto the fellowship of his Son Jesus Christ our Lord. (I Corinthians 1:4-9)

Tragically, there shall be no hope on that day for the wicked and those who rejected God's free offer of forgiveness and salvation through faith in the name of His Son Jesus Christ. The day of the Lord shall come upon them swiftly with great fury. Instantaneous global fire shall sweep billions of souls into Hell as did walls of water in the days of Noah. They will not know what hit them. One second they are gleefully on earth sinning against God. The next second they shall be bundled and burned by the reapers like trash thrown into a raging furnace. Too horrible to comprehend, their screams for mercy will never be heard by anybody outside Hell - including God. He will forget they ever existed. That is the ultimate Hell: Permanent separation from God with no hope of reconciliation, forever abandoned, and never remembered.

Five Virgins Refused to Invest Time, Effort, and Resources

The day of the Lord shall also come suddenly and unexpectedly to those who are religious but spiritually dull, lazy, complacent, and preoccupied with this world. They are represented in the parable as five foolish virgins.

Then shall the kingdom of heaven be likened unto ten virgins, which took their lamps, and went forth to meet the bridegroom. And five of them were wise, and five were foolish. They that were

147

foolish took their lamps, and took no oil with them: But the wise took oil in their vessels with their lamps. While the bridegroom tarried, they all slumbered and slept. And at midnight there was a cry made, Behold, the bridegroom cometh; go ye out to meet him. Then all those virgins arose, and trimmed their lamps. And the foolish said unto the wise, Give us of your oil; for our lamps are gone out. But the wise answered, saying, Not so; lest there be not enough for us and you: but go ye rather to them that sell, and buy for yourselves. And while they went to buy, the bridegroom came; and they that were ready went in with him to the marriage: and the door was shut. Afterward came also the other virgins, saying, Lord, Lord, open to us. But he answered and said, Verily I say unto you, I know you not. Watch therefore, for ye know neither the day nor the hour wherein the Son of man cometh. (Matthew 25:1-13)

Clearly, the bridegroom in this parable is Jesus. The event is the marriage of Jesus with His bride. According to Apostle John in Revelation 21:9-14, the bride is New Jerusalem. Bridesmaids don't marry the bridegroom but are important participants in the wedding ceremony. In the parable, half of the bridesmaids were ready for the wedding. The other half missed it because it caught them by surprise. The bridegroom unexpectedly showed up at an hour nobody was expecting. All 10 were surprised, but only five were ready. His sudden and unexpected arrival caught the other five bridesmaids totally by surprise. The door to the wedding was shut in their faces. Jesus told His disciples to watch because none of us know the day nor the hour when the Son of Man shall appear suddenly. Could 50% of the worldwide population of Christians miss the Parousia? Will the door to eternal life be slammed in the faces of one out two church members because they will not be ready for the Lord's sudden and unexpected return? It's a sobering thought that all Christians should seriously ponder.

What was the sin of the five foolish virgins? Their sin was not having more than enough oil for their lamps. Enough was not satisfactory. They needed more than enough! The wise virgins had oil in their lamps, and extra oil for the journey to the wedding. The foolish virgins only had oil in the lamps. They neglected to accumulate extra oil for the journey to the glorious marriage ceremony. They foolishly dismissed the possibility that the bridegroom could arrive at midnight, the darkest hour. Consequently, their lamps went out and left them stumbling in the darkness at midnight. Walking in pitch darkness cost them valuable traveling time to the wedding. Extra effort earlier in the day would have prevented the costly error at midnight which resulted in being denied entrance to the wedding event.

Most Bible teachers focus on the oil. They teach that the five foolish virgins did not have the Holy Spirit. The parable's focus, however, is the lamp, not the oil. The lamp is the Word of God.

Thy word is a lamp unto my feet, and a light unto my path. (Psalm 119:105)

The parable of the 10 virgins is about the Word of God. The five wise virgins represent Christians who have stored plenty of Holy Scriptures in their hearts. They will desperately need it for the perilous journey through gross darkness that will engulf this world at its midnight hour of existence. The five foolish virgins represent religious Churchianity members who thoughtlessly neglect to store ample supplies of the Word of God in their hearts and minds. The unexpected and sudden arrival of Jesus Christ will utterly shock them. They will demand that the five wise virgins - disciples of Jesus who prepared for the Final Day - give them whatever is necessary to get them to the end to meet the Bridegroom. True Christians, however, know that you can't fake it until you make it. The Word is either in you or it isn't. And you can't acquire it overnight. It requires countless hours of reading, studying, meditating, and praying until your soul is saturated with the Word, and remains saturated.

And what is the Word? Better still, who is the Word? The Word is Jesus Christ!

In the beginning was the Word, and the Word was with God, and the Word was God. The same was in the beginning with God. All things were made by him; and without him was not anything made that was made. In him was life; and the life was the light of men. And the light shineth in darkness; and the darkness comprehended it not. (John 1:1-5)

The five foolish virgins were late for the wedding because they had not prepared for the journey that came upon them suddenly and unexpectedly. They had some oil, but not enough oil. When the Final Day arrives, there will be many church members with some Word in their hearts and minds, but not enough for the midnight journey. Their minds will be cluttered with sport scores, news, information, investments, deals, money, conspiracy theories, recipes, gossip, TV sitcoms, porn, horoscopes, social media banter, and everything else they readily consumed each day.

When the five foolish virgins realized the stupidity of their actions, they pleaded with the five wise virgins to share their supply. They rebuffed their pressure. Instead, the five wise virgins told them to go buy more oil. Obviously, both the wise and foolish virgins knew the whereabouts of the merchant who sold oil. It was available to all who paid the price to obtain it. What we don't know is whether the oil merchant was open for business at midnight. Perhaps he would have agreed to open the store, but at a premium price. Truthfully, it did not matter. The five foolish virgins lost time traveling to the merchant to buy oil, and then heading toward the wedding party. It was the loss of valuable time that got them in trouble on the wedding day.

Imagine that a billionaire leaves you his or her estate in a will and you have one hour to arrive at the trustee's law office to claim the inheritance. Excitedly, you run to your automobile only to discover that the car's fuel tank is almost empty! Hurriedly, you drive around town looking for a place to buy gasoline, but all the stores are closed. Finally, you locate a place to fill up the gasoline tank and you break the speed limit and run through traffic lights as you race to the law office that is representing the deceased billionaire's estate. Frantically, you run through the parking lot and to head to the lobby of the building as you try to catch your breath. When you approach the building, you read the sign on the door: Closed! No matter how hard you rattle the doorknob and press the doorbell button, nobody will unlock the door. It's over! You missed your inheritance because you did not take time to fill up the gasoline tank earlier in the day when you had plenty of time to be ready for the call. In this imaginary scenario, nobody prevented you from buying fuel earlier. You didn't do it because being ready was not a priority.

God has one way to illuminate our journey through this life. It is His holy Word. Acquiring abundant amounts and storing it in your heart comes with a price. His Word must be pursued. You only pursue what you desire. The abundance of your heart is proof of what you desire and pursue. What overflows from your heart today? Is the Word of God, or is it entertainment, sports, news, politics, fashion, social acceptance, money, investments, fame, ambition, food, fun, sex, parties, or education? Your heart is full of something. It is not empty. You invested time, money, resources, and energy pursuing and acquiring it. Will it be sufficient to get you through the last segment of life's journey when the midnight cry "Jesus is coming!" is shouted by angels?

When the day of the Lord suddenly and unexpectedly explodes upon humanity, there will be no time to shop for oil to keep your lamp lit when "darkness shall cover the earth, and gross darkness the people." You will either have it or not. For those who keep their lamps lit, God promised that He "shall arise upon thee, and His glory shall be seen upon thee."

Arise, shine; for thy light is come, and the glory of the Lord is risen upon thee. For, behold, the darkness shall cover the earth, and gross darkness the people: but the Lord shall arise upon thee, and his glory shall be seen upon thee. (Isaiah 60:1-2)

For those who passionately pursued the Word of God at all costs, their journey will be in the Son's brightness. The outcome will be different, however, for those who wasted their time on the foolishness of this world. They will stumble in gross darkness and discover that the door has been closed in their faces. The grand wedding of all ages will begin without them. Jesus repeatedly emphasized the need for readiness:

Let your loins be girded about, and your lights burning; and ye yourselves like unto men that wait for their lord, when he will return from the wedding; that when he cometh and knocketh, they may open unto him immediately. Blessed are those servants,

whom the lord when he cometh shall find watching: verily I say unto you, that he shall gird himself, and make them to sit down to meat, and will come forth and serve them. And if he shall come in the second watch, or come in the third watch, and find them so, blessed are those servants. And this know, that if the goodman of the house had known what hour the thief would come, he would have watched, and not have suffered his house to be broken through. Be ye therefore ready also: for the Son of man cometh at an hour when ye think not. (Luke 12:35-40)

Slothful Servants Banished to Hell

Once again, we see the same instructions: Be dressed. Be ready. Keep your lamp lit. In this parable, however, Jesus reverses the order of the wedding instructions. This time He says we should be like men who are at their master's house waiting on him to return from a wedding feast. They are admonished to be dressed in readiness and have their lamps lit so that they may immediately open the door when he knocks. Jesus said servants who are alert when He arrives shall be blessed. The master shall serve them at *his* table! They are blessed by the Master because they were ready for his arrival. What about the slothful servants who were not ready?

Then Peter said unto him, Lord, speakest thou this parable unto us, or even to all? And the Lord said, Who then is that faithful and wise steward, whom his lord shall make ruler over his household, to give them their portion of meat in due season? Blessed is that servant, whom his lord when he cometh shall find so doing. Of a truth I say unto you, that he will make him ruler over all that he hath. But and if that servant say in his heart, My lord delayeth his coming; and shall begin to beat the menservants and maidens, and to eat and drink, and to be drunken; the lord of that servant will come in a day when he looketh not for him, and at an hour when he is not aware, and will cut him in sunder, and will appoint him his portion with the unbelievers. And that servant, which knew his lord's will, and prepared not himself, neither did according to his will, shall be beaten with many stripes. But he that knew not, and did commit things worthy of stripes, shall be beaten with few stripes. For unto whomsoever much is given, of him shall be much required: and to whom men have committed much, of him they will ask the more. (Luke 12:41-48)

The slothful servant foolishly surmised that his master's return would be delayed. He reasoned, "I have a lot more time to do what I want to do, not what my master instructed me to do. I will complete his instructions later." What happened to the slothful, disobedient servant who was not ready? It's not pretty. He was beaten with many stripes!

In the Gospel of our Lord according to St. Mark, Jesus continued with the same admonitions about His return: take heed, stay alert, fulfill your appointed assignment, be ready.

Take ye heed, watch and pray: for ye know not when the time is. For the Son of man is as a man taking a far journey, who left his house, and gave authority to his servants, and to every man his work, and commanded the porter to watch. Watch ye therefore: for ye know not when the master of the house cometh, at even, or at midnight, or at the cockcrowing, or in the morning: lest coming suddenly he find you sleeping. (Mark 13:33-36)

Living a life of spiritual readiness is not spending your days in dreaded fear that you will not be ready to meet Jesus upon His return. It doesn't mean forgoing your career development, acquiring an education, building a business, raising a family, enjoying time spent with friends and relatives, traveling, and recreation. God desires us to enjoy living. He desires us to love Him, love our neighbors, and love living. He doesn't, however, want us to love the world. The daily challenge to all Christians is to be in the world but not of the world.

Spiritual readiness simply means living each day - indeed each hour! - in the fear of the Lord, knowing that each of us must give an account someday for all that we have done and said in this world. God have mercy on us! It means we are aware that life is like a vapor that suddenly vanishes. Yes, we should be fully engaged in the affairs of life - family, church, career, education, recreation, and relaxation - but all for the glory of God.

Jesus said we must be dressed in readiness. Does the Bible tell us our wardrobe? Yes, it does. It is a suit of armor. We must wear all of it every day. Our biblical wardrobe is righteousness, salvation, truth, peace, faith, and the sword of the Spirit. When dressed in the armor of God, we can successfully withstand Satan in the evil day.

Jesus said we must be constantly ready - dressed with the armor of God and our path illuminated by the Word of God. Failure to obey His instructions will result in the forfeiture of our invitation to the great wedding.

Be alert! Be ready! Be dressed!

Have your lamp lit with plenty of oil for a treacherous journey in deep darkness at the midnight hour! Gross darkness shall encompass the people in the world in the runup to Jesus' return. You must store up extra oil to keep your lamp lit for a journey through gross darkness. We do not know when Jesus shall suddenly and unexpectedly burst into our dimension of time, space, and matter. It is the biggest secret in the universe. Only God the Father knows the date.

But of that day and hour knoweth no man, no, not the angels of heaven, but my Father only. (Matthew 24:36)

Thieves Don't Schedule Appointments

Jesus compares His second coming with the arrival of a thief in the night. How does a thief appear? Suddenly and unexpectedly! Thieves plunder homes after midnight when the owners are in a deep sleep and not prepared to readily react to a violent home invasion.

Thieves don't schedule appointments to rob you. Robbers don't send letters announcing their anticipated arrival time to ransack your house. The homeowner and police would be waiting for them to arrive. For the same reason, Jesus will not notify anybody of the day and hour He will burst through the world's front door and violently ransack humanity's home.

Watch therefore: for ye know not what hour your Lord doth come. But know this, that if the goodman of the house had known in what watch the thief would come, he would have watched, and would not have suffered his house to be broken up. Therefore be ye also ready: for in such an hour as ye think not the Son of man cometh. (Matthew 24:42-44)

Jesus didn't say it once. He didn't say it twice. He repeatedly taught His disciples to pay attention, stay alert, be ready, and keep their lamps lit.

Take ye heed, watch and pray: for ye know not when the time is. For the Son of man is as a man taking a far journey, who left his house, and gave authority to his servants, and to every man his work, and commanded the porter to watch. Watch ye therefore:

for ye know not when the master of the house cometh, at even, or at midnight, or at the cockcrowing, or in the morning: lest coming suddenly he find you sleeping. (Mark 13:33-36)

Remember, therefore, what you have received and heard; hold it fast, and repent. But if you do not wake up, I will come like a thief, and you will not know at what time I will come to you. (Revelation 3:3)

"Behold, I am coming like a thief. Blessed is the one who stays awake and keeps his clothes, so that he will not walk about naked and men will not see his shame." (Revelation 16:15)

The apostles taught Christians what they were personally taught by Jesus before the Ascension and by the Holy Spirit afterwards. Saint Paul wrote:

For yourselves know perfectly that the day of the Lord so cometh as a thief in the night. (I Thessalonians 5:2)

St. Peter repeated what he heard too.

But, beloved, be not ignorant of this one thing, that one day is with the Lord as a thousand years, and a thousand years as one day. The Lord is not slack concerning his promise, as some men count slackness; but is longsuffering to us-ward, not willing that any should perish, but that all should come to repentance. But the day of the Lord will come as a thief in the night; in the which the heavens shall pass away with a great noise, and the elements shall melt with fervent heat, the earth also and the works that are therein shall be burned up. (2 Peter 3:8-10)

Lollygagging Lot Almost Lost It

Whereas Jesus said His second coming will be as the days of Noah, He also compared it to the days of Lot. Sodom and

Gomorrah had sunk into immoral debauchery. Their sins were so gross that there was no way to save the inhabitants. Lot was an important leader in Sodom. He "sat at the gate," meaning he was a city elder, perhaps a city councilman. Lot acclimated to Sodom's vile sins. Although he did not participate in their sins, he wasn't revulsed by them either. He looked the other way as he sought to make a living and perform his civic duties. Perhaps he reasoned, "What people do in their private homes is their business. I can't let it affect my business." He also didn't want to provoke the city's powerful LGBTQ lobby to campaign against his re-election to the city council. Lot was, after all, the lone "conservative family values" representative in the city government. Therefore, Lot publicly tolerated the city's vile sins despite being privately troubled by it. Does it sound like today's politicians?

God chose to destroy all of them except Lot and his family. He sent an angel to notify Lot that both cities - Sodom and Gomorrah - were on track to be razed and reduced to ashes. Lot's proximity to Sodom's sins and his refusal to openly oppose them had dulled his spiritual senses. He was in danger but didn't perceive it. Even when an angel told him face-to-face that God would soon destroy the cities, Lot didn't respond with an alarmed sense of urgency. Instead, he took his time getting ready for the destruction that he was told was on its way. He deceived himself into thinking he had more time. The normalcy bias prevented him from acting on the angel's warning. "Certainly, God wouldn't do it now," Lot may have reasoned in his mind. The Bible doesn't tell us how long and why Lot stalled his flight from Sodom, but we can only imagine what he did after receiving an angelic notification of the cities' death sentence. Perhaps he went to his garage and casually sorted through the tools he wanted to take along. Whatever he did, it was stupid. Fire was on its way, but Lot was not on fire to go his way! His lack of urgency in the face of certain destruction required another angelic visitation. This time the angel physically escorted Lot and his family out of Sodom in the nick of time.

God sent notification to Lot that sudden destruction would soon strike his hometown. Lot chose, however, to rationalize what the angel meant. Perhaps he dug out of the closet his favorite Bible prophecy timeline chart he purchased years ago from an End Time prophecy teacher. Lot surmised that he had much more time than the angel said. Besides, as a respectable city official, he was expected to attend Sodom's LGBTQ Gay Pride Parade the coming weekend. As the only compassionate conservative elected to sit on the Sodom City Council, Lot solicited the good will and votes of Sodom's LGBT community in the upcoming city election to prove his devotion to diversity and inclusiveness, even though as a good man, he was privately troubled by his city's slide into debauchery. He was persuaded that Sodom could be reformed if they elected more family-values conservatives to the city council and appointed as judges. He proudly displayed a sign on his donkey cart that said, "God bless Sodom." Yes, it's true he did not personally approve of the lifestyles of his constituents, but his motto was "What happens in Sodom stays in Sodom." Hopefully it is obvious to the reader that the author is sarcastically comparing Lot to today's politically-minded family-values conservatives in many churches.

Jesus mentioned the days of Lot in His teachings about the End of the Age.

Likewise also as it was in the days of Lot; they did eat, they drank, they bought, they sold, they planted, they builded; but the

same day that Lot went out of Sodom it rained fire and brimstone from heaven, and destroyed them all. Even thus shall it be in the day when the Son of man is revealed. (Luke 17:28-30)

When did the fire and brimstone fall? Sudden destruction came immediately when the angel removed Lot and his family. This scripture clearly refutes John Nelson Darby's secret pre-tribulation rapture hoax. According to Darby's DPPZites, tribulation starts after the Christians are raptured to Heaven, and the fire does not consume the planet for another thousand years after the end of the tribulation. Does Darby's theology line up with Jesus' words about His Second Coming and the End of the Age?

Jesus said "...the same day that Lot went out of Sodom it rained fire and brimstone from heaven, and destroyed them all. Even thus shall it be in the day when the Son of man is revealed." (Luke 17:29-30)

Jesus' words are simple to comprehend. He said fire and brimstone rained down from heaven upon Sodom and destroyed them all. Our Savior stated it shall happen the same way when He returns. What does that mean? It means Jesus will return one time - suddenly and unexpectedly - to rescue His disciples. The moment they leave the earth, fire and brimstone will rain down on the planet and destroy everybody and everything. Christians will go up as the fire comes down. There will not be a long gap between the catching away of the saints and the fiery destruction of the wicked and the planet. Jesus will arrive like Indiana Jones in the Temple of Doom just in time to rescue his friends. Will you have faith in Him to do it when darkness covers the world?

The second coming of Jesus shall be a single event that shall suddenly and unexpectedly burst upon an unsuspecting human population on earth. God's chosen people - Israel the Church - will be fireproof. Angels shall evacuate them. Fire and brimstone, however, shall rain down upon the wicked. There will be no escape from destruction. There will not be a Jewish empire for 1,000 years. There will only be a Jesus empire forever! This old earth will be consumed by fire the instant the Church is gathered by the angelic reapers.

For Christian saints who keep the commandments, the second coming of Jesus Christ shall be an instantaneous divine deliverance from a world rotted by sin, and racked by unimaginable global persecution, tyranny, wars, and calamities.

It will be a different story for the rebellious. For all found lurking outside the Ark of Baptism when fire and brimstone rain down, the Lord's second coming shall be instantaneous judgment and eternal damnation. The wicked Synagogue of Satan that persecutes the churches in Smyrna and Philadelphia shall be damned to the Lake of Fire. All liars shall also find their place in the Lake of Fire. Homosexuals, heterosexual adulterers and fornicators, and all others who are sexually immoral, impure, and lewd shall be swept into the flames of Hell. Idolaters and sorcerers shall perish suddenly. People who stir up strife, hatred, dissension, rage, jealousy, selfishness, envy, and heresies shall quickly vanish and be transported by angels to the Lake of Fire. Murderers, drunkards, gluttons, and carousers shall join them too.

Jesus said He will come quickly. Quickly does not mean immediately or soon. It means the velocity Jesus will travel when He departs the City of Heaven for Earth. Faster than lightning, he shall come swiftly without any delay. With a sword (the Word) in His mouth, the Lord Jesus Christ shall make war against all who refused to repent of their sins before His arrival.

161

He which testifieth these things saith, Surely I come quickly. Amen. Even so, come, Lord Jesus. (Revelation 22:20)

Repent; or else I will come unto thee quickly, and will fight against them with the sword of my mouth. (Revelation 2:16)

Jesus Christ told us what we must do every day: Stay awake. Be alert. Be dressed for action. Keep your lamp lit. Know your assignment. Be diligent and faithful until the Master returns.

The Second Coming of Jesus on the Final Day shall be:

- Singular
- Sudden and unexpected.

CHAPTER 5

HIS SECOND COMING SHALL BE ATMOSPHERIC

THERE'S AN EARLY 19TH century idiom that says, "What goes up must come down." Of course, it refers to the law of gravity. When speaking of the second coming of Jesus Christ, we could say, "Who went up must come down."

Essentially, that's what the angels said to the men who watched the resurrected Messiah lift off from earth and soar into the sky like a SpaceX rocket blasting off from Cape Canaveral.

This author currently lives approximately 80 miles south of Cape Canaveral. One of the benefits of living along Florida's Treasure Coast (in addition to perpetual sunshine, beautiful beaches, palm trees, great fishing, wide rivers, turtles, tropical flowers, fresh citrus juices, dolphins, pelicans, and the annual aroma of orange blossoms in the air) is the excitement of watching rockets blast off from Cape Canaveral and streak across the sky.

Nighttime rocket launches are the best to experience. Wow! A magnificent fireball lights up the sky. People come out of their homes to watch it. Drivers pull their vehicles off the road and stand along highways and roads to observe the spectacular glowing object moving through the sky.

Whether daytime or nighttime, the first stage of the launch is awesome. The rocket is visible for only a few minutes. As it climbs higher into the atmosphere, spectators stretch their necks and refocus their eyes to follow the rocket that quickly disappears behind the clouds. After a few minutes, the rocket is gone and the excitement is over. There's nothing left to do but post photos on social media to let your friends know you saw it. Invisible to the people on earth, however, the rocket continues to soar upward on its way to outer space to accomplish its mission long after the people below stop watching it.

That's the way it was one day approximately 2,000 years ago. Jesus Christ - the Son of God - lifted off from "Cape Jerusalem." He soared into the daytime sky and was received by a cloud which whisked Him to a heavenly dimension from which He came to save us. In short, Jesus went home after successfully accomplishing His mission on earth. When He arrived in Heaven as a hero, Jesus took His seat at the righthand of His Heavenly Father and has interceded for the saints ever since.

Weeks earlier, He had been whipped, flogged, beaten, tortured, and crucified by the cruel and corrupt Romans to satisfy the blood-lust of the wicked and diabolical Jewish religious rulers who rejected their Messiah. He was buried, descended to the place of the dead, resurrected by God the Father, and appeared to many of His disciples over 40 days. During this 40-day interlude between His resurrection and ascension back to Heaven, Jesus imparted to the Apostles the Gospel of the Kingdom and the foundation of the Church.

Jesus' work on earth was finished. He said it on the cross. "It is finished." He didn't mean, "I'm dying. It's over." He meant that the Old Covenant between God and the Jews was over. A New Covenant had arrived. It is for everybody! He meant that Satan's death grip on humanity was finished, and that the redemption of mankind was accomplished. With His work on earth completed, Jesus was ready to return home. The Comforter would soon take His place on earth to supervise the mission of the Church, the preaching of the Gospel of the Kingdom, the salvation of lost souls, and the encouragement of the saints.

His disciples came together with Jesus. They asked Him if He planned to restore the political and military kingdom of Israel. His Jewish disciples' focus was on reclaiming real estate and political power. They yearned for Israel to once again be the dominant nation in the region. Unbelievable! After walking side-by-side with Jesus for three years, hearing Him teach about the Kingdom of God, and witnessing signs, wonders, and miracles - these Jewish men were still fixated on getting back their land and power. Nothing has changed in over 2000 years. Unsaved Jews today are still obsessed with land, wealth, and political power. They don't see the Kingdom of God because you must be born again through faith in Jesus Christ to see it. Thus, the veil remains over their eyes.

When His disciples eagerly asked Jesus, "Are we going to get back our land?" Jesus' reply was to tell them that it was none of their business:

When they therefore were come together, they asked of him, saying, Lord, wilt thou at this time restore again the kingdom to Israel? And he said unto them, *It is not for you to know the times or the seasons,* which the Father hath put in his own power. (Acts 1:6-7)

165

After informing them that restoring the nation of Israel was none of their concern, Jesus told them what He expected them to be busy doing in His absence:

But ye shall receive power, after that the Holy Ghost is come upon you: and ye shall be witnesses unto me both in Jerusalem, and in all Judaea, and in Samaria, and unto the uttermost part of the earth. (Acts 1:8)

Jesus told them to get ready for two things: They would be supernaturally energized by the Holy Spirit; and they would go, go, go! The Great Commission was ready to start. These guys needed to pack their bags and put on walking shoes. There wouldn't be time to hang out in Jerusalem. Besides, the non-believing Jews were going to make their lives miserable anyway. They would soon be compelled to hit the highway to escape deadly persecution by the Jews.

Three things awaited them: First, Jew-on-Jew violence would erupt when the Jewish Sanhedrin and synagogue rulers cracked down on the growing movement among Jews to believe that Jesus Christ had, indeed, risen from the dead and was their promised Messiah. Second, the Roman army would surround Jerusalem and destroy the temple, and slaughter the Jewish inhabitants. Third, God would take the kingdom away from the Jews and give it to another nation of people who would praise Him.

In other words, Jesus was saying to His disciples, "Boys, you have no idea what's coming because of your identification with me. Forget about a Jewish kingdom on earth. Get busy preaching the Kingdom of God. Get out of town and go as far as you can go. Preach the Gospel. Baptize believers. Make disciples. Cast out devils. Heal the sick. I'll be back later."

As soon as Jesus told them the Holy Spirit's power would come upon them and they would be witnesses for Him around the world, the resurrected Savior lifted off the ground. He soared higher and higher. Amazed as they gazed, the disciples' eyes were fixated on their Messiah as He vanished into the atmosphere. A cloud received Jesus and He was gone.

"Whoa! Dude, what just happened?" could have been Peter's first words spoken that none of the apostles recorded. If anybody said it, you know it was Peter – the Jewish redneck!

The Same Jesus Shall Return

Two angels suddenly appeared and asked the incredulous men a question. "Hey guys, why stand there gawking up into the sky?"

Furthermore, the angels informed the disciples that the "same Jesus" would return from Heaven. The "same Jesus" means the God-Man who departed the earth in a resurrected human body will be the same God-Man who returns to earth in a resurrected human body. This "same Jesus" will also return the "same way" that He left: In a cloud in the sky! His second coming shall be atmospheric.

"And when he had spoken these things, while they beheld, he was taken up; *and a cloud received him* out of their sight. And while they looked steadfastly toward heaven as he went up, behold, two men stood by them in white apparel; which also said, Ye men of Galilee, why stand ye gazing up into heaven? *this same Jesus, which is taken up from you into heaven, shall so come in like manner as ye have seen him go into heaven.* (Acts 1:9-11)

Who is coming again? "This same Jesus!"

The angels' words are a great promise of hope for mankind. The triumphant and victorious Jesus who went up will be the same Jesus who comes down. He will not be a facsimile, replica, clone, impersonator, imitation, lookalike, double, stand-in, mirror image, remake, nor a holographic image. The second coming of Jesus Christ shall not be a metaphysical phenomenon, nor shall it be a mystical religious experience. He will not appear in virtual reality. His appearance shall be very real! The king who returns will be the one and only Son of God who came to earth as God in human flesh, died for the sins of the human race, was crucified, died, buried, and resurrected from the dead! He will be the real deal.

Without a doubt, the second coming of Jesus Christ will be an atmospheric event. Just as he was whisked away from earth in a cloud after the resurrection, Jesus shall burst back into our atmosphere someday on the clouds. He left on a cloud. He shall return on clouds. Whoever goes up must come down. Jesus shall come down. He shall come down with fire.

The Biblical Significance of Clouds

Clouds have significance in the Bible. They are often associated with the glory of God. The Hebrew word for "cloud" means "covering." Throughout the Bible, the Hebrew word for "cloud" represents the divine presence of Almighty God. When God led the Hebrew people out of Egypt, His divine presence was in a cloud by day and fire by night.

And the Lord went before them by day in a pillar of a cloud, to lead them the way; and by night in a pillar of fire, to give them light; to go by day and night. (Exodus 13:21)

Moses met God in a cloud on Mount Sinai. God told Moses to "come up to Me into the mount." He promised to give Moses "tables of stone, and a law, and commandments" written by God that Moses was to teach to the Hebrews. Moses ascended the mountain and encountered Almighty God at the summit. The mountaintop was encased in a cloud of God's glory.

And Moses went up into the mount, *and a cloud covered the mount.* And the glory of the Lord abode upon mount Sinai, *and the cloud covered it six days: and the seventh day he called unto Moses out of the midst of the cloud.* And the sight of the glory of the Lord was like devouring fire on the top of the mount in the eyes of the children of Israel. *And Moses went into the midst of the cloud,* and gat him up into the mount: and Moses was in the mount forty days and forty nights. (Exodus 24:15-18)

When Moses left the mountaintop to return to base camp, he was horrified when he discovered the Hebrews dancing around a golden calf idol they made while he was meeting with the Creator of the universe. In a fit of fury, Moses tossed the stone tablets and broke them into pieces at the foot of the mountain. God responded by scheduling a morning meeting with Moses on the mountain. Almighty God arrived at the meeting in a cloud.

And the Lord descended in the cloud, and stood with him there, and proclaimed the name of the Lord. (Exodus 34:5)

In the Book of Leviticus, God's presence over the mercy seat was in the form of a cloud.

And the Lord spake unto Moses after the death of the two sons of Aaron, when they offered before the Lord, and died; and the Lord said unto Moses, Speak unto Aaron thy brother, that he come not at all times into the holy place within the veil before the mercy seat, which is upon the ark; that he die not: *for I will appear in the cloud upon the mercy seat.* (Leviticus 16:1-2)

In the 18th Psalm, King David beautifully described the awesomeness of Almighty God. David praised his Maker as his rock, fortress, deliverer, strength, buckler, horn of his salvation, and high tower in whom he trusted. In distress, David called upon the Lord. He cried unto his God. The Lord heard his plea for help. The earth shook and trembled. The foundation of the hills moved and were shaken because He was angry. Smoke came out of God's nostrils, and fire came out of His mouth. God bowed the heavens and came down. He came down hidden in the clouds.

God surprised David's enemies by riding upon a cherub and concealing His arrival to earth enshrouded in thick clouds. It was "lights out" for David's enemies. God caught them off guard and utterly surprised them. He came suddenly and unexpectedly. He came in the atmosphere hidden in clouds to rescue His beloved servant David.

And he rode upon a cherub, and did fly: yea, he did fly upon the wings of the wind. He made darkness his secret place; *his pavilion round about him were dark waters and thick clouds of the skies.* (Psalm 18:10-11)

Clouds are God's canopy. He wears them like a royal robe. If you've ever wondered what the Day of the Lord will look like, read Psalm 97. It's going to be an awesome thing to behold.

The Lord reigneth; let the earth rejoice; let the multitude of isles be glad thereof. *Clouds and darkness are round about him:* **righteousness and judgment are the habitation of his throne. A fire goeth before him, and burneth up his enemies round about. His lightnings enlightened the world: the earth saw, and trembled. (Psalm 97:1-4)**

Jesus Shall Come Like Lightning

Jesus' glorious appearing shall also be like lightning.

For as the lightning cometh out of the east, **and shineth even unto the west; so shall also the coming of the Son of man be. (Matthew 24: 27)**

How does lightning appear in the sky? Lightning appears unexpectedly and suddenly. It moves swiftly across the sky. Its brilliance illuminates the sky with dazzling flashes of light. It is furious and destructive. It humbles humans because it represents power that mankind cannot control. It sets on fire whatever it strikes.

Such shall be the coming of the Son of man when He appears suddenly and unexpectedly in the atmosphere. He shall move swiftly across the sky. Dazzling flashes of light from his glory will illuminate the sky above every continent. Glorious and mighty, Jesus' sudden and unexpected appearance in the clouds will humble every human because He represents a power that mankind cannot control. The Lord will set the world on fire.

As lightning flashes across the sky, so too will Jesus' arrival flash from east to west.

Have you ever noticed that Orthodox churches face east? Do you know why? Orthodox churches are built facing eastward because it is an ancient tradition grounded on the sure knowledge that Jesus' second advent shall be like lightning coming out of the east and shining unto the west. Likewise, Orthodox Christians pray facing eastward. It is their symbolic way of reminding themselves that our great hope is the second coming of our Lord and Savior, and that He shall first appear eastward in the atmosphere.

The second coming of Jesus will not be the first time His appearance is linked with the eastern atmosphere. How were the magi led to Bethlehem at the first advent of Jesus? When the wise men met with King Herod, they told him they came from the east and saw the Messiah's star in the east.

Now when Jesus was born in Bethlehem of Judaea in the days of Herod the king, behold, there came wise men from the east to Jerusalem, saying, Where is he that is born King of the Jews? *for we have seen his star in the east,* **and are come to worship him.** (Matthew 2:1-2)

In Old Covenant times, the prophet Ezekiel saw the glory of the Lord when facing east.

And the glory of the Lord came into the house by the way of the gate whose prospect *is toward the east.* (Ezekiel 43:4)

Daniel is another Old Covenant prophet who saw the Son of man arriving in the atmosphere. God gave Daniel visions at night about the Final Day.

I saw in the night visions, and, behold, one like the Son of man came *with the clouds of heaven,* **and came to the Ancient of days, and they brought him near before him.** (Daniel 7:13)

Whom did Daniel see in the visions? He saw one with the physical shape and likeness of a human man, but gloriously clothed in superhuman majesty like God. The Son of man is Jesus. The Ancient of days is God the Father. "They" are angels. Daniel saw the Son of man arriving with the clouds of heaven. The prophet saw the grand finale of the human saga. What he saw happening was atmospheric. Daniel saw the Final Day.

He Shall Come in the Clouds

Likewise, Jeremiah had a prophetic glimpse of the Final Day. The prophet saw Jesus coming in the clouds.

Behold, he shall come up as clouds, and his chariots shall be as a whirlwind: his horses are swifter than eagles. Woe unto us! for we are spoiled. (Jeremiah 4:13)

Numerous Bible scriptures confirm that the second coming of Jesus shall be an atmospheric event in the clouds:

Jesus saith unto him, Thou hast said: nevertheless I say unto you, Hereafter shall ye see the Son of man sitting on the right hand of power, *and coming in the clouds of heaven.* (Matthew 26:64)

And then shall they see *the Son of man coming in the clouds* with great power and glory. And then shall he send his angels, and shall gather together his elect from the four winds, from the uttermost part of the earth to the uttermost part of heaven. (Mark 13:26-27)

But he held his peace, and answered nothing. Again the high priest asked him, and said unto him, Art thou the Christ, the Son of the Blessed? And Jesus said, I am: and ye shall see the Son of man sitting on the right hand of power, *and coming in the clouds of heaven.* (Mark 14:61-62)

Behold, he cometh with clouds; and every eye shall see him, and they also which pierced him: and all kindreds of the earth shall wail because of him. Even so, Amen. (Revelation 1:7)

Immediately after the tribulation of those days shall the sun be darkened, and the moon shall not give her light, and the stars shall fall from heaven, and the powers of the heavens shall be shaken: and then shall appear the sign of the Son of man in heaven: *and then shall all the tribes of the earth mourn, and they shall see the Son of man coming in the clouds of heaven with power and great glory.* (Matthew 24:29-30)

It is "in the clouds" that the Body of Christ shall be joined with the Head of the Church. Apostle Paul encouraged the Church to be **"looking for that blessed hope, and the glorious appearing of the great God and our Savior. Jesus Christ; who gave himself for us, that he might redeem us from all iniquity, and purify unto himself a peculiar people, zealous of good works." (Titus 2:13-14)**

St. Paul the Apostle did not tell Christians to "be looking for the rapture so we can escape this hellhole." Paul did not say that "The Rapture" is our "blessed hope." Jesus is our blessed hope! His return is "his glorious appearing." Sadly, millions of evangelical Christians have been erroneously taught to await a secret appearance of Jesus to snatch them away from this world while everybody else is "left behind" for seven years of Hell on earth. There won't be anything secret about His return to earth. Jesus can't sneak in to snatch away the Christians even if He wanted to do it. It is impossible. Bolts of lightning flash in Heaven when Jesus gets up from His throne to walk to the other side of the room. He is God! He came the first time "lowly and meek." He'll come the second time with fire in His eyes. The universe will shake when Jesus cracks through the barrier that separates His Heavenly dimension from our physical dimension of time, space, and matter. All of creation will shout with glee, "He's back!"

Meeting in the Air

Apostle Paul told the Christians in Thessalonica not to be ignorant about the Lord's return.

But I would not have you to be ignorant, brethren, *concerning them which are asleep,* that ye sorrow not, even as others which have no hope. For *if we believe that Jesus died and rose again,*

even so them also which sleep in Jesus will God bring with him. For this we say unto you by the word of the Lord, that we which are alive and remain unto the coming of the Lord shall not prevent them which are asleep. For the Lord himself shall descend from heaven with a shout, with the voice of the archangel, and with the trump of God: and the dead in Christ shall rise first: *then we which are alive and remain shall be caught up together with them in the clouds, to meet the Lord in the air:* and so shall we ever be with the Lord. (1 Thessalonians 4:13-17)

There's going to be a trumpet blast and shout that shakes the universe! All graves – not some, but all - shall open. The graves of every human who ever lived from the beginning of time shall instantly pop open. Adam's grave shall open. Eve's grave too, along with the graves of Cain and Abel. Noah's grave shall open. The graves of Genghis Khan, all of Egypt's pharaohs, Adolf Hitler, Vladimir Lenin, and Fidel Castro shall pop open too. The graves of Mozart, Rembrandt, Picasso, da Vinci, Michelangelo, and van Gogh shall also spring open. Every grave! The saved and the unsaved. From Adam to the last human buried seconds before the last trumpet blares its first note, everybody will hear the wake-up call. What a scene it shall be on the Final Day. Sheer terror or indescribable joy will greet the awakened dead depending on their spiritual fate.

They're all coming out, but all are not going up. The righteous shall go up. Every man, woman, and child saved by faith in Jesus Christ and baptized in water in the name of the Father, the Son, and the Holy Spirit shall depart the earth in the same manner Jesus departed his disciples after the resurrection. They're going to a meeting in the air. Hallelujah! Glory be to God.

It will be a different story for the unsaved and wicked. They will be bundled and burned.

Whoever goes up must come down. The first Christians gazed upward toward Heaven when Jesus left the earth. The last Christians shall be gazing upward toward Heaven when Jesus returns to the earth. They will go up when He comes down.

The second coming of Jesus on the Final Day shall be:

- Singular
- Sudden and unexpected.
- Atmospheric

CHAPTER 6

HIS SECOND COMING
SHALL BE VISIBLE

T HE HOLY BIBLE CLEARLY teaches that the second coming of Jesus Christ will be seen by everybody on earth. The first chapter of the Apocalypse says, "Behold, he cometh with clouds; and every eye shall see him…"

How could that happen? Presently, there are over seven billion people alive on earth. How could seven billion people see the same thing happening in real time?

In the heyday of religious broadcasting via satellites, prominent Christian pastors, bible prophecy teachers, and religious broadcasting executives often said that global television broadcasting was the explanation. They surmised that the second coming of Jesus would be televised worldwide in real time. Broadcast TV stations and satellites, however, are quickly fading away into communication technology's yesteryear. Internet streaming is currently the up and coming technology for media content delivery systems. Regardless, all three video communication technologies - broadcasting, satellite, and streaming - require cameras to be fixed on an incoming object in the sky. Jesus would have to slow down considerably as he approaches the earth to give cameras enough time to zoom in and follow his entry into our atmosphere like a UFO spaceship landing in New York City's Central Park. Using media technology to explain how everybody on the planet will see Jesus when he returns also mandates that all seven billion people are awake and watching television or a mobile device at the same time. Forget this idea! It won't be on TV or your mobile cellphone.

How will everybody see Jesus returning to earth? The answer is quite simple.

Jesus Christ will be the only object lit up in the entire universe! You won't be able to miss him. He will be the grand star of the show. Every eye will be fixated on the glorious and marvelous arrival of the King of Kings and Lord of Lords.

Why will Jesus be the only object lit up in the universe? That's easy to explain too! Shortly before Jesus' grand entrance, Papa God will cut off the electricity to the whole universe by powering down the sun, moon, and stars. Lights out everywhere! Isaiah said darkness shall cover the earth, and gross darkness shall cover the people. The prophet saw the darkness of sorrow that will encompass the planet in the last days, the culmination of millenniums of sinfulness, rebellion, idolatry, sorcery, bloodshed, lewdness, and all other iniquities against God.

Jesus told us precisely when the universe will go dark. The lights will go out immediately after the days of great tribulation and just before the sign of the Son of man appears in heaven.

Immediately after the tribulation of those days shall the sun be darkened, and the moon shall not give her light, and the stars shall

fall from heaven, and the powers of the heavens shall be shaken: and then shall appear the sign of the Son of man in heaven: and then shall all the tribes of the earth mourn, *and they shall see the Son of man coming in the clouds of heaven with power and great glory.* And he shall send his angels with a great sound of a trumpet, and they shall gather together his elect from the four winds, from one end of heaven to the other. (Matthew 24:29:31)

If you accept Jesus Christ as an expert witness qualified to talk about the end of the world, then you must accept his timeline of events:

- The conclusion of great tribulation (no mention of seven years duration).
- Immediately thereafter, the sun will be darkened.
- The moon will not reflect any light because the sun went dark.
- The stars shall fall from heaven.
- The powers of heaven shall be shaken.
- The sign of the Son of man shall appear in heaven.
- ALL the tribes of the earth shall mourn, everybody will see the Son of man coming in the clouds of heaven with power and great glory.
- Jesus will deploy his angelic army with a mighty trumpet blast.
- The angels shall gather together his elect (born again disciples of Christ) from everywhere across the planet.

Every eye on earth - animals too! - will see Jesus Christ arriving in the clouds of heaven with power and great glory because the universe will be totally dark. The King of Kings shall be the only radiant object in the sky. Sinners will fry. Saints will fly.

Old Testament Prophet Isaiah Saw the Final Day

Old Testament prophet Isaiah saw the Final Day. He prophesied about the revelation God gave him. He cried out to the rebellious, stiff-necked Israelites:

For the stars of heaven and the constellations thereof shall not give their light: the sun shall be darkened in his going forth, and the moon shall not cause her light to shine. (Isaiah 13:10)

What day did Isaiah see in his spirit? He saw the Final Day. It is not unusual that an Old Testament prophet was given a divine revelation of the second coming of Jesus Christ. God has been speaking to mankind about the Final Day ever since Adam and Eve submitted to Satan shortly after the First Day. Ancient Jews had no excuse to reject Jesus, and neither do modern-day Jews. All the Jewish prophets foretold of the arrival of the Messiah and the Final Day. Thank God for the first-century Jews who believed on the name of Jesus as the Messiah. All of us should be eternally grateful for them, and we should honor their memory and legacy as saints and martyrs of the Church. Darby and Scofield lied when they said that Jesus failed in His mission to give the kingdom to the Jews. Thousands of Jews believed on the name of Jesus Christ as the Savior of the world. They did receive the kingdom! Because of them, the rest of us were graciously grafted into Israel.

Thousands of years ago, Isaiah said fallen humanity will howl when the Final Day arrives because it will mean their destruction. Extreme terror will overtake all sinners. Their hands will weaken, hearts melt, and pangs and sorrows shall grip them. The sudden, unexpected end of the world will fill their bodies with excruciating pains like a pregnant woman in childbirth. They will stare at each other in horrid bewilderment, their faces shall turn beet-red like they are on fire. When the Final Day bursts upon unrepentant sinners, it shall be cruel with God's wrath and fierce anger. He will empty the earth and destroy all sinners who rejected Jesus Christ.

Behold, the day of the Lord cometh, cruel both with wrath and fierce anger, to lay the land desolate: and he shall destroy the sinners thereof out of it. Howl ye; for the day of the Lord is at hand; it shall come as a destruction from the Almighty. Therefore shall all hands be faint, and every man's heart shall melt: and they shall be afraid: pangs and sorrows shall take hold of them; they shall be in pain as a woman that travaileth: they shall be amazed one at another; their faces shall be as flames. Behold, the day of the Lord cometh, cruel both with wrath and fierce anger, to lay the land desolate: and he shall destroy the sinners thereof out of it. (Isaiah 13:6-9)

In the 60th chapter of the Book of Isaiah, the prophet revealed what God will give His people after the Final Day. God's light will come to His people on earth when darkness covers the planet, and gross darkness envelops the inhabitants of earth. The blood-bought Church of the Redeemed shall arise and shine in the darkness! Why? Because their light will come to them. The Lord's glory shall rise upon them. It will be easy for the angelic reapers to know who is a sinner and who is a saint. Sinners will be trapped in darkness. Saints will glow with God's glory. They will twinkle like fireflies in a country pasture on a dark summer night.

Arise, shine; for thy light is come, and the glory of the Lord is risen upon thee. For, behold, the darkness shall cover the earth, and gross darkness the people: but the Lord shall arise upon thee, and his glory shall be seen upon thee. (Isaiah 60:1-2)

It gets even better! By the 14th verse of chapter 60, Isaiah reveals the gem God has planned for his children. It is the New Jerusalem, the Bride of Christ!

...and they shall call thee, The city of the Lord, The Zion of the Holy One of Israel. (Isaiah 60:14)

Isaiah went on and borrowed a page from John the Revelator in the Apocalypse. In his vision on Patmos island, John saw New Jerusalem coming down from Heaven. The city had no need of the sun, moon, and stars. Apostle John said God will be the light of the glorious city.

And the city had no need of the sun, neither of the moon, to shine in it: for the glory of God did lighten it, and the Lamb is the light thereof. (Revelation 21:23)

Let's rewind the prophetic time machine to the days of Isaiah. The Old Testament prophet saw the same thing that the New Testament apostle John saw in his vision. How could they match up? How could the Jewish Old Testament Bible match the Christian New Testament Bible? It is because God has been telling mankind the same story for millenniums of time. He's searching for men and women who believe Him. Indeed, God's desire is to be believed! Do you know any mother or father who doesn't want their sons and daughters to believe and trust them? Look at what Isaiah saw. It matches John's vision on Patmos.

The sun shall be no more thy light by day; neither for brightness shall the moon give light unto thee: but the Lord shall be unto thee an everlasting light, and thy God thy glory. Thy sun shall no more go down; neither shall thy moon withdraw itself: for the Lord shall be thine everlasting light, and the days of thy mourning shall be ended. (Isaiah 60:19-20)

Every Eye Shall See Jesus

The days of our mourning shall come to an end following the time of great tribulation. Jesus shall gather the saints unto Him in the sky, the angels will bundle and burn all sinners, the old planet will be torched and burned up, a new earth and heaven shall be created by God's spoken words, New Jerusalem shall come down from Heaven, God will pack up His stuff in Heaven and move to the new earth to live with his children in a new Garden of Eden. He will be their light forever.

The sun, moon, and the stars will become obsolete. There will be no need for them when Jesus returns. Their sudden extinguishing is why every eye shall see him on the Final Day.

Behold, he cometh with clouds; *and every eye shall see him,* and they also which pierced him: and all kindreds of the earth shall wail because of him. Even so, Amen. (Revelation 1:7)

"Every eye shall see him" refers to more than the people alive on earth when Jesus returns. It includes every human who ever lived. They too shall be present to see the Messiah's glorious appearing. Billions of people who previously lived and died will be standing alongside the living. It will be only elbow room across the planet. Everybody will be bumping into each other because the lights will be out in the universe. Is it any wonder why men's hearts will fail them for fear, and for looking after those things which are coming on the earth, when the powers of heaven shall be shaken?

John begins his statement by saying "behold." It means, "look, see!" See what? See the coming of Jesus! How is he coming? He is arriving with clouds. Clouds represent God's great glory. John said everybody shall see Jesus arriving with clouds, but he deliberately singled out a specific group of people: the people who pierced the Lord at Calvary.

The Jews and Romans who crucified Jesus shall see him and wail. Specifically, who shall see Jesus when he returns? Roman governor Pontius Pilate shall be standing on earth watching the arrival of the King of Kings and Lord of Lords. The Roman soldiers who whipped and beat Jesus will be there, along with the Roman soldiers who nailed him to the cross and tossed dice to win his robe.

Caiaphas and the members of the Sanhedrin will see him too. All the chief priests and elders of the people who took counsel against Jesus to put Him to death shall also be standing there when He arrives with clouds of great glory. Barabbas and Judas will also be among the Jews who will witness the return of the Son of God whom they crucified. Every Jew who shouted "crucify him!" will watch the return of Jesus. All the Jews, and their descendants, who arrogantly said, "His blood be on us, and on our children," shall witness the spectacular descent of the Son of God. Indeed, every unrepentant Jew who opposed and killed God's prophets, rebelled against God's sovereign rulership, mocked the name of Jesus Christ, and opposed the work of His one, holy, catholic, and apostolic church will be standing there to see with their eyes the arrival of the one they hated. His bloodshed shall be upon them as they demanded.

When Pilate saw that he could prevail nothing, but that rather a tumult was made, he took water, and washed his hands before the multitude, saying, I am innocent of the blood of this just person: see ye to it. Then answered all the people, and said, His blood be on us, and on our children. (Matthew 27:24-25)

Can anybody fathom the utter horror and shock that will be upon their faces? They spent centuries tossing and turning in their tormented graves, and suddenly their place of internment opens. They will climb out of their graves, tombs, vaults, caves, and even from the sea floor. Everything will be dark except one shining object in the sky. Jesus! The man they mocked and crucified will be hovering over them in the sky as the triumphant and victorious king to settle matters His way.

Old Testament prophet Zechariah saw the same thing New Testament apostle John saw about the Lord's return. They both saw the Jews who pierced Jesus' body mourn on the Final Day when he returns. Zechariah made it clear he was talking about the Jews because he said the people are the "inhabitants of Jerusalem."

All Who Pierced Jesus' Side Shall See Him

Zechariah said the Jews will look upon Jesus when He returns and mourn in bitter sorrow. They will be compelled to look upon the One whom their Jewish ancestors demanded to be crucified, who gleefully watched the Roman soldier pierce His side with a spear, and whom all unsaved Jews since the Crucifixion metaphorically pierced the Lord of Glory by their rejection of Him as their Messiah and by their unrepented sins. They should have mourned in sorrow for their sins and repented before the Final Day. It will be too late when He is seen by everybody. Their mourning shall be in vain.

And I will pour upon the house of David, and upon the inhabitants of Jerusalem, the spirit of grace and of supplications: and they shall look upon me whom they have pierced, and they shall mourn for him, as one mourneth for his only son, and shall be in bitterness for him, as one that is in bitterness for his firstborn. (Zechariah 12:10)

Every Jew alive today still has the opportunity to repent, believe on the name of Jesus Christ, and be baptized into his holy church - true Israel. Why follow rebellious ancestors to Hell? God's arms are opened wide. All sinners are welcomed to enter His kingdom by repenting and believing on the name of Jesus.

How do we know that Pontius Pilate, the Roman soldiers, Caiaphas, Barabbas, Judas, the chief priests and elders of the Jews, and all the other Jews who demanded Jesus' crucifixion will be standing on earth to witness the glorious return of the Messiah whom they crucified on a cross at Calvary?

Here's the proof: Apostle John said we should not marvel at the amazing truth that every grave will open in the hour of Jesus' coming. All dead humans since Adam and Eve will come out of their graves when they hear His glorious voice. It won't be only the saints who come out of their graves. All sinners will awaken from their sleep too. Resurrection Day is for everybody! The saints will be resurrected to eternal life, and the wicked shall be resurrected unto eternal damnation.

Marvel not at this: for the hour is coming, *in the which all that are in the graves shall hear his voice,* and shall come forth; *they that have done good,* unto the resurrection of life; *and they that have done evil,* unto the resurrection of damnation. (John 5:28-29)

And, behold, I come quickly; and *my reward is with me, to give every man according as his work shall be.* (Revelation 22:12)

Therefore, every human who ever lived will be startled out of their deep sleep when Jesus shouts. O what a shout it shall be on that day! Out of their graves they shall arise. The first thing their awakened eyes shall behold will be Jesus Christ coming with clouds of great glory. For sinners, the second thing they will see will be a giant angel with fiery eyes pointing his finger at them saying, "You're mine. Follow me. You're going to the everlasting lake of fire."

Their time out of the graves will be short lived. It will be like a peep breaking out of an eggshell and immediately snatched away by a menacing predator. If you are a peep coming out of your egg shell and the first thing you see is a hungry coyote licking his lips, you instantly know it's going to be a bad hair day. Get over it and accept your fate. You're going to be quickly devoured.

That's the way it will be on the Final Day when all graves open. Unsaved sinners and the wicked may have enough time to say, "What's up with this?" A fiery angel will grab them faster than you can say "Go to Hell." Who knows? Perhaps God will grant them time to stretch their legs and arms after being in the grave for a long time. They will quickly notice, however, that the world is utterly dark, terrorized people are screaming, and billions of humans are running into each other in the darkness trying to get away from the Son of Man in the sky riding upon a majestic stallion and leading a vast army of warrior angels.

Old Testament and New Testament scriptures both confirm that the arrival of Jesus Christ shall be visible to the entire human population on earth, including the living and the newly awakened dead. It will specifically impact the Jews and Romans who crucified the Lord by piercing his hands, feet, and side. Their wailing shall be utterly in vain. The Jews and Romans won't be the only people wailing on the Final Day. Every unrepentant sinner whose sins and iniquities pierced the tender heart of the Lord shall also wail and mourn on that dreadful day of the Lord.

When everybody sees Jesus, it will be too late to repent. Therefore, they will wail in remembrance and sorrow of their sins, and their refusal to repent and believe on the name of Jesus Christ as their savior when they had the opportunity to do it. Nothing will fill the world with greater despair and alarm than the sight of the Judge of the Universe arriving to pronounce judgment and sentencing upon unrepentant sinners, the wicked, and the rebellious.

Every Saint Shall See Jesus Too

There is good news for Christians. All Christians who ever lived shall see Jesus too!

Every devout Christian who loves Jesus Christ desires to be among the chosen generation that is alive on the Final Day to witness the glorious appearing of our blessed hope Jesus Christ. But it doesn't matter if you are still alive on earth that day, or whether your body died years or centuries earlier. Everybody will be there when He returns! O what a glorious meeting it shall be on the Final Day!

The living and the dead will be there. Saints and sinners too. The entire Church - Adam and Eve, Abel, Seth, Enos, Jared, Enoch, Methuselah, Lemech, Noah, Shem, Ham, Japheth, Abraham, Moses, Joshua, Ruth, Saul, David, Solomon, Daniel, Samuel, Ezra, Nehemiah, Esther, Job, Isaiah, Jeremiah, Ezekiel, Daniel, Hosea, Joel, Amos, Obadiah, Jonah, Micah, Nahum, Habakkuk, Zephaniah, Haggai, Zechariah, Malachi, Matthew, Mark, Luke, John, Peter, Paul, Timothy, Titus, James, Jude, and every Christian from every era will be standing alongside us on the Final Day. It will be a giant Family Day celebration!

All the mad monarchs who ever ruled nations and terrorized the people will be standing there to observe the arrival of King Jesus. Nimrod, Pontius Pilate, Herod the Great, Nero, Julius Caesar, Nebuchadnezzar, Genghis Khan, Tamerlane the Great, Vlad the Impaler, Henry VI, Mary, Queen of Scots, Ivan the

Terrible, Rudolf II, Napoleon, George III, Carlota of Mexico, Adolf Hitler, and Saddam Hussein will watch the arrival of Jesus Christ. Standing with them will be all the wicked men and women from every generation.

All the rulers of the earth who ever lived - great and not-so-great, righteous and wicked - will be brought out of the graves for the grand finale of the age of mankind. Gathered with them will be their kingdoms' inhabitants, their victims, and accomplices. Justice will be served.

St. Jude quoted pre-Flood prophet Enoch who said "Behold, the Lord cometh with ten thousand of his saints...." Behold literally means "be sure to see" or "don't miss this!" The Greek word is an exclamatory word telling the hearer that an observable, objective event will happen and the hearer or reader should make sure he or she sees it. If you heard a person point up to the sky and shout, "Look! See it!" you would immediately look up to see what was there. Therefore, Enoch said, "Look! See him! The Lord is coming."

According to Jude, Methuselah's father told us why we must see the Lord's visible return to earth, along with ten thousand of his angels. Jesus and the angels will arrive to execute judgment upon all the earth's inhabitants. They will also convince all ungodly people of their evil deeds which they committed in their human bodies, and their harsh words spoken by them against Jesus Christ.

And Enoch also, the seventh from Adam, prophesied of these, saying, Behold, the Lord cometh with ten thousands of his saints, to execute judgment upon all, and to convince all that are ungodly among them of all their ungodly deeds which they have ungodly committed, and of all their hard speeches which ungodly sinners have spoken against him. (Jude:14-15)

Jesus' Words Refute Darby's Rapture Hoax

The visibility of the Lord's second coming plainly refutes the doctrinal fallacy of "The Rapture" of Christian saints. John Nelson Darby's DPPZites insist that Jesus returns twice: First, he comes in a secret rapture of Christian saints before the start of tribulation. Second, they teach that Jesus returns seven years later in the Second Coming. The problem with the flawed theology is that it directly contradicts the words of Jesus Christ. Here is what the Lord said:

And there shall be signs in the sun, and in the moon, and in the stars; and upon the earth distress of nations, with perplexity; the sea and the waves roaring; men's hearts failing them for fear, and for looking after those things which are coming on the earth: for the powers of heaven shall be shaken. *And then shall they see the Son of man coming in a cloud with power and great glory.* And when these things begin to come to pass, then look up, and lift up your heads; for your redemption draweth nigh. (Mark 13: 25-28)

Based on the words of Jesus, here is the sequence of events as stated in Mark 13:

- There will be signs in the sun, the moon, and stars.
- There will be the distress of nations, and the inhabitants will be perplexed (puzzled, bewildered, mentally confused).
- Oceans will be turbulent, high waves roaring.
- Uncontrollable fear will cause many people to have heart attacks when they see strange, unusual, catastrophic events occurring on earth and in the sky.
- The powers of heaven shall be shaken.
- Then people shall see the Son of Man coming in a cloud with power and great glory.

190

- When these things start happening, the saints must look up and lift their heads because their redemption from this sin-laden world will be near.

Is it not abundantly clear that the saints of God (Christians) are present on the earth when the sun, moon, and stars go dark, the nations are distressed, people are perplexed, the oceans are turbulent and the sea waves roar, heart attacks grip multitudes, the powers of heaven are shaken, and all people see the Son of man coming in a cloud with power and great glory? Jesus said His disciples shall "look up" when these things happen because our redemption is coming.

Everything will occur in view of ALL the inhabitants of earth - saints and sinners. Let's look again at Matthew 24:29-31 which was discussed in the beginning of this chapter.

Immediately after the tribulation of those days shall the sun be darkened, and the moon shall not give her light, and the stars shall fall from heaven, and the powers of the heavens shall be shaken: and then shall appear the sign of the Son of man in heaven: and then shall all the tribes of the earth mourn, *and they shall see the Son of man coming in the clouds of heaven with power and great glory*. And he shall send his angels with a great sound of a trumpet, and they shall gather together his elect from the four winds, from one end of heaven to the other. (Matthew 24:29-31)

The sequence of events is:

- The conclusion of great tribulation.
- The sun will be darkened.
- The moon will not reflect any light because the sun went dark.
- The stars shall fall from heaven.

- The powers of heaven shall be shaken.
- The sign of the Son of man shall appear in heaven.
- ALL the tribes of the earth shall mourn, everybody will see the Son of man coming in the clouds of heaven with power and great glory.

In the gospel of our Lord according to St. Luke, we see the same pattern of End Time events. There is no mention of a secret pre-tribulation rapture of Christians followed seven years later by the second coming of Jesus Christ. There's nothing hidden, concealed, or mystical about the order of things on the Final Day. You don't need a "prophecy expert" to explain it. Simply read the Bible and believe it. If you are confused, it is because doctrines of men have permeated your mind. Ask God to remove the cognitive cobwebs.

Let's look at Apostle Luke wrote about the Final Day:

And there shall be signs in the sun, and in the moon, and in the stars; and upon the earth distress of nations, with perplexity; the sea and the waves roaring; men's hearts failing them for fear, and for looking after those things which are coming on the earth: for the powers of heaven shall be shaken. And then shall they see the Son of man coming in a cloud with power and great glory. *And when these things begin to come to pass, then look up, and lift up your heads; for your redemption draweth nigh.* (Luke 21:25-28)

Let's now list the sequence of events described by Apostle Luke:

- There shall be signs in the sun, the moon, and the stars.
- There will be the distress of nations, and the inhabitants will be perplexed (puzzled, bewildered, mentally confused).
- Oceans will be turbulent, high waves roaring.

- Uncontrollable fear will cause many people to have heart attacks when they see strange, unusual, catastrophic events occurring on earth and in the sky.
- The powers of heaven shall be shaken.
- Then people shall see the Son of man coming in a cloud with power and great glory.
- When these things start happening, the saints must look up and lift their heads because their redemption from this sin-laden world will be near.

Apostle Luke's account of Jesus' words is identical to Apostle Mark's version. Apostle Matthew's account of the Final Day matches the versions written by Luke and Mark, but Matthew also mentioned the sign of the Son of man in the sky, the mourning of all the tribes of the earth, and the mighty trumpet blast that signals to his angelic army that the time has arrived to gather the saints.

Now, let's combine the three accounts given by Matthew, Mark, and Luke as they quoted Jesus Christ about the Final Day:

- The conclusion of great tribulation.
- There will be signs in the sun, the moon, and stars.
- The sun will be darkened.
- The moon will not reflect any light because the sun went dark.
- The stars shall fall from heaven.
- Oceans will be turbulent, high waves roaring.
- Uncontrollable fear will cause many people to have heart attacks when they see strange, unusual, catastrophic events occurring on earth and in the sky.
- The powers of heaven shall be shaken.
- The sign of the Son of man shall appear in heaven.

- All the tribes of the earth shall mourn.
- All the tribes of the earth will see the Son of Man coming in the clouds of heaven with power and great glory.
- Jesus will deploy his angelic army with a mighty trumpet blast.
- The angels shall gather together his elect (the saved) from everywhere across the planet.
- When these things start happening, the saints must look up and lift their heads because their redemption from this sin-laden world will be near.

The Words That Made Caiaphas Furious

The three apostles also recorded another statement by Jesus made at His trial before the crucifixion. It is a very important addition to our understanding of the sequence of events on the Final Day. Jesus made a statement about His second coming while being interrogated by the Jewish chief priests, elders, and members of the council. They searched Jerusalem for Jewish liars who would make false accusations against Jesus, king of the Jews. None could be found. At the last minute, two Jewish liars stepped forward and swore that they heard Jesus make a terroristic threat to physically destroy the Jewish temple and rebuild it in three days. The Jewish high priest stood up and demanded an explanation from Jesus. The Lord said nothing. Angered by Jesus' silence, the Jewish high priest demanded that Jesus tell the Jewish tribunal whether he is the Christ, the Son of God. Jesus responded by telling them they would see something someday.

Now the chief priests, and elders, and all the council, sought false witness against Jesus, to put him to death; but found none: yea, though many false witnesses came, yet found they none. At

the last came two false witnesses, and said, This fellow said, I am able to destroy the temple of God, and to build it in three days. And the high priest arose, and said unto him, Answerest thou nothing? what is it which these witness against thee? But Jesus held his peace. And the high priest answered and said unto him, I adjure thee by the living God, that thou tell us whether thou be the Christ, the Son of God. Jesus saith unto him, Thou hast said: nevertheless I say unto you, Hereafter shall ye see the Son of man sitting on the right hand of power, and coming in the clouds of heaven. (Matthew 26:59-64)

Jesus could no longer remain silent when asked if He is the Christ, the Son of God. Further silence would have been interpreted as denial of His divinity. Jesus affirmed His divinity by essentially saying, "That's what people are saying about me." In other words, "That's the word on the street. I'm not denying what people are saying about me."

Surely the chief priests and elders were smoldering with indignation when they perceived that Jesus did not emphatically deny the claims of the public that He is the Anointed One, the long-promised Jewish Messiah, the Son of God. They seethed with rage and thought, "That's enough for me! He just refused to deny that he is the Son of God. I don't need to hear another word out of his mouth. Jesus must be executed!"

Jesus wasn't finished with Jerusalem's pompous Jewish rulers. He gave them another zinger that sent them through the roof with furious indignation. Paraphrasing Jesus, He said, "You're mad because I will destroy the temple and rebuild it in three days, and because I am the Christ, the Son of God. I've got news for you! Just wait until you see me on the Final Day. Your eyes will see something more shocking than the destruction of your Jewish temple!"

That sent Caiaphas over the top. He angrily ripped apart his clothing in disgust. He accused Jesus of blasphemy and asked his fellow Jewish henchmen what they wanted to do with Jesus. They promptly demanded the death penalty.

Then the high priest rent his clothes, saying, He hath spoken blasphemy; what further need have we of witnesses? behold, now ye have heard his blasphemy. What think ye? They answered and said, He is guilty of death. (Matthew 26:65-66)

What did Jesus tell Caiaphas he would witness that was more shocking than the destruction of the Jewish temple in Jerusalem?

Jesus stared directly into the eyes of Joseph ben Caiaphas, the high priest of the Sanhedrin, and said **"nevertheless I say unto you, Hereafter shall ye see the Son of man sitting on the right hand of power, and coming in the clouds of heaven."** In other words, Jesus said, "Caiaphas, I'm talking to you, big boy. Mr. Caiaphas, I will bring your old dead body out of its dusty, musty, rotten, stinking grave on the Final Day and make you stand on the earth and watch me return with clouds of great glory."

Jesus' words "nevertheless I say unto you" conveyed the message to Caiaphas and the Sanhedrin that "I have something more shocking to tell you." What would be more shocking than destroying and rebuilding the temple, and admitting you are the Son of God? Jesus said "You shall see...." See whom? You shall see the Son of man! What will Caiaphas see the Son of man doing? "Mr. Caiaphas, you and the Sanhedrin shall see the Son of man sitting on the right hand of power and coming in the clouds of heaven!"

He gave them advance notification that the innocent man they were going to crucify will come back someday in great power and glory. Jesus let them know his return would be visible. The spiritual dullness of the Jewish leaders prevented them from comprehending what Jesus told them. They did not discern that he informed them that he would someday bring them out of their graves to personally witness his glorious and triumphant return. When he returns, Jesus will be more than king of the Jews. He will be hailed as King of Kings, and Lord of Lords.

Jesus also enlightened the Sanhedrin that they will see him "sitting on the right hand of power." Why did it infuriate them? It was offensive enough to make Caiaphas rip apart his expensive tailor-made robe. The Jewish rulers knew precisely what Jesus implied. Among the Hebrews, the phrase "sitting on the right hand of power" signified that Jesus saw himself equal with Almighty God's divinity and royal nobility. The "right hand" signifies God's might and power. It represents the chief place of honor. "The power" speaks of the eternal Creator. "Sitting" denotes that his work is completed. Therefore, Jesus told the Jerusalem's chief Jews that they would someday see Him coming in clouds (God's divine glory), and sitting with might and power in the chief place of honor as a divine prince of Almighty God the Creator, and rightly chosen to judge mankind because His work is completed and His enemies are now under His feet. That's what made Caiaphas rip apart his robe!

Further implied in His response was the notion that He would "turn the tables" on them someday, meaning He will reverse His position with the Jews by turning his current position of disadvantage into a position of advantage at a later date. Paraphrasing

Jesus, He told the chief priests, "Presently I am a prisoner in your illegitimate court facing an unjust judgment for sins I did not commit. Boys, I've got news for you! Someday I'm going to switch positions with you. You will be a prisoner in my royal court! I will be the just and righteous Judge of the Universe on the Final Day. I will convict you of sins you did commit! You will be sentenced on the Final Day to eternal damnation in the everlasting lake of fire. Mark my words. You will see it someday."

The universal visibility of his second coming is a big deal to Jesus. He personally guarantees that every human who ever lived will be standing on earth in total darkness on the Final Day to personally see Him arrive in radiant brilliance as the triumphant king of the universe who will put all his enemies under his feet. The Final Day will be His day! All eyes shall be upon Jesus.

Throughout centuries, devout Christians have longed and hoped that their generation would see the second coming of Jesus Christ. They went to their graves with their hope unfulfilled. Here is some wonderful news! They will see Jesus return! It does not matter whether you are alive or in a grave on the Final Day. You will see Jesus! Every born again, baptized, Bible-believing, faith-walking, faith-talking, commandment-keeping disciple of Christ who ever lived will see him. They will be very alive when they awaken from their sleep on Resurrection Day. The entire Church of God - the Church militant and the Church triumphant - will be alive and united together on the Final Day. Perhaps the atmosphere shall reverberate with billions of voices joyfully singing, "All hail the power of Jesus' name, let angels prostrate fall."

All unrepentant sinners and wicked evildoers shall see him too. All the dead - saints and sinners - shall awaken from their graves to see His glorious arrival. The Jews and Romans who nailed him to the cross will be there too, along with every person throughout the ages who rejected Jesus, mocked Him, spat upon His holy name, and opposed His one, holy, catholic, and apostolic church. All shall see Jesus in His exalted glory when He returns. "Every eye shall see him" includes cattle, horses, elephants, rabbits, eagles, whales, rattlesnakes, ants, flies, gnats, even blind bats! The entire animal kingdom on earth shall see Jesus too.

When the entire human population is gathered - from Adam to the last baby born seconds before Jesus returns - an incomprehensible event will occur. Both saints and sinners, rich and poor, lowly and haughty shall bow their knees before the triumphant King Jesus and their mouths will audibly confess that He is Lord. Every knee means the animal kingdom too! Elephants, horses, lions, apes, squirrels, and turtles will bow before the King of Kings and confess that Jesus is Lord.

For it is written, As I live, saith the Lord, every knee shall bow to me, and every tongue shall confess to God. So then every one of us shall give account of himself to God. (Romans 14:11)

Jewish Ruling Class Knew They Were Murdering the Son of God

Caiaphas and the chief priests pretended they were shocked over Jesus' claim to be the Son of God, the Anointed One. They knew all along he was the promised Messiah. It was the real reason the Jewish rulers conspired to kill him. Jesus told us in the Parable of the Vineyard Owner that the Jewish rulers knew that Jesus is the Son of God. They murdered Jesus to steal His inheritance! They didn't know the crucifixion of Jesus would be used by God to take away the kingdom of God from the Jews and give it to non-Jews. It backfired on them. Instead of stealing Jesus' inheritance, they lost their position as God's chosen people.

After the crucifixion, resurrection and ascension of Jesus, the unbelieving Jews were on the outside of Israel looking it. The believing Jews, Greeks and Romans who confessed Jesus as Lord and were baptized into His church were inside Israel as rightful citizens of the kingdom of God. The Church did not replace Israel. Instead, God replaced the citizens of Israel! Almighty God kept the repentant Jews who believed on the name of Jesus, and He kicked out the rebellious Jews who rejected the Messiah. Furthermore, God enlarged the population of Israel by inviting non-Jews to enter the kingdom. Today, most Jews - including residents of the modern State of Israel - are not citizens of God's Israel. They could re-enter anytime, but are too stubborn, proud, and rebellious to do it.

In the parable, the vineyard owner (God the Father) had sent his son (Jesus) to his vineyard (Israel) to collect the harvest of fruit (souls, praise, and obedience) that rightfully belonged to him. The vineyard servants (the Jews) refused to obey the vineyard owner (God) by giving him the harvest (souls, praise, and obedience) that was due to him. The owner (God) sent many representatives (prophets and watchmen) to them (the Jews) seeking to acquire his rightful portion of the harvest. The vineyard servants (the Jewish rulers) killed them (the prophets and watchmen). Finally, the vineyard owner (God) sent his Son (Jesus) to collect the fruit that rightfully belonged him. He thought, "Surely they will respect and obey my son!" Instead, the vineyard servants (the Jewish rulers) said, "He sent his son (Jesus). Let's kill him and steal his inheritance!" What is the inheritance they lusted to possess? It was the Davidic kingdom and the physical land of Israel! Today, European Ashkenazi Jews claiming to be the descendants of the Jews who crucified Jesus now physically occupy the land, at the expense of Palestinian Christians (the true Semitic descendants of the early Christian saints who followed Jesus). Today's Zionist Jews are also madly driven to possess the Davidic kingdom of Greater Israel, an endeavor that will require perpetual war in the Middle East to conquer all the nations currently possessing real estate that previously belonged to ancient Israel. Caiaphas and his gang of rebels were fully aware that they were plotting to murder he Son of God!

Jesus told the Jews that all the prophets spoke of Him. Therefore, they had no excuse to justify rejecting Him. Daniel was one of the Old Testament prophets who prophesied about the Final Day. He said the archangel Michael, the great angelic defender of God's people (people of all races and nations who are disciples of Jesus), will stand up at a time when there will be trouble on earth unlike anything in world history. It will be *at that time* that God's people shall be delivered (everybody whose name is written in the book of life). Daniel said dead people sleeping in the dust of the earth shall awaken. Some will awake to everlasting life, others to shame and everlasting contempt. Once again, we see the same theme: All the graves shall be opened on the Final Day.

And at that time shall Michael stand up, the great prince which standeth for the children of thy people: and there shall be a time of trouble, such as never was since there was a nation even to that same time: and at that time thy people shall be delivered, every one that shall be found written in the book. And many of them that sleep in the dust of the earth shall awake, some to everlasting life, and some to shame and everlasting contempt. And they that be wise shall shine as the brightness of the firmament; and they that turn many to righteousness as the stars forever and ever. *But thou, O Daniel, shut up the words, and seal the book, even to the time of the end: many shall run to and fro, and knowledge shall be increased.* (Daniel 12:1-3)

Our Transformation Occurs When We See Jesus

The second coming of Jesus Christ shall be singular, sudden and unexpected, atmospheric, and visible. Every man, woman, and child on the planet shall behold his glorious arrival with the clouds. His glorious appearing shall streak across the sky as lightning from east to west. The atmosphere will radiate with His splendor and glory. All humans will stagger at the brightness of His coming. Saints will joyously shout in excitement. Most people, however, will wail and mourn in terror. There will be no place for sinners to hide.

The most important thing to know about his visible appearing is that we shall be transformed to be like Him when we see Jesus. Saint Paul said we shall be changed, in a moment, in the twinkling of an eye, at the last trump. Our corruptible bodies of human flesh shall put on incorruption of the resurrected body of our Lord and Savior. We shall trade our mortality for His immortality. This glorious transformation happens when we see Jesus as He is! He is glorious! Our miraculous transformation from mortal beings to immortal beings is synonymous with our eyes beholding His magnificence, purity, and glory.

...in a moment, in the twinkling of an eye, at the last trump: for the trumpet shall sound, and the dead shall be raised incorruptible, *and we shall be changed.* (1 Corinthians 15:52)

Apostle John wrote a fascinating declaration of hope about the Final Day. The beloved apostle said our Heavenly Father has bestowed upon Christians a wonderful privilege of sonship. We are now the children of God. The world, however, does not recognize us as children of God because they don't acknowledge God. Indeed, the full revelation of sonship has yet to be given to Christians. We know that we are God's children, but we do not comprehend how awesome it shall be when this world is finished and we are forever in the presence of God.

Presently, it does not appear in this world that we are children of God, but we must always know that when Jesus appears, we shall be like Him! (We shall be like him, but not equal. We are made in His image, not in His essence.) What will cause this transformation to miraculously happen? *John said we will become like Jesus when we see Him as he is!* Yes, we are presently children, but someday we shall reach full maturity in Christ. The bud blossoms into the flower! Buds need sunlight to bloom. We are buds today, but we will fully blossom into radiant flowers when the Son's light shines upon us. The fact that we are presently children of God gives us hope for our future when Christ returns.

Apostle John, however, added an "and" to this wonderful promise. The "and" is a morality clause in the promise of God. John added the caveat that qualifies who will receive this transformation. St. John the Apostle said every Christian that has this hope in Jesus will keep himself pure even as Jesus is also pure.

Behold, what manner of love the Father hath bestowed upon us, that we should be called the sons of God: therefore the world knoweth us not, because it knew him not. Beloved, now are we the sons of God, and it doth not yet appear what we shall be: *but*

we know that, when he shall appear, we shall be like him; for we shall see him as he is. And every man that hath this hope in him purifieth himself, even as he is pure. (1 John 3:1-3)

If you truly desire to be transformed on the Final Day to be like Jesus, you better do your best in this life to live a life that is pleasing to God. It may sound old fashioned these days, but "living right for God" will pay big dividends on the Final Day.

The Second Coming of Jesus on the Final Day shall be:

- Singular
- Sudden and Unexpected
- Atmospheric
- Visible

CHAPTER 7

HIS SECOND COMING
SHALL BE NOISY

JESUS CHRIST WILL NOT tiptoe quietly into our dimension of time, space and matter. He's going to make a scene. A big scene.

It will be noisy. The grand kick-off event will be the massive earthquake mentioned in Revelation 16:18. The Holy Bible describes the mighty earthquake as the worst and most powerful earthquake in human history. How much noise do you think the ripping of the earth's crust will make when the planet splits open? The violent shifting of tectonic plates and the splitting of the earth's crust will be heard worldwide.

And there were voices, and thunders, and lightnings; and there was a great earthquake, such as was not since men were upon the earth, so mighty an earthquake, and so great. (Revelation 16:18)

There will be lots of loud shouting, thundering, roaring, and trumpet blasts. Across the earth in every nation, there shall be shouts of "Hallelujah! Glory to God!" or "Oh God!" Angels sang during the first advent of Jesus Christ. Angels will shout during His second advent.

Everybody on earth will know that Jesus is back in town. He can't help it. It's simply Jesus being Jesus! It's not that Jesus intentionally makes awesome stuff happen. Spectacular stuff happens whenever He enters any place. During his brief earthly ministry, Jesus ruined every funeral He attended. Dead people woke up when Jesus entered the room! Why? Because Jesus is pure life! There's nothing in Him except life. Death cannot be in His presence.

He is glorious! When Jesus returns, the earth shall tremble and shake. And all the dead shall wake up to locate the source of the commotion. It will be too noisy to continue sleeping in the dust of the earth. You can't sleep when your casket is violently shaking.

The voice of thy thunder was in the heaven: the lightnings lightened the world: the earth trembled and shook. (Psalm 77:18)

The Old Testament prophet Daniel saw Jesus in the 2nd century BC. What a glorious sight he beheld! Daniel described the righteous king he saw in the vision:

And in the four and twentieth day of the first month, as I was by the side of the great river, which is Hiddekel; then I lifted up mine eyes, and looked, and behold a certain man clothed in linen, whose loins were girded with fine gold of Uphaz: his body also was like the beryl, and his face as the appearance of lightning, and his eyes as lamps of fire, and his arms and his feet like in color to polished brass, and the voice of his words like the voice of a multitude. (Daniel 10:4-6)

Centuries later, another man saw Jesus in a similar vision. It was about the Final Day. The vision came to John the Revelator when he was a prisoner on the Isle of Patmos years after the crucifixion, resurrection, and ascension of Jesus. Apostle John, who walked with Jesus during His earthly ministry, saw in his divine vision the same glorious king whom Daniel the prophet saw in a vision. John wrote:

And I turned to see the voice that spake with me. And being turned, I saw seven golden candlesticks; and in the midst of the seven candlesticks one like unto the Son of man, clothed with a garment down to the foot, and girt about the paps with a golden girdle. His head and his hairs were white like wool, as white as snow; and his eyes were as a flame of fire; and his feet like unto fine brass, as if they burned in a furnace; and his voice as the sound of many waters. And he had in his right hand seven stars: and out of his mouth went a sharp two-edged sword: and his countenance was as the sun shineth in his strength. And when I saw him, I fell at his feet as dead. And he laid his right hand upon me, saying unto me, Fear not; I am the first and the last: I am he that liveth, and was dead; and, behold, I am alive for evermore, Amen; and have the keys of hell and of death. (Revelation 1:12-18)

That's who is coming back to earth on the Final Day of the age of mankind. The noise of His glorious and triumphant re-entry to this world will disrupt all human activity. Indeed, His arrival shall disrupt the entire cosmos. All eyes shall be fixed upon him.

He shall speak like thunder, the sound of many waters, the voice of a multitude. Every ear shall hear Him and listen. He shall not be silent.

Our God shall come, and shall not keep silence: a fire shall devour before him, and it shall be very tempestuous round about him. (Psalm 50:3)

"It shall be very tempestuous round about him." What is a tempest? It is a violent commotion, disturbance, or tumult. In other words, Jesus will make a scene. And it will be noisy. It's impossible to make a silent scene. The noise of His arrival will drown out all other voices and sounds on the planet. Jesus will dominate everything. Humans have ignored God for thousands of years. Nobody will ignore Him on the Final Day. He has something to say and He will be heard.

When God the Father met with Moses on Mount Sinai to receive the Ten Commandments on stone tablets, the Hebrew people trembled over what they saw and heard on the holy mountain.

And all the people saw the thunderings, and the lightnings, and the noise of the trumpet, and the mountain smoking: and when the people saw it, they removed, and stood afar off. And they said unto Moses, Speak thou with us, and we will hear: *but let not God speak with us, lest we die.* And Moses said unto the people, Fear not: for God is come to prove you, and that his fear may be before your faces, that ye sin not. And the people stood afar off, and Moses drew near unto the thick darkness where God was. (Exodus 20:18-21)

Angelic Army Shall Make Lots of Noise

Like Father, like Son. Jesus looks, talks, and acts like his Papa. We should expect Him to resemble his Heavenly Father's traits, ways and mannerisms when He returns.

There's a reason Jesus will make so much noise. He is seriously ticked off by mankind's incessant wickedness. Lawsuits have already been filed in Heaven's court against all nations - including the USA and Israel. No nation is innocent. None shall escape judgment. No country will be granted immunity from prosecution. His judgment shall arrive with great noise. The thunderous slamming of His gavel will shake the universe.

A noise shall come **even to the ends of the earth;** *for the Lord hath a controversy with the nations,* **he will plead with all flesh;** *he will give them that are wicked to the sword,* **saith the Lord. (Jeremiah 25:31)**

A noise shall come! What shall be this noise? It is the tumultuous sound of a marching army advancing toward its enemy to slaughter its members.

Everybody will hear the roaring movement of the Lord of Hosts and His angelic army. Their marching will not be silent. This mighty army of angels shall gallop toward earth faster than greased lightning bolts. Their eyes, glowing with flames of fire, will search out the enemies of God. The army shall swoop down upon earth's sin-obsessed civilizations because Almighty God has a legal dispute with every nation.

Isaiah prophesied about the Day of the Lord. Isaiah heard the tumultuous noise of nations when they gather together for battle with the Lord. Yahweh shall command His sanctified ones, who rejoice in God's highness, to mete out His anger upon the wicked.

I have commanded my sanctified ones, I have also called my mighty ones for mine anger, even them that rejoice in my highness. The noise of a multitude in the mountains, like as of a great people; a tumultuous noise of the kingdoms of nations gathered together: the Lord of hosts mustereth the host of the battle. (Isaiah 13:3-4)

The warriors shall travel from a "far country" carrying "weapons of his indignation" to "destroy the whole land." The global population of unsaved souls shall howl when the Final Day arrives. It shall be a day of destruction for the global Babylonian empire - Nimrod's resurrected technological civilization that will proudly build a society that worships, obeys, and conforms to the image of the beast, perhaps an artificial intelligence god, a global brain. The wicked will howl when the warriors arrive to destroy them.

They come from a far country, from the end of heaven, even the Lord, and the weapons of his indignation, to destroy the whole land. Howl ye; for the day of the Lord is at hand; it shall come as a destruction from the Almighty. (Isaiah 13:5-6)

Isaiah said all hands shall be faint. Every heart shall melt. Like a pregnant woman in great distress, pangs of sorrow shall grip them. They shall be very afraid. Even the bravest, strongest men in the world will collapse and cry like sissies when they see the Lord. An instantaneous awareness will grip them that mankind's long running rebellion against God has ended abruptly.

Therefore shall all hands be faint, and every man's heart shall melt: and they shall be afraid: pangs and sorrows shall take hold of them; they shall be in pain as a woman that travaileth: they shall be amazed one at another; their faces shall be as flames. (Isaiah 13:7-8)

Destruction of the Wicked Shall be Noisy

Thunderous noise shall accompany the second coming of Jesus Christ. Today's self-centered, comfort-driven, convenience-obsessed, lukewarm church members do not like to hear it, but the Lord is coming back with wrath and fierce anger to destroy the wicked and their pride-centered civilization of rebellion against the Almighty. Righteous saints pre-marked by the angels for protection have no reason to fear the Final Day, though terrible it shall be for everybody else. The saints, however, shall be safely watching it from a high altitude.

Behold, the day of the Lord cometh, cruel both with wrath and fierce anger, to lay the land desolate: and he shall destroy the sinners thereof out of it. (Isaiah 13:9)

In one day, Almighty God will settle the score with mankind. Tucked away in God's infinite mind are billions of memories He accumulated over thousands of years observing mankind's never-ending wickedness: cruelty, idolatry, wars, abortions, injustice, thievery, lying, deception, betrayal, blasphemy, molestations, adultery, fornication, homosexuality, and countless other sins that were never forgiven because the guilty never expressed remorse, nor did they repent and change their ways.

He will deal with them in an instant. Bam! God will be back on earth! His furious wrath will be unleashed on the wicked because He has a controversy with all nations. The controversy against each nation is fully stated in shocking details in His lawsuits filed in Heaven's court. Jesus will arrive with the guilty verdict in hand to carry out the sentence - eternal damnation in the Lake of Fire! There won't be a trial. Only a sentencing hearing for the guilty.

None of these things will be done quietly. The angels will not whisper and tip-toe through each nation as they execute justice upon the world. The wicked will not bellow silent screams of anguish. Tumultuous noises will resound worldwide. The sun, moon, and the stars shall go dark. The simultaneous gasping of billions of people worldwide when the lights go out will be noisy! King Jesus shall punish sinners for their evil deeds, the wicked for their iniquity. How can it be done quietly? Have you ever heard the pitiful screams of an animal caught in a trap? Unimaginable shall be the volume of wailing coming out of the mouths of billions of sinners caught in God's snare on the Final Day. It will be a day of slaughter.

For the stars of heaven and the constellations thereof shall not give their light: the sun shall be darkened in his going forth, and the moon shall not cause her light to shine. And I will punish the world for their evil, and the wicked for their iniquity; and I will cause the arrogancy of the proud to cease, and will lay low the haughtiness of the terrible. (Isaiah 13:10-11)

Jerusalem Shall be Destroyed

The Final Day shall suddenly and unexpectedly sweep over the earth like a global thunderstorm of righteous indignation. Haughty, proud Zionists shall be utterly dismayed and stunned when the thunderstorm encompasses Jerusalem and the land of Israel too. The rebellious, proud, unbelieving, Christ-denying Jews will be compelled by God to drink from His cup of wrath. Sadly, many good Jewish men and women will perish on the Final Day because they believed their rabbis and the Talmud instead of emulating Abraham's faith. Woe to the Evangelical Zionists who refuse to tell Jews they must repent and believe on the name of Jesus Christ whom their ancestors crucified. God will bring evil on Jerusalem. Christ-hating Jews shall not go unpunished. Yahweh - the God of Israel! - shall call for a sword upon all the inhabitants of the earth, including the Zionist State of Israel. There will not be a Zionist Jewish kingdom on earth for 1,000 years. Old Jerusalem will disappear when Jesus returns because Planet Earth shall be entirely burned up in a ball of flames. When the smoke of the incinerated old earth clears away, there shall only be New Jerusalem, the eternal capital of the new earth.

Jeremiah told the Jews that Jerusalem will not go unpunished:

Therefore thou shalt say unto them, Thus saith the Lord of hosts, the God of Israel; Drink ye, and be drunken, and spew, and fall, and rise no more, because of the sword which I will send among you. And it shall be, if they refuse to take the cup at thine hand to drink, then shalt thou say unto them, Thus saith the Lord of hosts; Ye shall certainly drink. *For, lo, I begin to bring evil on the city which is called by my name, and should ye be utterly unpunished? Ye shall not be unpunished: for I will call for a sword upon all the inhabitants of the earth, saith the Lord of hosts.* (Jeremiah 25:27-29)

Wailing will be heard in more than the streets of Jerusalem and Tel Aviv, the self-proclaimed world capital of homosexuality. Terrified cries of torment will emanate from the White House, the Kremlin, Buckingham Palace, the Great Hall of the People, and every other palace of power in the world. Time will abruptly end for the occupants to rule nations on behalf of Satan.

O what a noisy day it shall be when our Lord Jesus returns to earth!

God instructed Jeremiah to prophesy about the Final Day. God will roar mightily! He shall shout to the angels to tread the blood out of all the inhabitants of the earth like vineyard workers crushing grapes. It's no wonder that human blood will flow so deep that it will reach the height of horses' bridles. Saint John saw a lake of human blood that was at least five feet deep and over 200 miles wide!

And the winepress was trodden without the city, and blood came out of the winepress, even unto the horse bridles, by the space of a thousand and six hundred furlongs. (Revelation 14:20)

A Worldwide Tumultuous Noise

A troublesome and tumultuous noise will sweep over the planet. Why? Because God has a controversy with all the nations. His controversy is a legal dispute, a quarrel with every nation past and present. He will openly litigate against them for all to see and understand His righteousness and fairness. The wicked shall be given to the sword for destruction. This noisy storm of violence against the wicked shall be like a great whirlwind that starts along the coasts and quickly encompasses all nations. The dead bodies of the wicked shall litter every nation like mounds of putrid, fly-covered animal dung.

Therefore prophesy thou against them all these words, and say unto them, *The Lord shall roar* from on high, and *utter his voice* from his holy habitation; *he shall mightily roar* upon his habitation; *he shall give a shout,* as they that tread the grapes, against all the inhabitants of the earth. *A noise shall come even to the ends of the earth; for the Lord hath a controversy with the nations,* he will plead with all flesh; he will give them that are wicked to the sword, saith the Lord.

Thus saith the Lord of hosts, Behold, evil shall go forth from nation to nation, and a great whirlwind shall be raised up from the coasts of the earth. And the slain of the Lord shall be at that day from one end of the earth even unto the other end of the earth: they shall not be lamented, neither gathered, nor buried; they shall be dung upon the ground. (Jeremiah 25:30-33)

God will make noises, and the wicked will make noises too. Have you ever participated in an old-time country farm butchering of livestock? Hogs, cattle, goats, and sheep squeal in anguish and terror when their foreheads are shot or hammered, and their throats are slit open with a sharp butcher knife. No farmer with a heart enjoys it. The animals' screams and terrorized eyes will haunt your mind for days after the slaughter. It's enough to make you become a vegetarian.

God instructed Jeremiah to warn the worthless preachers that their day of slaughter is coming too. Yes, the preachers who refused to preach! Cowardly and corrupt preachers shall find no place to flee from the noisy slaughter. His fierce anger will cut them down on the Day of the Lord. They refused to tell the people to repent of their sins. They live their best lives now, but their worst life is ahead. Pulpit pansies will perish along with the wicked in the Lake of Fire. Worthless preachers shall howl forever.

Howl, ye shepherds, and cry; and wallow yourselves in the ashes, ye principal of the flock: for the days of your slaughter and of your dispersions are accomplished; and ye shall fall like a pleasant vessel. And the shepherds shall have no way to flee, nor the principal of the flock to escape. *A voice of the cry of the shepherds, and an howling of the principal of the flock, shall be heard, for the Lord hath spoiled their pasture.* And the peaceable habitations are cut down because of the fierce anger of the Lord. He hath forsaken his covert, as the lion: for their land is desolate because of the fierceness of the oppressor, and because of his fierce anger. (Jeremiah 25:34-38)

Operation Babylon: The Destruction of Sodom and Egypt

Jesus will come back to earth with an army of Heavenly angels. Angels are noisy too. They won't heed Federal Aviation Administration restrictions on aircraft engine noise. The FAA will be out of business on the Final Day when Heaven's air force bursts through our atmosphere to fulfill God's military mission: Rescue the righteous. Slaughter the wicked.

Ezekiel heard the noise made by angels. Their wings make the noise of great waters, as the voice of the Almighty. Their wings also make the noise of spinning wheels and of a great rushing.

And when they went, *I heard the noise of their wings, like the noise of great waters, as the voice of the Almighty, the voice of speech, as the noise of an host:* when they stood, they let down their wings. (Ezekiel 1:24)

I heard also *the noise of the wings of the living creatures* that touched one another, *and the noise of the wheels* over against them, *and a noise of a great rushing.* (Ezekiel 3:13)

In the New Testament Bible, the Apostle Peter said the Final Day shall come suddenly and unexpectedly as a thief in the night. Our beloved and bold St. Peter said the heavens shall pass away with a great noise, and the earth shall be burned up. John Nelson Darby's Evangelical Zionists have a big gaping hole in their eschatology. How can there be a 1,000-year Jewish kingdom centered in Jerusalem when the old city and the planet will be destroyed by fire when the Lord returns? Either the Evangelical Zionists are wrong, or St. Peter is wrong. Apostle Peter wrote that the earth and heavens will burn up on the Final Day when the Lord returns as a thief in the night.

But the day of the Lord will come as a thief in the night; in the which the heavens shall pass away with a great noise, and the elements shall melt with fervent heat, the earth also and the works that are therein shall be burned up. (2 Peter 3:10)

The truth is evident: Old Testament scriptures about the Final Day are consistent with the New Testament scriptures about the Lord's second advent: Jesus shall come back suddenly and unexpectedly with a shout and trumpet blast, Jesus shall roar, an army of angels shall noisily accompany him like a great rushing, they shall slaughter the wicked, there shall be much howling on the earth, and if that's not enough, the angels will set the place on fire on their way out the door and burn up everything and everybody. Nobody and nothing will survive the angels' righteous rampage.

In military terms, the Lord's return is Operation Babylon. The Commander of Heaven's Armies will come to wipe out prosperous and influential Babylon, Nimrod's reconstituted global empire built upon decadence, pride, lewdness, perversion, adultery, fornication, homosexuality, pornography, sorcery, witchcraft, pharmacia, genetic manipulations, perpetual warfare, bloodshed, violence, abortions, fraud, theft, and deception.

How big of a military operation is Operation Babylon? Its noise shall move the earth! Every nation shall hear the cry of Babylon's crash when the angelic army launches its B-Day assault against the Great Harlot.

At the noise of the taking of Babylon the earth is moved, and **the cry is heard** among the nations. (Jeremiah 50:46)

The final destruction of Babylon will be like the destruction of Sodom and Gomorrah and neighboring towns. The Lord declared: "No one will be there; no one will inhabit it." So too shall be the fate of Babylon on the Final Day.

Babylon is noisy too. She proudly makes noises of sin, rebellion, sorcery, witchcraft, murder, lewdness, adultery, fornication, homosexuality, thievery, and war. Jesus Christ shall silence the sins of Babylon. Waves of angelic avengers will bombard her walls. Jerusalem shall fall. The angels' voices shall roar around the world

217

as they carry out God's command to destroy the Harlot. Her voice shall fall silent because complete silence is evidence of depopulation. No Babylonian citizens will be permitted to live.

Because the Lord hath spoiled Babylon, *and destroyed out of her the great voice;* when her waves do roar like great waters, a noise of their voice is uttered... (Jeremiah 51:55)

Angelic Trumpet Blasts Are Noisy Too

The Lord's second advent shall be preceded by noisy trumpet blasts from seven angels following the opening of the seventh seal in Heaven. Before the seven angels sound their trumpets, there will be voices, and thunderings, and lightning, and an earthquake on earth. Lots of noise and commotion! No doubt, it will be attributed to extreme climate change! People will ignore the signs because apostasy and spiritual rebellion will be rampant in many Babylonian churches. There will be non-stop sinning until the angels commence their non-stop slaying of the wicked. The slaughter begins when Jesus Christ bursts into the sky above us like an exploding meteor. Slaughtering is very noisy.

And when he had opened the seventh seal, there was silence in heaven about the space of half an hour. And I saw the seven angels which stood before God; and to them were given seven trumpets. And another angel came and stood at the altar, having a golden censer; and there was given unto him much incense, that he should offer it with the prayers of all saints upon the golden altar which was before the throne. And the smoke of the incense, which came with the prayers of the saints, ascended up before God out of the angel's hand. And the angel took the censer, and filled it with fire of the altar, and cast it into the earth: *and there were voices, and*

thunderings, and lightnings, and an earthquake. And the seven angels which had the seven trumpets prepared themselves to sound. (Revelation 8:1-6)

The first four angels will sound their trumpets. Each trumpet blast will be followed by spectacular events on earth:

- Hail and fire mingled with blood.
- One-third of the planet's trees and all the grass burned up.
- A mountain-size rock burning with fire shall be cast into the sea.
- One third of the sea struck by the burning rock shall become blood; one-third of sea creatures are killed; and one-third of the ships are destroyed.
- A great burning star called Wormwood shall fall from heaven, burning like a lamp. One-third of the rivers and one-third of the fountains of water shall become bitter.
- One-third of the sun, moon, and the stars shall be smitten and darkened.

Upon the fourth angel's trumpet blast, John heard an angel flying through the midst of heaven shouting a great and ominous warning to every human on Planet Earth.

And I beheld, and heard an angel flying through the midst of heaven, *saying with a loud voice,* **Woe, woe, woe, to the inhabitants of the earth** *by reason of the other voices* **of the trumpet of the three angels,** *which are yet to sound!* (Revelation 8:13)

The Roar Heard Around the World

There's another mighty sound when the Lord returns. His roar! A lot of folks will have heart attacks when they hear it. He shall roar from on high as the angels tread the blood out of the wicked as grapes. His roar is the battle cry that commences Operation Babylon. It originates in Heaven from whence He will manifest His anger against mankind's perpetual sin and rebellion. God roars from His habitation - meaning Heaven - upon mankind's habitation, meaning earth. It shall be as a goat in a pasture unaware that a mighty lion is crawling toward it through the tall grass. Suddenly, the lion stands up and roars. It is too late for the goat to flee. The lion pounces upon it and devours its victim. Likewise, sudden and unexpected destruction shall come upon the wicked. They won't see it coming because their minds are dulled and defiled by sins. Saved Christians, however, will be constantly alert, astutely observant, eagerly anticipating, and vigilantly ready for the Lord's return.

Therefore prophesy thou against them all these words, and say unto them, *The Lord shall roar from on high, and utter his voice from his holy habitation; he shall mightily roar upon his habitation; he shall give a shout,* **as they that** *tread the grapes,* **against all the inhabitants of the earth. (Jeremiah 25:30)**

Yahweh is the commander of Heaven's armies and a mighty warrior. He has been patient with mankind and longsuffering of our sinful nature for thousands of years. The last time His patience expired over mankind's ceaseless wickedness was the Great Flood. He regretted ever making mankind, and thus He destroyed all life on the land. God hit the reset button and spared the fish and only eight humans - Noah and his family - and the animals that entered Noah's Ark. Jesus said as the days of Noah were, so shall be His second coming.

Almighty God is loving, kind, generous, patient, long-suffering, and quick to forgive. Christians, however, give little thought to how much God remembers since the Garden of Eden. He is the Ancient of Days, but he is not senile. His sharp mind remembers every unrepented sin since the days of Adam and Eve like it happened an hour ago. Every murder, abortion, robbery, assault, theft, adultery, fornication, homosexual act, rape, molestation, lie, fraud - indeed, every sin! - is fresh in God's memory. (Let us rejoice that all repented sins are forever forgotten!)

We cannot fathom the pain, anguish, and anger that Almighty God has kept in reserve for the Final Day. All of it will gusher from deep inside His being in a mighty roar that will shake the heavens and earth.

The Lord shall go forth as a mighty man, he shall stir up jealousy like a man of war: he shall cry, yea, roar; he shall prevail against his enemies. (Isaiah 42:13)

The Lord also shall roar out of Zion, and utter his voice from Jerusalem; and the heavens and the earth shall shake: but the Lord will be the hope of his people, and the strength of the children of Israel. (Joel 3:16)

And he said, The Lord will roar from Zion, and utter his voice from Jerusalem; and the habitations of the shepherds shall mourn, and the top of Carmel shall wither. (Amos 1:2)

Who is this roaring King of glory? He is Yahweh, the Lord strong and mighty, the Lord mighty in battle. He shall come to save His people Israel, the one, holy, catholic and apostolic church - the holy Christian nation of people who love Him and keep His commandments. His people - true Israel - are waiting for the noisy sound of a great trumpet blast and a glorious shout!

For the Lord himself shall descend from heaven with a shout, with the voice of the archangel, and with the trump of God: and

221

the dead in Christ shall rise first: then we which are alive and remain shall be caught up together with them in the clouds, to meet the Lord in the air: and so shall we ever be with the Lord. (I Thessalonians 4:16-17)

Everybody Will Hear the Bridegroom's Shout to Open All Graves

Why will Jesus shout? He will shout with joyous elation. "That day" will have finally arrived. And that day is the Final Day. Almighty God will release his Son to bring forth "the Bride, the wife of the Lamb," which is the New Jerusalem. Jesus Christ is the head of the Church. The saints are the body of Christ. The Bridegroom's head will not go alone to the wedding ceremony. The Bridegroom's body will be joined to the head. New Jerusalem is the bride, the Lamb's wife. The saints (the body of Christ) are not marrying Jesus (the head). Together, the head and body are marrying New Jerusalem. The holy city thus fulfills God's promise to the Church in Revelation 3:12.

And I John saw the holy city, new Jerusalem, coming down from God out of heaven, *prepared as a bride adorned for her husband.* (Revelation 21:2)

And there came unto me one of the seven angels which had the seven vials full of the seven last plagues, and talked with me, saying, *Come hither, I will shew thee the bride, the Lamb's wife.* And he carried me away in the spirit to a great and high mountain, *and shewed me that great city, the holy Jerusalem,* descending out of heaven from God, having the glory of God: and her light was like unto a stone most precious, even like a jasper stone, clear as crystal… (Revelation 21:9-11)

Him that overcometh will I make a pillar in the temple of my God, and he shall go no more out: and I will write upon him the name of my God, *and the name of the city of my God, which is new Jerusalem, which cometh down out of heaven from my God: and I will write upon him my new name.* (Revelation 3:12)

There's going to be a grand wedding party! All those wearing the proper wedding garments are cordially invited to attend the celebration. Wise virgins with extra oil for their lamps will find their way through the darkness at the midnight hour to greet the Bridegroom. Fools will miss it as they frantically seek to acquire additional oil to light their lamps for the journey in darkness to the wedding. Be alert! Be ready! Be diligent! Jesus is coming!

The arrival of the wedding day necessitates Jesus dispatching legions of reapers (angels) to bundle the wicked for perpetual burning, and to gather His elect from every nation to dwell in New Jerusalem on the new earth. A mighty trumpet blast shall signify the time for Heaven's angels to gather all righteous souls on earth.

And he shall send his angels *with a great sound of a trumpet,* and they shall gather together his elect from the four winds, from one end of heaven to the other. (Matthew 24:31)

Meanwhile, all of mankind in graves since the Garden of Eden shall be suddenly awakened by Jesus' glorious shout that He is coming again.

The mass grave opening will not be confined to only departed Christian saints. All dead bodies shall hear His voice and come out of their graves. Adam and Eve, Cain and Abel, Enoch, Methuselah, Moses, Jeremiah, Genghis Khan, George Washington, Adolf Hitler, Mother Teresa, Billy Graham, Winston Churchill, Elvis Presley, John Wayne - everybody who ever lived. All the people buried one minute before the great trumpet blast will pop out too. They will set the world record for the shortest time in a grave.

When will the dead come out of their graves? When they hear Jesus' shout! It will be the shout heard around the world.

Marvel not at this: for the hour is coming, *in the which all that are in the graves shall hear his voice, and shall come forth*; they that have done good, unto the resurrection of life; and they that have done evil, unto the resurrection of damnation. (John 5:28-29)

And what about the Christians who are alive on the earth when Jesus returns? What happens to them? And when? A radical change is necessary because flesh and blood cannot inherit the Kingdom of God and dwell eternally in New Jerusalem.

Now this I say, brethren, that flesh and blood cannot inherit the kingdom of God; neither doth corruption inherit incorruption. Behold, I shew you a mystery; *We shall not all sleep, but we shall all be changed, in a moment, in the twinkling of an eye, at the last trump: for the trumpet shall sound,* and the dead shall be raised incorruptible, and we shall be changed. (I Corinthians 15:50-52)

First, all saints who are in repose in Christ shall come out of their graves and will be given incorruptible bodies. Next, the blessed generation of saints living on earth when Jesus comes back shall be changed in a moment, in the twinkling of an eye, and given incorruptible bodies too. When do these things happen? These things happen when the last trumpet sounds its glorious clarion call to the Church to come up into the air to meet King Jesus! Our mortal bodies are replaced with immortal bodies when our eyes see Jesus. It happens when the last trumpet is heard. The Lord's second coming shall be noisy!

Such shall be the day when Isaiah's prophecy is fulfilled: God will swallow up death, wipe away tears from all faces, and vanquish from the earth the rebuke of his people Israel, the holy Christian Church.

He will swallow up death in victory; and the Lord God will wipe away tears from off all faces; and the rebuke of his people shall he take away from off all the earth: for the Lord hath spoken it. (Isaiah 25:8)

In his vision on Patmos island, Apostle John saw another sign in heaven. It was great and marvelous. He saw seven angels who had the seven last plagues that would be poured out upon the rebellious human population. The seven plagues contained the wrath of God. John saw what looked like a sea of glass mingled with fire: and them that had gotten the victory over the beast, and over his image, and over his mark, and over the number of his name. They stood on the sea of glass, holding harps of God. The saints sang the Song of Moses, the servant of God, and the song of the Lamb. They sang:

Great and marvelous are thy works, Lord God Almighty; just and true are thy ways, thou King of saints. Who shall not fear thee, O Lord, and glorify thy name? for thou only art holy: for all nations shall come and worship before thee; for thy judgments are made manifest. (Revelation 15:3-4)

These are the saints who shall be viciously attacked by one of the horns upon the head of the fourth beast. The saints of God - the Holy Christian Church, true Israel - shall shout with joy when King Jesus arrives to save them from the beast. This blood-soaked tumultuous age of mankind will suddenly end. Thousands of years of wars, violence, bloodshed, disease, hatred, suffering, pain, tears, and death will abruptly end. Our blessed hope shall come for His beloved Church. The wise virgins will arrive in time for the wedding of the Bridegroom and New Jerusalem. The foolish virgins will miss the grand gala.

At the first advent of Jesus Christ, the daughter of Zion greatly rejoiced and shouted. Israel's king had come riding on a donkey bringing salvation to the world (Zechariah 9:9). When the second advent of Jesus Christ arrives, the inhabitants of New Zion shall cry out and shout, for great is the Holy One of Israel who shall be in the midst of his assembly (Isaiah 12:6). The daughter of New Zion shall gleefully sing joyous songs of praise and adoration. She shall be glad and rejoice with all her heart because the Lord has taken away her judgments and cast out her enemy. The king of Israel will be home forever (Zephaniah 3:14-15). The righteous shall be glad in the Lord and rejoice. All who are upright in heart shall shout for joy (Psalm 32:11).

There will be one more source of noise when Jesus returns. All of creation will sing and shout: the heavens, the earth, angels, the saints, and even the animals. What a happy day it shall be for the righteous! The heavens and the earth shall sing! The mountains shall break forth in singing (Isaiah 44:23), and the animals shall sing praises to King Jesus too. Yes, the animals shall talk! They shall glorify the Lord. They will sing praises to their Creator! Animals did not sin against God. They suffered death because of the sins of Adam and Eve. In the restoration of all things, we must consider the possibility that God will restore them on the new earth. The entire animal kingdom shall worship God! What a sound the animals shall make when they sing to Jesus Christ. They will joyfully sing for being delivered from their bondage to mankind's sins on earth.

And every creature which is in heaven, and on the earth, and under the earth, and such as are in the sea, and all that are in them, heard I saying, Blessing, and honor, and glory, and power, be unto him that sitteth upon the throne, and unto the Lamb for ever and ever. (Revelation 5:13)

All of God' beautiful creation was made for His glory. The universe, planets, stars, humans, animals, mountains, trees, oceans - everything exists for God's glory. All of Creation is obligated to praise Him. It is the duty and privilege of everybody, and everything, made by God to praise him.

The arrival of Jesus Christ shall be very noisy. The destruction of the wicked will be noisy too. And life in New Jerusalem shall be noisy. The homes, streets, parks, and amphitheaters of the eternal capital city of New Israel shall be filled with continuous shouts of happiness and joyful singing as the saints praise the Lamb of God throughout everlasting eternity.

And after these things *I heard a great voice* of much people in heaven, saying, Alleluia; Salvation, and glory, and honor, and power, unto the Lord our God: for true and righteous are his judgments: for he hath judged the great whore, which did corrupt the earth with her fornication, and hath avenged the blood of his servants at her hand. And again they said, Alleluia. And her smoke rose up for ever and ever. And the four and twenty elders and the four beasts fell down and worshipped God that sat on the throne, saying, Amen; Alleluia.

And a voice came out of the throne, saying, Praise our God, all ye his servants, and ye that fear him, both small and great. And I heard as it were the voice of a great multitude, and as the voice of many waters, and as the voice of mighty thunderings, saying, Alleluia: for the Lord God omnipotent reigneth. Let us be glad and rejoice, and give honor to him: for the marriage of the Lamb is come, and his wife hath made herself ready. And to her was granted that she should be arrayed in fine linen, clean and white: for the fine linen is the righteousness of saints. And he saith unto me, Write, Blessed are they which are called unto the marriage supper of the Lamb. And he saith unto me, These are the true sayings of God. (Revelation 19:1-9)

The Second Coming of Jesus on the Final Day shall be:

- Singular
- Sudden and Unexpected
- Atmospheric
- Visible
- Noisy

CHAPTER 8

HIS SECOND COMING
SHALL BE DISRUPTIVE

I F ELVIS PRESLEY WROTE a song about the Final Day, he'd sing that there will be a "whole lotta shaking going on."

The moment Jesus Christ enters our physical dimension, there will be brilliant lightning, deafening thunder, violent earthquakes, great noises, storms, tempests, and raging fires.

And the angel took the censer, and filled it with fire of the altar, and cast it into the earth: and there were voices, and thunderings, and lightnings, and an earthquake. (Revelation 8:5)

Jesus creates a scene wherever he goes. When he stands up in Heaven, lightning bolts flash as he walks to the other side of the throne room. Thousands of angels bow down crying "Holy, holy, holy!" It's just a normal day in Heaven.

The same is to be expected when the King of Kings enters our physical dimension. Jesus cannot tiptoe through the backdoor of the natural dimension of our reality and not be seen or heard. It is

229

impossible. He is God! His glory and greatness are too much for our physical world. The natural world will shake and tremble in His presence. His reentry into our realm will violently disrupt the universe. The cosmos will rupture. Jesus won't have to make it happen. Stuff just happens when he arrives on the scene.

The earth shall quake before them; the heavens shall tremble: the sun and the moon shall be dark, and the stars shall withdraw their shining: and the Lord shall utter his voice before his army: for his camp is very great: for he is strong that executeth his word: for the day of the Lord is great and very terrible; and who can abide it? (Joel 2:10-11)

There was a day ages ago when Jerusalem's idolatry and debauchery came to a sudden and swift end. Her people didn't see it coming. Isaiah, however, forewarned the inhabitants of Jerusalem that God would visit them in their state of sinful rebellion. He called the city Ariel. The prophet cried out:

Woe to Ariel, to Ariel, the city where David dwelt!... (Isaiah 29:1)

Isaiah warned that God would distress Jerusalem. There would be heaviness and sorrow. The Lord's army would encamp about the city and lay siege to it. The proud city would be greatly humbled. Brave men whisper in fear of what is happening to Jerusalem. Their faint and shrill voices shall come from the earth as the voice of spirit-charmers or necromancers.

And then Isaiah gave Jerusalem's arrogant inhabitants the really bad news. God would visit them in their state of prideful sin:

Thou shalt be visited of the Lord of hosts with thunder, and with earthquake, and great noise, with storm and tempest, and the flame of devouring fire. (Isaiah 29:6)

Such shall be the day of the Lord, but on a grand scale beyond human comprehension.

The prophet Joel saw "that day," the final visitation of God to earth when God would do more than disrupt time: He will abolish time as we presently know it. There can't be 24-hour days and 365-day years after the earth, moon, and sun are destroyed.

Although "the day of the Lord" and "that day" refer to numerous visitations of God to humanity over thousands of years, Joel spoke of the final visitation. It will be the final "day of the Lord." Confirming that Joel's prophecy referred to the Final Day of the Lord, Apostle Peter quoted Joel in the Book of Acts of the Apostles.

Blow ye the trumpet in Zion, and sound an alarm in my holy mountain: let all the inhabitants of the land tremble: for the day of the Lord cometh, for it is nigh at hand; a day of darkness and of gloominess, a day of clouds and of thick darkness, as the morning spread upon the mountains: a great people and a strong; there hath not been ever the like, neither shall be any more after it, even to the years of many generations. (Joel 2:1-2)

And it shall come to pass afterward, that I will pour out my spirit upon all flesh; and your sons and your daughters shall prophesy, your old men shall dream dreams, your young men shall see visions: and also upon the servants and upon the handmaids in those days will I pour out my spirit. *And I will shew wonders in the heavens and in the earth, blood, and fire, and pillars of smoke. The sun shall be turned into darkness, and the moon into blood, before the great and the terrible day of the Lord come. And it shall come to pass, that whosoever shall call on the name of the Lord shall be delivered: for in mount Zion and in Jerusalem shall* *be deliverance, as the Lord hath said, and in the remnant whom the Lord shall call.* (Joel 2:28-32)

Compare Joel's prophecy with the words of Apostle Peter after the resurrection and ascension of Jesus. The Jews were told that the only way to salvation was by repentance of sins and faith in the name of Jesus whom the Jews had crucified.

But Peter, standing up with the eleven, lifted up his voice, and said unto them, Ye men of Judaea, and all ye that dwell at Jerusalem, be this known unto you, and hearken to my words: for these are not drunken, as ye suppose, seeing it is but the third hour of the day. But this is that which was spoken by the prophet Joel; *And it shall come to pass in the last days, saith God, I will pour out of my Spirit upon all flesh: and your sons and your daughters shall prophesy, and your young men shall see visions, and your old men shall dream dreams: and on my servants and on my handmaidens. I will pour out in those days of my Spirit; and they shall prophesy: and I will shew wonders in heaven above, and signs in the earth beneath; blood, and fire, and vapor of smoke: the sun shall be turned into darkness, and the moon into blood, before that great and notable day of the Lord come: and it shall come to pass, that whosoever shall call on the name of the Lord shall be saved.* (Acts 2:14-21)

Speaking through the fiery prophet, God told the Israelites what would happen *before* the day of the Lord. These things shall be part of the warm-up act before the King of Glory steps out on the center stage of the universe:

And I will shew wonders in the heavens and in the earth, blood, and fire, and pillars of smoke. The sun shall be turned into darkness, and the moon into blood, before the great and the terrible day of the Lord come. (Joel 2:30-31)

Now is the time of salvation! This is the hour to cry out to Jesus and seek forgiveness of sins. People must go to the Cross and submit before the great and terrible day of the Lord arrives. Nobody will be saved after He returns. You must be baptized into His holy church before He arrives. He is coming to pick up family members only.

And it shall come to pass, that whosoever shall call on the name of the Lord shall be delivered: for in mount Zion and in Jerusalem shall be deliverance, as the Lord hath said, and in the remnant whom the Lord shall call. (Joel 2:32)

The Gospel is Disruptive

The first advent of Jesus Christ was very disruptive. It produced cosmic happenings. An angelic choir in the night-time sky over Bethlehem proclaimed to shepherds the birth of the Savior. Later, a delegation of wise men came from the east to Jerusalem seeking to worship the newborn Christ child. A mysterious star brightly "went before them" and led them to the house in Bethlehem where the infant Messiah lived with Mary and Joseph. (The Magi did not go to the manger where Jesus was born.) Joseph was led by angels in dreams to flee Bethlehem, and later to depart Egypt.

Likewise, the introduction of the gospel disrupted the world. Old Testament prophet Haggai pointed the Israelites to the coming of the Messiah. Haggai said God would shake the heavens, and the earth, and the sea, and the dry land; and all nations when Jesus is born on earth as God in human flesh. He prophesied that the glorious incarnation of the Son of God was Heaven's response to "the desire of all nations." The miraculous virgin birth of Jesus and the preaching of the Gospel of the Kingdom would agitate the world and "shake all nations."

God's introduction of the Christian gospel of the kingdom was more significant and momentous than His giving the Law to Moses on Mount Sinai, thus making the rejection of the gospel more dangerous than breaking the Law. The giving of the Law on Mount Sinai shook the mountain and nearby vicinities. The introduction of the Christian gospel, however, would shake the nations of the world. Foretelling of the resurrection of Jesus and the destruction of the Jewish temple, Haggai said the Messiah's unsurpassed glory would be superior to the glory and splendor of the gold and silver in the Jewish temple in Jerusalem.

For thus saith the Lord of hosts; Yet once, it is a little while, *and I will shake the heavens, and the earth, and the sea, and the dry land; and I will shake all nations, and the desire of all nations shall come:* and I will fill this house with glory, saith the Lord of hosts. The silver is mine, and the gold is mine, saith the Lord of hosts. The glory of this latter house shall be greater than of the former, saith the Lord of hosts: and in this place will I give peace, saith the Lord of hosts. (Haggai 2:6-9)

Jesus's earthly ministry was disruptive. He performed supernatural miracles that suspended the laws of physics. He turned water into wine. He made new eyeballs with mud. He fed thousands of men, women, and children with a handful of bread loaves and fish. He cured the incurable. He cast out demons. He raised the dead.

Staying true to his ways, Jesus' departure from this world also disrupted the planet. Darkness fell over the land when Jesus was crucified by the Romans to satisfy the delirious bloodlust of the Jews to murder the Son of God.

Now from the sixth hour there was darkness over all the land unto the ninth hour. (Matthew 27:45)

Many other strange occurrences shocked the people of Jerusalem on the day the Jews and Romans killed the Messiah. As Jesus' divine soul was violently separated from His human body, a mighty earthquake shook Jerusalem. Rocks split apart. The massive, thick curtain in the temple was ripped from top to bottom. Graves were opened. Dead saints came out of the graves and walked on Jerusalem's streets and were seen by many.

Jesus, when he had cried again with a loud voice, yielded up the ghost. And, behold, the veil of the temple was rent in twain from the top to the bottom; *and the earth did quake, and the rocks rent; and the graves were opened; and many bodies of the saints which slept arose, and came out of the graves after his resurrection, and went into the holy city, and appeared unto many.* **Now when the centurion, and they that were with him, watching Jesus, saw the earthquake, and those things that were done, they feared greatly, saying, Truly this was the Son of God. (Matthew 27:50-54)**

And, behold, there was a great earthquake: **for the angel of the Lord descended from heaven, and came and rolled back the stone from the door, and sat upon it. (Matthew 28:2)**

If His crucifixion and resurrection triggered earthquakes, atmospheric darkness, and supernatural phenomena, should we not expect even more spectacular disruptions when He returns?

His Second Advent Will Disrupt the Cosmos

Indeed, the second advent of Jesus Christ shall disrupt the cosmos. Let's start with the warm-up to the Big Event. Jesus called it "the beginning of sorrows." After walking out of the temple in Jerusalem, Jesus was asked privately by His disciples three questions:

- When will the temple be destroyed?
- What shall be the signs of your coming?
- What shall be the signs of the end of the age?

He responded by giving them a very detailed description of what will happen regarding all three questions. The problem today is that many people mistakenly omit the first question about the temple's destruction. They wrongly interpret his comments about the future destruction of the temple as a prophecy about the second coming. Whenever you read Matthew 24, always keep in mind that Jesus is answering all three questions asked by the disciples. At the time they were asked, all three questions concerned future events. The temple was destroyed in 70AD, thus fulfilling the prophecy. Therefore, the answer to the first question has already happened, but it was a future event at the time the disciples questioned Him. His comments about the abomination of desolation standing in the temple, and warnings to flee the city were about the destruction of the Jewish temple. What we are discussing today are the two remaining questions: What shall be the signs of his coming, and what shall be the signs of the end of the age?

He said we should expect to see people coming in his name claiming to speak for him, but deceiving many. We will hear of wars and rumors of wars. Nations shall rise against nations, and kingdoms against kingdoms. There will also be great earthquakes here, there, everywhere; plus, famines and pestilences. Such things are only the beginning of sorrows. Calamities much more horrible shall come.

Jesus-haters shall gather up Jesus-lovers to afflict them, and to kill many. Jesus-lovers shall be despised by Jesus-haters throughout the world for the sake of the name of Jesus Christ. When Christians are hated and killed worldwide, the resolve of many spiritually weak Christians will buckle and collapse. Their faith shall melt in the furnace of adversity. Such are they who shall be offended by strong Christians who refuse to draw back from the true apostolic faith despite severe persecution and cruel executions. Thus, Babylonian Churchianity members will betray true Christians who stand for righteousness while living in a vile, disgusting, sin-obsessed world that is on a collision course with Almighty God. Courageous disciples of Christ should be on guard now for signs that a spirit of Judas is operating among Evangelical Zionists.

As the world races toward the Final Day, it's going to to be identified with Jesus Christ. Many Christians who foolishly believe they will be removed from earth in a secret rapture before the start of the great tribulation will succumb to the temptation to deny Jesus Christ as God. Those who endure to the end shall be saved. The end of the age shall come when the gospel of the kingdom of God is preached in all the world as a witness. Only a portion of the worldwide church will still be in the game in the last inning. Intense social, economic, and political pressure will be too much for many weak Christians to endure. Cowardly, timid, fearful, and faithless church members will have their part in the lake that burns with fire and brimstone.

For many shall come in my name, saying, I am Christ; and shall deceive many. And ye shall hear of wars and rumors of wars: see that ye be not troubled: for all these things must come to pass, but the end is not yet. For nation shall rise against nation, and kingdom against kingdom: and there shall be famines, and pestilences, and earthquakes, in divers places. All these are the beginning of sorrows.

Then shall they deliver you up to be afflicted, and shall kill you: and ye shall be hated of all nations for my name's sake. And then shall many be offended, and shall betray one another, and shall hate one another. And many false prophets shall rise, and shall deceive many. And because iniquity shall abound, the love of many shall wax cold. But he that shall endure unto the end, the same shall be saved. And this gospel of the kingdom shall be preached in all the world for a witness unto all nations; and then shall the end come. (Matthew 24:5-14)

In addition to great earthquakes in many places, Jesus also said there shall be fearful sights and great signs from heaven. "Fearful sights" means terrifying things.

...and great earthquakes shall be in divers places, and famines, and pestilences; and fearful sights and great signs shall there be from heaven. (Luke 21:11)

But wait, there's more! There will be signs in the cosmos too. On earth, nations will be totally stressed out and bewildered about what's happening. And sea waves shall roar. Politicians will tell frightened voters that the environment is crashing because of extreme climate change. People will believe anything but the Bible. Most will stubbornly refuse to repent and call upon the name of the Lord to be saved.

And there shall be signs in the sun, and in the moon, and in the stars; and upon the earth distress of nations, with perplexity; the sea and the waves roaring... (Luke 21:25)

What explains such bizarre cosmic disruptions of the universe's natural order? Creation's groaning will eventually become a scream of anguish pleading with the Creator to deliver it from the crushing burden of accommodating mankind's sins for thousands of years.

In Matthew 24:8, Jesus said the things coming upon the earth (earthquakes, famines, pestilences, wars, deception) are the beginning of sorrows. The "beginning of sorrows" means "the beginning of travail pangs."

Who or what will be in labor? Who or what will suffer birth pangs? It is God's beautiful creation that presently seeks deliverance from man's awful sins. Creation was never intended to coexist with sin. Sin is a foreign substance - a virus that entered creation at the fall of Adam and Eve and made it sick. Apostle Paul said the whole creation - the entire universe! - is groaning in travail caused by the proliferation of sin. Creation shall be delivered from the bondage of man's sin on the Final Day.

...because the creature itself also shall be delivered from the bondage of corruption into the glorious liberty of the children of God. For we know that the whole creation groaneth and travaileth in pain together until now. (Romans 8:21-22)

Planet Earth's Popeye Moment

This author loved to watch Popeye cartoons every weeknight after elementary school. Popeye was cool. He was a happy, easy-going, skinny sailor who tried his best to get along with everybody. Popeye's good-natured personality, however, was always challenged by mean, nasty bullies such as Brutus. In each cartoon, Popeye would reach his tipping point. He would shout, "That's all I can stands. I can't stands no more!" Now that's when the cartoon hero would whip out a big can of spinach, squeeze it until the lid popped off, gulp down all the spinach, flex his big muscles, and go after Brutus with vengeance. For Brutus, it was "lights out." The big bearded goon would find himself knocked out on the floor seeing twinkling stars and hearing chirping birds. And Popeye went on his way in each cartoon episode whistling a happy tune, and often holding hands with his girlfriend Olive Oyl. End of story.

Planet Earth is rapidly approaching Popeye's tipping point. The planet will shout to God, "That's all I can stands. I can't stands it no more!" It will be "lights out" for sinful mankind. End of story. God will speak into existence a new earth that will whistle a happy tune for eternity. A perpetual happy ending!

Strange things are already happening, yet few people are connecting the dots to Matthew 24. Earthquakes have happened since Noah's Flood, but our planet is now experiencing "great earthquakes" as prophesied by Jesus. The Great Sumatra-Andaman Earthquake of December 26, 2004, struck the Indian Ocean with a whopping 9.1 magnitude. It generated a terrifying tsunami that suddenly and unexpectedly swept hundreds of thousands of people into the sea. The power of the quake moved the earth off its axis, and shortened the day. Likewise, the deadly magnitude 8.9 super-quake that struck Japan in April 2011 moved the earth off its axis by four inches, and shifted Japan's main island by eight feet. A magnitude 8.8 mega-quake that struck Chile in March 2010 also shifted the planet off its axis and shortened the day.

Yes, our planet is speaking to God now. It is groaning in travail like a pregnant woman suffering painful birth pangs. Someday, however, it will beg for immediate relief from mankind's unbearable burden of sins. Did you know that our planet can speak? Planet Earth has a mouth. And blood has a voice. Innocent blood speaks to God through the earth's mouth. The Bible says so in its account of Cain's murder of his brother Abel over their offerings to God.

And the Lord said unto Cain, Where is Abel thy brother? And he said, I know not: Am I my brother's keeper? And he said, What hast thou done? *the voice of thy brother's blood crieth unto me from the ground. And now art thou cursed from the earth, which hath opened her mouth to receive thy brother's blood from thy hand...* (Genesis 4:9-11)

For thousands of years, proud and rebellious men and women did not know that Almighty God had placed deep in the bowels of the earth His explosive charges that are set to detonate at the appointed time. The mega seismic convulsion scheduled by God for the end of the age will be the mother of all earthquakes. The Bible says the earth is resting on invisible pillars:

...for the pillars of the earth are the Lord's, and he hath set the world upon them. (I Samuel 2:8)

Mankind has a date with destiny when God will suddenly and unexpectedly knock the earth off its pillars. Isaiah prophesied the earth will be moved off its axis and rock back and forth like a drunkard. It will be ripped up and removed like a flimsy hut in a windstorm. Isaiah saw the day when the earth totters under the weight of mankind's unceasing, accelerating, and worsening iniquity. The planet will be removed. Why? Because the transgressions of mankind shall be heavy upon it. The earth shall split wide open, be thoroughly shaken, tremble, fall, and not rise again.

The earth is utterly broken down, the earth is clean dissolved, the earth is moved exceedingly. The earth shall reel to and fro like a drunkard, and shall be removed like a cottage; and the transgression thereof shall be heavy upon it; and it shall fall, and not rise again. (Isaiah 24:19-20)

That day will spring upon the unsaved human population suddenly and unexpectedly, like a thief in the night bursting into a home after midnight while its drunken inhabitants snooze. Three things shall pounce upon them: Fear, a pit, and a snare. The snare is God's trapping net. Escaping the cosmic disruption will be impossible. Judgment is unavoidable. Only the saints whose foreheads are sealed by the angels will be spared and rescued when the foundations of the earth shake. Everybody else is going to the pit.

Fear, and the pit, and the snare, are upon thee, O inhabitant of the earth. And it shall come to pass, that he who fleeth from the noise of the fear shall fall into the pit; and he that cometh up out of the midst of the pit shall be taken in the snare: for the windows from on high are open, and the foundations of the earth do shake. (Isaiah 24:17-18)

One reason why God will be wroth with furious indignation is mankind's ongoing destruction of His beautiful planet that He lovingly made for mankind. Beginning in the Twentieth Century with the invention of the atomic bomb, mankind has ventured into a realm it has never been since the Garden of Eden: The ability to destroy the earth. Powerful nations possess military weapons beyond the comprehension of most people. Intercontinental ballistic missiles, submarines, and warplanes are armed with warheads capable of destroying our planet multiple times over. Russia boasts it has a fleet of terrifying drone submarines carrying nuclear-armed torpedoes that can generate a massive tsunami wave to wipe out the entire coast of North America. As terrifying as these weapons are to sensible people, they pale in destructive power when compared to new top-secret weapons that have yet to be deployed in warfare.

Despite official denials, we must assume that some nations also possess stockpiles of biological and chemical warfare agents, including terrifying biological agents that kill targeted ethnic groups while sparing others. Weather warfare is another method that madmen will employ to destroy our planetary home. The militaries of the world's most powerful nations are also expanding their arsenals into outer space. Imagine the horrors of future wars fought with armies of self-energizing human flesh-eating robotic warriors, genetically modified cyborg soldiers, and directed-energy scalar weapons. Furthermore, scientists are tinkering with Creation by creating genetically modified creatures that have never existed in human history. The Nephilim have returned as they were in the days of Noah.

This is madness! We are permitting politicians, scientists, animal testing research laboratories, defense contractors, and powerful corporations to destroy God's planet. There is coming a day when the Creator will put an end to their lunacy. God will destroy the people who are destroying His earth!

And the nations were angry, and thy wrath is come, and the time of the dead, that they should be judged, and that thou shouldest give reward unto thy servants the prophets, and to the saints, and them that fear thy name, small and great; *and shouldest destroy them which destroy the earth.* (Revelation 11:18)

Rebellious, sin-obsessed mankind will make such a mess of our planet that there will be no way to save it. Jesus said God will shorten the days of tribulation because it shall be so great that no flesh could survive. "No flesh" includes the animal kingdom. Furthermore, the planet's soil is soaked in blood! Blood has a voice and the earth has a mouth. The blood is speaking to God every hour through the earth's mouth pleading for justice. God has no choice but to start over. He will make a new planet. The Holy Bible calls it "the restitution of all things." It will be the restoration of His glorious creation.

Repent ye therefore, and be converted, that your sins may be blotted out, when the times of refreshing shall come from the presence of the Lord; and he shall send Jesus Christ, which before was preached unto you: *whom the heaven must receive until the times of restitution of all things, which God hath spoken by the mouth of all his holy prophets since the world began.* **(Acts 3:19-21)**

Satan, his demons - which are the disembodied spirits of the Nephilim - and his human progeny disrupted the Creator's beautiful, wonderful plan for mankind. There's coming a day when God will stupendously and permanently disrupt their destructive plans for His creation. He will end the old creation and start over. Many troubling things in modern society can be easily understood by recognizing that Satan's minions – spiritual and human – are madly driven to mar, defile, and destroy all things that are good: the environment, culture, art, music, values, theater, sports, entertainment, families, and education. Almighty God is very aware of the destruction of His planet. He is coming someday to destroy those who have destroyed His beautiful earth.

Mankind's damage to the planet and its blood-saturated soil will necessitate the obliteration of Planet Earth. The earth shall be dissolved by fire. God will create a new earth that is not deformed by mankind's endeavors nor soaked with blood. How will God create a new earth, and how long will it take him to do it? He will create the new earth the same way He created the old earth - and in the same amount of time. He will speak it! It won't take a lot of time to do it. He can speak, "Let there be a new earth!" Our Heavenly Father still has it going on. He may be ancient, but He is still the one and only Creator. He is as much God today as he was when he spoke this present world into existence. When Jesus returns, however, Father will be done with His old creation. Behold, he makes all things new!

But the day of the Lord will come as a thief in the night; in the which the heavens shall pass away with a great noise, and the elements shall melt with fervent heat, the earth also and the works that are therein shall be burned up.

Seeing then that all these things shall be dissolved, what manner of persons ought ye to be in all holy conversation and godliness, looking for and hasting unto the coming of the day of God, wherein the heavens being on fire shall be dissolved, and the elements shall melt with fervent heat? Nevertheless we, according to his promise, look for new heavens and a new earth, wherein dwelleth righteousness. (2 Peter 3:10-13)

Mother of All Earthquakes Reserved for Jerusalem

Although there will be great earthquakes in many places of the world as we approach the end, God has one special earthquake scheduled for that wicked city Jerusalem, which the Bible calls Sodom and Egypt. It's going to be a doozy. You don't want to be riding in a Evangelical Zionist tour bus in Jerusalem on that day. Sorry, but the tour company will not issue refunds to any survivors.

God still remembers the day they crucified His son. At the appointed hour, his fury shall explode on Jerusalem and the city's wicked Kabbalah wizards, rabbis, Freemasons, proud politicians, bloodthirsty military commanders, treacherous intelligence agents, and greedy businessmen. Almighty God will send an extreme mega earthquake that will strike Jerusalem with vengeance, splitting the "great city" into three parts. Simultaneously, there shall be a collapse of cities worldwide. God will remember Babylon (Jerusalem) and make her lick every drop from His cup of wrath. The disruptive earthquake is part of the grand finale of the age of mankind.

And *the great city was divided into three parts, and the cities of the nations fell:* and great Babylon came in remembrance before God, to give unto her the cup of the wine of the fierceness of his wrath. (Revelation 16:19)

The Jerusalem quake will be preceded by the seventh angel pouring out his vial into the air, and a great voice. The voice originates from the temple of heaven, from the throne. Therefore, it is Almighty God, not an angel or prophet, who makes a powerful proclamation just before the earthquake that will devastate Jerusalem. He says, "It is done." God the Father will echo the words of God the Son on the Cross at Calvary when Jesus cried, "It is finished!" Our Heavenly Father will shout "It is done!" to signify the final destruction of Babylon the Great, and the harlot's entire Satanic empire on earth. It also signifies the end of the age of mankind and this present world.

And the seventh angel poured out his vial into the air; and there came a great voice out of the temple of heaven, from the throne, saying, It is done. (Revelation 16:17)

Jerusalem, along with her tabernacle of Moloch star god Remphan (the so-called Star of David), shall be destroyed by God in His final judgment on Satan's Babylonian civilization. Jerusalem is Babylon the Great, "the great city," the harlot, the city that kills

God's prophets, the city that crucified our Lord, the capital of the synagogue of Satan.

In the Old Testament, God often called rebellious and idolatrous Jerusalem a harlot, and promised that divine judgment would cut her down.

...but if ye refuse and rebel, ye shall be devoured with the sword: for the mouth of the Lord hath spoken it. *How is the faithful city become an harlot! it was full of judgment; righteousness lodged in it; but now murderers.* (Isaiah 1:20-21)

Speaking through Old Testament prophet Ezekiel, God accused Jerusalem of being worse than a harlot. He said the city is so vile it is like a prostitute that pays men for sex!

How weak is thine heart, saith the Lord God, seeing thou doest all these things, the work of an imperious whorish woman; in that thou buildest thine eminent place in the head of every way, and makest thine high place in every street; and hast not been as an harlot, in that thou scornest hire; but as a wife that committeth adultery, which taketh strangers instead of her husband! *They give gifts to all whores: but thou givest thy gifts to all thy lovers, and hirest them,* that they may come unto thee on every side for thy whoredom. (Ezekiel 16:30-33)

The 17th chapter of the Apocalypse describes Mystery Babylon as a great whore with whom the kings of the earth have committed fornication, and the inhabitants of the earth have been made drunk with the wine of her fornication. John is shown a woman sitting upon a beast, full of names of blasphemy. Furthermore, John said the great city has a name written upon her forehead: MYSTERY, BABYLON THE GREAT, THE MOTHER OF HARLOTS AND ABOMINATIONS OF THE EARTH.

The Apocalypse mentions the "great city" 10 times. Each scripture refers to Mystery Babylon that shall be destroyed by God. One of the 10 verses clearly identify Mystery Babylon, the great city. It is Jerusalem - the city that crucified Jesus Christ! Furthermore, the Bible calls Jerusalem "Sodom and Egypt."

And their dead bodies shall lie in the street of the great city, which spiritually is called Sodom and Egypt, where also our Lord was crucified. (Revelation 11:8)

Crucifying the Son of God was to be expected of the people of Jerusalem. They have a long history of murdering God's holy prophets. Jesus accused them to their faces of being murderers. Apostle Paul accused them too. And Stephen accused them of killing God's prophets. Indeed, the Jews murdered Stephen the moment he accused them of killing the prophets!

Wherefore ye be witnesses unto yourselves, *that ye are the children of them which killed the prophets.* (Matthew 23:31)

Woe unto you! for ye build the sepulchers of the prophets, *and your fathers killed them.* (Luke 11:47)

***Lord, they have killed thy prophets*, and digged down thine altars; and I am left alone, and they seek my life. (Romans 11:3)**

Which of the prophets have not your fathers persecuted? and they have slain them which shewed before of the coming of the Just One; of whom ye have been now the betrayers and murderers: who have received the law by the disposition of angels, and have not kept it. When they heard these things, they were cut to the heart, and they gnashed on him with their teeth. But he, being full of the Holy Ghost, looked up steadfastly into heaven, and saw the glory of God, and Jesus standing on the right hand of God, and said, Behold, I see the heavens opened, and the Son of man standing on the right hand of God. *Then they cried out with a loud voice, and stopped their ears, and ran upon him with one accord, and cast him out of the city, and stoned him:* and the witnesses laid down their clothes at a young man's feet, whose name was Saul. And they stoned Stephen, calling upon God, and saying, Lord Jesus, receive my spirit. And he kneeled down, and cried with a loud voice, Lord, lay not this sin to their charge. And when he had said this, he fell asleep. (Acts 7:52-60)

It Won't be the First Time God Splits Apart Jerusalem

It will not be the first time God divides Jerusalem into three parts. He did it in the days of Ezekiel. God instructed Ezekiel to shave his head and beard with a sharp knife. The sharp knife represented the sword of war that was coming to Jerusalem. God's judgment would be a time of calamity and ruin. Even in modern times, most Arab societies consider shaving off a man's hair and beard to be an act of utter humiliation.

God told the prophet to weigh the cut hair and beard on balances, and accurately divide the hair into three parts. The cutting of his hair represented God removing His grace and glory from Jerusalem. Each pile of hair cut by the sword represented a third of Jerusalem. One third of the city was burned in a fire. A second third of Jerusalem was cut to pieces with swords. The remaining third of the city was scattered to other nations like chaff in the wind. Symbolically, Ezekiel's head represented the chief Jewish rulers of the city. His hair represented the citizens. The hair cut from his head represented the survivors who became refugees when they were cut off from the city.

And thou, son of man, take thee a sharp knife, take thee a barber's razor, and cause it to pass upon thine head and upon thy beard: then take thee balances to weigh, and divide the hair. Thou shalt burn with fire *a third part* in the midst of the city, when the days of the siege are fulfilled: and thou shalt take *a third part*, and smite about it with a knife: and *a third part* thou shalt scatter in the wind; and I will draw out a sword after them. Thou shalt also take thereof a few in number, and bind them in thy skirts. Then take of them again, and cast them into the midst of the fire, and burn them in the fire; for thereof shall a fire come forth into all the house of Israel. Thus saith the Lord God; *This is Jerusalem: I have set it in the midst of the nations and countries that are round about her.* (Ezekiel 5:1-5)

The cataclysmic extreme worldwide earthquake shall be triggered by God's roar. His Majesty the King shall roar in righteous indignation because He is wroth with sinful humans who repeatedly rejected His generous offer of mercy, forgiveness, adoption, and eternal life made possible by repentance, faith in the name of the crucified and resurrected Jesus Christ, and baptism into his holy church.

The Lord shall go forth as a mighty man, he shall stir up jealousy like a man of war: *he shall cry, yea, roar;* he shall prevail against his enemies. (Isaiah 42:13)

The wrath expressed by the King of the Universe shall be as the roaring of a mighty lion which strikes its prey suddenly and unexpectedly. Yahweh's anger will manifest as a roar from Heaven because He has a legal dispute with all the nations that must be settled. Jeremiah heard the roar from heaven in his spirit when he prophesied:

The Lord shall roar from on high, and utter his voice from his holy habitation; he *shall mightily roar upon his habitation; he shall give a shout, as they that tread the grapes, against all the inhabitants of the earth.* A noise shall come even to the ends of the earth; *for the Lord hath a controversy with the nations,* he will plead with all flesh; he will give them that are wicked to the sword, saith the Lord. (Jeremiah 25:30-31)

God's roar from Heaven will physically shake the earth.

The Lord also shall roar out of Zion, and utter his voice from Jerusalem; *and the heavens and the earth shall shake:* but the Lord will be the hope of his people, and the strength of the children of Israel. (Joel 3:16)

The Old Testament prophet Habakkuk said that when God stands up to judge, He measures the earth, drives asunder the nations, the mountains are scattered, and the hills bow. Habakkuk said when the mountains see God, they tremble; and the sun and moon stand still as the light of His arrows go by, and the shining of His glittering spear. God shall march through the world in indignation, threshing the wicked, and going forth for the salvation of His people.

He stood, and measured the earth: he beheld, and drove asunder the nations; and the everlasting mountains were scattered, the perpetual hills did bow: his ways are everlasting. (Habakkuk 3:6)

The mountains saw thee, and they trembled: the overflowing of the water passed by: the deep uttered his voice, and lifted up his hands on high. *The sun and moon stood still in their habitation:* at the light of thine arrows they went, and at the shining of thy glittering spear. *Thou didst march through the land in indignation, thou didst thresh the heathen in anger.* Thou wentest forth for the salvation of thy people, even for salvation with thine anointed; thou woundedst the head out of the house of the wicked, by discovering the foundation unto the neck. (Habakkuk 6:10-13)

Accompanying the splitting asunder of Jerusalem by a mega-earthquake prior to the second coming of Jesus Christ, every island and mountain on Planet Earth shall disappear! If that's not disruptive enough, massive hailstones, estimated to be over 100 pounds each, will rain down on nations signifying God's heavy judgments upon unrepentant sinners. People too stubborn and proud to repent will blaspheme God for the hailstorm and die in their rebellion.

And every island fled away, and the mountains were not found. And there fell upon men a great hail out of heaven, every stone about the weight of a talent: and men blasphemed God because of the plague of the hail; for the plague thereof was exceeding great. (Revelation 16:20-21)

God Will Rewind Time to Genesis 1

The greatest disruption that happens when Jesus Christ returns is the reversal of Creation! God rewinds His time machine to the first words in the Book of Genesis.

In the beginning God created the heaven and the earth. And the earth was without form, and void; and darkness was upon the face of the deep... (Genesis 1:2)

Watch what happens near the end. There will be a super-fast rewind and the world will go back in time! Jeremiah saw it!

I beheld the earth, and, lo, it was without form, and void; and the heavens, and they had no light. I beheld the mountains, and, lo, they trembled, and all the hills moved lightly. *I beheld, and, lo, there was no man, and all the birds of the heavens were fled.* (Jeremiah 4:23-25)

"Whoa! This can't be true," cry the modern-day Bible prophecy experts with their elaborate prophecy charts in their hands. "There is much more that must happen: The Jews will rule the earth for 1,000 years, people will marry and have children on earth, Satan will be released from the bottomless pit at the end of the Millennial kingdom, the Great White Throne of Judgment will follow, and then New Jerusalem comes down from Heaven."

You can chuck into the trash bin your Evangelical Zionist prophecy books and timeline charts. It will be "lights out" for this rotten old world when Jesus Christ returns. He will rewind His time machine to the opening sentences in the Book of Genesis. The earth will be without form, and void; there will be no sun, moon, or stars in the heavens; there won't be any humans and wildlife on the planet! Through judgment, God reverses creation. It will happen because God has already decreed it.

For this shall the earth mourn, and the heavens above be black: because I have spoken it, I have purposed it, and will not repent, neither will I turn back from it. (Jeremiah 4:28)

Time will end! There will be no need of it after Jesus Christ returns. Eternity shall begin. Neither will there be need of the sun, moon, and stars. All of them shall become obsolete at the end of history and the consummation of all things. Jesus shall be our light forever in New Jerusalem!

And the city had no need of the sun, neither of the moon, to shine in it: for the glory of God did lighten it, and the Lamb is the light thereof. (Revelation 21:23)

You can't ignore the fact that the cosmos will be disrupted by the second coming of Jesus Christ. Jesus will initiate a universal blackout immediately after the days of Satan's tribulation against the saints come to an end. The time of great tribulation is Satan's wrath against God's church. The day of the Lord is God's wrath against Satan and his wicked humans. When Satan's persecution of Christians is concluded, it will be God's turn to do His stuff to Satan and his followers. What will happen? God will pull the plug and cut off the universe's electricity. Why waste electricity when you're ready to implode the entire building? A demolition expert knows that he or she must first cut off the electrical power prior to imploding a building. In this case, the demolition contractor is Almighty God. He will shut down all stars prior to imploding the universe. He will recall and rescind His words spoken in Genesis.

Immediately after the tribulation of those days shall the sun be darkened, and the moon shall not give her light, and the stars shall fall from heaven, and the powers of the heavens shall be shaken... (Matthew 24:29)

It wasn't the first time the Jewish Sadducees and Pharisees heard that Almighty God will someday turn out the lights in the universe. They knew that Jesus was referring to Isaiah's prophecies about the Medes' destruction of Babylon, a type of the final "day of the Lord" at the end of the age. In the Last Days, Jerusalem is identified in the Apocalypse as "the great city," the harlot, Mystery Babylon. Isaiah prophesied that her people will howl, their hearts shall melt, they shall be afraid: pangs and sorrows shall grip them, their faces shall be inflamed, because the day of the Lord has arrived and it shall come as a destruction from the Almighty.

Howl ye; for the day of the Lord is at hand; it shall come as a destruction from the Almighty. Therefore shall all hands be faint, and every man's heart shall melt: and they shall be afraid: pangs and sorrows shall take hold of them; they shall be in pain as a

woman that travaileth: they shall be amazed one at another; their faces shall be as flames. Behold, the day of the Lord cometh, cruel both with wrath and fierce anger, to lay the land desolate: and he shall destroy the sinners thereof out of it. *For the stars of heaven and the constellations thereof shall not give their light: the sun shall be darkened in his going forth, and the moon shall not cause her light to shine.* And I will punish the world for their evil, and the wicked for their iniquity; and I will cause the arrogance of the proud to cease, and will lay low the haughtiness of the terrible. (Isaiah 13:6-11)

Isaiah uttered numerous prophecies about great cosmic disruptions that will accompany the final Day of the Lord. He said "the moon shall be confounded, and the sun ashamed" (Isaiah 24:23), and the "sun shall be no more thy light by day, neither for brightness shall the moon give light unto thee" (Isaiah 60:19). And he told the Israelites why they would no longer need the sun and moon: "but the Lord shall be unto thee an everlasting light, and thy God thy glory" (Isaiah 60:19). He was speaking of New Jerusalem, the true eternal capital city of Israel, the Christian church.

How dreadful shall the wrath of God be for unrepentant sinners and the wicked when the Final Day catches them by surprise? The magnitude of the cosmic disruption is unimaginable. Mountains will be removed. Islands will disappear. The seas will roar. The sun, moon, and stars will turn to darkness. The planet will be ripped apart by a worldwide earthquake. The pillars holding the earth in space will be removed. The planet will be tossed to and fro in space like a drunkard. Massive hailstones shall pummel the wicked as they hide in caves seeking to escape the Lord's indignation as the blood of hundreds of millions of aborted babies cries out from the soil for revenge and justice. His angels shall crush the wicked as grapes.

The great cosmic disruption caused by Jesus' second coming is mentioned throughout the Holy Bible in verses about the awesome might of God, His sovereignty over His creation, and the final day of the Lord. The following items are a partial list of Biblical events that dramatically illustrate the powerful disruptive nature of the Lord's second coming:

- There shall be a great shaking in the land of Israel, all creatures shall shake at God's presence, the mountains shall be thrown down. (Ezekiel 38:19-20)

- God will overturn and remove mountains in his anger, shake the earth out of her place and its pillars, command the sun not to rise, and seal up the stars. (Job 9:5-8)

- When the heathen nations rage, their kingdoms shall be removed. The earth shall melt when He utters His voice. (Psalm 45:6)

- His stare at the earth will trigger earthquakes. His will touch hills and set off volcanic eruptions. (Psalm 104:32)

- The earth shall quake, the heavens shall tremble, the sun and moon shall be dark, and the stars withdraw their shining when the Lord utters His voice before His army. (Joel 2:10-11)

- There shall be wonders in the heavens and in the earth: blood, and fire, and pillars of smoke, the sun shall be turned into darkness, and the moon into blood. (Joel 2: 30-32)

- The sun and the moon shall be darkened, and the stars shall withdraw their shining. (Joel 3:15)

- The stars of heaven and the constellations will cease giving light, the sun shall be darkened, and the moon will cease to shine. (Isaiah 13:10)

- The moon shall be confounded, and the sun ashamed. (Isaiah 24:23)

- When God's thunderous voice is heard in Heaven, lightnings will lighten the world, and the earth will tremble and shake. (Psalm 77:18)

- When God comes on the scene, he shall not keep silent. A fire will devour His enemies as he goes forth. There shall be a tempest around Him. (Psalm 50:3)

- The earth trembles at the presence of the God of Jacob. (Psalm 114:7)

- An unstoppable army shall invade, a fire devours everything before them, and a flame behind them sets everything on fire. Mankind lost the Garden of Eden, the paradise that God lovingly prepared for them. (Joel 2:3)

- God will rain upon the wicked snares, fire, brimstone, and a horrible tempest. (Psalm 11:6)

- The judgments given to mankind when the first three angels pour out their bowls will be like the plagues of Egypt. The first bowl shall release noisome and grievous sores upon all people who received the mark of the beast and worshipped his image. The second bowl shall turn the sea to blood and kill everything in it. The third bowl will turn rivers and fountains of water into blood.

- The fourth angel's bowl shall be poured out upon the sun: power shall be given to him to scorch men with fire.

- The fifth angel will pour out his vial upon the seat of the beast; and his kingdom will be full of darkness, and they will gnaw their tongues for pain.
- The sixth angel will pour out his vial upon the Euphrates river and it shall dry up.
- The seventh angel will pour his vial into the air. God will shout from Heaven, "It is done." There shall be voices, thunder, and lightning. An extreme mega-earthquake will strike Jerusalem and split the city into three parts, the cities of nations shall fall, islands and mountains shall disappear.

The second coming of Jesus on the Final Day shall be:

- Singular
- Sudden and unexpected
- Atmospheric
- Visible
- Noisy
- Disruptive

CHAPTER 9

HIS SECOND COMING SHALL BE FIERY

JESUS WILL COME WITH a flaming fire!

When the Lord and his angelic special forces commandos suddenly and unexpectedly kick open sinful mankind's front door, they will burst into Babylon and all her daughters with flamethrowers the size unlike anything seen by men.

Everything shall be set ablaze! People, houses, skyscrapers, parliaments, palaces, military bases, shopping malls, universities, schools, museums, vehicles, aircraft, ships, bridges, nuclear power facilities, film studios, farms, ranches, forests, mountains, theaters, cafes, restaurants, hair salons, clothing boutiques, candy stores, nightclubs, stock exchanges, banks, shrines, temples, mosques, churches, cities, nations - everything!

He's coming to burn abortionists. He's coming to burn child molesters. He's coming to burn pornographers. He's coming to burn rapists. He's coming to burn homosexuals, adulterers, fornicators, and sexually immoral men and women. He's coming to burn liars and deceivers. He's coming to burn the wicked. He's coming to burn warmongers. He's coming to burn swindlers and thieves. He's coming to burn those who oppress the poor and weak. He's coming to burn murderers and those who shed innocent blood. He's coming to burn people who cheat widows out of their houses and savings. He's coming to burn drunkards, drug addicts, and gluttons. He's coming to burn perverted preachers and deviant deacons. He's coming to burn Judaizers. He's coming to burn all antichrists who deny that Jesus Christ came to earth as God in human flesh. He's coming to burn revilers. He coming to burn those who cause strife and division in His church. He's coming to burn idolaters, witches, warlocks, sorcerers, gurus, mystics, astrologers, necromancers, numerologists, diviners, soothsayers, occultists, New Agers, and members of secret societies. He's coming to burn the greedy, the jealous, the envious, and those who covet. He's coming to burn those who destroy His earth. He's coming to burn all humans who rejected His gracious offer of forgiveness and salvation through faith in His Son Jesus Christ.

Will anybody be safe? Yes, all living saints marked by angels, and all departed saints dwelling peacefully in blissful repose in the presence of God. Born again Christians whose names are written in the Book of Life have no reason to fear that they will experience God's fiery wrath. His wrath is reserved for the wicked and unsaved. Angels will douse this planet with a flammable liquid that cannot be extinguished by men, and Jesus will light the match.

God's consuming fire will be preceded by a spectacular separation of souls. First, all the graves shall be opened. There's going to be a big meeting. Every human who ever lived will come out of their graves and tombs to join those who are alive on the Final Day. Second, angelic reapers shall seize the wicked, bundled them, and take them away to be burned later in the lake of fire. Next, the righteous souls who come out of their graves shall be caught up to meet the Lord in the air. Shortly thereafter, all the righteous saints left behind will also be caught up to join their fellow triumphant saints to greet and escort our royal King Jesus.

Immediately, all humans from the beginning of time will be segregated into two camps: Saved and unsaved. Sheep and goats. Righteous and unclean. Saints and sinners. Citizens of New Jerusalem and citizens of the Lake of Fire. Your group designation is decided now in this life before Jesus returns. Get in the right line for the correct mark!

...and before him shall be gathered all nations: and he shall separate them one from another, as a shepherd divideth his sheep from the goats: and he shall set the sheep on his right hand, but the goats on the left. (Matthew 25:32-33)

The Final Day encompasses the darkening of the cosmos, the appearance of the sign of the Son of Man, the Second Coming of Jesus, the opening of all graves, the bundling of the wicked, the catching up of the saints, the separation of souls as sheep and goats, the great white throne of judgement of the wicked, the casting of Satan and the wicked into the lake of fire, the works of the saints placed in the crucible to be tried by fire, the fiery destruction of the earth, the rolling up of the cosmos like a scroll, the creation of a new earth and heavens, the descent of New Jerusalem, and Almighty God moving into His new place with His children. It will be an awesome day that will happen faster than a second. Time will end when the time maker appears on the scene. God doesn't need the silly clocks and calendars of puny men to accomplish all His objectives according to His schedule. Who are we to tell Him to slow down and take a thousand years to do it? Do you think God is unable to do everything instantaneously?

The good news is that the Church shall escape God's wrath upon the wicked. The fire shall not burn righteous men, women, and children who are saved by faith in Jesus Christ. Glorified bodies will not burn. The saints, however, shall feel the heat on their feet as they are caught up into the atmosphere to meet our glorious King Jesus. They will know that the triumphant Church was rescued by Jesus a split second before the fireball engulfed the planet. As saints gaze at the burning planet below them, each man and woman will say, "There but for the grace of God, go I."

Operation Bundle and Burn

Jesus' arrival will swiftly usher in judgment upon the world as a mighty flood. It will come suddenly and unexpectedly as in the days of Noah. People were sinning like there was no tomorrow. And they were right! There was no tomorrow for them. The sky turned black. Brilliant streaks of lightning flashed across the sky. Ominous claps of thunder reverberated above. A deluge of heavy rain fell nonstop for 40 days and nights. The earth's crust was ripped asunder by mighty earthquakes. Fountains deep inside the planet were released through massive fissures in the planet's crust and flowed like mighty rivers onto the earth's surface. All drowned except Noah and his family, and the creatures that dwelt in water.

Another flood is scheduled for mankind. A flood of fire! The commander of Heaven's armies will signal to the angels that it is time to commence Operation Bundle and Burn. Prior to the incineration of the planet, an astonishing aerial armada of angelic reapers shall descend with the Lord. Tens of millions of them will fill the sky. The reapers will fan out across continents in search of men and women who have the mark of the beast, or the name of the beast, or the number of his name. Heaven's law enforcement officers will apprehend all rebels and lawbreakers who rejected or ignored the merciful King's sin amnesty.

First, however, they will snatch up unrepentant sinners and vile, wicked people who pop out of their graves when Jesus shouts. Sleepy time will be over. The wicked dead will be startled out of their sleep in their dusty graves. There will be no time to yawn for those who will be awakened from death. As quickly as dead people shoot out of their graves, angelic reapers will snatch them faster than lizards eating crickets. It will be "off to the fire pit" to be flame-broiled for eternity! The Bible says they will be bundled and burned. It will be no different than a gardener who pulls weeds, bundles them in piles, and tosses them into a fire pit to ensure that the seeds never reproduce.

If a man abide not in me, he is cast forth as a branch, and is withered; and men gather them, and cast them into the fire, and they are burned. (John 15:6)

After lassoing and bundling startled, dazed, and freaked out dead sinners awakened from their graves, the angelic reapers will quickly turn their attention to the terrified living sinners who will be running, screaming, cursing, and trying to hide from the fury of the Lord. They won't go far. Not even deep caves will provide cover from God's wrath. Indeed, the wicked will beg cave rocks to fall and crush them. Better to be crushed by boulders than captured by angels with fiery eyes and glistening swords.

And the kings of the earth, and the great men, and the rich men, and the chief captains, and the mighty men, and every bondman, and every free man, hid themselves in the dens and in the rocks of the mountains; and said to the mountains and rocks, Fall on us, and hide us from the face of him that sitteth on the throne, and from the wrath of the Lamb... (Revelation 6:15-16)

It won't matter whether they are crushed or captured. They are going to Beelzebub's Barbeque Pit located at 666 Beast Street, Hell. They'll be turning forever on skewers over roaring flames and hot coals. They'll have plenty of time to remember their sins, their rejection of God's forgiveness through faith in Jesus Christ, and even worse, they'll have eternity to contemplate their complete separation from God who will no longer remember they ever existed! They will forever fry in black fire. Hell's flames are invisible because the darkness is so great that not even roaring fires can produce light in a world totally separated from God.

Let them be blotted out of the book of the living, and not be written with the righteous. (Psalm 69:28)

The present age is a repeat of the pre-flood age. Mankind's wickedness and evil is increasing. The earth is filled with violence and bloodshed. Just as creation is moaning for release from mankind's sins, God too will reach His "Popeye point" when He wails, "That's all I can stands. I can't stands no more!" Once again, God will regret ever making mankind. The second time, however, will be different that the first global judgment. In the first worldwide judgment, God destroyed the wicked with water. The second global judgment will be accomplished with fire. The first time God spared the earth. The second time he will destroy the planet with fire and start over.

In his second epistle to the church in Thessalonica, Saint Paul wrote that Jesus and his angels shall come back to earth in flaming fire to take vengeance on humans who do not know God, nor obey the Gospel of our Lord Jesus. They shall be punished with everlasting destruction from the presence of the Lord. They shall be punished by fire and separated from God forever. Could there be a worse punishment?

...when the Lord Jesus shall be revealed from heaven with his mighty angels, in flaming fire taking vengeance on them that know not God, and that obey not the gospel of our Lord Jesus Christ: who shall be punished with everlasting destruction from the presence of the Lord, and from the glory of his power; when he shall come to be glorified in his saints, and to be admired in all them that believe (because our testimony among you was believed) in that day. (2 Thessalonians 1:7-10)

John the Baptist bravely warned the Jewish elite about the day when God separates all humans into two groups: wheat and chaff. The chaff shall burn up with unquenchable fire.

And now also the axe is laid unto the root of the trees: *therefore every tree which bringeth not forth good fruit is hewn down, and cast into the fire.* I indeed baptize you with water unto repentance: but he that cometh after me is mightier than I, whose shoes I am not worthy to bear: he shall baptize you with the Holy Ghost, and with fire: whose fan is in his hand, *and he will thoroughly purge his floor, and gather his wheat into the garner; but he will burn up the chaff with unquenchable fire.* (Matthew 3:10-12)

Jesus Told Us in the Parables about Operation Bundle and Burn

Insight into "Operation Bundle and Burn" is found in the parable of the sower. Ordinarily, most people acquainted with this parable think it is only about sowing the Word of God. Yes, the primary focus is about the reception or rejection of God's word in the hearts and minds of people. There's an important revelation in the parable, however, about the Lord's second advent to earth. It is about the reapers.

The parable of the sower in found in Matthew 13, Mark 4, and Luke 8. In the Gospel according to St. Mark, Jesus said understanding the parable of the sower is the key to understanding all His other parables. If you don't understand the Parable of the Sower, you won't understand anything else about the Kingdom of God. Interestingly, Matthew 13 begins with the Parable of the Sower, the cornerstone to understanding the Kingdom of God, but concludes with the people of His hometown of Nazareth rejecting Jesus. Obviously, they didn't get it. If you truly desire to understand the kingdom of God, the second coming of Jesus, and the consummation of all things, it is paramount that you diligently seek to first understand the parable of the sower. Nazareth's citizens did worse than reject the Word of God. They rejected the one who is the Word!

And he said unto them, Know ye not this parable? and how then will ye know all parables? (Mark 4:13)

Although known as the parable of the sower, its focus is the condition of the soils in which the sower spreads his seed. Almighty God is the sower and Lord of the Harvest. The seed is the Word of God. The soil represents the spiritual hearts of mankind: the wayside, stony places, thorns, and good soil. Seed that fell on good soil produced a bountiful harvest, 30 to 100 times more fruit.

Without skipping a beat, Jesus immediately taught them the next parable. It too was about a sower and the seed he scattered.

Another parable put he forth unto them, saying, The kingdom of heaven is likened unto a man which sowed good seed in his field: but while men slept, his enemy came and sowed tares among the wheat, and went his way. But when the blade was sprung up, and brought forth fruit, then appeared the tares also. So the servants of the householder came and said unto him, Sir, didst not thou sow good seed in thy field? from whence then hath it tares? He said unto them, An enemy hath done this. The servants said unto him, Wilt thou then that we go and gather them up? But he said, Nay; lest while ye gather up the tares, ye root up also the wheat with them. Let both grow together until the harvest: and in the time of harvest I will say to the reapers, Gather ye together first the tares, and bind them in bundles to burn them: but gather the wheat into my barn. (Matthew 13:24-30)

Keep in mind that Jesus said understanding the parable of the sower is the master key to understanding all the other parables. Thus, the Master Teacher taught them another parable about the sower, the seed, and the harvest. It is about the second coming of Jesus and the end of the age of mankind. After the crowd departed, Jesus and His disciples entered a house. The puzzled disciples asked Jesus to explain the parable of the tares of the field. Jesus gave them this explanation:

He answered and said unto them, He that soweth the good seed is the Son of man; the field is the world; the good seed are the children of the kingdom; but the tares are the children of the

wicked one; the enemy that sowed them is the devil; the harvest is the end of the world; and the reapers are the angels. As therefore the tares are gathered and burned in the fire; so shall it be in the end of this world. *The Son of man shall send forth his angels, and they shall gather out of his kingdom all things that offend, and them which do iniquity; and shall cast them into a furnace of fire: there shall be wailing and gnashing of teeth.* Then shall the righteous shine forth as the sun in the kingdom of their Father. Who hath ears to hear, let him hear. (Matthew 13:37-43)

The Great Separation of Souls

It is the great separation of souls! All human souls who ever lived will be separated into two groups: wheat and tares. All graves will open when Jesus shouts. Every dead person shall come out of his or her grave. The awakened dead and those living when Jesus returns shall be separated by the reapers. Everybody will receive a subpoena to appear in court. Christians marked by angels will be excused because their court file folders will be empty. There will be no record of any sins that must be punished.

For unrepentant sinners, however, it will be a short court hearing. The court hearing's only purpose will be to pronounce sentencing of the guilty. They will arrive in Heaven's court as pre-convicted and declared guilty by reason of their rejection of God's sin amnesty - the forgiveness of sins through faith in Jesus Christ. The Supreme Judge of the Universe shall pronounce the sentence: eternity in the everlasting lake of fire, complete separation from God, and the blotting out of their names from God's memory forever. Angels will gather up and remove from God's kingdom all who offend Him. The weeds will be quickly bundled and burned in the lake of fire. They will be destroyed in the lake of fire. Their physical resurrected bodies will burn forever in extreme agony.

So shall it be at the end of the world: the angels shall come forth, and sever the wicked from among the just, and shall cast them into the furnace of fire: there shall be wailing and gnashing of teeth. (Matthew 13:49-50)

For the Son of man shall come in the glory of his Father with his angels; and then he shall reward every man according to his works. (Matthew 16:27)

Thou hast rebuked the heathen, thou hast destroyed the wicked, thou hast put out their name for ever and ever. (Psalm 9:5)

When does the judgment of humans occur? Is it 1,000 years after the second coming or immediately when the Lord gloriously appears in the sky?

John Nelson Darby's Evangelical Zionists say it happens 1,000 years after the second coming of our Lord. Jesus Christ said it happens immediately. He said angels shall gather out of his kingdom all things that offend, and all who do acts of iniquity. They shall be cast into the furnace of fire. No thousand-year intermission is scheduled.

God is presently allowing the tares to grow and flourish alongside the wheat. It's always been that way. Born again, baptized, commandment-keeping Christians are the wheat. They are found in every Christian church in the world. They are prohibited from pulling up the tares (which are also found in every Christian church in the world). Christians may identify and expose them, but they are not authorized to rip them out of the ground. Only God can do it.

God does not punish the wicked now because He is waiting until the end of the age. He is allowing the weeds to grow with the wheat. If God sends judgment now upon the wicked, the wheat will suffer too. Besides, some tares are darnel, a weed that has striking similarities to wheat. Only an expert can detect the difference between darnel and wheat. An amateur gardener could mistakenly pull up wheat thinking it is darnel. Satan planted many darnel weeds in thousands of churches. Some of them are growing tall behind pulpits! Let the professionals pull up the tares. The angels will get the job done correctly on the Final Day.

In another parable, Jesus said His angels will separate the wicked from the saints as a fisherman keeps the good fish and throws away the bad. Where do bad fish go? Into the furnace of fire!

Again, the kingdom of heaven is like unto a net, that was cast into the sea, and gathered of every kind: which, when it was full, they drew to shore, and sat down, and gathered the good into vessels, but cast the bad away. *So shall it be at the end of the world: the angels shall come forth, and sever the wicked from among the just, and shall cast them into the furnace of fire: there shall be wailing and gnashing of teeth.* (Matthew 13:47-50)

The New Testament Bible clearly states that there will be a great separation of souls that will happen suddenly, without warning, at the end of the age when Jesus returns. Only baptized, commandment-keeping saints will be ready for it. In Jesus' long answer to the disciples' questions about the destruction of the temple, the second coming, and the end of the age (Matthew 24 and 25), our Lord mentioned the separation of souls. He called the two groups "goats and sheep."

In Matthew 25, Jesus said the entire human population beginning with Adam will be separated into two groups. First, all souls shall be convened according to their respective nations. All the Chinese people who ever lived in history will be gathered. Likewise, all the people who ever lived in the British Isles will congregate together. And the same for all the citizens of France, Switzerland, Finland, Russia, Kenya, Uganda, Nigeria, Syria, Iraq, Israel, Thailand, Cambodia, Australia, and every nation presently or previously on earth. Every member of countless indigenous tribes around the world will assemble according to their respective tribes - Cherokee, Comanche, Eskimo, Arawak, Caribs, Tucanoan, Maasai, Pygmies, Canaanites, and thousands more presently or previously on the earth. It will be the biggest United Nations general assembly in world history.

Next, Jesus shall separate the people in each nation into two groups: Sheep and goats. The sheep will be instructed to move to His right side. The goats will be ordered to stand on His left side. If you go right, life will be good forever. If you go left, you'll exit through the door marked "Eternal Damnation."

When the Son of Man comes in His glory, and all the holy angels with Him, then He will sit on the throne of His glory. Before Him will be gathered all nations, and He will separate them one from another as a shepherd separates his sheep from the goats. He will set the sheep at His right hand, but the goats at the left. (Matthew 25:31-33)

What happens to the goats on the left? They will be barbecued!

Then He will say to those at the left hand, 'Depart from Me, you cursed, *into the eternal fire*, prepared for the devil and his angels.' (Matthew 25:41)

The sheep and goats will go in two different directions and stay in their respective dwelling places for eternity. No objections

271

shouted by the goats will be allowed by the Judge of the Universe. He will instruct the court's bailiffs to swiftly escort the goats to the fiery pits of Hell. The righteous shall be led to their beautiful luxurious residences in New Jerusalem. Both goats and sheep made their choices for eternity while living on earth.

And these shall go away into everlasting punishment: but the righteous into life eternal. (Matthew 25:46)

All the Dead Shall Come Out When They Hear Jesus Shout

Apostle Paul told us what will happen at the end of the age of mankind. Here's the sequence of events:

- Jesus Christ shall descend from Heaven to earth with a shout, with the voice of the archangel, and with the trump of God.
- The dead in Christ shall rise first.
- Those who are alive on earth shall be caught up together with them (the dead in Christ) to meet Jesus in the air.
- The saints shall remain forever with the Lord.

But I would not have you to be ignorant, brethren, concerning them which are asleep, that ye sorrow not, even as others which have no hope. For if we believe that Jesus died and rose again, even so them also which sleep in Jesus will God bring with him. For this we say unto you by the word of the Lord, that we which are alive and remain unto the coming of the Lord shall not prevent them which are asleep. For the Lord himself shall descend from heaven with a shout, with the voice of the archangel, and with the trump of God: and the dead in Christ shall rise first: then we which are alive and remain shall be caught up together with them in the clouds, to meet the Lord in the air: and so shall we ever be with the Lord. Wherefore comfort one another with these words. (1 Thessalonians 4:13-18)

It won't be only the dead in Christ who awaken from their graves. All dead humanity - from Adam to the last human who died seconds before Jesus shouts - shall be awakened by his shout and God's trumpet blast. All bodies shall come out of their graves - the bodies of the righteous and the bodies of unsaved sinners.

Marvel not at this: for the hour is coming, in the which *all that are in the graves shall hear his voice, and shall come forth;* they that have done good, unto the resurrection of life; and they that have done evil, unto the resurrection of damnation. (John 5:28-29)

All will come out, but all will not go up! The saved saints will go up to meet the Lord in the air. Unsaved sinners will be bundled and burned forever in Hell's raging furnace. In the Gospel of our Lord according to St. Luke, Jesus gave us another example of souls separated at the End of the Age. The people taken shall be bundled and burned. Those remaining shall be saved.

And as it was in the days of Noah, so shall it be also in the days of the Son of man. They did eat, they drank, they married wives, they were given in marriage, until the day that Noah entered into the ark, and the flood came, and destroyed them all. Likewise also as it was in the days of Lot; they did eat, they drank, they bought, they sold, they planted, they builded; but the same day that Lot went out of Sodom it rained fire and brimstone from heaven, and destroyed them all. Even thus shall it be in the day when the Son of man is revealed. In that day, he which shall be upon the housetop, and his stuff in the house, let him not come down to take it away: and he that is in the field, let him likewise not return back. Remember Lot's wife. Whosoever shall seek to save his life shall lose it; and whosoever shall lose his life shall preserve it. I tell you, in that night there shall be two men in one bed; the one

273

shall be taken, and the other shall be left. Two women shall be grinding together; the one shall be taken, and the other left. Two men shall be in the field; the one shall be taken, and the other left. And they answered and said unto him, Where, Lord? And he said unto them, Wheresoever the body is, thither will the eagles be gathered together. (Luke 17:26-37)

Imposters Will be Spotted at the Wedding by Their Clothing

Jesus also gave us a parable about a wedding feast that shows us another example of the coming great separation of souls. In the gospel of our Lord according to St. Matthew, Jesus told the disciples that a separation will happen when the wedding feast is ready to begin.

Then saith he to his servants, The wedding is ready, but they which were bidden were not worthy. Go ye therefore into the highways, and as many as ye shall find, bid to the marriage. So those servants went out into the highways, and gathered together all as many as they found, both bad and good: and the wedding was furnished with guests. And when the king came in to see the guests, he saw there a man which had not on a wedding garment: and he saith unto him, Friend, how camest thou in hither not having a wedding garment? And he was speechless. *Then said the king to the servants, Bind him hand and foot, and take him away, and cast him into outer darkness; there shall be weeping and gnashing of teeth. For many are called, but few are chosen.* (Matthew 22:8-14)

Jesus gave us a description of the final moments prior to His appearance. He said:

"Immediately after the tribulation of those days shall the sun be darkened, and the moon shall not give her light, and the stars shall fall from heaven, and the powers of the heavens shall be shaken: and then shall appear the sign of the Son of man in heaven: and then shall all the tribes of the earth mourn, and they shall see the Son of man coming in the clouds of heaven with power and great glory. And he shall send his angels with a great sound of a trumpet, and they shall gather together his elect from the four winds, from one end of heaven to the other." (Matthew 24:29-31)

Apostle Peter Warned That Scoffers Will Ridicule the Promise of Jesus' Return

Among the wicked population of that momentous Final Day shall be scoffers who will mock God and His preachers of righteousness and ridicule the promise of our Lord's Second Coming. Apostle Peter forewarned what to expect as we approach the Final Day.

This is now the second letter that I am writing to you, beloved. In both of them I am stirring up your sincere mind by way of reminder, that you should remember the predictions of the holy prophets and the commandment of the Lord and Savior through your apostles, knowing this first of all, that scoffers will come in the last days with scoffing, following their own sinful desires. They will say, "Where is the promise of his coming? For ever since the fathers fell asleep, all things are continuing as they were from the beginning of creation." (2 Peter 3:1-4)

As mankind marches toward its Final Day, many will deliberately ignore crucial information: Noah's Great Flood! Peter and his fellow apostles taught the Church that someday mockers and scoffers would arise in society to ridicule the preaching of the Lord's return.

This second epistle, beloved, I now write unto you; in both which I stir up your pure minds by way of remembrance: that ye may be mindful of the words which were spoken before by the holy prophets, and of the commandment of us the apostles of the Lord and Savior: *knowing this first, that there shall come in the last days scoffers, walking after their own lusts, and saying, Where is the promise of his coming? for since the fathers fell asleep, all things continue as they were from the beginning of the creation.* (2 Peter 3:1-4)

St. Peter the Apostle prophesied that in the Last Days people will be willingly ignorant that God flooded the world with water ages ago, and that he will burn the planet in the next global judgment. Peter said the earth and heavens that exist now are merely in storage awaiting the biggest fire in history. The entire planet and the atmosphere will be engulfed in flames.

For this they willingly are ignorant of, that by the word of God the heavens were of old, and the earth standing out of the water and in the water: whereby the world that then was, being overflowed with water, perished: but the heavens and the earth, which are now, by the same word are kept in store, reserved unto fire against the day of judgment and perdition of ungodly men. (2 Peter 3:5-7)

Nobody will survive the flood of fire except those who were sealed in the ark of baptism. Apostle Peter compared baptism into the Church with entering Noah's ark.

For Christ also hath once suffered for sins, the just for the unjust, that he might bring us to God, being put to death in

the flesh, but quickened by the Spirit: by which also he went and preached unto the spirits in prison; which sometime were disobedient, *when once the longsuffering of God waited in the days of Noah, while the ark was a preparing, wherein few, that is, eight souls were saved by water. The like figure whereunto even baptism doth also now save us (not the putting away of the filth of the flesh, but the answer of a good conscience toward God,) by the resurrection of Jesus Christ:* who is gone into heaven, and is on the right hand of God; angels and authorities and powers being made subject unto him. (1 Peter 3:18-22)

Apostle Peter warned that people should not foolishly think that God is forgetful or slow to fulfill His promises. He is holding back the Final Day to give sinful men and women more time to repent and be saved through faith in the name of Jesus Christ and baptism into His church. God does not desire to punish the wicked. He desires that all be saved. God's sin amnesty commenced at the Cross on Calvary's hill. The unconditional pardon of all sins is readily available to any and all who will come to Jesus seeking forgiveness and salvation. The sin amnesty ends when the Final Day begins.

The Final Day Shall Come as a Thief in the Night

Every passing day brings us one day closer to the cancellation of the sin amnesty. Saint Peter said the Final Day shall come suddenly and unexpectedly - like a thief entering your home after midnight, sets your house on fire, and you burn up in your sleep!

The Lord is not slack concerning his promise, as some men count slackness; but is longsuffering to us-ward, not willing that any should perish, but that all should come to repentance. *But the day of the Lord will come as a thief in the night; in the which*

277

the heavens shall pass away with a great noise, and the elements shall melt with fervent heat, the earth also and the works that are therein shall be burned up. (2 Peter 3:9-10)

Therefore, how shall we live knowing that this earth shall be dissolved by a consuming fire from Heaven? In what spiritual state should we be found by Jesus Christ upon His glorious return? Peter said our conversations and behavior, before both men and God, must be holy and godly. Our thoughts, words, prayers, and actions must attest to an earnest, heartfelt yearning for Jesus Christ to return. All of mankind - the living and the dead, the saved and the damned - shall see with their eyes the fiery destruction of the cosmos on the Final Day. Thus, Apostle Peter exhorts all men and women by asking, "Since you will see everything dissolved by fire, what kind of person ought you be now while you are still living?"

Seeing then that all these things shall be dissolved, what manner of persons ought ye to be in all holy conversation and godliness, looking for and hasting unto the coming of the day of God, *wherein the heavens being on fire shall be dissolved, and the elements shall melt with fervent heat?* **Nevertheless we, according to his promise, look for new heavens and a new earth, wherein dwelleth righteousness.** (2 Peter 3:11-13)

Payday is coming when God will give to every man and woman who ever lived in the history of the world their just rewards for the way they lived on earth. Persecutors of the righteous should take heed! God will punish those who caused trouble for Christians who sought to live holy lives for God. As the antichrist forces greatly persecute the saints of God, the Lord will spring a reversal upon them. He will transfer the affliction and pain they impose upon the Church to themselves, but in greater measure. Simultaneously, the afflicted righteous will be given rest. It will happen suddenly and unexpectedly when Jesus returns one time in the atmosphere and is revealed in blazing fire.

...seeing it is a righteous thing with God to recompense tribulation to them that trouble you; and to you who are troubled rest with us, when the Lord Jesus shall be revealed from heaven with his mighty angels... (2 Thessalonians 1:6-7)

In his second epistle to the church in Thessalonica, Apostle Paul said God's "mighty angels (whom Psalms 104:4 says God makes ministers of flaming fire) will arrive in "flaming fire" to take "vengeance" on all who do not know God, and did not obey the gospel of Jesus. They shall be sentenced to everlasting destruction, separated from the presence of the Lord and His glory and power.

...in flaming fire taking vengeance on them that know not God, and that obey not the gospel of our Lord Jesus Christ: who shall be punished with everlasting destruction from the presence of the Lord, and from the glory of his power; when he shall come to be glorified in his saints, and to be admired in all them that believe (because our testimony among you was believed) in that day. (2 Thessalonians 1:8-10)

Psalm 21:9 says God shall make His enemies "as a fiery oven in the time of thine anger...swallow them up...and the fire shall devour them."

Psalm 97:3 says a fire goes before God "and burneth up his enemies."

Psalm 104:4 describes God's angels as His minister of "flaming fire."

Psalm 106:18 declares that "a fire was kindled" amidst the Hebrews who worshipped the golden calf, and "the flame burned up the wicked."

Angelic Reapers Will First Yank Out the Weeds

Jesus told his disciples what will happen when this present age's time is up and judgment is rendered upon the wicked on the Final Day. He described the righteous as wheat, and the wicked as tares (weeds).

Another parable put he forth unto them, saying, The kingdom of heaven is likened unto a man which sowed good seed in his field: but while men slept, his enemy came and sowed tares among the wheat, and went his way. But when the blade was sprung up, and brought forth fruit, then appeared the tares also. So the servants of the householder came and said unto him, Sir, didst not thou sow good seed in thy field? from whence then hath it tares? He said unto them, An enemy hath done this. The servants said unto him, Wilt thou then that we go and gather them up? But he said, Nay; lest while ye gather up the tares, ye root up also the wheat with them. Let both grow together until the harvest: and in the time of harvest I will say to the reapers, *Gather ye together first the tares, and bind them in bundles to burn them: but gather the wheat into my barn.* (Matthew 20:24-30)

When the Final Day arrives, you don't want to be bundled and burned. Instead, you must be among the wheat gathered into the Lord's barn.

Noah preached righteousness and repentance for many years as he constructed the ark. His warnings of impending judgment were ignored as people shamelessly sinned without fear of God.

People heard Noah's preaching, but they scoffed at his sermons and mocked him as a foolish man. Something came upon the earth, however, that nobody had ever seen nor imagined: a worldwide flood. It came suddenly and unexpectedly. Nobody, except Noah and his family, were prepared to escape sudden destruction.

Jesus said his second coming shall be as the days of Noah. He shall come suddenly and unexpectedly, and with fire! In the Apocalypse, Jesus said he would come quickly.

Behold, I come quickly: blessed is he that keepeth the sayings of the prophecy of this book. (Revelation 22:7)

Many people mistakenly interpret Jesus's words to mean that He will come soon. More than two thousand years have passed since Jesus said it; therefore, it does not mean his return will be soon. Instead, a paraphrase of His words would say, "My travel time from Heaven to Earth shall be extremely short. I will arrive quickly...faster than light. Don't let my sudden arrival catch you by surprise."

The flood came quickly. So too will the fire.

The message of repentance and forgiveness through faith in Jesus Christ has been preached for over 2,000 years. Present-day scoffers foolishly mock warnings that God will judge this wicked world like He did in the days of Noah. In fact, today's scoffers deny that Noah's Great Flood ever happened!

Their rebellious unbelief, however, will not hold back the next flood. Rain will not fall from the sky. It will be fire. It will come quickly and suddenly.

On that Final Day...

- **Every tree that bringeth not forth good fruit is hewn down, and cast into the fire. (Matthew 7:19)**

281

- And whosoever was not found written in the book of life was cast into the lake of fire. (Revelation 20:15)

- ...if any man build upon this foundation gold, silver, precious stones, wood, hay, stubble; every man's work shall be made manifest: for the day shall declare it, because it shall be revealed by fire; and the fire shall try every man's work of what sort it is. If any man's work abide which he hath built thereupon, he shall receive a reward. If any man's work shall be burned, he shall suffer loss: but he himself shall be saved; yet so as by fire. (1 Corinthians 3:12-15)

- And whosoever shall offend one of these little ones that believe in me, it is better for him that a millstone were hanged about his neck, and he were cast into the sea. And if thy hand offend thee, cut it off: *it is better for thee to enter into life maimed, than having two hands to go into hell, into the fire that never shall be quenched: where their worm dieth not, and the fire is not quenched.* (Mark 9:42-44)

- ...and to you who are troubled rest with us, when the Lord Jesus shall be revealed from heaven with his mighty angels, in flaming fire taking vengeance on them that know not God, and that obey not the gospel of our Lord Jesus Christ... (2 Thessalonians 1:7-8)

When the Final Day arrives, there shall be only one safe place: In Christ!

When Christ, who is our life, shall appear, then shall ye also appear with him in glory. (Colossians 3:4)

The Second Coming of Jesus on the Final Day shall be:

- Singular
- Sudden and unexpected

- Atmospheric
- Visible
- Noisy
- Disruptive
- Fiery

CHAPTER 10

HIS SECOND COMING SHALL BE GLORIOUS

HIS FIRST ARRIVAL ON earth attracted little attention. Yes, a small number of shepherds watching sheep on the hillsides outside Bethlehem saw and heard angels singing in the nighttime sky. At first, those eyewitness accounts stirred excitement among the town's inhabitants. As the years passed by, however, the amazing stories faded into folklore told by old men and women to children. Besides, the family - Joseph, Mary, and their child Jesus - moved away from Bethlehem to Nazareth. The singing angels, the bright star, and the wise men were old news.

His second arrival will be a global showstopper. The first time, few people on earth were aware of His arrival. The second time, everybody will know He's back. The first time, Jesus brought grace. The second time, He will bring glory.

For the grace of God that bringeth salvation hath appeared to all men, teaching us that, denying ungodliness and worldly lusts, we should live soberly, righteously, and godly, in this present world; *looking for that blessed hope, and the glorious appearing of the great God and our Savior Jesus Christ;* who gave himself for us, that he might redeem us from all iniquity, and purify unto himself a peculiar people, zealous of good works. (Titus 2:11-14)

The humble Savior who came with grace for the forgiveness of sins is the same Savior who will come again with great glory for the final judgment of sins and the consummation of all things.

The saving work of Jesus Christ began at the Cross: He willingly bore our sins, died to pay the ransom for our souls, descended to the place of the dead, rose from the grave, and ascended to Heaven to intercede for us. We now wait for Jesus to return in great glory to deliver us from God's wrath that will be poured out upon the wicked, and to usher in the full manifestation of the Kingdom of God.

We look back to the first advent of Jesus Christ to remind ourselves of God's grace bestowed upon sinners by purchasing our redemption. We look forward to the second advent of Jesus Christ with anticipation of our redemption being completed. Your salvation will be completed when your physical body is glorified to permanently house your born-again spirit. Your physical body will be glorified when your eyes see Jesus in the air. The second coming of Jesus Christ will transform your mortal physical body to be like His glorious resurrected body. Thus, your salvation needs both advents of Jesus Christ to be complete because your physical body is still subject to death, which is the curse that came upon all life because of sin.

For our conversation is in heaven; *from whence also we look for the Savior, the Lord Jesus Christ: who shall change our vile body, that it may be fashioned like unto His glorious body,* according to the working whereby he is able even to subdue all things unto himself. (Philippians 3:20-21)

The Last Days began with the first advent of Jesus Christ and concludes with the second advent of our Lord. St. John the Apostle saw both manifestations of Jesus Christ. The apostle traveled and lived daily with Jesus during our Lord's ministry on earth. With his physical eyes, John saw Jesus in a human body that knew hunger, thirst, weariness, and pain. Apostle John, however, was also shown in a vision Jesus Christ as He is in Heaven - the Savior who will return to earth for the Church.

Who did John see in the vision on Patmos island? He saw a glorious king! His hair is white as snow. He eyes are like flames of fire. His feet are like polished brass. His voice sounds like many rivers.

And I turned to see the voice that spake with me. And being turned, I saw seven golden candlesticks; and in the midst of the seven candlesticks one like unto the Son of man, clothed with a garment down to the foot, and girt about the paps with a golden girdle. His head and His hairs were white like wool, as white as snow; and His eyes were as a flame of fire; and His feet like unto fine brass, as if they burned in a furnace; and His voice as the sound of many waters. And he had in His right hand seven stars: and out of His mouth went a sharp two-edged sword: and His countenance was as the sun shineth in His strength. And when I saw him, I fell at His feet as dead. And he laid His right hand upon me, saying unto me, Fear not; I am the first and the last: I am he that liveth, and was dead; and, behold, I am alive for evermore, Amen; and have the keys of hell and of death. (Revelation 1:12-18)

Three of Jesus' disciples saw the glory of the Lord. Jesus took Peter, James, and John, His brother, up to a high mountain. Jesus was transfigured before their eyes. His face was as bright as the sun. His clothing was white as light. Moses and Elijah appeared and talked with Jesus.

Jesus is no longer the suffering servant. He is now the King of Glory! Every human will see Jesus coming in the clouds with power and great glory. His glorious appearing shall happen immediately after the tribulation and the darkening of the sun, moon, and stars. The cosmic theater lights will be dimmed so that the star of the show can make His grand entrance onto the center stage. There will be no seats in the house with an obstructed view. Every view will be center orchestra seats. Every eye shall see him! It will be the King Jesus Show starring Jesus Christ.

Immediately after the tribulation of those days shall the sun be darkened, and the moon shall not give her light, and the stars shall fall from heaven, and the powers of the heavens shall be shaken: and then shall appear the sign of the Son of man in heaven: and then shall all the tribes of the earth mourn, *and they shall see the Son of man coming in the clouds of heaven with power and great glory.* And he shall send His angels with a great sound of a trumpet, and they shall gather together His elect from the four winds, from one end of heaven to the other. (Matthew 24:29-31)

***Behold, he cometh with clouds; and every eye shall see him,* and they also which pierced him: and all kindreds of the earth shall wail because of him. Even so, Amen. (Revelation 1:7)**

Why will the second advent of Jesus Christ be glorious? His triumphant return will be glorious for one reason only: Jesus is glorious! Therefore, everything He does is glorious.

How can we imagine a future event that is unimaginable? How can we comprehend the arrival of a king who is incomprehensible?

There is no historical event in mankind's past to reference as an example of what will happen on the Final Day. No human in history ever saw anything comparable to the grand and glorious arrival of the King of Glory. Waves of unending praise and thunderous ovations shall resound as the saints of God worship the King of Kings and Lord of Lords. There will be nobody left to stop us from worshipping Jesus with all our heart, mind, and soul. How long will the first standing ovation last? None of us know. Unrestrained and joyous cheering, shouting, singing, and worshipping of our triumphant King will fill the heaven above New Jerusalem forever.

Old Testament Prophet Isaiah Saw Jesus

The Bible gives us glimpses of the Almighty God's magnificent glory. Old Testament prophet Isaiah saw the Lord's glory. Isaiah saw Jesus! It happened in a vision in the year that King Uzziah died. The scripture does not indicate whether the vision occurred before or after Uzziah died. We only know it happened in the same year. We also don't know if Isaiah meant the king's physical death or the civil death of his kingship due to the leprosy that ravished His body. We simply know that the prophet used the year of the king's civil or physical death to mark the time of the vision. One thing we know, however, is that Old Testament prophet Isaiah saw Jesus Christ. How do we know it? We know it because Apostle John said the deity was Jesus Christ.

These things said Isaiah, when he saw His glory, and spake of him. (John 12:41)

The vision is described in the sixth chapter of the Book of Isaiah. The prophet saw Jesus Christ sitting upon a throne, high and lifted up, and His majestic robe filled the ornate temple in Heaven.

Above the throne were six-winged seraphim that shouted, "Holy, holy, holy, is the Lord of hosts: the whole earth is full of His glory."

In the year that king Uzziah died I saw also the Lord sitting upon a throne, high and lifted up, and His train filled the temple. Above it stood the seraphim: each one had six wings; with twain he covered His face, and with twain he covered His feet, and with twain he did fly. And one cried unto another, and said, Holy, holy, holy, is the Lord of hosts: the whole earth is full of His glory. (Isaiah 6:1-3)

Isaiah did not describe the Divine Essence of the trinitarian Godhead. No man has seen the face of Almighty God and lived. In the New Covenant age, the physical manifestation of God given to mankind to behold with their eyes is Jesus Christ, the last Adam. Likewise, the Old Covenant prophet Isaiah was given the manifestation of Yahweh in the personhood of the Messiah, our Lord Jesus Christ.

Interestingly, Isaiah also did not describe the form and appearance of Jesus. Instead, he described the physical setting around Jesus. He beheld the Lord's stately and majestic throne. It was "high and lifted up." He said the Lord was clothed in a spectacular royal robe. Isaiah was particularly amazed by the grandeur and size of the majestic garment's flowing skirt that filled the holy temple. Isaiah was awestruck by the seraphim that flew above the throne crying, "Holy, holy, holy is the Lord of hosts: the whole earth is full of His glory."

Moses Saw God's Goodness

The Israelites knew that nobody had ever seen the face of God and lived. Moses had an encounter with Almighty God shortly after the Hebrews greatly sinned by dancing naked around a golden calf idol. Moses took the tabernacle of the congregation and pitched it far from the camp of the rebellious Hebrews. The Hebrews who sincerely sought God went out unto the tabernacle. Moses went too. When the people saw Moses enter into the tabernacle, a cloud-like pillar descended and stood at the door of the tabernacle while Moses talked to God. Seeing the pillar, the Hebrews rose up and worshipped God. The Book of Exodus says God spoke to Moses as a man speaks to a friend. For a moment, Moses had regained the superb privilege and lofty position enjoyed by Adam and Eve who spoke with God daily in the Garden of Eden as friends.

And Moses took the tabernacle, and pitched it without the camp, afar off from the camp, and called it the Tabernacle of the congregation. And it came to pass, that everyone which sought the Lord went out unto the tabernacle of the congregation, which was without the camp. And it came to pass, when Moses went out unto the tabernacle, that all the people rose up, and stood every man at His tent door, and looked after Moses, until he was gone into the tabernacle. And it came to pass, as Moses entered into the tabernacle, the cloudy pillar descended, and stood at the door of the tabernacle, and the Lord talked with Moses. And all the people saw the cloudy pillar stand at the tabernacle door: and all the people rose up and worshipped, every man in His tent door. And the Lord spake unto Moses face to face, as a man speaketh unto His friend. And he turned again into the camp: but His servant Joshua, the son of Nun, a young man, departed not out of the tabernacle. (Exodus 33:7-11)

What did Moses say to his friend, Almighty God? After securing God's restoration of the Hebrew people, Moses boldly made one personal request: He asked to see God's glory! His soul hungered to see God's face. He craved the immediate knowledge of Almighty God which is reserved for angelic spirits and the souls of saints who have departed this world. Moses previously had an encounter with God on the mountain, yet it did not satisfy his soul's hunger for God. Moses craved a deeper experience with his Maker, the almighty Creator of the universe.

Moses cried to God, "I beseech Thee! Show me thy glory."

Yahweh could not fully grant the heartfelt request of His servant and friend Moses. God did, however, allow Moses to see and experience all the divine presence that a mortal human can handle and remain alive on earth. He gave Moses a fleeting glimpse of a portion of His glory. What Moses saw was God's goodness. Moses' eyes beheld only the afterglow of the glory of God's backside as He walked past him. Had Moses seen anything more he would have instantly dropped dead because his mortal body's neurons would have been overwhelmed and short circuited from an electrical overload.

And the Lord said unto Moses, I will do this thing also that thou hast spoken: for thou hast found grace in my sight, and I know thee by name. *And he said, I beseech thee, shew me thy glory. And he said, I will make all my goodness pass before thee,* **and I will proclaim the name of the Lord before thee; and will be gracious to whom I will be gracious, and will shew mercy on whom I will shew mercy. And he said, Thou canst not see my face: for there shall no man see me, and live. (Exodus 33:17-20)**

God's goodness and glory are inseparable. Wherever God's goodness is made known, so too is His glory. Likewise, whenever His glory is revealed, God's goodness is also present.

As Moses met God at the rock in Horeb, we meet God through Christ the Rock. It was through the incarnation of Jesus Christ in Mary's womb and His birth in Bethlehem that God revealed Himself to mankind. Blessed Mary's undefiled womb was the holy Ark of the New Covenant.

When the Virgin Mary gave birth to the Christ child, a heavenly choir of angels sang in the nighttime sky above Bethlehem, "Glory to God in the highest, and on earth peace, good will toward men." God's glory returned to earth to announce that mankind could have peace and reconciliation with their Maker through faith in the only begotten Son of God.

If we hunger to see God the Father, we must first see God the Son. Jesus said:

No man hath seen God at any time; the only begotten Son, which is in the bosom of the Father, he hath declared him. (John 1:18)

Ye have neither heard His voice at any time, nor seen His shape. (John 5:37)

Not that any man hath seen the Father, save he which is of God, he hath seen the Father. (John 6:46)

And Jesus cried out and said, "He who believes in Me, does not believe in Me but in Him who sent Me. "He who sees Me sees the One who sent Me. (John 12:44-45)

When the day of His crucifixion drew near, Jesus prepared His disciples that he would depart to return to His Father in Heaven. In reassuring them, Jesus admonished them to not allow their hearts to be troubled. He promised that he was going home to prepare a place for them. Jesus said, "and if I go and prepare a place for you, I will come again...." Thomas asked how they would know the way there. Jesus replied by declaring that He *is* the way! Jesus said no human can come to the Father except by him.

Philip demanded, "Show us the Father." Jesus answered him:

...Have I been so long time with you, and yet hast thou not known me, Philip? *he that hath seen me hath seen the Father;* **and how sayest thou then, Shew us the Father? (John 14:9)**

His heart's cry "Show us the Father" was identical to Moses asking God to "show me Thy glory." Yahweh spoke with Moses as a friend. Jesus spoke with Philip as a friend. If you see God, you will first see His glory. If you see the Son, you will see His glory. The full revelation of Almighty God to mankind in this present age is found only in Jesus Christ, the Son of God. Jesus is the bread of life and living water that abundantly satisfies our hungry, thirsty souls that long to be reconnected with the divine Creator who walked with Adam and Eve in the Garden of Eden and spoke with them as friends.

Ye are my friends, *if ye do whatsoever I command you.* **Henceforth I call you not servants; for the servant knoweth not what His lord doeth:** *but I have called you friends;* **for all things that I have heard of my Father I have made known unto you. (John 15:14-15)**

During the Old Testament times, it was upon the rock in Horeb that Yahweh granted Moses' desire to see His goodness and glory. In New Testament times, it is only upon Christ the Rock that we can see God's goodness and glory. When Jesus returns on the Final Day, all humans will see the fullest and brightest display of His glory. We will not look at His backside as He passes by. Everybody will see His radiant face as He arrives on clouds of great glory.

...and then shall appear the sign of the Son of man in heaven: and then shall all the tribes of the earth mourn, *and they shall see* *the Son of man coming in the clouds of heaven with power and great glory.* (Matthew 24:30)

Jesus saith unto him, Thou hast said: nevertheless I say unto you, *Hereafter shall ye see the Son of man sitting on the right hand of power, and coming in the clouds of heaven.* (Matthew 26:64)

And then shall they see the Son of man coming *in the clouds with great power and glory.* (Mark 13:26)

And Jesus said, I am: and ye shall see the Son of man *sitting on the right hand of power, and coming in the clouds of heaven.* (Mark 14:62)

Blow the Trumpet in Zion

Clouds have always been associated with God's glory. Biblical references to clouds describe the presence of God on earth. In the magnificent exodus of the Hebrews out of Egypt, God told Moses he would come to him in a thick cloud that the people may hear when God spoke to Moses.

And the Lord said unto Moses, *Lo, I come unto thee in a thick cloud,* that the people may hear when I speak with thee, and believe thee forever. And Moses told the words of the people unto the Lord. (Exodus 19:9)

God descended from Heaven to Mount Sinai for a divine visitation with the Hebrew people. His arrival was heralded by lightning and thunder, a thick cloud, the voice of the trumpet, fire, smoke, and an earthquake.

And it came to pass on the third day in the morning, *that there were thunders and lightnings, and a thick cloud upon the mount, and the voice of the trumpet exceeding loud; so that all the people that was in the camp trembled.* And Moses brought forth the people out of the camp to meet with God; and they stood at the nether part of the mount. *And mount Sinai was altogether on a smoke, because the Lord descended upon it in fire: and the smoke thereof ascended as the smoke of a furnace, and the whole mount quaked greatly.* (Exodus 19:16-18)

The same things will happen when Jesus Christ returns on the Final Day. In the Apocalypse vision seen by Apostle John on the island of Patmos, the apostle saw and heard lightnings, thundering, voices, great hail, and a mighty earthquake. As the Hebrews heard "the voice of the trumpet exceeding loud," all inhabitants of the earth shall hear the last trumpet blast when Jesus descends from Heaven to earth with a mighty shout. He will come with clouds. All who rejected Christ and persecuted His church shall wail.

Behold, he cometh with clouds; and every eye shall see him, and they also which pierced him: and all kindreds of the earth shall wail because of him. Even so, Amen. (Revelation 1:7)

Old Testament prophet Joel foretold of the wondrous event. He said the saints should blow the trumpet in Zion, sound an alarm in God's holy mountain, and let all the inhabitants tremble for the day of the Lord is coming. The saints are to shout, "Repent! The day of the Lord is coming!"

In the second chapter of the Book of Joel, the prophet said the day of the Lord "is nigh at hand." It will be a day of darkness and of gloominess, a day of clouds and thick darkness. He saw an army coming that mankind had never seen in history, nor would ever see again. They will torch everything as they march across the earth. A great fire will devour everything before them, and a mighty flame will burn after they marched through the land. Nothing shall escape their military march through all nations. The earth will quake before God's army. The heavens above shall tremble as the sun, moon, and stars go dark. Joel said the Lord shall utter His voice before His army, for His camp is bigger and mightier than humans can comprehend. He said the day of the Lord is great and very terrible, and nobody can live through it.

Joel prophesied that "it shall come to pass afterward" that God shall pour out His spirit upon all flesh. Sons and daughters shall prophesy, old men shall dream dreams, and young men shall see visions. Joel said God will show wonders in the heavens and in the earth. There shall be blood, fire, and pillars of smoke. The sun shall be turned into darkness, and the moon into blood. All of it shall happen before the great and terrible day the Lord comes. The good news is Joel's assurance that "whosoever shall call on the name of the Lord shall be delivered: for in mount Zion and in Jerusalem shall be deliverance."

Apostle Peter quoted prophet Joel on the Day of Pentecost when the Holy Spirit was given to the Church. When the men and women of Jerusalem marveled at the sight and sound of Spirit-filled saints speaking in other languages as they came out of the upper room, Peter told them, "But *this is that* which was spoken by the prophet Joel..." The Jews immediately knew that "this" (the disciples speaking in other languages known by others hearing them) was "that" (the Lord pouring out His spirit on all flesh).

Speaking about the coming day of the Lord, Old Testament prophet Joel said the priests of God must "blow the trumpet in Zion, sanctify a fast, call a solemn assembly, gather the people, sanctify the congregation, assemble the elders, gather the children...." He said the ministers of the Lord should weep and pray that the people be spared.

"Sanctify the congregation" means the people who claim to be Christians must clean up their lives before the Lord returns. Christians must repent of their sins, and turn from their wicked ways, and abstain from unlawful sensual pleasures outside marriage. In short, they must embrace holiness.

Almighty God Desires to Live with the Saints on a New Earth

As goodness is synonymous with God's glory, so too is holiness. The essence of the glory of the Lord is the magnificent radiance of His holiness. The Lord is a morally perfect spiritual being without sin and cannot be in the presence of sin. He is separated from all sin; thus, He is holy.

What does this mean for us and the second coming of Jesus? It means everything! Without holiness, no man or woman claiming to be a Christian shall see the Lord when He returns.

Follow peace with all men, *and holiness, without which no man shall see the Lord…* (Hebrews 12:14)

It is the responsibility of all Christians to prepare themselves for the Final Day. Daily repentance is necessary in the life of all Christians because "all have sinned, and come short of the glory of God." There must be true repentance of personal sins, genuine sorrow for sinful ways in their lives, and forsaking all such sins as proof that they have truly repented. Jesus shall return on clouds of great glory, and His glory is the radiance of His holiness. Without holiness, no man or woman shall see the Lord. Therefore, the Church must be holy! Our Lord Jesus Christ will present to God the Father "a glorious church, not having spot, or wrinkle, or any such thing; but that it should be holy without blemish." In other words, we must be holy.

Wherefore, beloved, seeing that ye look for such things, *be diligent that ye may be found of him in peace, without spot, and blameless.* (2 Peter 3:14)

Husbands, love your wives, even as Christ also loved the church, and gave himself for it; that he might sanctify and cleanse it with the washing of water by the word, *that he might present it to himself a glorious church, not having spot, or wrinkle, or any such thing; but that it should be holy and without blemish.* (Ephesians 5:25-27)

In Old Covenant times, the tabernacle was the portable dwelling place of God transported by the Hebrews from the Exodus until the conquest of Canaan. It was also known as the Tent of the Congregation. The tabernacle was sanctified by God's glory. It was in the glorified, holy tabernacle that God met with the children of Israel.

And there I will meet with the children of Israel, and the tabernacle shall be sanctified by my glory. (Exodus 29:43)

In the New Covenant age, Jesus Christ is our high priest and our perfect tabernacle, a tabernacle not made with human hands. Jesus is the temple of God. God meets with the children of Israel (the Church) in the glorified, holy tabernacle who is Jesus Christ, the resurrected Savior of the world. Apostle Peter referred to Jesus as a "living stone." Surely, St. Peter was referencing Isaiah 28:16 in which God declares that He will "lay in Zion for a foundation a stone, a tried stone, a precious cornerstone, a sure foundation..."

The New Testament temple is not a physical building in Jerusalem constructed with expensive stones and gold. The new temple is built upon a living stone, a sure foundation, chosen by God. Apostle Peter's "living stone" is not a breathing rock with eyes, a mouth, and a heartbeat. It is the resurrected Son of God, Jesus Christ, who is alive forever. The living stone Jesus Christ was chosen by Almighty God as the sure foundation upon which God would build a new temple constructed with lively stones. Such lively stones are born again Christians who keep the commandments. From the foundation to the roof, the entire New Testament temple is composed of living materials. Together, Jesus and His disciples form a spiritual house, a holy priesthood, who offer up spiritual sacrifices made acceptable to God by Jesus Christ.

To whom coming, as unto a living stone, disallowed indeed of men, *but chosen of God,* and precious, *ye also, as lively stones, are built up a spiritual house, an holy priesthood,* to offer up spiritual sacrifices, acceptable to God by Jesus Christ. (1 Peter 2:4-5)

Thus, the physical bodies of born again, baptized, commandment-keeping disciples of Jesus Christ are "lively stones" because the Holy Spirit dwells inside them. Apostle Paul asked Christians in Corinth if they understood that their physical bodies have been joined to Jesus' resurrected body, and that they have bought with a price.

Know ye not that your bodies are the members of Christ? shall I then take the members of Christ, and make them the members of an harlot? God forbid. What? know ye not that he which is joined to an harlot is one body? for two, saith he, shall be one flesh. *But he that is joined unto the Lord is one spirit.* Flee fornication. Every sin that a man doeth is without the body; but he that committeth fornication sinneth against his own body. *What? know ye not that your body is the temple of the Holy Ghost which is in you, which ye have of God, and ye are not your own? For ye are bought with a price: therefore glorify God in your body, and in your spirit, which are God's.* (1 Corinthians 6:15-20)

Apostle John the Revelator heard a great voice from Heaven proclaiming that the tabernacle of God is with men, and He shall dwell with them and be their God. The Old Covenant's tabernacle of the congregation - the tent of meeting - was a tented palace for Israel's true king. It was a miniature Garden of Eden: The entrance faced east and was guarded by cherubim, the lampstand represented the Tree of Life, and the law represented the Tree of Knowledge of Good and Evil. The tabernacle represented God's house among His people Israel. During His earthly ministry, Jesus Christ – the Word of God - tabernacled with God's people. He dwelt among them, and the people beheld His glory. He was and is and shall forever be full of grace and truth.

And the Word was made flesh, and dwelt among us, (and we beheld his glory, the glory as of the only begotten of the Father,) full of grace and truth. (John 1:14)

In the Old Covenant age, the tabernacle was a tent where God's Spirit resided among the people of Israel. While Jesus Christ was physically on the earth, He was the tabernacle. On the Day of Pentecost, the Holy Spirit tabernacled in the physical bodies of the saints and continues to this day to dwell inside the bodies of all saints. In the eternal age to come, something more awesome will happen! Apostle John heard "a great voice out of Heaven." The heavenly voice called upon hearers to "behold," meaning to fix their eyes upon and observe with great attention something spectacular to observe.

And I heard a great voice out of heaven saying, Behold, the tabernacle of God is with men, and he will dwell with them, and they shall be His people, and God himself shall be with them, and be their God. (Revelation 21:3)

What is the spectacular thing we should behold? It is Almighty God relocating his official personal address from the City of Heaven to New Jerusalem, the new Garden of Eden. The tabernacle of God will be with the saints and Yahweh shall once again dwell in the Garden of Eden with the humans He made. No more shall there be a separation between the Creator and the saved children made in His image. They will live together in the same city. We shall be His people, and He shall be our God.

Jesus' Glory Was Made Known Through Miracles

During Jesus' earthly ministry, St. John the Apostle said the Word was made flesh, and dwelt among us - and humans beheld the glory of Jesus. John described Him as "full of grace and truth."

How was Jesus' glory made known to mankind? It was through the miracles performed by Jesus. His first miracle was done by Jesus on behalf of His mother. He turned average water into great wine at a wedding feast. The miracle was the first ray of hope for mankind that emanated from the Word of God arriving on earth in human flesh to dwell among men. The Messiah who can change water into wine can also change wine into blood in the Eucharist, the great thanksgiving feast of holy communion with the Lord. In the Old Testament, wine was a symbol of gladness. In the New Testament, wine is the emblem of our Savior's blood shed for the remission of sins. Thus, the new wine is an emblem of our gladness representing God's forgiveness of our sins through the shed blood of Jesus. The choice of a wedding feast as the venue to perform His first miracle on earth also points to the great wedding feast that God will convene when the Bridegroom is married to His bride New Jerusalem.

This beginning of miracles did Jesus in Cana of Galilee, *and manifested forth his glory*; and his disciples believed on him. (John 2:11)

Each miracle manifested the glory of Jesus. People believed on Him as the Messiah. Although the miracles were stunning and impressive, the greatest manifestation of the Lord's glory was not the miracles. Then as it still is today, His greatest display of His glory is His love for humanity. The greatest display of Jesus' love for mankind was His willingness to be sacrificed on a wooden cross for the sins of the world. Jesus' greatest miracles are seen in the salvation of lost souls. He can take people out of the vilest sins and place them in His kingdom of light. Nothing compares with such miracles of grace. Yes, He can turn water into wine, but even greater, Jesus turns whinos into winners. Jesus saves.

Believers glorify Jesus by living holy lives, separated from the world's filth. Holy living and loving everybody glorify Jesus Christ and inspires sinners to believe on the name of Jesus. God's divine plan is to dwell (tabernacle) with His holy people (the Church, true Israel) in New Jerusalem for eternity. If you desire to dwell with God, you must live a holy, sanctified life now. No sinful person will be permitted to enter God's tabernacle. Flesh and blood cannot inherit the Kingdom. You must be born again by the Spirit and baptized into Christ's church. Corrupt souls cannot inherit that which is incorruptible.

The time for repentance and the embrace of holiness is before you take your last breath on earth or before the Final Day when Jesus returns to earth on clouds of great glory. He will descend from Heaven with a shout, with the voice of the archangel, and with the trump of God.

Our Transformation Occurs
When We See Jesus in His Glory

The dead in Christ shall rise from their graves. Immediately thereafter they who are alive on earth when Jesus returns on clouds of great glory shall join with the resurrected saints and all shall meet the Lord in the air. The victorious Church shall be glorified. We shall be glorified when we see His glory! The wicked shall perish in the brilliance of His revealed glory. The righteous shall be instantly glorified as they meet Jesus in the clouds of great glory.

St. Paul the Apostle said not every Christian shall die. There will be a chosen generation of saints who will never experience physical death and the grave. They will be the saints who shall join in the air the resurrected saints who will come out of their graves when Jesus returns. All Christians - both those who are alive and those who are resurrected - shall be changed in a moment, in the twinkling of an eye when the last trump is heard. Our mortal bodies of flesh and blood shall be exchanged for new immortal bodies that shall never age, become weary or sick, nor die.

When does this great exchange of bodies occur? Apostle Paul said it will happen for those counted worthy of inheriting the kingdom when Jesus Christ *"shall come to be glorified in His saints,* and to be admired in all them that believe...in that day."* (2 Thessalonians 1:10)

All unsaved sinners shall suffer a different fate on that Final Day. For them, Jesus Christ shall be **"revealed from heaven with His mighty angels, in flaming fire taking vengeance on them that know not God, and that obey not the gospel of our Lord Jesus Christ."** (2 Thessalonians 1:7-8) The unsaved **"shall be punished** with everlasting destruction from the presence of the Lord, and from the glory of His power…" (2 Thessalonians 1:9)

On the Final Day, the wicked shall be scorched with great heat and they will blaspheme the name of God because of the many plagues upon the earth. They will stubbornly refuse to repent and give Him glory. The Final Day will not be glorious for them.

The Son of God shall come in His glory, along with all His holy angels. He shall sit upon the throne of His glory. In the glory of His Father, Jesus shall reward every man and woman according to their works in this life on earth. When He comes in the glory of His father, he shall be ashamed of whoever was ashamed of Him and His words while living in this adulterous and sinful world.

Born again saints will be partakers of the glory that shall be revealed, obtain the salvation which is in Christ Jesus with eternal glory, the hope of His calling, the riches of the glory of His inheritance in the saints, and the hope of glory, which is Christ in them.

The Apocalypse gives us a vivid picture of life in heaven. Every living being glorifies God. The 24 elders sing, **"Thou art worthy, O Lord, to receive glory and honor and power: for thou hast created all things, and for thy pleasure they are and were created.** (Revelation 4:11)

A heavenly choir too numerous to count - ten thousand times ten thousand, and thousands of thousands - will sing with a loud voice, **"Worthy is the Lamb that was slain to receive power, and riches, and wisdom, and strength, and honor, and glory, and blessing."** (Revelation 5:12)

When the consummation of all things is completed, every animal, bird, and fish shall also sing to glorify Jesus. The creatures will sing, **"Blessing, and honor, and glory, and power, be unto him** that sitteth upon the throne, and unto the Lamb for ever and ever" (Revelation 5:13). Creation has been made new! Even mammals, birds, and fish sing to glorify Jesus.

The second coming of Jesus Christ shall be glorious on a scale that humans cannot imagine is possible. His glory is the magnificent radiance of His holiness. Only the holy shall see God and inherit the kingdom. Our physical bodies shall be glorified (transformed by the resurrection to be made immortal, thus suitable to dwell with God) when we meet him in the clouds of His great glory. When Jesus Christ shall appear, we shall also appear with him in glory! The spotless Church shall share in the magnificent radiance of His holiness. The head of the one, holy, catholic and apostolic church shall be united with His body - the saints of God. And so all Israel shall be saved.

When Christ, who is our life, shall appear, *then shall ye also appear with him in glory.* (Colossians 3:4)

Whoso eateth my flesh, and drinketh my blood, hath eternal life; *and I will raise him up at the last day.* (John 6:54)

The Second Coming of Jesus on the Final Day shall be:
- Singular
- Sudden and unexpected
- Atmospheric
- Visible
- Noisy
- Disruptive
- Fiery
- Glorious

CHAPTER 11

HIS SECOND COMING SHALL BE JUDGMENTAL

WHEN THE FINAL DAY arrives God shall judge the secrets of all people. He will do it by Jesus Christ, according to His gospel.

...in the day when God shall judge the secrets of men by Jesus Christ according to my gospel. (Romans 2:16)

Jesus Christ is both the mediator of our salvation, and the mediator of our judgment. God the Father has committed to Jesus Christ the "authority to execute judgment" on the Final Day "because He is the Son of Man."

...and hath given him authority to execute judgment also, because he is the Son of man. (John 5:27)

The judgment of all men and women who lived on earth from the beginning of time will occur on the Final Day. All will stand before the Supreme Judge of the Universe. The Second Coming, the Day of the Lord, the Last Day, the Judgment Seat of Christ, and the Great White Throne of Judgment are synonymous. Together they are the Final Day. It all happens when Jesus returns. Every human will be judged and rewarded accordingly for what he or she rightly deserves.

For the Son of man shall come in the glory of his Father with his angels; and then he shall reward every man according to his works. (Matthew 16:27)

Most Evangelical Zionist theologians and prophecy teachers spread these events out over 1,000 years, but almost all traditional orthodox Christian theologians and Bible scholars hold to the ecclesiastically historic view that all judgment takes place when Jesus returns. Neither theologians nor intellectuals can comprehend it because our limited carnal human minds cannot fathom the absence of time as it has existed since Creation. The same God who made time can suspend it, abolish it, or refashion it for a new age.

What is the purpose of time? We determine the hours and days by the length of the earth's rotation, and years by the length of the earth's revolving around the sun. A mean solar day represents the average length of the period of time during which the earth makes one complete rotation on its axis. An hour is a period of time equal to one twenty-fourth of a mean solar day. A year represents the time the earth completes its orbit around the sun, which is 365 ¼ solar days. The earth's seasons are due to its axial tilt. The passing of seasons affects the planet's hours of daylight, weather, temperature, vegetation, and soil fertility.

Time as we presently know it will cease to exist on the Final Day. The sun, stars, and moon shall disappear. Therefore, the objects we use to measure time will vanish. How can we have hours, days, and years when the earth, sun, and the moon no longer exist?

Undoubtedly, Evangelical Zionist theologians and studious students of Bible prophecy charts will strenuously object to the assertion that time will cease to exist when Jesus Christ returns. Their John Nelson Darby-inspired eschatology demands that God must keep the sun, moon, and stars brightly lit for another thousand years to accommodate the Jewish rulership of the world. Although pious people arrogantly think they know everything about God's plan for the end of the age, the truth is that God does not need nor seek permission from humans to do anything! The Creator asked Job "Where were you when I laid the foundations of the earth? Who has determined its measurements? To what are its foundations fastened? Or who laid its cornerstone when the morning stars sang together?"

There is an appointed day ahead which no man or woman can avoid appearing in the Creator's courtroom.

And the times of this ignorance God winked at; but now commandeth all men everywhere to repent: because he hath appointed a day, in the which he will judge the world in righteousness by that man whom he hath ordained; whereof he hath given assurance unto all men, in that he hath raised him from the dead. (Acts 17:30-31)

Chapter 7 described the great separation of souls that will happen on the Final Day. The entire human population since the beginning of time will be separated according to their respective nations.

Angelic bailiffs will organize billions of humans according to their nationality. The names of ancient nations, kingdoms, and empires long forgotten will be called out by angels: "Citizens of Sparta, follow me. Citizens of Scythia, go with him." Another angel will shout, "All citizens of the Roman Empire, follow me!" Hovering over the crowd like a drone, an angel will instruct the citizens of the Kingdom of Ararat to follow the signs. The same will happen for citizens of modern nations: The United States of America, Canada, Mexico, Peru, Cayman Islands, Great Britain, Iceland, Spain, Moldova, Russia, China, Thailand, Australia, Kenya, Nigeria, Israel, and Jordan. Angels will lead them to their designated areas. Once separated into their respective national groupings, citizens of each nation will be subdivided into two groups: sheep and goats. Angels will shout, "Goats go to the left! Sheep go to the right!" Here's an important tip: If you go left on the Final Day, things will not go well for you. You don't want to be a goat on the Final Day. You still have time to choose the right side. It's your choice. Nobody is predestined to be a goat except Satan and the fallen angels.

"When the Son of Man comes in His glory, and all the holy angels with Him, then He will sit on the throne of His glory. Before Him will be gathered all nations, and He will separate them one from another as a shepherd separates his sheep from the goats. He will set the sheep at His right hand, but the goats at the left. (Matthew 25:31:33)

The Judge will ask the sheep and goats the same set of questions. He will not ask: "Did you attend church every week? Did you tithe? Did you teach Sunday School? Did you stand with Israel? Which political party did you support in the elections?" No, Jesus will ask us questions about mercy and kindness. Both sheep and the goats will be questioned by Judge Jesus: Did you feed the hungry? Did you give water to the thirsty? Did you provide housing for the homeless? Did you clothe the destitute? Did you visit sick people? Did you visit prisoners and comfort them? Yikes! Are you prepared to answer those questions?

310

To those who correctly answer the questions, Jesus will say to the sheep on His right: "Inherit the kingdom prepared for you!" The just Judge of the Universe will turn to the goats on His left and banish them to the lake of everlasting fire. The sheep will be escorted into the land of eternal life, but the goats will be led away into eternal punishment.

"Then the King will say to those at His right hand, 'Come, you blessed of My Father, inherit the kingdom prepared for you since the foundation of the world. (Matthew 25:34)

Depart from Me, you cursed, into the eternal fire, prepared for the devil and his angels. (Matthew 25:41)

"And they will go away into eternal punishment, but the righteous into eternal life." (Matthew 25:46)

If you are not doing acts of mercy for the poor, hungry, thirsty, naked, sick, and imprisoned, there is still time to mend your ways and obey the Lord's commandments. He is coming for those who keep His commandments. Jesus said the proof of your love for Him is your obedience to His commandments. The Book of Hebrews declares that "without faith it is impossible to please God…" James, the brother of Jesus, said true Christians must be "doers of the word and not hearers only." James also defined religion that is "pure and undefiled before God" as this: "to visit the fatherless and widows in their affliction and to keep oneself unstained by the world."

Trees That Don't Produce Good Fruit are Cut Down and Burned

Faith and good works cannot be separated. We are not saved by good works. Good works, however, are proof of our salvation. A life devoid of good works of mercy and charity is evidence that a person claiming to be religious has no justifying faith in Jesus Christ. James said faith without works is dead, meaning there is no life in the person's faith. A living tree produces good fruit. A tree that produces no good fruit is not worth keeping. It will be cut down and tossed into the fire.

Every tree that bringeth not forth good fruit is hewn down, and cast into the fire. (Matthew 7:19)

James asked the saints how they would benefit by saying they have faith but ignore church brothers and sisters who need clothing and food. To James, shooing away needy brothers and sisters with a pious prayer, but refusing to give them what they need, has no spiritual benefit for your soul.

James said a man may say, "You have faith and I have works." His answer holds true today. James replied:

Show me your faith without your works, and I will show you my faith by my works. You believe that there is one God; you do well. The demons also believe and tremble. But do you want to be shown, O foolish man, that faith without works is dead? Was not Abraham our father justified by works when he offered his son Isaac on the altar? Do you see how faith worked with his works, and by works faith was made perfect? The Scripture was fulfilled which says, "Abraham believed God, and it was reckoned to him as righteousness," and he was called the friend of God. You see then how by works a man is justified, and not by faith only. Likewise, was not Rahab the prostitute justified by works when she received the messengers and sent them out another way? As the body without the spirit is dead, so faith without works is dead. (James 2:18-26)

Perhaps you are asking why a book about the Second Coming of Jesus Christ is discussing good works of mercy for the poor, hungry, thirsty, naked, sick, and imprisoned. The answer is plain and simple: As explained earlier, every human will be separated into groups according to his or nationality. Once there, each nation's population will be subdivided between sheep and goats. Both goats and sheep will be asked the same questions about acts of mercy. The sheep shall enter into eternal life, the goats will plunge headfirst into the lake of fire. Jesus said those who love Him keep His commandments. Saint John heard in the vision on Patmos a voice proclaim that whosoever does the commandments of Jesus has the right to the tree of life, and they may enter through the gates into the city.

On the Final Day, Jesus will return for every Christian who kept His commandments. They shall enter through the gates of New Jerusalem because God has graciously conferred upon them the right to feast on the fruit of the Tree of Life. Dogs (meaning vile, filthy, depraved, wicked men and women), sorcerers, sexually immoral heathens, murderers, idolaters, and liars will be prohibited from entering the city. They shall dwell forever encased inside invisible flames of black fire.

Blessed are they that do his commandments, that they may have right to the tree of life, and may enter in through the gates into the city. For without are dogs, and sorcerers, and whoremongers, and murderers, and idolaters, and whosoever loveth and maketh a lie. (Revelation 22:14-15)

Increase in Scoffers and Mockers is Sign the Final Day is Near

In recent decades, Biblical morality in Western nations has become an outdated concept from a bygone era. Even more unpopular is the topic of judgment of sins. Talking about morality and judgment of sins is a guaranteed way to reduce the number of social invitations you receive. As technology-centric societies move away from Biblical morality, the more people behave like the ancient Israelites without a king: "Every man did that which was right in his own eyes." Modern sociologists call it "situational ethics." God calls it rebellion.

Western societies have been overtaken by an aberrant political movement that despises Biblical morality and ridicules the belief that an all-seeing God will judge everybody someday. This movement also exalts as socially virtuous new definitions of "tolerance" and "inclusiveness." In their warped minds, "tolerance" means validating any behavior or lifestyle deemed acceptable by social revolutionaries. Furthermore, politically correct "inclusiveness" demands that morally upright men and women accept the beliefs and behavior of immoral men and women as socially acceptable and normal.

Zealots promoting a Mao-like cultural revolution angrily reject any notion that there exists a sinless, morally perfect God who will judge the lives of humans. They laugh at the Holy Bible as a moral code for mankind. They scoff at Christians who believe that Jesus Christ was resurrected from the dead and shall return in glory.

An unholy alliance of cultural communists, atheist academics, Jewish journalists, zany zealots, liberal lawyers, and deep pocket devils have deliberately decimated traditional Western societies and constructed a caustic culture that viciously defames and mauls any person who dares to defy their mantra of tolerance and inclusivity. Sadly, many Christian churches in Western nations have buckled under the immense social, political, legal, and financial pressure to acquiesce to the demands of the anti-God "thought police." Consequently, many pastors privately tremble at the threat of being labeled "intolerant and judgmental" by wicked men and women who are enemies of the Cross. It should be the other way! Wicked men and women should tremble because righteous men are preaching God's word. Because righteous men and women stopped boldly preaching the Word of God in Western Christian nations, the tares now outnumber the wheat in most of those countries. Fearless preaching is the only method to combat wicked weeds.

Western nations, once bastions of traditional Christianity, have become hotbeds of hostility against Biblical morality and the disciples of Jesus Christ. As bizarre as is this movement of political-correctness, Christians should not be surprised by its appearance. The Bible foretold it would manifest as we approach the Final Day. The Bible calls them "scoffers." Scoffers arrogantly and foolishly mock, jeer, deride, scorn, and ridicule people, things, and/or beliefs that they don't accept, like, or understand.

Apostle Peter said we must know that scoffers will appear in the last days. They will be driven by their pursuit of carnal lusts. Mockingly, these Last Days scoffers are presently taunting Christians who are proclaiming that Jesus will return to judge all mankind. "Where is the proof that your Jesus god will return?" they arrogantly ask with derisive laughter. "The world has been the same since its creation," they arrogantly post on social media.

...knowing this first, that there shall come in the last days scoffers, walking after their own lusts, and saying, Where is the promise of his coming? for since the fathers fell asleep, all things continue as they were from the beginning of the creation. (2 Peter 3:3-4)

In saying "knowing this first" Apostle Peter told the saints they could be assured the scoffers would appear in the final stage of the world's existence. Indeed, it would be a sure sign that Jesus' return is near. His emphatic statement of their future appearance was an instruction to the Church that Christians must prepare for the scoffers. Peter is saying to the Church, "Trust me saints. It's going to happen! They are coming some day! You can count on it. And when they show up in large numbers, it means we are close to the Final Day."

If Apostle Peter were amongst us today, the beloved saint would shout: "They're here!" Shockingly, the biggest populations of scoffers and mockers are in nations with a Christian heritage. Satan sowed tares among the wheat in each of those nations, and now the tares outnumber the wheat. They arrogantly sneer in the faces of righteous preachers warning people to repent of their sins, believe on the name of Jesus, and be baptized into the Church. They laugh at Biblical prophecies of the second coming of Jesus. They live selfishly to satisfy their sexual lusts and carnal pleasures with no restraints of morality.

St. Paul the Apostle advised his protege Timothy to prepare the saints for vile people in the last days. He said, "in the last days perilous times shall come." The beloved apostle said people in the last days shall be:

"...lovers of their own selves, covetous, boasters, proud, blasphemers, disobedient to parents, unthankful, unholy, without natural affection, trucebreakers, false accusers, incontinent, fierce, despisers of those that are good, traitors, heady, high-minded, lovers of pleasures more than lovers of God; having a form of godliness, but denying the power thereof: from such turn away." (2 Timothy 3:1-5)

316

The apostle's warning to the Church is this: when you see people commonly acting as such, take heed because it means living amongst such people will be full of grave risk and danger. Be on guard! Today we see millions of law-abiding Christian men and women compelled to obtain government permits to lawfully carry firearms for their personal protection. Protection from whom? Protection from people who refuse to allow God's moral code to self-govern their lives! Even worse, many churches employ armed security guards during religious services as houses of worship have become targets of deranged men with guns, swords, and knives plotting to carry out mass murder. Shockingly, pastors have been shot or stabbed while preaching or officiating the Lord's Supper, and bombs have exploded in sanctuaries filled with men, women, and children worshipping God. Surely, we are living in perilous times that requires the supernatural protection of God to escape such madness.

The rapid social acceptance of sexual sins and blatantly immoral behavior in Western nations is intimidating many sincere pastors, evangelists, and Bible teachers who know what the Word of God says about such things. As earnest students of the Bible, they know that sexually immoral people - both homosexual and heterosexual - will not enter the kingdom of God. Yet, if they boldly preach it from their pulpits, they risk provoking walkouts by church members with family members who have joined the modern sexual revolution. Or, they face pressure from church deacons, trustees, and donors who threaten to withhold donations or even terminate the pastor's employment if he continues "upsetting" church members who have family members involved in sexual sins. Righteous pastors are also intimidated by church members who

317

fear their church will be branded in their city as "homophobic" and "intolerant" by radical Cultural Marxists and the local news media.

What should pastors do when confronted by intimidation from inside and outside the Church? They must preach the truth! They must fear God more than men. Men can injure or kill your physical body, but God can cast your soul and body into the Lake of Fire!

Fear them not therefore: for there is nothing covered, that shall not be revealed; and hid, that shall not be known. What I tell you in darkness, that speak ye in light: and what ye hear in the ear, that preach ye upon the housetops. And fear not them which kill the body, but are not able to kill the soul: but rather fear him which is able to destroy both soul and body in hell. (Matthew 10:26-28)

Spineless preaching produces feeble jellyfish-like disciples who cannot stand up. Increasingly, a growing number of churches in Western nations tolerate an "anything goes" attitude toward doctrine, beliefs, and behavior. "Judging" has become unfashionable in a politically correct culture of unbridled tolerance. Many deceived church members are hearing another Jesus calling. They are following a fake Jesus. Their imaginary Jesus is cool, socially acceptable, and very non-judgmental. He offends nobody and is liked by everybody. People who follow and obey the real Jesus, however, are labeled as offensive, divisive, mean-spirited, and bigoted cultural Neanderthals from another age. Therefore, their voices must be silenced in this new age of tolerance and inclusiveness.

Jesus' Words Shall Judge Sinners on the Final Day

With Cultural Marxists at one extreme, Babylonian Churchians are at the other extreme. Babylonian Churchians slyly confront righteous Christians by partially quoting Jesus. They say, "Jesus said he didn't come to judge the world." That's true, but it's not a complete quote, nor is it a doctrinally sound understanding of what Jesus meant. In His first advent, Jesus' mission was to go to the Cross as the sacrificial lamb on Passover. A way had to be made for mankind to be reconciled to their Maker. Jesus did not come to judge sinners, but to save them. Jesus said people must choose whether to receive or reject His words. His word will judge them on the Final Day.

And if any man hear my words, and believe not, I judge him not: for I came not to judge the world, but to save the world. He that rejecteth me, and receiveth not my words, hath one that judgeth him: the word that I have spoken, *the same shall judge him in the last day.* (John 12:47-48)

In this age of grace, which is the time of God's sin amnesty, each of us judge ourselves by our response to Jesus' words. We either believe and obey Him, or we disbelieve and disobey Him. (Many people claim to believe Jesus' words, yet disobey them. Obedience is proof of belief!) There is no middle ground. Whenever people reject Jesus' words, they reject God's gracious offer of mercy and forgiveness of sins. They judge themselves as damned for eternity.

During the great expanse of time between the Cross and the second advent of Jesus Christ, God is saying to mankind, "According to your words, so be it." God gave humanity a choice: eternal life or eternal death. Beginning with Adam and Eve, all humans were given by God a free will to make choices. The Spirit of the Lord is crying out to humanity, "Choose life and live!" Jesus Christ, however, is the stumbling block to rebellious Jews and foolishness to rebellious non-Jews. They desire to choose life, but stubbornly refuse to submit to the lordship of Jesus Christ. Therefore, they judge themselves to spend eternity in the Lake of Fire.

I call heaven and earth to record this day against you, that I have set before you life and death, blessing and cursing: therefore choose life, that both thou and thy seed may live... (Deuteronomy 30:19)

Today's Babylonian Churchians desperately seek to avoid controversy. Opposing abortion is too controversial. Opposing same-sex marriage is very controversial too. Standing against the tide of transgenderism is risky. It could get you in trouble with city officials, local news reporters, and political activists. Pulpit preaching that says Christians must abstain from sexual relations prior to marriage may offend and chase away cohabitating couples who are "checking out" the church to see if they want to attend. Telling church members that viewing pornography in the privacy of their homes is sinful may agitate influential church members who don't want their secret sins revealed. Admonishing church members not to watch movies that contain violent, sexual, profane, and/or occult content is condemned as meddling in personal affairs. Yes, preaching righteousness and holiness is very controversial and divisive. Jesus and the apostles would not be welcomed to preach and teach in most churches today.

Every Christian fellowship has both Christians and Churchians among its congregation. Christians conform to the image of the Son. Babylonian Churchians conform to the image of the world. Christians are wheat. Churchians are tares. Age doesn't matter. A young Christian sincerely seeking to follow Christ can be seated next to an old Churchian who has slyly played the religious game for decades. Many church tares excel in concealing their identity by mimicking the wheat. Tares are not always in the congregation. Sometimes they are found behind the pulpit or on the board of elders. All churches have wheat and tares growing side by side until the Final Day. The angels will separate them. Tares will be bundled and burned.

It's true that Jesus did not come to judge people. He came to save them. He'll do the judging on His next visit to earth. Jesus did, however, come the first time to divide families, friends, religious institutions, cities and nations into two groups: His disciples and His enemies. The second time He comes to earth, the conquering King will gather all who separated themselves unto Him for salvation. Sheep on the right, goats on the left!

You won't have a choice where you will stand in the courtroom before the Great Judge. The angels will assign your spot. You chose your future spot now while living on earth by being a sheep or a goat. You have free will to be a sheep or goat. Nobody is predestined by God to be damned to the lake of fire. Therefore, you will be judged on the Final Day by your response to the Word of God while you lived on earth. If you end up in the goat pen, you will have nobody to blame but yourself. Likewise, if you end up in the sheep pasture, you will have nobody to thank but Jesus! We are unable to save ourselves from damnation in Hell. Jesus did all the work necessary for us to be saved and delivered from eternal spiritual death. We can only choose to believe or reject the Word of God. God's word will judge you on the Final Day. Choosing to believe and obey Jesus' words is what makes you a sheep.

In His first advent, Jesus also did not come to bring peace on earth. Instead, He came to send a sword to divide nations, cities, and families. Wielding His sword of the Word, Jesus drew a sharp line in society's sand and asked, "Are you with me or against me?" He is still asking the same question today.

Think not that I am come to send peace on earth: I came not to send peace, but a sword. (Matthew 10:34)

He that is not with me is against me; and he that gathereth not with me scattereth abroad. (Matthew 12:30)

The sword of truth divides nations, cities, families, and churches. The Word of God is an instrument of war, sharper than any two-edged sword, that pierces "even to the dividing asunder of soul and spirit, and of the joints and marrow, and is a discerner of the thoughts and intents of the heart. Fearless, uncompromised preaching of the Word of God automatically produces division, hostility, stress, and tension. Such things are not the product of the Gospel, but the response from mankind's wickedness and enmity toward God's holiness.

At first glance, there seems to be a paradox in what angels sang announcing the birth of Jesus, and in the words of Jesus as an adult. Hovering over Bethlehem's shepherd fields, angels sang "Glory to God in the highest, and on earth peace, good will toward men." Decades later, Jesus proclaimed, "Think not that I am come to send peace on earth: I came not to send peace, but a sword." How can there be both peace on earth and a sword? Is the Bible inconsistent? Did Jesus not know God's original plan? Was Jesus radicalized in his thirties? Did He develop a bad attitude?

There is no conflict between the two statements. The angels sang correctly, and Jesus spoke truthfully. Both were in unison with the Father's will. When the angels sang, "peace on earth, good will toward men," they were joyfully announcing that thousands of years of hostility between God and mankind was over. Humanity had been separated from God since the fall of Adam and Eve in the Garden of Eden. When sin entered them, the immediate consequence was spiritual death and separation from God, plus physical death in all life forms on earth. Animals and plants suffer death because of humanity's sins.

Sin greatly proliferated. Wicked human societies around the world were in direct opposition to God's original plan at Creation. By default, they adopted Satan as their spiritual father. Their Heavenly Father, however, loved humanity too much to allow them to be forever lost. He had a plan. He sent His son to earth in human flesh to live a sinless life in a human body, and to be sacrificed as the Lamb of God on Passover for the remission of sins of all who believed on His name. With the first advent of the Messiah, God made a way for mankind to be reunited with their Maker through the forgiveness of their sins by repentance, faith in the name of Jesus, and baptism into the church, which is the true Israel. The angels joyfully sang to proclaim that God was extending goodwill from Heaven to sinful humans. It is a gift of merciful salvation. He yearns to bestow grace on sinners to receive the gift of salvation.

Jesus Reconciled Fallen Mankind to Almighty God

Through the death, burial, and resurrection of Jesus Christ, Almighty God has reconciled us to Himself. To be reconciled means that a quarrel has been settled. God has a long-running controversy with the nations. He has made a way for their citizens to be reconciled to Himself, but most people reject His gracious offer of reconciliation. Reconciliation also means that two or more parties have been brought into agreement and harmony. To be reconciled with somebody means they are no longer your enemy but restored as your friend. God desires to call every human His friend. First, however, they must be reconciled to God through faith in Jesus Christ. He is the only way to obtain reconciliation with our Heavenly Father. Sadly, billions of humans have chosen to burn in Hell rather than to be reconciled with God because reconciliation requires repentance of sins, submission to God's authority, and obedience to His commandments. They stubbornly prefer to burn than bow.

And all things are of God, who hath reconciled us to himself by Jesus Christ, and hath given to us the ministry of reconciliation; to wit, that God was in Christ, reconciling the world unto himself, not imputing their trespasses unto them; and hath committed unto us the word of reconciliation. (2 Corinthians 5:18-19)

Jesus commenced His public ministry by being baptized by John the Baptist in the Jordan river. He was installed into His ministerial office by being washed with water as Aaron and his sons washed the Hebrew priests at the door of the tabernacle of the congregation.

And Moses brought Aaron and his sons, and washed them with water. (Leviticus 8:6)

Our Lord showed us the way we must follow: Through Trinitarian baptism we enter the one, holy, catholic, and apostolic Church. As men were admitted into the synagogue (Israel) as Israelites through public circumcision, Christians are admitted into the Church (Israel) through public baptism. When Jesus came out of the water, the Holy Spirit gently descended upon Him like a dove. A voice from heaven said, "This is my beloved Son, in whom I am well pleased."

Therefore we are buried with him by baptism into death: that like as Christ was raised up from the dead by the glory of the Father, even so we also should walk in newness of life. (Romans 6:4)

Jewish Rulers Plotted to Steal Jesus' Inheritance

Israel's stiff-necked Jewish rabbis pushed back against the young Messiah who drew large crowds of adoring and curious followers yearning to see and hear something new and fresh about God.

There was opposition. The Jewish rulers vehemently opposed the Son of God. They are still opposing Him today. Jesus' growing popularity threatened the pious Jewish religious establishment who had a monopoly on religion and its lucrative revenue. They had no intention to share it with an uneducated son of a carpenter from the no-good town of Nazareth who was, according to them, conceived out of wedlock. Regardless, the crowds grew as Jesus proclaimed the kingdom of God. The more Jesus proclaimed the kingdom, the more the priests and Pharisees wanted to kill him. They had to eliminate the competition. They plotted to steal His inheritance.

Jesus' ministry went through the land like a whirlwind. Families were ripped apart, friendships were shattered, and business relationships ruptured by the ensuing controversy over whether Jesus was a profound prophet sent by God or a looney lunatic. As opposition intensified, Jesus did not back off. He did not give people any wiggle room to straddle the fence and play on both sides of the controversy. In fact, he doubled down. He warned people that associating with Him would cost them dearly. They risked being disowned and rejected by their closest family members.

For I am come to set a man at variance against his father, and the daughter against her mother, and the daughter in law

against her mother in law. And a man's foes shall be they of his own household. He that loveth father or mother more than me is not worthy of me: and he that loveth son or daughter more than me is not worthy of me. And he that taketh not his cross, and followeth after me, is not worthy of me. He that findeth his life shall lose it: and he that loseth his life for my sake shall find it. (Matthew 10:35-39)

His comments hearkened back to the words of the Old Testament prophet Micah. He too lived in an age of universal corruption. Nobody could be trusted. No relationship was secure, not even blood family members. Prophetically, Micah described the same state of universal lawlessness that Apostle Paul told Timothy would characterize the world in the last days.

For the son dishonoreth the father, the daughter riseth up against her mother, the daughter in law against her mother in law; a man's enemies are the men of his own house. (Micah 7:6)

Bold, fearless preaching of the gospel of the Kingdom of God automatically results in division among the hearers. Some believe God's word, others reject it. Some who reject it revolt against those who believe it. Their love of sin, lusts, sensual pleasures, idols, liquor, drugs, superstitions, power, social status, and money compel them to attack people who are willing to surrender their sins to the lordship of Jesus Christ. Consequently, there will be continuous contentious conflicts between the two groups. Stubborn goats fight with docile sheep. Rebellious sinners are offended by repentant sinners who submit their lives to God and turn away from their wicked ways. Instead of confronting their own sins, they attack the disciples of Jesus who obey Him in thought, word, and deed by living holy lives in the sight of God.

The Gospel of the Prince of Peace Causes Division

How ironic is it that the Prince of Peace causes commotion and division everywhere His gospel is proclaimed? Jesus said there are two groups of people in the world: People who are with Him, and people who are against Him. Whoever is not with Jesus is automatically against Him. And whoever does not assist Jesus in gathering lost souls into His kingdom is automatically helping Satan scatter lost souls to damnation.

He that is not with me is against me: and he that gathereth not with me scattereth. (Luke 11:23)

There's no middle ground. His demand for fidelity and loyalty are much greater than most modern Christians realize. Jesus espouses the same demand for loyalty as did his Old Testament namesake Joshua who shouted to the Hebrews to choose the god they would serve. Interestingly, Joshua accused the Hebrews of worshiping false gods before Noah's Flood! There was no waffling in Joshua's mind. He served the God of Moses who delivered the Hebrews out of Egypt.

And if it seem evil unto you to serve the Lord, _choose you this day whom ye will serve;_ whether the gods which _your fathers served that were on the other side of the flood,_ or the gods of the Amorites, in whose land ye dwell: _but as for me and my house, we will serve the Lord._ (Joshua 24:15)

Yes, it is true that Jesus did not come the first time to judge sinners. His first visitation to earth was to save mankind, but His second visitation will be to judge mankind. Almighty God's sin amnesty disappears the moment the Final Day appears. There will be no gap between God's two economies. The transition from mercy to judgment is instantaneous. Only God the Father knows when it will happen. Apostle Peter said God's patience is longsuffering because He is not willing that any soul perish, but desires that all humans come to Him in a humble spirit of repentance. The door to God's mercy and forgiveness, however, will violently slam shut on the first second of the Final Day, never to open again for any human pleading for Yahweh to spare them from the endless agony of Hell. Now is the accepted time. Now is the day of salvation.

As opposition to His message intensified, Jesus not only doubled down in His rhetoric, He cranked it up too. He told the people that He came to send fire upon the earth, and He wished it was already burning! How more radical could he talk? Today, he would be tracked by law enforcement agencies as a dangerous revolutionary. Jesus would be banned from social media platforms for spewing violent, inflammatory "hate speech." His bank account would be frozen, and his assets seized on criminal charges of domestic terrorism.

I am come to send fire on the earth; and what will I, if it be already kindled? But I have a baptism to be baptized with; and how am I straitened till it be accomplished! (Luke 12:49-50)

In various Bible scriptures, fire represents adversity or persecution. It also signifies holy zeal for God. To paraphrase the Lord's remarks, Jesus said, "I came to send fire on the earth, and oh how I wish it was already burning!"

At first, His words appear to be a strange utterance from the Son of God. He said it immediately after talking about the faithful and wise servant, and the unfaithful and foolish servant. Speaking of the last days, Jesus said the faithful and wise servant will be found serving "meat in due season" when the master of the house returns. The unfaithful, foolish servant will not prepare himself for the master's return. Such a person shall be severely punished because he knew the Lord's will but did not do it.

There are instances in the Gospels when the Last Adam's sacred humanity was briefly unveiled. Jesus gave us a glimpse of his feelings, the innermost thoughts of His compassionate heart when He wished the fire was already burning on earth. He mentioned a baptism that He had to experience, and that He was determined to carry on His ministry until the baptism was accomplished.

It was His baptism in blood on the Cross! Gazing into the future, Jesus' humanity shone through His words as he contemplated the terror of the cruel crucifixion the Jews and Romans were preparing for Him. He had to get through it. As God, He could endure the cross. As a man, He dreaded the crucifixion's awful pain and agony. Yet, Jesus was determined to successfully complete His mission.

There could be no salvation for fallen humanity if there was not a resurrection. There could be no resurrection if there was not a death. There could be no death if there was not a crucifixion. There would be no crucifixion if there was not a sacrificial lamb on Passover. There would be no sacrifice if Jesus did not willingly go to Jerusalem to be killed by the Jews and Romans. It had to be done!

He longed to get it done and over with, and to unleash the holy fire of the gospel of the kingdom of God. His suffering on the cross would kindle the fire that would perpetually burn around the world until He comes again. Jesus also knew that the preaching of the gospel would start the process of separating goats and sheep. Nations, cities, towns, neighborhoods, and families would be split apart over their allegiance to or rejection of Him. The fiery gospel will burn until the Final Day, dividing and separating people. This fire does not originate on earth. It is a holy fire sent from Heaven!

Suppose ye that I am come to give peace on earth? I tell you, Nay; but rather division: for from henceforth there shall be five in one house divided, three against two, and two against three. The father shall be divided against the son, and the son against the father; the mother against the daughter, and the daughter against the mother; the mother in law against her daughter in law, and the daughter in law against her mother in law. (Luke 12:51-53)

Jesus foreknew that the unleashed gospel would incense the world to strike against all people who declare their allegiance to Him. Rebellious reprobates gleefully slander, revile, persecute, attack, imprison, even kill the devout Christian saints. Before the Final Day arrives, Christians will be persecuted and hated in every nation. Only those who endure to the end shall be saved.

And ye shall be hated of all men for my name's sake: but he that endureth to the end shall be saved. (Matthew 10:22)

Then shall they deliver you up to be afflicted, and shall kill you: and ye shall be hated of all nations for my name's sake. (Matthew 24:9)

How strange is it that the gospel of peace provokes hatred and violence everywhere it goes? Jesus knew that the introduction of the New Covenant gospel would spread like a holy fire through nations as the apostles and disciples obeyed his great commission to go into all the world and preach the gospel of the kingdom of God, making disciples of all people, and baptizing converts in the name of the Father, and the Son, and the Holy Spirit. The gospel, however, had to clash with the world's love of sin. Indeed, if there is no opposition, the true gospel has not been preached.

The Final Day Shall Come When the Gospel is Preached in All the World

The Final Day shall come when this gospel of the kingdom - the gospel that causes division, strife, fire, and persecution! - shall be preached in all the world for a witness unto all nations.

And this gospel of the kingdom shall be preached in all the world for a witness unto all nations; and then shall the end come. (Matthew 24:15)

Why is the preaching of the gospel a witness unto all nations? It constitutes evidence placed in their legal file folders in Heaven's Court to be opened on the Final Day. Jesus said his holy angels will gather all the nations before him on the Final Day. He will separate the people in each nation into two groups: Jesus' sheep and Satan's goats. They will be questioned by the Great Prosecutor. Each nation's legal folder will contain evidence that the gospel of the kingdom was preached within their respective borders. Enoch, Methuselah, and Noah preached the gospel before the Great Flood. Apostle Paul wrote that the gospel was preached unto Abraham too.

And the scripture, foreseeing that God would justify the heathen through faith, preached before the gospel unto Abraham, saying, In thee shall all nations be blessed. (Galatians 3:8)

Therefore, no human since the beginning of time will have an excuse on the Final Day to escape their rightful guilty verdict. They were offered mercy and forgiveness during the long sin amnesty but rejected it when they rejected Jesus. The Judge shall swiftly render a judgment. The court's angelic bailiffs will promptly carry out the Judge's sentence upon the guilty. They shall be bundled and burned.

When the Son of man shall come in his glory, and all the holy angels with him, then shall he sit upon the throne of his glory:

and before him shall be gathered all nations: and he shall separate them one from another, as a shepherd divideth his sheep from the goats: and he shall set the sheep on his right hand, but the goats on the left. (Matthew 25:31-33)

How long shall this final judgment take? Puny men cannot fathom God's magnificence and the greatness of His stupendous plan. When Jesus returns on the Final Day, time will cease to exist in its present form. Jesus doesn't wear a Rolex. Mankind's fixed measurements of time shall instantly cease. The second coming has no seconds. Neither is the Final Day a day. It will only be now! The Final Day's length of time, as we presently know it, will be as short or long as necessary for Almighty God to do all that His Word says will happen when Jesus Christ returns. Seconds, minutes, hours, days, months, years, and millenniums will cease to exist. Apostle Peter was speaking of the Final Day when He wrote:

But, beloved, be not ignorant of this one thing, that one day is with the Lord as a thousand years, and a thousand years as one day. (2 Peter 3:8)

The great I Am shall preside on a great white throne. Earth and heaven will vanish from His face because there will no longer be a place for them in His new world order. The books will be opened, including the book of life. The sea, and death and Hell will surrender to God the dead which were in them. Based on the words written in those books, the dead shall be judged according to their works on earth. Death and hell shall be cast into the Lake of Fire. Every human whose name was not found in the book of life will be tossed in there too.

And I saw a great white throne, and him that sat on it, from whose face the earth and the heaven fled away; and there was

found no place for them. And I saw the dead, small and great, stand before God; and the books were opened: and another book was opened, which is the book of life: and the dead were judged out of those things which were written in the books, according to their works. And the sea gave up the dead which were in it; and death and hell delivered up the dead which were in them: and they were judged every man according to their works. And death and hell were cast into the lake of fire. This is the second death. And whosoever was not found written in the book of life was cast into the lake of fire. (Revelation 20:11-15)

The judgment seat of Christ, a great white throne, a book of life, an examination and verdict of every person's lie on earth, eternal life for some, eternal damnation for others - oh my, it sounds very judgmental! Apostle Paul said "we must all appear before the judgment seat of Christ." The definition of "must" means "to be required or compelled to, as by the use or threat of force." Attendance before the judgment seat of Christ is mandatory. Each person who ever lived shall justly receive from God appropriate rewards or punishments based on the things done while their soul dwelt in their physical body on earth. What has your body done? The time for repentance is now.

For we must all appear before the judgment seat of Christ; that every one may receive the things done in his body, according to that he hath done, whether it be good or bad. (2 Corinthians 5:10)

Our "idle words" shall be judged too. What are idle words? It means useless talk. Pointless, useless, spontaneous banter that has no purpose, nor produces anything good. It also includes false, malicious, slanderous statements that injure others. Human beings were made in the God's image. God spoke the universe into existence.

Words have power. Humans, however, waste much of their lives uttering words that are contrary to the Word of God. Jesus did not say we will be condemned for our "idle words." Instead, He said we shall give an account to God for such talk.

But I say unto you, That every idle word that men shall speak, they shall give account thereof in the day of judgment. (Matthew 12:36)

Judge Jesus Will Preside on the Final Day

The Judge will do all the judging on Judgment Day. The judge is Jesus. Because the Son of God is also the Son of Man, our Heavenly Father has given Jesus Christ high and sovereign power to govern all things, and to sit on the great white throne to judge all secrets in the hearts of men and women. He shall judge us according to the word of the truth of the Gospel. The courtroom examination will include more than our outward deeds and words. The Judge will introduce into our trial all of our secret and hidden thoughts, desires, and motives - both good and evil. Apostle Paul said the secrets of our heart shall be made manifest "in the day when God shall judge the secrets of men by Jesus Christ" according to His gospel. Thus, our true character shall be on display for all to see.

A Final Day judgment of our lives on earth is not a new concept introduced by early Christianity. Knowledge of it existed since the fall of Adam and Eve. King Solomon wrote about it.

For God shall bring every work into judgment, with every secret thing, whether it be good, or whether it be evil. (Ecclesiastes 12:14)

Fortunately for fallen humanity, there is Good News for repentant sinners who place their faith in Jesus Christ and know they are justified because of what Jesus did for them on the Cross.

If you live by faith in Jesus Christ knowing that you are justified by Him and made righteous (meaning, in right standing with God), you will finish your journey by still having faith in King Jesus. You will stand before the judgment seat of Christ justified by His righteousness! You will not be condemned for sins you committed on earth because there is now no condemnation for those who are in Christ Jesus. The Judgment Seat of Christ is not the place where salvation is awarded or denied. That determination is done by humans while alive on earth based on how they responded to the gospel. For Believers, our sins will be revealed at the judgment seat of Christ as transgressions forgiven by God, washed away by the blood of the Lamb of God. On that Final Day, all Christians will finally comprehend the fulness of the work of grace that Jesus did for us.

Our court file folder marked "Sins" will be empty because our transgressions were expunged. Expungement means criminal offenses were erased by the court as though they never happened. It is not probation, which means the defendant is guilty of crimes but will not justly serve an appropriate prison sentence. Expungement is much better than probation or even "not guilty." It means that in the eyes of the court no crimes ever occurred! You will be declared sinless!

Our Works on Earth Must Pass the Test of Fire on the Final Day

It will be a different story, however, regarding the court folder marked "works." That folder will not be empty. Our works on earth must pass the test of fire, and our eternal rewards will depend on the results of the fire test.

According to the grace of God which is given unto me, as a wise master builder, I have laid the foundation, and another buildeth thereon. But let every man take heed how he buildeth thereupon. For other foundation can no man lay than that is laid, which is Jesus Christ. Now if any man build upon this foundation gold, silver, precious stones, wood, hay, stubble; every man's work shall be made manifest: for the day shall declare it, because it shall be revealed by fire; and the fire shall try every man's work of what sort it is. (1 Corinthians 3:10-13)

Sins and works are two different matters. The Greek word "ergon," according to Strong's Concordance, means "work, task, employment; a deed, action; that which is wrought or made, a work." It refers to the actions we took, the things we did with the precious time God allotted us over our lifetime. Indeed, this is one of the most significant verses in the Bible about the eternal worth of our works during our lifetime on earth.

God gives all humans the same amount of time: 24 hours each day. Wealthy people do not receive more time than poor people. Successful people do not have more hours each day than non-productive people. Generous people don't have more time than stingy people. Each day has 1,440 minutes. Some people consciously devote their daily allotted minutes to achieving their goals, while others waste away their daily minutes on frivolous matters. Would you insert a rare gold coin into a vending machine for a candy bar or soft drink? That's what we do every time we waste a golden hour on frivolous nonsense.

The quantity of our works shall not be the determining factor when our works are tested by fire. Nor will it be the economic value of our works that count. The only thing that will matter on the Final Day shall be the eternal value of our work on earth. Specifically, a holy fire will test the building materials we used to construct our works that were built upon "the foundation." And what is the foundation? It is the "faith which was once delivered unto the saints." The foundation is the gospel of the kingdom.

Apostle Paul described himself as a "wise master builder" who laid the foundation. Referring to the gospel, the apostle said every man and woman must take heed how he or she builds upon the foundation. The materials available to us to build upon the foundation of the gospel are described symbolically as "gold, silver, precious stones, wood, hay, stubble." Three will quickly go up in smoke. Three will survive the flames, minus some dross that accumulated along the way.

On the Final Day, all of us must watch our life's works, achievements, accomplishments, and use of the precious gift of time be placed in God's crucible. A crucible is the hollow area at the bottom of a furnace where a substance is subjected to extremely high temperatures. What did we do with the precious gospel delivered once unto the saints? What materials did we use to build upon the pure foundation put in place by the apostles? Did we build structures composed of man-made doctrines, errors, or even heresies and idolatry? The fire will reveal the components of our construction materials. Will it sizzle or shine?

In particular, every man and woman involved in Christian ministry must daily ponder the test of fire that awaits them on the Final Day. What was the end result of your preaching, teaching, writing, speaking, and activities in your home, church, ministry, business, and workplace? Did your words truly convict people of the necessity of repenting of their sins and following Jesus? Did your words and works make converts for Christ, or recruits for your denomination? Did you persuade people to become citizens of the kingdom, or patriot activists for your nation? Did your words and actions inspire people to stand for Jesus, or stand for your favorite politician? Did you seek people's votes more than their souls? What were your true motives in religious affairs? Were the things you taught and did in God's name genuine and pure? Did your lifestyle glorify God to the people you met? Did people see Jesus in you? How many lost souls over your lifetime on earth were influenced by you to repent of their sins and believe on the name of Jesus Christ? Did you teach the Apostles' Doctrine or your denomination's doctrines?

Your works are going into the flaming furnace. Will they survive or go up in smoke? Apostle Paul said if our works survive the fiery test, we shall receive an eternal reward from God. Your reward will be the appropriate wages you earned. If our works burn up, our soul will be narrowly saved with great difficulty like a person who must pass through flames to escape from a burning house. Entering the kingdom of God naked and covered in soot is, however, preferable to entering the Lake of Fire fully clothed! Nevertheless, many Christians will sadly leave behind a pile of ashes as a monument to their lives on earth. Their lifetime of toil will be rendered worthless; thus, they shall receive no eternal rewards. They shall eternally pay for their mishandling of the precious things of God while on earth because their rewards will be negligible or nonexistent. Their position in the kingdom of God shall be fixed forever at a lowly state. Other saints will dwell in New Jerusalem at much higher levels based on their works on earth. The quality of your works on earth will follow you for eternity in New Jerusalem. There will be no way to go back to earth to do it again and make things better the second time.

The test of fire of our works on earth shall happen on the Final Day when Jesus Christ suddenly and unexpectedly arrives on clouds of great glory after the sign of the Son of man appears in heaven and the sun, moon, and stars go dark.

If any man's work abide which he hath built thereupon, he shall receive a reward. If any man's work shall be burned, he shall suffer loss: but he himself shall be saved; yet so as by fire. Know ye not that ye are the temple of God, and that the Spirit of God dwelleth in you? If any man defile the temple of God, him shall God destroy; for the temple of God is holy, which temple ye are. (1 Corinthians 3:14-17)

Today's Religious People Behave
Like Ancient Israelites

The day of the Lord is Judgment Day for every human alive and who ever lived. Why are so few professing Christians concerned about it? Fixated on the affairs of daily living, they neither contemplate giving an account of their lives, nor show genuine grief over the fate of billions of lost souls on the Final Day. Why do they show little regard for such weighty matters? Perhaps they are not grieved by knowing that billions of souls are not ready for the Final Day because they too are not ready for it.

They are living carefree lives in the world with little regard about their thoughts, words, and deeds in this life. Multitudes of church members are foolishly following religious hucksters teaching them to pursue worldly gain as the standard to measure God's blessings in their lives. Even worse, church members are divorcing their spouses, watching pornography, committing fornication or adultery, aborting babies to hide their sexual sins, stealing from their employers, swindling money from fellow church members, lying, slandering, reading their horoscope, watching movies that contain violence and nudity and occultism, consuming intoxicating beverages, and a host of other sinful ways. They do it because their church pastor does not preach against such sins. Regardless, all will appear before the Great Judge.

Such Christian church members are no different than the ancient Israelites who freely sinned and went to the temple to tell each other they were saved and delivered because they were God's chosen people. In the days of Jeremiah, the people of Judah greatly grieved the Lord by their sinful ways while deceiving themselves into believing they were saved because of their ethnic race. Nothing has changed over thousands of years. The Jews continue to think today that they are saved because of their race. The temple was destroyed in 70AD and they still don't get it. Some people are slow learners. Even worse, many hardcore Zionist Jews foolishly fantasize about building a third temple.

The prevalent idolatry, sexual lewdness, and dishonesty of the Israelites were more than the Lord could endure. He had enough of their sinful acts. God commanded Jeremiah to deliver a stern message to the Israelites: Amend your ways and stop trusting in your lies. The Lord told the people to stop insulting Him by chanting "the temple of the Lord" when they entered the temple after committing vile sins against God in the privacy of their homes and shops. Yahweh was disgusted with their pious hypocrisy. The priests lied to the people and gave them a false sense of security. God let them know that the sanctity of the Temple did not guarantee them protection from his divine wrath. The guilty would be punished regardless of their Temple attendance.

The word that came to Jeremiah from the Lord, saying, Stand in the gate of the Lord's house, and proclaim there this word, and say, Hear the word of the Lord, all ye of Judah, that enter in at these gates to worship the Lord. Thus saith the Lord of hosts, the God of Israel, Amend your ways and your doings, and I will cause you to dwell in this place. Trust ye not in lying words, saying, The temple of the Lord, The temple of the Lord, The temple of the Lord, are these. (Jeremiah 7:1-4)

How does the behavior and words of ancient rebellious Jews differ from what is said and done in many Christian churches each week? Is it different than a modern-day church deacon or elder committing adultery and idolatry with his eyes by secretly watching pornography in his home on Saturday night, and going to church on Sunday to act religious in front of the congregation? Is it different than a Christian woman who murders the reputations of other Christians by gossiping and slandering them, yet teaches a church Sunday School class about the Sermon on the Mount? Is it different than a church music director attending a Freemason lodge meeting on Tuesday night to pay homage to Baphomet the goat god, and then leading the church worship and praise music on Wednesday night? The porn-consuming deacon, the slanderous Sunday School teacher, and Masonic music director each go to church chanting "The Church of the Lord!" while refusing to repent and turn from their wicked ways.

The Spirit of the Lord is speaking to members of Southern Baptist, Methodist, Church of God, Catholic, Pentecostal, Anglican, Presbyterian, Assemblies of God, Orthodox, Lutheran, Calvary Chapel, Reformed, Charismatic, non-denominational churches, and every other denomination around the world to repent of their sins, and turn from their wicked ways, and stop deceiving themselves by thinking they are saved when they live like the devil. They are defiling the temple of God - their physical bodies. God is calling to them to stop it now. The Final Day is coming! All will stand before the Great Judge.

Behold, ye trust in lying words, that cannot profit. Will ye steal, murder, and commit adultery, and swear falsely, and burn incense unto Baal, and walk after other gods whom ye know not; and come and stand before me in this house, which is called by my name, and say, We are delivered to do all these abominations? (Jeremiah 7:8-10)

God Told Them to Consider Shiloh's Rubble

Jeremiah was a street preacher. He stood at the gate in Jerusalem, most likely the entrance to the inner court, and delivered a doozy of a sermon. It sizzled so much that King Jehoiakim sought to kill him. The fiery prophet flawlessly and fearlessly delivered precisely the words God commanded him to speak to the people of Judah as they flocked to the city on a religious fast day to make their appearance in the temple. The Lord accused the sinful, hypocritical Jews of making the temple a den of thieves. God said, "I have seen it with my own eyes!"

Yahweh gave them an instruction to help them understand what He was saying: "Get on your donkeys and ride over to Shiloh. Look around and tell Me what you see. Try to find the town! It's not there anymore. Consider your ways!"

After the conquest of Canaan, Shiloh was for a brief time the central place of worship of Yahweh, the Holy God of Israel. The

Ark of the Covenant was kept there. Over time, however, Shiloh lost its purity. It was defiled by idolatry, the kidnapping of virgin girls, and the sins of Eli and his sons. Something happened to Shiloh. It was destroyed, perhaps by the Philistines in 1050 BC. When and how Shiloh was destroyed is not the important thing to know. The essential lesson is this: If God destroyed Shiloh (Israel's first holy city), could not the same fate befall Jerusalem?

Is this house, which is called by my name, become a den of robbers in your eyes? Behold, even I have seen it, saith the Lord. But go ye now unto my place which was in Shiloh, where I set my name at the first, and see what I did to it for the wickedness of my people Israel. (Jeremiah 7:11-12)

The people of Judah foolishly believed they would be protected from God in the temple of the Lord they profaned by their vile sins. They believed their own lies. They told themselves that temple attendance counted more than holy living. Their worst sin was religious schizophrenia! They simultaneously worshipped idols and the Holy God of Israel! What were they thinking?

Prior to his temple gate sermon, Jeremiah had already told the people what God decreed for them. He cried out to the "children of Benjamin" to gather themselves "to flee out of the midst of Jerusalem." Why should they flee the holy city? Because "evil appeareth out of the north, and great destruction." God revealed to Jeremiah that Judah would be militarily invaded by a 'great nation" from the north. The invaders were cruel and would show no mercy to the Jews as they captured the city with bows and spears. Their wives, houses, and fields would be seized by the invaders.

Time had run out for Judah. Soon it would be "lights out" for them. Sudden and unexpected judgment would sweep them away in their sins. God repeatedly sent righteous preachers and prophets to warn them, but they stubbornly refused to repent. Oftentimes, the Jews beat or killed God's prophets and watchmen. Why did they do it? They harmed the prophets because they didn't believe God would really do what He threatened to do to the Jews. Therefore, God had no other option but to harshly judge them. Despite repeated warnings, the judgment suddenly and unexpectedly swept them away because the people chose not to listen to God's pleas for repentance. They were spiritually deaf.

Thus saith the Lord, Stand ye in the ways, and see, and ask for the old paths, where is the good way, and walk therein, and ye shall find rest for your souls. *But they said, We will not walk therein.* **Also I set watchmen over you, saying, Hearken to the sound of the trumpet.** *But they said, We will not hearken.* **Therefore hear, ye nations, and know, O congregation, what is among them. Hear, O earth: behold,** *I will bring evil upon this people, even the fruit of their thoughts, because they have not hearkened unto my words, nor to my law, but rejected it.* **(Jeremiah 6:16-19)**

What happened to them? God started their mornings by speaking to them, but they would not answer him. Consequently, the Lord vowed to do to Jerusalem and the temple the same thing He did to Shiloh: They were cast out of the sight of the Lord. The Babylonian army invaded Jerusalem and plundered and defiled Solomon's temple. The war's Jewish survivors were taken to Babylon as slaves.

The Holy God of Israel is still pleading with sinners - Jews and Gentiles - to repent. He is crying out to sinful humans in every nation to ask for the old ways and walk in the good ways where they shall find rest for their souls. The Final Day is coming.

Unrepented sin must be judged. Now is the time of God's gracious and merciful sin amnesty. All sinners must hear His voice pleading with them to act wisely by accepting his merciful offer of forgiveness and eternal salvation.

Come now, and let us reason together, saith the Lord: though your sins be as scarlet, they shall be as white as snow; though they be red like crimson, they shall be as wool. If ye be willing and obedient, ye shall eat the good of the land: but if ye refuse and rebel, ye shall be devoured with the sword: for the mouth of the Lord hath spoken it. (Isaiah 1:18-20)

Pre-Flood Preachers Warned About the Final Day

St. Jude gave us a glimpse into antediluvian history with a fascinating fragment of his knowledge of Enoch's prophecies about the Final Day. Clearly, the apostles and early church fathers possessed knowledge of pre-flood prophecies that have been lost over time. The Bible does not reveal to us how Jude knew these things. Perhaps he possessed an authentic copy of the Book of Enoch or memorized the story that was handed down orally over thousands of years. It doesn't matter. What matters is that the Holy Spirit inspired Jude to write it so we are aware today that such knowledge was commonly known in those days.

Jude's amazing assertion verifies that the first advent of Jesus Christ was revealed to Adam, and the second advent of the Lord was revealed to Enoch! (Enoch was identified by Jude as "seventh from Adam," thus distinguishing him from Cain's son Enoch who was third from Adam.) His reference to Enoch also signifies that God imparted knowledge to mankind after Adam's fall in the Garden that there would be a Final Day when Almighty God returns to earth to eradicate sin from his creation, and to justly judge all unrepentant sinners who joined Satan's rebellion by rejecting the Lordship of Jesus Christ. From age to age, each generation of men and women have known in their hearts there is a holy Creator of the universe. The doctrine of a final judgment has been known since the days of Adam and Eve.

Moses told us in the Book of Genesis that Enoch walked with God and was taken up into Heaven, thus his body never experienced death. Enoch was a righteous man whom God used, along with Noah, to preach repentance to the wicked population dwelling on earth after the fall of Adam and Eve. God has always had a faithful and obedient congregation of saints (true Israel, the Church) representing him on earth preaching repentance, righteousness, holiness, and the Final Day judgment. Such servants are present today on every continent as a witness to all nations in preparation for the Final Day.

Enoch, Noah's great-grandfather, looked beyond the Great Flood which had not yet occurred. The Flood was the first world-wide judgment on sinners, yet Enoch saw the Final Day! According to Jude, Enoch prophesied that the Lord will come with ten thousand angels (thus meaning an innumerable multitude) to execute judgment upon all, and to convince the ungodly of their ungodly deeds and hard words. Among those mentioned are murmurers, complainers, those who seek to fulfill their lusts, people who speak boastful words, and those who desire to be admired.

And Enoch also, the seventh from Adam, prophesied of these, saying, Behold, the Lord cometh with ten thousands of his saints, to execute judgment upon all, and to convince all that are ungodly

among them of all their ungodly deeds which they have ungodly committed, and of all their hard speeches which ungodly sinners have spoken against him. These are murmurers, complainers, walking after their own lusts; and their mouth speaketh great swelling words, having men's persons in admiration because of advantage. (Jude 14-16)

St. Jude, the servant of Jesus Christ and brother of James the Just, said God will come on the Final Day to "execute judgment upon all." The judgment is meant to "convince all that are ungodly among them of all their ungodly deeds which they have ungodly committed, and of all their hard speeches which ungodly sinners have spoken against him."

The "ungodly among them" who commit "ungodly deeds" means people who willfully commit acts they know are sinful, delight in them, and purposefully persevere in committing such sins. Sinners guilty of "hard speeches" against God are blasphemers and all who mock, scoff, and ridicule the Holy Bible, God's laws and ways, righteousness, holiness, and sacred things. Such sinners are "murmurers and complainers" who are never satisfied with the blessings God has bestowed upon them. They always want more, pretentiously believe they are entitled to possess more, and continually express their discontent with their lot in life. They walk after their own lusts. Their mouths speak "great swelling words," meaning they boast of themselves. God will come to execute such people whose thoughts, words, and deeds are continually against the Lord with no fear or regret. Great shall be their eternal agony that commences on the Final Day. Their Final Day horror will never end! Over and over shall their bodies, which will be resurrected unto death on the Final Day, burn up in hell's flames, only to reappear to burn up again and again forever. Their physical bodies are never annihilated by Hell's furious flames but must suffer forever with no hope of escape. What sinful pleasure or unjust gain is worth the pain and anguish?

The Book of Enoch, still accepted to this day by Ethiopia's ancient orthodox churches as inspired canon written by Enoch, declares there shall be "no salvation" for "all of you sinners," but only "a curse." The righteous "elect," however, shall be blessed with "light and joy and peace." The elect "shall inherit the earth." God will bestow wisdom upon the elect, and "they shall all live and never again sin."

The Book of Enoch's first chapter opens with a declaration that the prophecy is written to bless "the elect and righteous, who will be living in the day of tribulation, when all the wicked and godless are to be removed." Therefore, the Book of Enoch refutes James Nelson Darby's false doctrine that Christians will be raptured away and never experience the time of great tribulation. Jesus said it is the wicked who will be taken first by the reapers. The book describes Enoch as "a righteous man, whose eyes were opened by God" to see "the vision of the Holy One in the heavens" which was revealed to him by angels. The angels told him everything, and from them he understood what he was shown and told it was "not for this generation, but for a remote one which is to come."

What did the angels show Enoch? The pre-Flood prophet said "the Holy Great One will come forth from His dwelling, and the eternal God will tread upon the earth, (even) on Mount Sinai." He will "appear in the strength of His might from the heaven of heavens." When God appears on earth again, "all shall be smitten with fear." Even the watchers (angels) "shall quake." Enoch said "great fear and trembling shall seize" the people worldwide. High mountains will shake, and high hills will be made low. Mountains and hills shall melt like wax next to a flame.

Enoch prophesied "the earth shall be wholly rent in sunder," meaning it shall be ripped apart. All the inhabitants living on the earth when the Lord returns shall perish because "there shall be judgment on all" mankind.

O what a different outcome for Christians! Enoch said, "But with the righteous He shall make peace." The Lord "will protect the elect, and mercy shall be upon them." They "shall all belong to God, and they will be prospered, and they shall all be blessed." And God "will help them all," and "light shall appear unto them." God will "make peace with them."

Whether or not you accept the Book of Enoch as inspired scripture, its prophecies resemble Old Testament and New Testament scriptures themes about the Final Day: God will return to earth to judge all sin. The planet will be ripped apart. Mountains and hills shall disappear. The wicked shall be executed. The elect shall be protected by His mercy and blessed by His goodness. God's wrath is for the wicked, not the elect.

St. Jude tells us to remember the "words which were spoken before of the apostles of our Lord Jesus Christ." In particular, he is referring to Paul and Peter who both warned that mockers and scoffers would appear on earth in the runup to the Final Day. Such fools pursue their lusts. They mock holy things, have no fear of God, treat sacred matters with irreverence, laugh at admonitions to repent of their sins, and reject warnings that a day of judgment shall come to mankind. Likewise, they scoff at those who believe on the name of Jesus Christ to save their souls, and eagerly wait for His return to earth. Consumed and driven by their sensual lusts, such men and women separate themselves from God, His commandments, and His holy universal church. Instead, they join themselves with Satan, his demons, and all who do works of iniquity. They consciously choose to be damned.

But, beloved, remember ye the words which were spoken before of the apostles of our Lord Jesus Christ; how that they told you there should be mockers in the last time, who should walk after their own ungodly lusts. These be they who separate themselves, sensual, having not the Spirit. (Jude 17-19)

According to St. Jude, some of these sinners can be saved by making a difference in their lives by showing compassion to them. Others must be saved with fear. They must be pulled out of Hell's fire! All wise farmers know that different crops are harvested with different tools and methods. Christians need discernment to know whether a sinner needs compassion or fear to make the decision to repent and follow Jesus. Isaiah said God will not break a bruised reed, not quench the smoking flax. He shall bring forth judgment unto truth. Jude said some sinners need to be loved into the kingdom, and others need Hell scared out of them.

And of some have compassion, making a difference: and others save with fear, pulling them out of the fire; hating even the garment spotted by the flesh. (Jude 22-23)

The Final Day fire is coming, and the church needs to get busy loving people into the kingdom or pulling them out of Hell. Time is running out!

St. Jude alluded to the warnings by Apostles Paul and Peter about scoffers and mockers in the final days of the age of mankind. Peter said scoffers shall come in the last days, eagerly pursuing their sensual lusts, and mockingly deride the truth that Jesus Christ is coming back to earth. With smirky grins, they obnoxiously ask, "Where is this Jesus you say is coming back?" They jab at Christians by saying, "Nothing has changed since the beginning of the world. Tomorrow will be the same as today." Showing no fear of Almighty God, such insolent men and women will mock devout Christians in the last days, saying "We've heard this stuff all our lives. Now we are old, and nothing happened. I'm going to enjoy life and ignore the religious nuts." St. Peter forewarned us to be ready for them as we approach the Final Day.

This second epistle, beloved, I now write unto you; in both which I stir up your pure minds by way of remembrance: that ye may be mindful of the words which were spoken before by the holy prophets, and of the commandment of us the apostles of the Lord and Savior: knowing this first, that there shall come in the last days scoffers, walking after their own lusts, and saying, Where is the promise of his coming? for since the fathers fell asleep, all things continue as they were from the beginning of the creation. (2 Peter 3:1-4)

People Who Mock the First Day Will Also Mock the Final Day

The Final Day fire is coming, but the proud, haughty, and foolish people of this world do not know it, nor do they desire to know it. Their daily lives are controlled by their stomachs, genitals, digital devices, and bank accounts. Suddenly and unexpectedly, the reapers shall appear and carry them off to the Lake of Fire.

And I will say to my soul, Soul, thou hast much goods laid up for many years; take thine ease, eat, drink, and be merry. But God said unto him, Thou fool, this night thy soul shall be required of

thee: then whose shall those things be, which thou hast provided? (Luke 12:19-20)

According to St. Peter, lack of knowledge or awareness that Jesus Christ is coming will not be the chief reason that people will be deluded. Indeed, it's just the opposite! People willfully choose to be ignorant. They claim the world has been the same since the beginning of time. Their foolishness is the combined product of having no fear of God, their rejection of His word, and their denial that He is the Creator of the universe. In other words, a growing number of people embrace a godless, humanistic worldview that exalts Darwinian evolution to explain how the universe and life began.

Apostle Peter said the earth, heavens and water were created by God's spoken word at Creation. The same word that formed the universe, stars, and planets is the same source of power that unleashed the Great Flood. Looking unto the Final Day, St. Peter said the present heavens and earth are kept preserved now by the same word of God, and reserved to be consumed by fire on the day of judgment and the destruction of wicked humans. Dissolving the universe by fire will not impose upon God's abilities. It will demand no more effort on His part than speaking words like He did to commence the Great Flood.

In these last days, people brazenly deny that another global judgment will strike mankind because they reject the reality of the first worldwide judgment on sinful humanity. If they comprehended the terrible judgment rendered upon mankind by the Great Flood's worldwide wall of water, they would not irreverently and callously disbelieve the Bible's promise of a Final Day flaming flood of fire.

Writing to the church in Rome, Paul the Apostle said "the wrath of God is revealed from heaven against all ungodliness and unrighteousness of men" because God placed inside all humans an innate awareness of the Creator. "From heaven" shows that the judgment is a divinely inflicted penalty against iniquity. "Against all ungodliness and unrighteousness" means the judgment is decreed by the Great Judge of the Universe for offenses against Almighty God and His code of moral behavior. Most humans refuse or neglect to give God the honor, glory, and gratitude that He rightfully deserves. They worship idols and/or the creation, but not the Creator.

Apostle Paul said that the invisible things of God are plainly seen! How can you plainly see invisible things?

The "invisible things of God" refer to the attributes of the Godhead that cannot be perceived by human senses of sight, hearing, touch, smell, and taste. Neither can the invisible things of God be understood by human intellect and reasoning. Yet, Paul said the invisible is visible. As long as there has been a universe, and men and women to observe it, God's existence has been discernable to mankind.

Furthermore, Paul said humans have an understanding of the invisible things of God made possible by the things God made. Creation speaks to mankind every minute of each day: Worship the Creator! Humans can obtain some understanding of God's greatness by beholding, observing, studying, and appreciating the splendor of His creation.

Regardless of atheists' lies, all true sciences are the study of creation. Man is still trying to figure out how the universe came into existence and continues to function with incomprehensible perfect precision and order. Great universities, research laboratories, and space observatories together spend vast amounts of money each year seeking to understand the origin of the universe, the beginning of life, physics, biology, and genetics. European nations invested tens of billions of euros in constructing CERN's Large Hadron Collider and have launched plans to spend more billions of euros to build the Future Circular Collider. Why did scientists construct CERN in Switzerland? They were searching for the God particle! Known as the Higgs boson, the God particle is the elusive boson that is crucial to modern mankind's understanding of the structure of matter.

Many of the greatest minds on earth nobly devote their lives to pursuing knowledge and understanding of the universe, yet steadfastly refuse to acknowledge and glorify the Creator. They proudly boast of their knowledge, not realizing they have become fools. They foolishly seek answers that omit God so that human intelligence can be exalted. Like Nimrod, they are purposely constructing a Babylonian technological ziggurat to reach Heaven and overthrow God. Their technological Tower of Babel, however, will not survive the Final Day's fire.

God's wonderful creation is so stupendous, beautiful, and amazing that even atheists, agnostics, and idol-worshippers know in their hearts that it is too marvelous to have come into existence without a divine designer, yet their carnal minds stubbornly refuse to give God the glory and worship He rightfully deserves from the human creatures He made. Every sunrise and sunset, and snow-covered mountains, rainbows, fields of wildflowers, cheerful songbirds, smiling infants, innocent kittens, deep canyons - all of creation proclaims the glory of God. No excuse will prevail on the Final Day for people to claim they did not know that God exists.

Give God glory now while you have breath and a heartbeat to do it! Our purpose for living is to glorify God.

Hopefully, some may snap out of their delusion before they die or the Lord returns, but most will harden their hearts and stiffen their necks in rebellious opposition to God's sovereign rulership over their lives and the universe. Such rebels will stubbornly set their faces like flint to proudly and defiantly march to Hell. There is no hope for such fools.

For this they willingly are ignorant of, that by the word of God the heavens were of old, and the earth standing out of the water and in the water: whereby the world that then was, being overflowed with water, perished: but the heavens and the earth, which are now, by the same word are kept in store, reserved unto fire against the day of judgment and perdition of ungodly men. (2 Peter 3:5-7)

There is an Appointed Time When the Earth Shall be Destroyed by Fire

Apostle Peter said Christians should not forget an important truth: There is no time in Heaven. One day is the same as a thousand days as far as God is concerned. He is the great I AM! Heaven does not possess, nor does it need, clocks and calendars. Time does not exist in Yahweh's dimension. In fact, God made time for mankind's sake. Apostle Peter also reminded us that God isn't late fulfilling His promises. To men, it appears that God is taking a long time to fulfill Biblical prophecies, meaning the return of Jesus and the consummation of all things. Over 2,000 years have passed in human history since the crucifixion and resurrection of Jesus because God is patient and merciful. He's giving fallen mankind more time (while time still exists) to repent before unleashing His wrath upon unrepentant sinners. God does not desire sinners to perish. He yearns to save all men and women. Despite His patience with sinful humanity, there is an appointed time when the heavens shall disappear, the elements of the universe shall melt, and the earth shall be burned up. When that appointed time arrives, time itself will disappear because humans will no longer need it.

But, beloved, be not ignorant of this one thing, that one day is with the Lord as a thousand years, and a thousand years as one day. The Lord is not slack concerning his promise, as some men count slackness; but is longsuffering to us-ward, not willing that any should perish, but that all should come to repentance. But the day of the Lord will come as a thief in the night; in the which the heavens shall pass away with a great noise, and the elements shall melt with fervent heat, the earth also and the works that are therein shall be burned up. (2 Peter 3:8-10)

St. Peter the Apostle asked a penetrating question: If you understand that everything shall be consumed by fire on the Final Day, what kind of person ought you to be now in your daily living and conversations? How many people ponder this question daily as they interact with others and conduct their affairs in this world?

He said our conversation and behavior must be holy and godly. Apostle Peter further stated that Christians must look for and speed up the coming of the Final Day wherein the heavens shall be dissolved by raging fire and the elements of the universe shall melt with fervent heat. Our anticipation of our Lord's second coming is based on His promise of new heavens and a new earth where the righteous shall dwell with God forever. Seeing that we yearn for such things, St. Peter admonishes the church to be diligent that Jesus Christ shall find each of us on that day to be in peace, without spot, and blameless.

Seeing then that all these things shall be dissolved, what manner of person ought ye to be in all holy conversation and godliness, looking for and hasting unto the coming of the day of God, wherein the heavens being on fire shall be dissolved, and the elements shall melt with fervent heat? Nevertheless we, according to his promise, look for new heavens and a new earth, wherein dwelleth righteousness. Wherefore, beloved, seeing that ye look for such things, be diligent that ye may be found of him in peace, without spot, and blameless. (2 Peter 3:11-14)

God's Warning to the Edomites Who Persecute His People

Based on God's past judgment of nations, we can reasonably conclude that the Final Day will follow established Biblical patterns of divine actions. For example, God judged the kingdom of Idumea, also known as Edom. The Edomites were descendants of Esau, twin brother of Jacob. Jacob's name was changed to Israel, and Esau's name became Edom. God told Ezekiel that the Edomites had a "perpetual hatred" of Israel and used the sword to shed innocent blood. Therefore, a great calamity (judgment) came suddenly and unexpectedly upon the Edomites.

Isaiah called all nations to come and hear, indeed let the earth hear too, how the Lord's indignation burst upon the Edomites. If Isaiah were here today, he would post on social media this message: "Attention all nations! The Great Judge of the universe has issued a court summons. Pay attention to this warning. Almighty God shall judge every nation with the same fury He unleashed upon Edom for making war against His people. Look around. Can you find the kingdom of Edom? It vanished! A worldwide judgment will spring upon all nations suddenly and unexpectedly on the Final Day. The wicked shall be executed with divine swords bathed in blood. The whole earth shall emit a wretched stench coming from their carcasses, and their blood will melt the mountains. The sun, moon, and stars will disappear as violent convulsions reverberate throughout the cosmos. The heavens shall be rolled together like a parchment scroll. The sword of the Lord shall come down on all who persecuted and opposed my Son and His Church. All the inhabitants of the earth will tremble and wail.

Come near, ye nations, to hear; and hearken, ye people: let the earth hear, and all that is therein; the world, and all things that come forth of it. For the indignation of the Lord is upon all nations, and his fury upon all their armies: he hath utterly destroyed them, he hath delivered them to the slaughter. Their slain also shall be cast out, and their stink shall come up out of their carcasses, and the mountains shall be melted with their blood. And all the host of heaven shall be dissolved, and the heavens shall be rolled together as a scroll: and all their host shall fall down, as the leaf falleth off from the vine, and as a falling fig from the fig tree. For my sword shall be bathed in heaven: behold, it shall come down upon Idumea, and upon the people of my curse, to judgment. (Isaiah 34:1-5)

The Old Testament Edomites represent the kingdom of the Son of Perdition, the enemies of the New Testament Church, true Israel. Isaiah prophesied that the Lord's vengeance will be expressed in a day of global judgment, and the year of recompenses for the controversy of Zion. Jeremiah prophesied that a noise shall come even to the ends of the earth; for the Lord has a controversy (a quarrel) with the nations. He will give the wicked to the sword. Hosea said the Lord has a controversy (a quarrel) with all the inhabitants of the land because there is no truth, nor mercy, nor knowledge of God in the land. Micah cried out to the mountains and the foundations of the earth to hear the Lord's controversy (quarrel) with the Jews. Nobody can fathom the awful fury and doom that will strike the enemies of the one, holy, catholic, and apostolic Church - God's true Israel. Her enemies shall be consumed by fire when the Lord returns to deliver the saints. Until the Final Day arrives, however, the Church must patiently wait, even as she is persecuted, for the glorious appearing of our blessed hope.

The King of Kings shall return to earth because His Father has a controversy with the nations, and He's going to end it on His terms. A negotiated settlement with sinful mankind will not be offered. Total surrender will be the only option on the Final Day. Every knee shall bow before His only begotten Son. Jesus will prove that He is the Messiah promised to mankind since Adam's fall in the Garden of Eden, prophesied by the prophets, and proclaimed by the preachers. All liars, deniers, scoffers, mockers, deceivers, and enemies of the Cross who opposed Jesus Christ and His Church shall be permanently silenced.

And the nations were angry, and thy wrath is come, and the time of the dead, that they should be judged, and that thou shouldest give reward unto thy servants the prophets, and to the saints, and them that fear thy name, small and great; and shouldest destroy them which destroy the earth. (Revelation 11:18)

And I heard another out of the altar say, Even so, Lord God Almighty, *true and righteous are thy judgments.* (Revelation 16:7)

The Second Coming of Jesus on the Final Day shall be:

- Singular
- Sudden and unexpected
- Atmospheric
- Visible
- Noisy
- Disruptive
- Fiery
- Glorious
- Judgmental

CHAPTER 12

HIS SECOND COMING
SHALL BE FINAL

D O YOU COMPREHEND THE finality of the Final Day? Final means the end, the termination of something, the conclusion.

What comes to an end? What is terminated? What is concluded on the Final Day?

Life as humans have known it since the Garden of Eden will cease to exist the very moment Jesus Christ enters our dimension. The curtain will fall on the age of mankind, never to be reconstituted in its present state.

It won't only be the age of mankind that ends. The earth, sun, moon, stars - indeed, the entire cosmos - shall vanish forever. Jesus' last words on the Cross were "It is finished." Perhaps when He returns Jesus will take a final look at His universe and declare, "It is finished!"

And he said unto me, It is done. **I am Alpha and Omega, the beginning and the end. I will give unto him that is athirst of the fountain of the water of life freely. (Revelation 21:6)**

Comprehension of the finality of the Final Day is clouded for millions of Evangelical Zionists in the United States of America, and wherever post-Reformation, Zionist-centric, pseudo-Evangelicalism has spread around the world through their missionary endeavors. According to their prophecy teachers, God's prophetic timeline will play out over a span of 1,007 years *before* the start of eternity!

Occultist John Nelson Darby, the chief Evangelical Zionist prophecy guru, crafted his esoteric eschatology in the 19th century to justify the removal of the Christian church from the earth, and the establishment of a political state of Israel so that Zionists could rule the planet from Jerusalem for 1,000 years.

Sadly, Darby's deeply flawed doctrines spread far and wide in the second half of the twentieth century. They infected the minds of millions of sincere Christians who were taught that Darby's Dispensational, Pre-Millennial, Pre-Tribulation, Zionism (DPPZism) is Biblically accurate and in harmony with the Church's teachings since the days of the Apostles.

A second book would be required by this author to fully describe the fallacies of their Darby-inspired cultish doctrines. A cursory examination of their popular prophecy timeline charts quickly reveals a dazzling array of incomprehensible events that they say must happen to fit into Darby's systematic theology. The average Christian cannot comprehend their prophecy timeline charts because it requires many years of cult-like indoctrination to memorize the storyline crafted by the Evangelical Zionists. For most Christians exposed to Darbyism, his end time theology is a ball of tangled knots rolled up inside their brains that make it difficult to see the marvelous simplicity of the second coming of our Lord and Savior Jesus Christ.

Evangelical Zionists' Amazing
End Time Prophecy Predictions

Modern-day rapture sects have competing variations of Darby's End Times model. Although various factions have spun their own versions, the most commonly accepted storyboard is as follows:

- The 70th week of Old Testament prophet Daniel's prophetic vision has been floating in timelessness since 539 BC. According to Evangelical Zionists, God separated the seventieth week from the previous sixty-nine weeks. The long expanse of time is the "church age." (Please recall that DPPZites teach that Israel and the Church are separate entities, and that God formed the Church during a great intermission between Jesus' failure to persuade the Jews to follow Him and the eventual restoration of the Jewish kingdom.) Evangelical Zionists teach that the 70th week does not start until the end of the "church age" at which time God's Heavenly People (saved Gentiles) will be removed from the earth in "The Rapture."

- In His first advent to earth, Jesus failed in His mission to convince the Jews that He was their king.

- The Jews convinced the Romans to crucify Jesus because He claimed to be the Son of God and vowed to destroy the temple.

- God called "time out" on His failed plan to establish the Jewish kingdom. He paused His "prophetic time clock" to give the Jews more time to get ready for their kingdom.

- Realizing His original planned failed, God implemented Plan B. During the intermission, God changed His focus to saving non-Jews (gentiles) until the Jews were ready to accept Jesus as their Messiah and King.

363

- God established "the Church" for gentiles.
- The gentile "church age" has existed for over 2,000 years but will reach its climax when "the times of the gentiles" (the church age) are over and God is ready to return to His main focus: establishing a Jewish empire ruled from Jerusalem, "the eternal capital of Israel."
- God's "prophetic time clock" was restarted on May 8, 1948, when the State of Israel was established in Palestine. (Another DPPZite camp teaches that it will restart after "The Rapture.")
- God's "Heavenly People" (gentile Christians) will be secretly and mysteriously removed from the earth by an appearance of Jesus that cannot be seen by unsaved people. Only "rapture ready" Christians will see Jesus and be snatched up in "The Rapture."
- God's "Heavenly People" will be transported to Heaven to wait out the events that will transpire on earth.
- The unsaved will be "left behind" on earth.
- At this point, life on earth will become weird. Lots of crazy stuff starts happening.
- The Holy Spirit will be removed from the earth.
- Immediately after "The Rapture," the identity of "the Antichrist" will be revealed.
- After the Antichrist is made known, "the Great Tribulation" will begin and last precisely seven years.
- During the seven-year Great Tribulation, "the Antichrist" will implement the Mark of the Beast system of buying and selling.
- The Tribulation Temple will be built by the Jews in Jerusalem.

- The Sanhedrin will restart animal sacrifices in the newly built temple. (You can insert anywhere at this point the appearance of the spotless red heifer. No rapture tale is complete without the red heifer!)
- "The Antichrist" will deceptively sign a peace treaty with the State of Israel that he intends to violate.
- "The Antichrist" will enter the new temple and declare himself as a god, thus desecrating it as the Abomination of Desolation.
- The Seven Seals will be opened by Jesus in Heaven.
- The Four Horsemen of the Apocalypse will start galloping around the world releasing famines, wars, pestilences.
- Cataclysmic natural events will occur on earth. The earth will tremble.
- Martyred souls under the altar in Heaven will cry out for justice.
- 144,000 Jews will be sealed by God to preach to those left behind after the rapture.
- The gospel of the kingdom will not be heard by everybody before "The Rapture." The gospel will be preached to everybody left behind after "The Rapture." The gospel will be preached worldwide by the 144,000 Jewish male virgins. People who missed "The Rapture" when the Evangelical Zionists go to Heaven will have a second chance to be saved before the second coming of Jesus.
- The seven trumpets will sound to start great natural judgments on earth.
- Hail and fire mixed with blood will pummel the people on earth.
- A burning mountain will be thrown into the sea.

- The star Wormwood will strike the seas.
- A third of the sun, moon, and stars will go dark.
- A mighty plague of locusts will be unleashed to torment mankind.
- Four Angels will be released.
- Two Jewish witnesses will be killed in the streets of Jerusalem.
- There will be great woe on earth and worship in Heaven.
- A war will erupt in Heaven.
- Satan will fall from Heaven.
- The Beast will rise from the sea.
- Another Beast will rise from the earth.
- The Seven Bowls will be poured out onto the earth.
- Seas, rivers, and streams will turn to blood.
- The Sun will scorch people with fire.
- Darkness will cover the earth.
- The Euphrates River will dry up.
- 200,000,000 soldiers will march across the dried Euphrates riverbed.
- A river of blood will flow 200 miles long, as high as a horse bridle.
- A massive worldwide earthquake will rip apart the planet.
- Major armies of the world will surround the political State of Israel in the Middle East.
- The Battle of Armageddon will commence. The State of Israel will be the center of the massive military conflict. Israel will not have the military might to defeat its enemies.
- Realizing their fate is doomed without a miracle, the Israeli Jews will have a "come to Jesus moment" and cry out to

Jesus to save them. Millions of Israelis will suddenly become Messianic Jews. (No explanation about what happens to Jews in Miami, Los Angeles, New York City, and London. Do they survive the calamities that strike the earth before the Armageddon war? If not, will their souls be saved?)

- False religion will collapse.
- Babylon will be destroyed. (Most DPPZites believe that the Roman Catholic Church is Babylon.)
- At this point in time, the Second Coming of Jesus (which the DPPZites say is different from the Rapture) will occur to save the Jews, punish the enemies of Israel, destroy "the Antichrist," and defang the Beast.
- Jesus will inaugurate "The Millennial Kingdom" - a 1,000-year Jewish kingdom on earth headquartered in Jerusalem. Jews get more land than the West Bank, Gaza, and East Jerusalem. They now own the entire planet!
- The human population during the Millennial Kingdom will be composed of three groups: Heavenly People, Earthly People, and Tribulation Saints. (You may need a diagram to sort out this stuff.) The Heavenly People are the Evangelical Zionists who go to Heaven in "The Rapture" before "The Great Tribulation." The Earthly People are the Jews. The Tribulation Saints are the sinners who will be saved by the preaching of the 144,000 Jewish male virgins during "The Great Tribulation" which will last for seven years.
- The Heavenly People (Evangelical Zionists) who go to Heaven in "The Rapture" will receive their glorified bodies. The Jews (Earthly People) will receive their glorified bodies at the Second Coming of Jesus which will occur seven years

367

after "The Rapture" of Evangelical Zionists. The Tribulation Saints (people who will be saved during "The Great Tribulation") will receive their glorified bodies a thousand years after the Second Coming. (Some Rapture cultists teach that the Jews will not receive their glorified bodies until the end of the 1,000 years, but will rule the earth anyway because they are Jews.)

- The Tribulation Saints are saved mortals without glorified bodies who will go through all the natural life cycles: grow, mature, age, marry, procreate, die.

- Babies born during the Millennial Kingdom will inherit the Adamic fallen nature, meaning they will commit sins.

- Tribulation Saints without glorified bodies will rapidly replenish the earth with unsaved children over 1,000 years. There could be billions of them by the end of the Millennial Kingdom.

- Jesus will rule the Tribulation Saints with an iron scepter to keep them under control because they will live in natural bodies with their fallen Adamic sin nature.

- Because there will be tens of millions - possibly billions - of Tribulation Saints and their offspring living in their sinful natural bodies that are not glorified, Jewish priests will be needed to intercede to Jesus on their behalf. Therefore, there will be rampant sin throughout the Millennial Kingdom. Jesus will have a mess to deal with for a thousand years. His second coming will not fix the sin problem.

- Things get worse: Satan will be turned loose near the end of the Millennium to deceive people again. (There is debate among DPPZites over whether Heavenly People (Evangelical

Zionists) and Earthly People (Jews) can be deceived by Satan at the end of the millennium. Some DPPZites believe that only the offspring of Tribulation Saints living in their mortal human bodies will be vulnerable to Satan's deception.)

- Satan gathers a vast number of saved people without glorified bodies for one final, big rebellion against God. No kidding! DPPZites teach that people will fight against God after the Second Coming of Jesus! Many will turn against God despite living on earth with Jesus for 1,000 years.

- God will stop the rebellion by sending fire from Heaven.

- Satan will be defeated again.

- Graves will be opened and all unsaved people will be called out of the ground and sea. (DPPZites say this happens at the end of the 1,000-year kingdom!)

- Unsaved people will stand before the Great White Throne of Judgment.

- God's "Heavenly People" will not be present for the reading from the books of judgment.

- Unsaved sinners will be cast into the Lake of Fire.

- Satan cast into the Lake of Fire.

- Death and Hades will be cast into the Lake of Fire.

- God will renovate the old earth and makes it "new." He does not destroy the earth with fire, but gives the old planet a total makeover by patching the holes in the earth's crust made by the mega-earthquakes and nuclear explosions, and by slapping a new coat of paint on the surface to make everything green again.

- The New Jerusalem will come down from Heaven to the newly decorated earth.

Wow! Is your head spinning? An obsession with wild and elaborate prophecy timelines as described above is akin to watching action movies that are 90% dazzling, stunning special effects. Your eyes are fixated on monsters, meteors, and mayhem. After leaving the theater you can't explain the film's storyline to your friends. All you can talk about are monsters, meteors, and mayhem.

Do you desire to know this author's prophetic timeline? Here it is: JESUS!

The Final Day is all about Jesus Christ, the glorious Messiah, Savior, Son of God, King of Kings, and Lord of Lords. If you take your eyes off the star of the show, you will only see the clowns. The purpose of clowns is to divert the audience's attention long enough for something else to be ready to happen on the main stage. Stay focused on Jesus Christ until the end. He is the main attraction. Everything else is a distraction.

Four Ways Not to Read the Apocalypse

Sadly, the proliferation of "End Time" ministries in recent decades has contributed to a disturbing misunderstanding and misuse of the word "apocalypse." It does not mean the cataclysmic destruction of the earth. People often describe natural calamities and disasters as "apocalyptic." Apocalypse simply means the unveiling (the revealing) of somebody or something. The Holy Bible's final book is the Apocalypse, or the Book of the Revelation of Jesus Christ. The book does not reveal "apocalyptic" destruction in the Last Days. It reveals Jesus Christ and His holy Church to mankind.

People who sincerely believe the grandiose prophecy timeline as described above, or some variation of it, commit four serious errors in their reading and interpretation of the Apocalypse: They read the Book of the Revelation of Jesus Christ in a literal, linear, chronological, and futuristic manner.

First, Evangelical Zionists mistakenly read the Apocalypse literally. Thus, you must believe that an actual physical monster will rise from the ocean, and the beast must have seven heads, tens horns, and ten crowns. You must also believe there will be four literal horsemen on galloping horses crisscrossing the planet unleashing war, famines, and mayhem everywhere they travel. Furthermore, you must literally believe a strange hybrid critter shall appear that looks like a leopard, has feet like a bear, and a lion's mouth. Clearly, these things are symbolic representations of real things. The Apocalypse uses images, symbols, pictures, and figures to describe literal events and to convey literal truth. You must, however, discern when the Apocalypse uses symbols and images to describe things that are literal.

Second, Evangelical Zionists mistakenly use a linear method to read the Revelation of Jesus Christ. A linear reading can be deceiving. "Linear" pertains to lines and length. For example, a line that starts on the left side extends to its end on the right side. Your eyes are following a straight line from left to right. That's linear thinking. Thus, rapture enthusiasts read the Apocalypse from left to right, seeing its contents only as a sequence of spectacular events. Linear thinking easily leads people to the third error.

Third, Evangelical Zionists emphatically insist that the events in the Book of the Revelation of Jesus Christ are in chronological order. If Event A is in Chapter One and Event E is in Chapter Three, it must mean that Events B, C, and D follow Event A and precede Event E. Right? Wrong! The Apocalypse is not a chronological timeline of futuristic events. Apostle John described things he had already seen, things "which are" happening in his time, and things "which shall be hereafter." John of Patmos placed these events into four categories to describe them to readers: seven seals, seven trumpets, seven thunders, and seven vials. Each category has a different length of time to be fulfilled. Some are fulfilled over a short timeline. Some are fulfilled over a long timeline. Some short timeline prophecies are embedded inside long timeline prophecies. Reading the Apocalypse in a chronological order limits the reader from seeing the vision's big picture.

Fourth, Evangelical Zionists are religious futurists. They see most prophecies as future events. They mistakenly interpret the Book of the Revelation of Jesus Christ as apocalyptic predictions of future events linked to world news. What they miss is the realization that some things in the Apocalypse have already occurred, some are happening as we live, and other things shall be fulfilled before the end of the age of mankind. The Apocalypse is a true story spread across thousands of years.

Many people also fail to grasp the principle of dual fulfillment, meaning some prophecies have a short-term and a long-term fulfillment. People who are always waiting on prophecies to be fulfilled in the future often miss how a prophecy was already fulfilled. Instead, they devote endless hours talking about "prophecies in the news," but neglect to live out prophecy now by letting Jesus Christ rule and reign in and through them today to establish and expand the kingdom of God on earth. They are always waiting for "something big to happen" on earth in the future, but they seldom do anything meaningful on earth now for God's kingdom. They fool themselves into believing that their present-day obsession with the future is a legitimate ministry for God. In truth, it is an inexcusable waste of precious time that could be devoted to preaching the Gospel in all nations, and feeding the hungry, giving water to the thirsty, clothing the naked, and visiting sick people in hospitals and inmates in prison. Few, if any, sinners have been saved while attending a Bible prophecy conference, but the rapture industry has generated billions of dollars in revenue over the last 50 years.

Today's Evangelical Zionists eerily resemble yesterday's Pharisees. The Pharisees knew the scriptures. They memorized the Messianic prophecies and could talk for hours about their understanding of the coming Messiah. Yet, when the Messiah arrived and stood there in front of the Jewish religious rulers, they argued with Jesus! They told Jesus that they knew more than Him about the coming Messiah. Israel's religious leaders made a career talking about the Messiah, but they totally missed Him when He arrived. Sadly, many Evangelical Zionists leaders may miss the Messiah the second time He arrives. They are obsessed with "The Rapture" and the State of Israel, not the Second Coming of Jesus Christ and His kingdom.

The Apocalypse is God's Love Story

The best way to read and interpret Apostle John's vision is to see it as God's love story about the Church. The Book of the Revelation of Jesus Christ (the Apocalypse) reveals God's extraordinary love of human beings, and His mercy and grace to redeem them from the fall of mankind in the Garden of Eden. That's why the Bible starts in Genesis with God living with humans in the first Garden of Eden and concludes in the Apocalypse with God living with humans in the last Garden of Eden. The tree of life is in the Garden of Eden and New Jerusalem.

The Apocalypse is the Revelation of Jesus Christ, not the Revelation of Scary End Time Prophecies. It's all about Jesus! The entire Bible - Old and New testaments - is about Jesus Christ. It's not about ancient Israel. It is about the Ancient of Days! It is not only about the Jews in the modern State of Israel who have been circumcised in their flesh. It is about all true Israelites whose hearts have been circumcised - the people of the promise, the call-out ones, the ecclesia - who have followed and obeyed God by faith throughout the ages since the Book of Genesis. Reading it in a literal, linear, chronological, futuristic manner blinds the eyes of readers from beholding the beauty of God's love story.

Old Testament prophet Daniel saw the wonderful end of the story too. Daniel saw the majestic and triumphant King Jesus Christ coming with the clouds of heaven as the Son of Man, meaning the Judge of mankind. He approached the Ancient of Days who gave His Son dominion, and glory, and a kingdom, that all people, nations, and languages should serve Him forever.

I beheld till the thrones were cast down, and the Ancient of days did sit, whose garment was white as snow, and the hair of his head like the pure wool: his throne was like the fiery flame, and his wheels as burning fire. A fiery stream issued and came forth from before him: a thousand thousands ministered unto him, and ten thousand times ten thousand stood before him: the judgment was set, and the books were opened. I beheld then because of the voice of the great words which the horn spake: I beheld even till the beast was slain, and his body destroyed, and given to the burning flame. As concerning the rest of the beasts, they had their dominion taken away: yet their lives were prolonged for a season and time. I saw in the night visions, and, behold, one like the Son

of man came with the clouds of heaven, and came to the Ancient of days, and they brought him near before him. And there was given him dominion, and glory, and a kingdom, that all people, nations, and languages, should serve him: his dominion is an everlasting dominion, which shall not pass away, and his kingdom that which shall not be destroyed. (Daniel 7:9-14)

The Day of the Lord is the Final Day of the long saga that began at Creation. It is about Jesus Christ ushering in the finality of the age of mankind, conquering death and Hades, making His enemies His footstool, casting Satan into the everlasting lake of fire, receiving His inheritance (saved souls), presenting the kingdom back to our Heavenly Father, the consummation of all things, and restoring saved humanity to the Garden of Eden to dwell forever with God the Father, the Son, and Holy Spirit in New Jerusalem on the new earth.

The Final Day Shall Be Like a Thief in the Night

Many Evangelical Zionists mistakenly think that Jesus is the thief who comes in the night. Not so! Apostle Peter said, "the day of the Lord will come as a thief in the night." The day of the Lord is the Final Day. It is the Lord's sudden and unexpected arrival (Parousia) that ushers in the Final Day. The Final Day is the grand finale of the age of mankind. It includes the Second Advent of Jesus Christ, the darkening of the cosmos, the opening of the graves, the bundling of the wicked to be burned, the catching up of the saints to meet the Lord in the air, the gathering of all humanity by respective nations, the separation of souls as goats and sheep, the great throne of judgment, the testing of the saints' works on earth, the rolling up of the universe as a scroll, the melting of the elements of the universe, the burning of the earth, the creation of a new earth and heavens, the arrival of New Jerusalem, the restitution of all things, and the start of eternity with God.

The Final Day will explode suddenly and unexpectedly upon mankind and this rebellious world. For the wicked and unprepared, the day of the Lord will come as a thief breaking down their backdoor after midnight. They will be snoring away their lives in a deep state of spiritual delusion, unaware that time has run out for sinful humanity.

But the day of the Lord will come as a thief in the night; in the which the heavens shall pass away with a great noise, and the elements shall melt with fervent heat, the earth also and the works that are therein shall be burned up. (2 Peter 3:10)

Immediately the heavens shall pass away with a great noise, and the elements shall melt with fervent heat, and the earth and everything built upon it shall be incinerated by fire. Take heed! There will be no secret rapture, no seven years of tribulation, no second chance to be saved, no third temple and animal sacrifices, no 1,000 year Jewish kingdom, no babies born in a millennial kingdom, no people living in natural bodies with the Adamic sin nature, and no second chance for Satan to deceive the nations. There will only be the sudden arrival of Jesus Christ to gather His sheep and establish His everlasting Kingdom.

Satan's Wrath Against the Church

Before Jesus arrives, however, there will be vicious, ruthless, violent, and intense Satanic persecution of the saints before the Final Day. Its duration will be an unknown number of days of great tribulation. Jesus never said it will last precisely seven years. The seven-year number is a concoction of John Nelson Darby which he achieved by pasting together Old Testament and New Testament scriptures to make them say something that isn't there. That's classic Darbyism!

What did Jesus say?

...for then shall be great tribulation, such as was not since the beginning of the world to this time, no, nor ever shall be. And except those days should be shortened, there should no flesh be saved: but for the elect's sake those days shall be shortened. (Matthew 24:21-22)

Jesus did not say "for then shall be the Great Tribulation that shall last seven years." He said there will be "great tribulation" such as was not since the beginning of the world to this time, nor shall ever be again. His prophecy is an example of dual fulfillment. Jesus referred both to the fall of Jerusalem in 70AD, and the days of trouble immediately preceding the Second Coming of the Lord. His comment about great tribulation was in response to three questions asked by His disciples: When will the temple be destroyed? What are the signs of the end of the age? What are the signs of your second coming?

The tribulation spoken of by Jesus in the New Testament scriptures parallels Daniel's vision in Old Testament scriptures. He too saw an unparalleled time of trouble coming to the world "such as never was since there was a nation even to that same time." Michael the Archangel told Daniel that "his people shall be delivered, every one that shall be found written in the book," meaning the Book of Life.

And at that time shall Michael stand up, the great prince which standeth for the children of thy people: and there shall be a time

of trouble, such as never was since there was a nation even to that same time: and at that time thy people shall be delivered, every one that shall be found written in the book. (Daniel 12:1)

Nobody can imagine or accurately describe the persecution that Satan will unleash upon Christ's Church in the final days of the world. It will be the great climax of the age of mankind, the culmination of Satan's war against God that started when Lucifer tempted Eve to sin against God in the Garden of Eden.

And the dragon was wroth with the woman, and went to make war with the remnant of her seed, which keep the commandments of God, and have the testimony of Jesus Christ. (Revelation 12:17)

This book's author believes, but humbly acknowledges other interpretations as deserving equal consideration, that the woman in Revelation 12:17 represents four referents: Eve, Israel, Mary, and the Church. The seed is singular, not plural. Thus, the seed is Jesus. The remnant of her seed represents all Christians throughout the ages, the Church Triumphant and the Church Militant.

Evangelical Zionists adamantly insist they will be taken away by "The Rapture" to escape "The Great Tribulation." For the record, they accurately teach that God's wrath is not stored up for Christians. This author wholeheartedly agrees. Their fanatical devotion to "The Rapture" doctrine and their prophecy timeline charts, however, blinds them from seeing the simplicity of how Christians will be spared from God's wrath.

Their Rube Goldberg contraption has innumerable moving parts that must be meticulously and perfectly synchronized to make their marvelous wonder machine work as they envision. If one cog fails to function precisely on time, none of their Amazing Prophecy Machine's components will work as they promise.

Currently, at the time of this book's publication in 2020, Evangelical Zionists are seeking to orchestrate the building of the "Tribulation Temple" in Jerusalem. Without a third temple, their "Antichrist" boogeyman cannot go into it and proclaim himself as a god (an event that Evangelical Zionists insist will happen). They also eagerly anticipate a war with Iran, a tragic event that has not yet happened at the time of this book's publication. They foolishly think God needs their help to fulfill Biblical prophecies. Therefore, Evangelical Zionists enthusiastically support radical Zionist Jews who scorn the name of Jesus, seek to regain the territory of ancient Greater Israel, build a third temple in Jerusalem, and restart animal sacrifices. These Zionist goals are blasphemous and repugnant to Almighty God. Disciples of Christ should plead with Jews to stop rebelling against God, denying the name of Jesus as their Savior, and seeking an earthly Jewish kingdom. Jesus Christ is our Promised Land. He is our temple. He is the Lamb of God sacrificed once to take away the sins of the world.

Evangelical Zionists mistakenly confuse tribulation with wrath. Tribulation means calamity and suffering. Wrath means violent, passionate punishment. Satan's wrath will bring great tribulation upon the saints. God's wrath shall bring great tribulation upon the wicked. The saints will not be delivered from Satan's wrath. The wicked will not be delivered from God's wrath. The saints will be instantly removed from the earth immediately before the wrath of God is poured out upon the wicked. Satan's kingdom shall come to a sudden climactic end, but the saints' kingdom shall suddenly come to a glorious beginning. Satan's future is perpetual torment in the everlasting lake of fire, but Jesus' kingdom shall have no end.

As the Days of Noah

Jesus said His return shall be as the days of Noah. People will be living daily lives as usual. They will be eating, getting drunk, marrying and divorcing, buying and selling, lying and stealing, committing sexual sins, etc. Just another day in Paradise Lost. Jesus said His arrival will catch them by surprise just as the Great Flood arrived suddenly and unexpectedly to wash away sinners into Hades.

But of that day and hour knoweth no man, no, not the angels of heaven, but my Father only. But as the days of Noah were, so shall also the coming of the Son of man be. For as in the days that were before the flood they were eating and drinking, marrying and giving in marriage, until the day that Noah entered into the ark, and knew not until the flood came, and took them all away; so shall also the coming of the Son of man be. (Matthew 24:36-39)

Nobody - including Jesus and the angels - knows the day and hour that the Final Day will erupt upon mankind. Only God the Father knows the super-secretive sealed date. Sinners will be sinning like crazy right up to the moment God releases Jesus to depart Heaven and violently burst into our dimension riding upon a white horse in clouds of great glory. He shall descend from Heaven to earth with a shout at the last trumpet blast. The Lion of Judah will roar!

What happens before His arrival in clouds of great glory?

Societies around the world will worsen as men and women seek to finally throw off and escape from the "shackles" of morality placed on them by God at the beginning of the world. Christianity will be spurned and ridiculed as a religious relic from ancient times, not the belief system of modern, educated, technologically advanced people. The ancient spirit of Nimrod will be mighty upon the earth. Educated, wealthy, influential men and women will conspire and collaborate to complete Nimrod's construction of Babylon's ziggurat. Their Tower of Technology will usher in a new world order of global governance, a techno-religion that worships an AI god, scientists and technocrats revered as temple priests, social acceptance of every imaginable sexual deviancy, radical new forms of marriage and family, a total surveillance state, biometric identification of all humans, cashless transactions using barcode tattoos in or on the skin of people, tens of millions of people dwelling in micro-apartments living their lives in continuous virtual reality, a man-made Genesis that creates new lifeforms, synthetic biology, cyborgs, robots, and artificial intelligence. Satan's dreamworld will become mankind's nightmare.

As social decadence deepens, hostility will worsen toward true Christians. Godless people will hate God's people. New Nimrods will excitedly perceive that the time has finally arrived to revive the ancient Luciferian empire that existed before the Great Flood. All barriers will be knocked down for the completion of the mighty construction project. The greatest barrier will be Christianity. The New Nimrods will wage war to eliminate every vestige of Christianity from their Techno-Babylonian civilization. Rapid advancements in technology will be the driving force that empowers the New Nimrods to locate, identify, track, and punish followers of The Way. Bible-believing Christians will be ostracized from society. A global social credit score system will penalize people who believe in Jesus Christ and associate with His disciples. Association with Jesus and Christians will be costly in the closing days of mankind. Christians will gather in digital catacombs to worship the Lord. Near the end of time, Christians will be hunted as wild game in some nations. The spirit of Nimrod, the mighty hunter of men, shall appear on earth again.

True Christians will Preach Creationism Again

At the same time, there will be a revival of Creationism among devout Christians. The Holy Spirit will inspire them to teach, preach, declare, and emphasize that Almighty God is the Creator of the Universe. The revival of Creationism will be inspired by the first of three angels who encircle the earth prior to the Final Day. The first angel tells the inhabitants of the earth to fear God and worship Him as the Creator. The second angel announces the destruction of Babylon. The third angel warns that whosoever receives the mark of the beast and worships the beast and his image shall be cast into the everlasting lake of fire.

And I saw another angel fly in the midst of heaven, having the everlasting gospel to preach unto them that dwell on the earth, and to every nation, and kindred, and tongue, and people, saying with a loud voice, *Fear God, and give glory to him; for the hour of his judgment is come: and worship him that made heaven, and earth, and the sea, and the fountains of waters.* **(Revelation 14:6-7)**

As we approach the Final Day, creationism will be restored to its rightful place in the preaching of the gospel of the kingdom of God. There will be a strong pushback by the heroic and faithful "Church of Smyrna" and "Church of Philadelphia" to undo the damage done by the teaching of Charles Darwin's theory of evolution. In the Apocalypse, Jesus spoke to seven churches in Asia. There were many other churches, but He confined His remarks to seven. The seven churches represent the entirety of Christ's orthodox catholic church throughout the world. "Catholic" is an adjective, not a noun. All early churches were "catholic" in the sense that they preached and taught the original Apostles' doctrine, the same true gospel that was taught in all places at all times. No legitimate church deviated from the true catholic faith as delivered once by the Apostles. If a church was not "catholic" it was automatically deemed as heretical.

Jesus reprimanded five of the seven churches for their failure to defend the true catholic faith. Only the churches in Philadelphia and Smyrna received His approval. Regarding the approach to the end of time, one possible explanation may be that five-sevenths of professing Christians in the world will be lukewarm or outright apostate before Jesus returns. Thus, only two-sevenths of Christians worldwide will be holding onto the Apostles' doctrine. Christians who represent the churches in Philadelphia and Smyrna in the last days shall be viciously persecuted by the Synagogue of Satan (fake Jews) for daring to reinstate creationism on the earth, defending the right to life, and for fearlessly proclaiming Jesus Christ as the Son of God and the true Messiah.

Many Christians will once again boldly proclaim that Almighty God is the Creator of Heaven and Earth. There will be an awareness that the true gospel of the kingdom cannot be properly preached by omitting the truth in the Book of Genesis. The full gospel includes creationism. If Christians dare to tell sinners the end is coming, it will be necessary to tell them who created the beginning. Jesus Christ is the Alpha and Omega, the beginning and the end. If there is a Final Day, there had to be a First Day. If there was a first day, there must be a Creator. A supernatural anointing will fall upon Christians who bravely and boldly teach creationism as an essential component of the full gospel of the kingdom.

A revival of creationism will be accompanied by a renewed fear of God. Bold evangelists will preach the fear of God because He is the Creator. They will be rejected, scorned and betrayed by the apostate churches. Such a revival led by the Holy Spirit in the closing hours of the Last Days will be the catalyst for inflamed hostility toward Christians. Their preaching will infuriate and provoke the New Nimrods by reminding them of three things:

- Almighty God is the Creator of the universe and all life. He spoke and it happened.
- He judged mankind with a Great Flood and destroyed Lucifer's empire on earth. He spoke and it happened.
- The heavens and earth are kept in store and reserved, by the same word of God spoken at Creation and the Great Flood, unto fire against the day of judgment and perdition of ungodly men and women. He shall speak again, and it shall happen.

The New Nimrods are Building a Technological Tower of Babel

The angel who encircles the earth proclaiming that mankind must fear God and worship the Creator shall preach the "everlasting gospel." It is the same gospel yesterday, today, and forever. Enoch said the gospel was known to Adam! Nimrod, Babel's mighty ruler and chief architect of the tower of Babel, was Noah's great grandson. Surely, he heard firsthand from Great Grandfather Noah the true story of the worldwide Flood. Likewise, Nimrod also heard firsthand accurate descriptions of the civilization that was wiped out by the Great Flood. Nimrod, revered by Freemasons as the founder of their Satanic secret fraternity, longed to revive the Luciferian civilization that God drowned in a deluge.

Josephus described Nimrod as "a bold man, and of great strength of hand." According to the great Jewish historian, Nimrod excited the people to "an affront and contempt of God." The founder of Babylon persuaded the population not to glorify God. Neither did Nimrod want people to recognize the Creator as the source of their happiness. Nimrod taught the people that they were the source of their own happiness and success. He also introduced tyranny as a form of government. Nimrod saw no other way to turn mankind away from the fear of God except by bringing them into total subjection to his rule. He devised a government in Babylon that compelled people to depend on it to supply all their needs. Josephus also recorded that Nimrod vowed to seek revenge on God for destroying the pre-flood civilization of his forefathers. Furthermore, Nimrod taught his citizens that submitting to God was a sign of cowardliness.

The New Nimrods are active on earth today. The masters of Mystery Babylon are eagerly constructing a Tower of Technology that exudes contempt for God the Creator. The New Nimrods are telling people they are the source of their own happiness and success. Wealthy technocrats seek to impose global tyranny upon billions of people by using artificial intelligence, continuous surveillance of all speech and actions, social credit scores, weaponized drones, robotic police officers and soldiers, some form of a mark on people's hands or foreheads necessary to conduct financial transactions, a virtual disconnect from reality, laboratory creation of hybrid human-animal Nephilim-like creatures and non-human intelligent species, and a new religion centered upon the worship of an AI god.

The new Luciferian civilization will not fare better than its pre-flood predecessor. It shall be consumed by a flood of flames on the Final Day. God's long-running controversy with the nations will end abruptly. The New Nimrods will be bundled and burned along with their technology gods.

The New Nimrods will seethe with hatred of the Holy Name of Jesus Christ. Our Lord warned us that Christians "shall be hated of all men" for His name's sake. Jesus cautioned the saints to "take heed to yourselves," meaning Christians must be careful about their personal safety as they seek to fulfill their duty to preach the gospel. Jesus said Christians will be apprehended and taken to councils, referring to the ecclesiastical courts of the Jews such as the Sanhedrin. People who boldly confess faith in the name of Jesus Christ shall be beaten in Jewish synagogues. They will also be brought before rulers and kings, meaning civil government authorities. Sadly, Christians will be betrayed by close family members and apostate Christians. Such betrayals will result in numerous executions of true Christians. Swift executions will be carried out on saints convicted of "hate speech." The saints who endure the persecution to the end, however, shall be saved.

But take heed to yourselves: for they shall deliver you up to councils; and in the synagogues ye shall be beaten: and ye shall be brought before rulers and kings for my sake, for a testimony against them. And the gospel must first be published among all nations. But when they shall lead you, and deliver you up, take no thought beforehand what ye shall speak, neither do ye premeditate: but whatsoever shall be given you in that hour, that

speak ye: for it is not ye that speak, but the Holy Ghost. Now the brother shall betray the brother to death, and the father the son; and children shall rise up against their parents, and shall cause them to be put to death. And ye shall be hated of all men for my name's sake: but he that shall endure unto the end, the same shall be saved. (Mark 13:9-13)

The loyalty, devotion, and boldness of Jesus' true disciples in the Last Days will enrage the enemies of the Cross. Their bitter contempt and loathing of true Christians, courageous and uncompromised, will provoke them to unrestrained acts of violence against disciples of Jesus who refuse to be silenced by persecution. The vicious violence will be worse than anything Nero's wicked mind imagined such as nailing Christians to crosses and burning them at night as street lights. The more the New Nimrods laboriously strive to rebuild Lucifer's pre-Flood civilization, however, the louder the authentic saints will proclaim the full gospel of the kingdom of God. Consequently, anti-Jesus zealots will unleash unimaginable fury upon the confessing ecclesia in every nation.

Despite the persecution, God's resilient people will joyfully suffer and endure extreme persecution for their identification with the only name under heaven given among men whereby people must be saved. This chosen generation – a royal priesthood, a holy nation, a peculiar people - will boldly revive creationism by emphatically declaring that Almighty God is the Creator of the universe and all life. They will loudly warn the New Nimrods that their Babylonian Tower of Technology will collapse and burn. As billions of humans willingly receive the mark of the beast, courageous saints will warn the foolish that they shall reap an eternal curse for worshipping the beast and His image and receiving the mark of his name. Shockingly, many apostate churches will serve as neighborhood "chipping centers" in cities to assist their congregations' transition into the new world of seamless Internet of Things technology and artificial intelligence.

And I saw thrones, and they sat upon them, and judgment was given unto them: and I saw the souls of them that were beheaded for the witness of Jesus, and for the word of God, and which had not worshipped the beast, neither his image, neither had received his mark upon their foreheads, or in their hands; and they lived and reigned with Christ a thousand years. (Revelation 20:4)

For discerning saints who remain spiritually awake, worldwide hatred of the name of Jesus Christ and His disciples will be a "canary in the coalmine" early warning indicator that the Final Day is quickly approaching. They will keep plenty of oil in store for their lamps as they see the midnight darkness blanketing the world. Sadly, apostate church members will not discern the severity of the deepening darkness because they too will be immersed and mesmerized by Babylon's dazzling digital entertainment and deceived by doctrines of devils.

Unrepentant sinners and the wicked certainly will not see the Final Day rapidly coming upon them. Saints who remain awake and vigilant, however, will long for it. Things will become so dire and dark in this world that true Christians will beg God to end it. Jesus is coming for those who are eagerly "looking for that blessed hope, and the glorious appearing of the great God and our Savior Jesus Christ." They are represented in the Parable of the Ten Virgins as the five wise virgins who were ever eager and ever ready for the midnight cry that the bridegroom was on his way for the wonderful wedding party.

"The Rapture" is Not the Falling Away

The "wise virgins" will distinctly discern the stunning and rapid advancement of apostasy in many churches: the falling away from the ancient apostolic faith, the rejection of sound doctrine, the embrace of aberrant lifestyles, the reluctance to preach against sin, idolatry, and the onset of extreme spiritual coolness among Christians who previously were on fire for God.

Let no man deceive you by any means: for that day shall not come except there come a falling away first, and that man of sin be revealed, the son of perdition; who opposeth and exalteth himself above all that is called God, or that is worshipped; so that he as God sitteth in the temple of God, shewing himself that he is God. (2 Thessalonians 2:3-4)

Many prominent Evangelical Zionists teach that Apostle Paul was prophesying about "The Rapture." They ludicrously say that evangelical Christians will "fall away" from the earth when they are taken up in "The Rapture" to escape the ensuing tribulation.

The DPPZites commit the very sin Apostle Paul warned against doing, meaning deceiving people about the second coming of Jesus Christ. The great apostle said, "Let no man deceive you by any means..." Apostle Paul said "that day" - the Final Day! - shall not come before two things happen: a worldwide departure from God's truth and the public unveiling of the man of sin, the son of perdition.

The falling away (apostasy) does not occur among followers of non-Christian religions. They can't fall away from the truth when they have never known the truth. Who falls away from the truth? Only people who previously knew the truth - the Lord

Jesus Christ, the Word made flesh. Therefore, the falling away represents Christians who walk away from Jesus Christ, the Holy Bible, the Apostles' doctrine, and the ancient creeds. Thus, they become apostates.

"That day" also will not arrive until the second requirement is fulfilled: the revealing of the man of sin, the son of perdition. The Holy Bible uses the same Greek word for the revealing of the man of sin and it often does for the revealing of Jesus Christ: apocalypsis. The man of sin (commonly known as the Antichrist) will be as clearly revealed to true Christians as the son of perdition (destruction) as is Jesus Christ is revealed to us as the Son of God. There will be no doubt in the hearts and minds of God's people that the man of sin has been revealed. He will be more than an opponent of Jesus Christ. He will be our Lord's hideous rival. He will mimic Jesus. As Jesus is God incarnate, so too will the man of sin be Satan incarnate. He will be Satan in human flesh, the spiritual leader of the worldwide apostasy, the spiritual and political king of the New Nimrods.

Another erroneous teaching of the Evangelical Zionists is that the Jews must build a third temple in Jerusalem, and the "Antichrist" must enter it to declare himself as a god. There is no prophecy in the New Testament that says a third temple will be built before Jesus returns. Likewise, there is no prophecy in the New Testament that the Jews will return to Jerusalem to establish the political state of Israel. Jesus Christ fulfilled all of God's promises to Israel. Regarding the temple, the New Testament Bible clearly says that the physical bodies of Christians are the temple of God. We, the Christians, are the body of Christ. We are lively stones in the temple, which is Jesus Christ, the chief cornerstone.

When Apostle Paul said the man of sin sits in the temple of God, he meant that the man of sin will be seated in the temple of apostates, meaning their physical bodies. He will shew himself to them to be their god. The man of sin will oppose Almighty God and exalt himself above all that is called God or that is worshipped. Artificial intelligence will be his Unholy Spirit.

Prior to the revealing of the man of sin, the "wise virgins" will discern the world's frightening open and unashamed embrace of Satan. Outright adoration of Satan will become commonplace in the years ahead as the New Nimrods build a Luciferian society in eager anticipation of his return as ruler of this world through Satan's incarnation in the man of sin. Thus, the saints will discern that Satan's release from the bottomless pit to deceive the nations will be imminent. Satan's freedom from the bottomless pit and the reign of the son of perdition are congruent.

Satan will be Loosed Before the Second Coming of Jesus

Following the triumph of Jesus over Satan, which was accomplished by His resurrection, the devil has been bound in the bottomless pit. Since Satan's public humiliation on Resurrection Day, God has restrained him from deceiving the nations. The divine restraint is intended to prevent Satan from hindering people from hearing the Good News. The Good News is the wonderful proclamation of reconciliation: God and mankind has been reconciled through Jesus Christ. Forgiveness of sins, eternal salvation, citizenship in the Kingdom of God, and friendship with God are the primary promises in the New Covenant between God and mankind. Because God loves mankind, the New Covenant is a gift from Him. Jesus did the work on the Cross. To receive the free gift, fallen men and women need only repent of their sins against God, believe on the name of Jesus Christ to save them, turn from their wicked ways, and be baptized into Christ's church.

How is Satan restrained? He is restrained by fearless and bold preaching of the Gospel of the Kingdom of God. When Christians are fearless and bold, and the Gospel is preached purely without mixture, the chains around Satan are tightened. The reverse, however, happens when Christians are timid, corrupt, cowardly, complacent, and/or apostate. Satan's chains are loosened (but not broken) whenever the Gospel is not preached purely and boldly. Cowardly and complacent Christians extend the chain that restrains Satan, thus giving him extra room to move about to hinder people from being saved.

After His ascension to Heaven, Jesus has ruled and reigned in and through His glorious church to reveal God the Creator to humans in every nation. Sadly, the doctrines of DPPZism have deceived millions of Evangelical Zionists. They have no awareness that Jesus desires to rule and reign through them now. Instead, they foolishly wait for their imaginary rapture pooka to appear to whisk them away to Heaven where they will rule and reign with Christ after His second coming. Therefore, they make themselves of little use to God in this present life because they do not know who they are now in Christ. They surrendered their identity as true Israel to people who despise Jesus. They traded their birthright for a bowl of porridge.

Prior to the Final Day, the old serpent will be loosed for a short season to once again deceive the nations. (Darby's DPPZites teach this will happen 1,000 years after the second coming!) Unimaginable tribulation will vex the saints when Satan unleashes his full fury against them as fallen mankind sprints toward the grand climax of world history. Fortunately, God will shorten those days for the elect's sake. Otherwise, no flesh (human and animal) would survive.

Virtual Reality Technology Will Usher in World of Unlimited Sinning

For confessing Christians, life on earth will become sheer madness. It will seem as though they are living in an insane asylum where the inmates successfully revolted and overthrew the administrators and security officers. None of us can fathom how wicked, decadent, bizarre, bloodthirsty, and lewd human society will become prior to the Second Coming of Jesus. Wickedness will reach extreme depths of depravity that God-fearing people have never witnessed, nor thought could ever happen. Extreme wickedness and the unabashed worship of Satan will become the "new norm" of society. Even Noah would be shocked if he could see it.

At the time of this book's publication in 2020, mankind is rapidly approaching the greatest explosion of sinful behavior since the days of Noah. Virtual reality and artificial intelligence will be parents that give birth to this new age of debauchery. Neither the wicked or unrepentant sinners will see the Final Day coming because they will be delirious with unrestrained sinful pleasures made possible by and experienced in virtual reality. They will boast that the New Nimrods and their Tower of Technology have finally freed mankind from God's restraints of morality. For the first time in human history, men and women will be free to commit any sin imaginable by doing it in virtual reality. Their sexual lusts, wildest fantasies, bloodlusts, and carnal cravings will be fulfilled beyond anything they imagined could ever happen in real life. People will be empowered in virtual reality to do whatever wicked acts their hearts desire. Lewd heterosexual and homosexual sexual acts, group sex, sex with children, sex with animals, necromancy, erotic encounters with strangers, acts of violence, bloody fistfights, murder, seances, any unlawful act imaginable to sinful men and women will be declared lawful if committed in virtual reality.

VR will be hailed as a crime-prevention technology because people will be encouraged and permitted to commit criminal acts in a Westworld-like virtual reality. Thus, pedophiles will be free to molest children in virtual reality, and society will affirm their contribution to society by keeping their primal urges and needs confined to VR. Testosterone-charged young men will be encouraged and permitted to fight to the death in VR cages. There will be no limits placed on the combatants' ability to inflict pain and injury to their VR opponents. Unimaginable sadistic acts will be allowed in VR because we will be told that "such crimes are not real."

Present-day digital pornography will transition from an observatory to a participatory activity. Married men and women will be permitted and encouraged to have adulterous relationships inside VR, thus demonstrating their exemplary social behavior by limiting their infidelity to virtual activity. People will freely choose as their cybernetic sexual companions artificially intelligent humanoid robots with realistic skin texture and body temperature, or real humans in different cities or continents wearing bodysuits fitted with sensors for physical sensations and connected via the Internet for remote erotic encounters.

Satan's New Nimrods will salaciously satisfy the deepest carnal desires of sinners. Digital addiction will pale in comparison to VR addiction. Dopamine rushes and surging hormones in the bodies of VR users will produce instant addictions as they experience for the first time the ecstasy of unrestrained sinning in virtual reality. Multitudes of humans around the world will be demonically possessed through virtual interaction with real demons that will inhabit VR avatars.

Sadly, many weak Christians will fall back into deadly sin because the lure of unrestrained pleasure will be too much to resist. They will succumb to temptations to experience lurid things presently prohibited in physical reality. Satan will whisper in their ears, "Do it. You want it. It is not sin because it isn't real." The sin, however, will be real in their hearts and minds even though their physical bodies never physically touch other physical bodies. Their souls will be defiled by their virtual connection.

Ye have heard that it was said by them of old time, Thou shalt not commit adultery: but I say unto you, That whosoever looketh on a woman to lust after her hath committed adultery with her already in his heart. (Matthew 5:27-28)

Flee fornication. Every sin that a man doeth is without the body; but he that committeth fornication sinneth against his own body. (1 Corinthians 6:18)

Fortunately, there will be a remnant of Christ's church that will cry out to the world to repent before the Final Day arrives. Christians who dare to speak against the New Nimrods' Techno-Babylonian society will be hated, vilified, mocked, ridiculed, ostracized, imprisoned, and even killed. It will be in virtual reality that the enemies of the Cross return to the demonic violence heaped upon saints in the first four centuries of the Church. Their vehement hatred of Jesus Christ and contempt for His disciples will drive them to flog and beat Christians in virtual reality. Yes, Christians will be attacked by mobs in virtual reality. They will be told that Christians are not welcomed in VR. They will be consigned to digital ghettos. When their bloodlust reaches the boiling stage, Satan will turn them loose to commit real acts of A Clockwork Orange-like dystopian ultra-violence against Christians in physical reality including savage beatings, torture, murder, and destruction of property.

Once again, God the Creator will regret ever making humanity. The world's evil nature and repulsive sinful behavior will remind Him of the days of Noah. The Creator will conclude that the wickedness of man is great in the earth, and that every imagination of the thoughts of men's hearts is only continuous evil. God's heart will be grieved.

And the Lord said, I will destroy man whom I have created from the face of the earth; both man, and beast, and the creeping thing, and the fowls of the air; for it repenteth me that I have made them. (Genesis 6:7)

May every saint pause to humbly reflect on the wonderful assurance that the ecclesia shall find grace in the eyes of the Lord. He shall deliver His people of the promise (New Jerusalem) from Satan's wrath, and protect them as Noah and his family were shielded in the ark from the global storm of judgment.

God Will Implode the Entire Universe and Start Over

What shall be the sequence of events? What happens first? When does each prophetic event occur and in what order? How much time do these things require to happen? Why does it matter?

Nobody knows when Jesus will return, nor does anybody know precisely how the end of the world shall transpire. We have the Word of God to illuminate our minds to understand as much as is possible for mortal human beings. In the end, however, God will do it His way and in His time. The main thing to know is that our wonderful Heavenly Father will surely rescue us from this collapsing civilization. How and when He does it is His sovereign prerogative. Our only obligations are to be spiritually ready, eagerly awaiting His return, and faithfully tending our Father's business.

Here's what we know: Suddenly the sky will change. The sun, moon, and stars will go dark. The kingdom of the Prince of Darkness on earth will suddenly be covered in darkness and his people in gross darkness. Have you ever been in a theater or auditorium during an electrical blackout? Imagine a universal blackout! Billions of people will gasp simultaneously around the world. Fear will grip all who are outside the ecclesia of God. Joyous anticipation shall sweep over the saints who immediately turn their eyes upward because they will instantly know that their redemption is drawing nigh.

Can you imagine the eerie sound of global moaning sweeping over the planet when the sign of the Son of man appears in the sky? Yes, the wicked will wail, but the saints will worship! The appearance of the sign of the Son of man in the sky will produce joyful shouts of praise from the lips of saints on every continent. The victorious voices of millions of saved saints will saturate the atmosphere with universal proclamations of "King Jesus! We worship You." It will be far different for the wicked and unrepentant sinners. The sign of the Son of man in the sky will produce horrific fear and dread in their hearts and mind.

As explained in the previous chapters of this book, God will darken the sun, moon, and stars because He is finished with them. When Jesus enters our universe, He will power down the lighting. The angels will go from room to room (solar systems and galaxies) throughout the universe and turn off the lights forever. They will never shine again. When the Final Day arrives, God will be finished with the entire cosmos! He will create something new. He is still the Creator!

When a business owner of a tall building decides to implode it so that he or she can build something new on the site, the last thing done is the cutoff of electrical power in the building before the implosion. That's precisely what Jesus will do when He arrives. He will cut off the electricity to the sun, moon, and stars. It will happen immediately prior to Him imploding the universe. When the lights go out, the next thing to happen will be angels rolling up the universe. That's why Old Covenant prophet Isaiah and New Covenant apostle John both saw the universe dissolved and rolled up like a parchment scroll. A parchment scroll is rolled up to be put away or discarded. God will roll up the universe and discard it on the Final Day!

And all the host of heaven shall be dissolved, and the heavens shall be rolled together as a scroll: **and all their host shall fall down, as the leaf falleth off from the vine, and as a falling fig from the fig tree. (Isaiah 34:4)**

And the heaven departed as a scroll when it is rolled together; **and every mountain and island were moved out of their places. (Revelation 6:14)**

Old Covenant Isaiah and New Covenant John both saw the heavens rolled together like a scroll and vanish. Isaiah said the "host of heaven" will fall down like a leaf falling from the vine, or a falling fig from the tree. Micah saw the Lord come forth out of His place and tread upon the high places of the earth, and the mountains turned molten under Him. St. John the Revelator saw every mountain and island moved out of their places when the heavens were rolled together as a scroll.

Why will the Creator destroy His creation? The explanation is as simple as this: There's coming a day when God will be done with this old universe. It belongs to Him. He made it and He can do with it as He pleases. God is not obligated to request permission from humans to discard His property. There will be no need to keep the present earth! No Mercury, Venus, Mars, Jupiter, and Saturn! No Neptune or any other planet, star, comet, asteroid, black hole, solar system, galaxy, or universe. The entire universe will be disposed of in God's trash bin.

How will God do it? He created it by His spoken words and He can abolish it by His spoken words. Perhaps God will merely inhale back into Himself the words He spoke at Creation. Somehow the present universe will cease to exist. One thing is certain: Destroying the universe will not require any heavy lifting on God's part. He will not break into a sweat doing it. God will merely speak it out of existence the same way He spoke it into existence.

When Jesus Christ cracks through the barrier that separates our dimension from Heaven, every eye shall see Him. Moments before His sudden arrival, the sign of the Son of man shall appear in the sky. All lights in the universe will be extinguished. Daytime and nighttime will instantly cease to exist the moment God shuts down the sun, moon, and stars. Isaiah said darkness shall cover the earth. Boom! Suddenly Jesus Christ will hover above the planet.

He will glow with glory. Every eye shall see Him no matter where on earth they are standing.

It's no wonder why men and women will suffer massive heart attacks when Jesus Christ returns. They won't have time to die later. It will be over quickly. Instant death, however, will not provide them an easy escape from the Great Judge. They will be dead only a short time. When Jesus opens all the graves, they will suddenly pop to life again and stare in the face fearsome angelic reapers. Jesus' interstellar traveling entourage, the angels who will travel with Him from the City of Heaven to earth, will rapidly bundle and burn the wicked. Years of laughing at preachers and scoffing at the notion of a future Judgment Day will strike terror in the hearts of sinners who suddenly realize that the Creator of the universe is rapidly dismantling it.

...men's hearts failing them for fear, and for looking after those things which are coming on the earth: for the powers of heaven shall be shaken. (Luke 21:26)

Our Heavenly Father will give His Son a long list of tasks to complete. He and the angels will be busy on the Final Day. Jesus' To-Do list on the Final Day includes:

- Turn off the lights throughout the universe.
- Go to the far end of the universe and roll it up as a parchment scroll destined for the trash bin.
- Trigger a massive earthquake that rips apart the earth's crust.
- Destroy Babylon.
- Open all the graves - saints and sinners.
- Catch up into the sky the resurrected saints who were asleep in their graves.

- Catch up into the sky the saints who are alive on the earth when Jesus returns.
- Separate all humans according to their respective nations.
- Subdivide all humans in their respective nations: sheep will go to the right and goats will go to the left.
- Question all humans about their compassion on earth. Did you feed Christ, give Him water, clothe Him, visit Him?
- Convene Heaven's court and preside over the judgement seat of Christ. Decree judgment on unrepentant sinners and the wicked.
- Cast unrepentant sinners and the wicked into the Lake of Fire.
- Reward the saints according to their works.
- Torch the earth and consume it with fire.
- Speak into existence a new earth and a new heaven.
- Bring forth the City of New Jerusalem.
- Relocate His throne and personal belongings from Heaven to His new home in New Jerusalem.

Wow! What a busy Final Day it shall be for Jesus. How long will it take to be completed? Days, months, years, centuries, a millennium? None of the above!

When the Time Maker arrives, time departs. Every time zone in the universe will automatically default to Jesus Time. Will there be a new measurement of time in the new heaven and earth? Only God knows. One thing is certain: The Final Day is the last day!

But, beloved, be not ignorant of this one thing, that one day is with the Lord as a thousand years, and a thousand years as one day. (2 Peter 3:8)

For a thousand years in thy sight are but as yesterday when it is past, and as a watch in the night. (Psalm 90:4)

Final Means It Is Over...End of Story

Many sincere, devout religious people cannot grasp the finality of "final." Final means it is over. Está terminado! C'est fini! Es ist vorbei! È finita! Het is gedaan! No matter the language spoken, it means the same: It is over!

Humans - including saved, born again Christians - subconsciously resist the realization that God has appointed a day to end the universe, judge every human, and start over. St. Peter the Apostle said people are willfully ignorant of the fact that the Pre-Flood world was previously covered with water, and the present world is kept in store and reserved unto fire against the day of judgment.

For many Evangelical Zionists, "The Rapture" is their imaginary great escape out of this world, a fantasy that permits them to evade persecution and affliction for their faith in Jesus Christ, and thus evade their duty to refuse the mark of the beast, and to overcome the devil through the blood of the lamb and the word of their testimony. Besides, if they somehow miss "The Rapture," they'll have a seven-year gap to get a second chance to be saved during the Great Tribulation. Man-made doctrines, however, do not match up with the God-inspired Bible. Jesus Christ will return one time. And when He does return, He will burn the earth with fire so hot that even the ashes will dissolve. The old earth must dissolve to make way for the new earth. Consider the words of Apostle Peter:

Seeing then that all these things shall be dissolved, what manner of persons ought ye to be in all holy conversation and

godliness, looking for and hasting unto the coming of the day of God, wherein the heavens being on fire shall be dissolved, and the elements shall melt with fervent heat? Nevertheless we, according to his promise, look for new heavens and a new earth, wherein dwelleth righteousness. (2 Peter 3:11-13)

No doubt that Apostle Peter heard Jesus' words ringing in his ears when he warned that the day of the Lord will strike suddenly like the Great Flood. Jesus said His second coming shall be as it was in the days of Noah. It was business as usual for the world's population of avid sinners. They did not see the judgment coming, although Noah had faithfully preached and warned them for decades. People mocked Noah and scoffed at his holiness preaching. According to Jesus, the people continued in their sinful lifestyles *until the day Noah and his family entered the ark and the flood arrived suddenly and unexpectedly.* It was their Final Day! The flood did not arrive seven years after Noah and his family entered the ark. The flood came suddenly and unexpectedly immediately after Noah entered the ark and the hatch was sealed. Divine judgment was all around them, but did not touch them. Today, our ark is baptism into Christ's church.

For Christ also hath once suffered for sins, the just for the unjust, that he might bring us to God, being put to death in the flesh, but quickened by the Spirit: by which also he went and preached unto the spirits in prison; which sometime were disobedient, *when once the longsuffering of God waited in the days of Noah, while the ark was a preparing, wherein few, that is, eight souls were saved by water. The like figure whereunto even baptism doth also now save us* (not the putting away of the filth of the flesh, but the answer of a good conscience toward God,)

by the resurrection of Jesus Christ: who is gone into heaven, and is on the right hand of God; angels and authorities and powers being made subject unto him. (1 Peter 3:18-22)

Likewise, Jesus cited Lot's escape from Sodom. On *the same day* that Lot departed the wicked city, *fire and brimstone rained down* from heaven upon the inhabitants. It too was their Final Day. Now here is the key: Jesus said "even thus shall it be in the day when the Son of man is revealed." When God removes sealed saints from the earth, fire will consume the planet *on the same day!* The Final Day will explode upon mankind the moment the church is taken away - not seven years later.

And as it was in the days of Noah, so shall it be also in the days of the Son of man. They did eat, they drank, they married wives, they were given in marriage, *until the day that Noah entered into the ark, and the flood came, and destroyed them all.* Likewise also as it was in the days of Lot; they did eat, they drank, they bought, they sold, they planted, they builded; *but the same day that Lot went out of Sodom it rained fire and brimstone from heaven, and destroyed them all. Even thus shall it be in the day when the Son of man is revealed.* (Luke 17:26-30)

St. Jude warned the wicked their fate shall be eternal fire if they do not repent. He cited as examples the inhabitants of Sodom and Gomorrah, and neighboring cities Admah and Zeboim, who were addicted to immoral sexual lusts which could be satisfied because the inhabitants enjoyed prosperity and plenty of leisure time. Jude's admonition to all hearers of his words is that the destruction of these cities is a stark reminder and warning to flee all sexual immorality - heterosexual, homosexual, bisexual, and transsexual.

Even as Sodom and Gomorrah, and the cities about them in

like manner, giving themselves over to fornication, and going after strange flesh, are set forth for an example, suffering the vengeance of eternal fire. (Jude 1:7)

The Bible is true and without error. Clearly, numerous scriptures tell us that the world will be destroyed when Jesus returns. There cannot be a Jewish kingdom in Jerusalem ruling the world for 1,000 years because old Jerusalem will vanish in the consuming flames from Heaven. Jesus's words are not in error. Revelation 20 has been misinterpreted by well-meaning Christians who think they know something the ancient church did not know. The Holy Bible tells us that the world will be destroyed when Jesus returns, not a thousand years later. Jesus said it shall be destroyed on the same day He removes the saints.

Heaven and earth shall pass away: but my words shall not pass away. (Mark 13:31)

...for the fashion of this world passeth away. (1 Corinthians 3:31)

And the world passeth away, and the lust thereof: but he that doeth the will of God abideth forever. (1 John 2:17)

God Will do a New Thing

The Creator of the present universe is eager to do a new thing. This wonderful "new thing" will be unprecedented in human history. It shall spring forth like fresh new grass. The Divine Creator will bring forth a bud that will blossom with unspeakable beauty. God will make a way in the wilderness for His chosen people, the people of promise, the saints who love and obey Jesus Christ. The ecclesia has always been pilgrims passing through this world looking for a city which has foundations, whose builder and maker is God. He will suddenly change their environment. He will deliver them from this old dying world, and refresh them with new rivers of pure water to satisfy their thirsty souls. God promised to provide for His people in the wilderness on their journey from Babylon to Jerusalem just as He provided for the Hebrews on their way from Egypt to Canaan. We can rest assured that our Heavenly Father will provide us a safe passage on our journey from Mystery Babylon to New Jerusalem.

Isaiah saw it thousands of years ago. What did he see? He saw God deliver Israel out of Babylon and bring them into Jerusalem.

Behold, I will do a new thing; now it shall spring forth; shall ye not know it? I will even make a way in the wilderness, and rivers in the desert. (Isaiah 43:19)

The "new thing" started in Bethlehem with the birth of the Messiah. It blossomed at Calvary. It flowed from the upper room on Pentecost. It shall come to fruition on the Final Day when the Creator abolishes this present world and creates a new world where He will dwell forever with the sealed saints who believed on the name of Jesus Christ to save them from eternal damnation.

Speaking of the promised Messiah, Jeremiah asked the Israelites how long would they backslide. Speaking of the Christ Child in the Virgin Mary's undefiled womb, the prophet said the Lord had created a new thing on earth. The "new thing" is Jesus! It's all about Jesus. Get your eyes off Israel and the Jews in the Last Days. Fix your eyes upon Jesus! He is the only star of the show. People from all races and nations - including the Jews and Israel - are invited to the wedding feast. You must, however, RSVP the bridegroom's Heavenly Father now and confirm your seat. Walk-ins will not be permitted to enter on that glorious wedding day. Proper attire will be required.

How long wilt thou go about, O thou backsliding daughter? for the Lord hath created a new thing in the earth, A woman shall compass a man. (Jeremiah 31:22)

Apostle John saw in the Patmos vision a "new heaven and a new earth." Where were the old heaven and earth? Where did they go? John said the first heaven and the first earth had passed away and no longer existed. Neither did the sea remain.

And I saw a new heaven and a new earth: for the first heaven and the first earth were passed away; and there was no more sea. (Revelation 21:1)

If there is a first heaven and the first earth, there must be another heaven and another earth that follow. The hope of a new beginning for mankind runs throughout the Bible, from Genesis to the Apocalypse. Abraham did not long for a political kingdom with hundreds of square miles of physical territory under control by his descendants. He sojourned (lived temporarily) in the land of promise as somebody living in a strange country. He didn't build a permanent house. Instead, he lived in temporary tents. Think about it! Abraham lived in the physical land God promised him, but he treated it as a strange country that wasn't his home. Why? The beloved patriarch of our faith was looking for a city whose builder and maker is God! Abraham, who was not Jewish, yearned to live in New Jerusalem. A Zionist political State of Israel meant nothing to Abraham. New Jerusalem is the ecclesia of God in a new and perfect state. Think about it. We shall live with Abraham in New Jerusalem! It is the city he was yearning to find. He is our example of being justified by faith.

By faith he sojourned in the land of promise, as in a strange country, dwelling in tabernacles with Isaac and Jacob, the heirs

with him of the same promise: for he looked for a city which hath foundations, whose builder and maker is God. (Hebrews 11:9-10)

One of the keywords that run throughout the Holy Bible is "new." God spoke frequently in the Bible about "new" things: a new song, new wine, a new moon, a new cart, new gate, a new thing, new fruit, new bottles, new covenant, new testament, new mercies, new heart, new spirit, new tongues, new commandment, new creature, new man, new heavens, new earth, new Jerusalem.

Our Heavenly Father always had a plan to redeem fallen humans and restore them to the Garden of Eden. The prophets foretold of the double blessing God would give the saints: The Messiah and a new earth whereupon to worship Him absent the presence of rebellious sinners and the Tempter. Isaiah saw in his spirit the new heavens and new earth. He said the old cosmos would be forgotten. We will not remember this present life. All those whose names were blotted out of the Book of Life shall also be forgotten forever. God does not desire us to grieve throughout eternity in remembrance of our relatives and friends who did not enter the Kingdom of God, but instead are trapped in the everlasting lake of fire.

For, behold, I create new heavens and a new earth: and the former shall not be remembered, nor come into mind. (Isaiah 65:17)

The new Jerusalem can only be situated on a new earth that is under a new heaven. Life on the First Day after the Final Day will be entirely new. Nobody can imagine what the saints will see and experience on the first day after the Final Day. It is incomprehensible! The first day after the Final Day shall bring forth God's final seat where He shall remain for eternity. The Ancient of Days will even cast away His holy temple that currently dwells in Heaven.

There will be no need of a temple in New Jerusalem because God is the temple! Christians are the living stones of the temple. We shall dwell together for eternity with no separation.

But as it is written, Eye hath not seen, nor ear heard, neither have entered into the heart of man, the things which God hath prepared for them that love him. (1 Corinthians 2:9)

The Restitution of All Things

This is not a strange, new doctrine. This is the Gospel! The holy prophets have spoken it since the world began. The apostles spoke it too. The Church did not start in Jerusalem on the day of Pentecost. Jesus Christ has always been preached to fallen men and women since the Garden of Eden.

...and he shall send Jesus Christ, which before was preached unto you: **whom the heaven must receive until the times of restitution of all things,** *which God hath spoken by the mouth of all his holy prophets since the world began.* (Acts 3:20-21)

The Heavenly Father sent His only begotten Son to earth to atone for mankind's sins and to make a way for fallen men and women to be restored to spiritual life. "He shall send Jesus Christ," meaning the Savior who was always promised by God from the beginning of the world to save people, to redeem people, to teach people, to gather His people to Himself, to judge the world, and to punish the wicked.

"Whom the heaven must receive..." means that the resurrected Savior's abode is in Heaven until the Final Day. Immediately after Jesus commissioned the apostles to be His witness "unto the uttermost part of the earth," He was taken up "and a cloud received him out of their sight."

"Whom the heaven must receive" also signifies that Jesus was exalted and clothed with glory and power when He ascended from the earth to Heaven. In His place, the Holy Spirit - our Comforter and Advocate - was sent to represent Him on earth as the only Vicar of Christ until the second coming of the Lord, to assist the Church (ecclesia) in the great commission of preaching the gospel of the kingdom to all nations as a witness, to encourage the saints, and to be an advocate of the saints. Jesus is in Heaven. The Holy Spirit oversees the one, holy, catholic, and apostolic church in her glorious endeavors to fulfill the Master's great commission.

"Until the times of restitution of all things" means that Jesus Christ must remain in Heaven until the Final Day. God's long-running controversy with the nations will end abruptly. He will settle the score in His favor. No appeals for another trial will be heard by the Great Judge. His decrees are absolute and non-negotiable. Jesus shall avenge the iniquities committed against His Heavenly Father since the fall of Adam and Eve. He will judge the living and the dead. The wicked shall be given the punishment they justly deserve. He will avenge all injustices on earth committed since the beginning of the world. Every man and woman - great and lowly, rich and poor, famous and unknown - shall bow their knees and confess with their tongues that Jesus Christ is Lord of Lords and King of Kings. He shall exalt His glorious Church. He shall heal and restore Creation to its true order and splendor without sin and death. The victorious, triumphant conquering King Jesus will present the kingdom to Almighty God. The restitution of all things is the completion of the work of Jesus Christ. The new creation will have peace and order as it was in the beginning of the old creation.

You will not find a temple in New Jerusalem, nor shrines and altars. God will no longer dwell in a temple in Heaven, nor will He dwell in a temple on earth. Almighty God and His Son are our temple.

And I saw no temple therein: for the Lord God Almighty and the Lamb are the temple of it. (Revelation 21:22)

The sun, moon, and stars will vanish on the Final Day because their purpose will be completed. New Jerusalem shall have no need of them. The city will be illuminated by God's glory and Jesus' light.

And the city had no need of the sun, neither of the moon, to shine in it: for the glory of God did lighten it, and the Lamb is the light thereof. (Revelation 21:23)

The restitution of all things is beyond the comprehension of the most educated, intelligent theologians, philosophers, intellectuals, and scientists in the world. Who can imagine and describe the first day after the last day? It would be marvelous and wonderful if God would rewind His time machine to Genesis 1:27-28 and restart there. What a wonderful place to start over!

So God created man in his own image, in the image of God created he him; male and female created he them. And God blessed them, and God said unto them, Be fruitful, and multiply, and replenish the earth, and subdue it: and have dominion over the fish of the sea, and over the fowl of the air, and over every living thing that moveth upon the earth. (Genesis 1:27-28)

Imagine life without sin! No devil, no temptations, no demons, no evil, no violence, no wars, no disease. No death, only life! Imagine the animal kingdom restored to its wonderful beauty. No wild beasts, no predators, no carnivores, and no poisonous serpents.

If God takes us back to the original Garden of Eden it would be stupendous and astounding. Living with God in an abundantly beautiful and peaceful garden environment - never to experience any of the troubles that have plagued humans since the fall of Adam and Eve - would be a tremendously gracious gift from our Heavenly Father. But wait, there's more!

God will go beyond restoring Creation to its original state. The great Creator will create again! God promised He would do it for us. God will not remodel our present planet. He will create something wonderful and new for us.

Nevertheless we, according to his promise, look for new heavens and a new earth, wherein dwelleth righteousness. (2 Peter 3:13)

And I saw a new heaven and a new earth: for the first heaven and the first earth were passed away; and there was no more sea. (Revelation 21:1)

Jeremiah Saw God Rewind Time to Genesis

Jeremiah saw the Final Day. The Old Testament prophet saw the earth as it was in its primitive state in Genesis 1:2, described by Moses as "without form, and void; and darkness was upon the face of the deep." What caused it to happen? Judgment! God gave Jeremiah a fleeting glimpse of the Final Day. Gazing into the faraway future, the prophet saw the arrival of the day of the Lord and the judgment that will be wrought upon mankind's wicked world. All was gone. The earth returned to its primitive state at the beginning of time. Using the same Hebrew words in Genesis 1:2, Jeremiah saw the planet's formlessness, emptiness, nothingness, and confusion. Earth was without beauty and surrounded by stark darkness. Jeremiah saw no light in the universe.

Jeremiah's ministry was focused on preaching a warning of divine judgment if the people of Israel did not repent of their evil ways. God, however, revealed something to Jeremiah infinitely more shocking than the impending destruction of Israel. The Old Testament prophet saw the destruction of the entire planet!

Jeremiah saw God rewinding His time machine! He received a prophetic glimpse of the Final Day when the Creator will be finished with His old creation, and will rewind time to its primordial starting point.

I beheld the earth, and, lo, it was without form, and void; and the heavens, and they had no light. (Jeremiah 4:23)

Yes, Jeremiah saw the ultimate judgment of sin and rebellion: the complete abolition of the existing cosmos. It must be abolished to make way for a new cosmos - a new creation. The Creator will not slap a fresh coat of paint on our old planet marred by massive earthquakes, volcanic eruptions, meteor strikes, massive hailstones, pestilences, famines, and wars involving nuclear, biological, chemical, and scalar weapons. Even worse, this present planet's soil is soaked with blood. The earth has a mouth and blood has a voice. The blood of innocent humans killed since the murder of Abel is continually crying out to God for justice. Our old earth is already beyond repair. No refurbishment will suffice. It is only fit for a fire - flames so hot that even the cinders and ash vanish.

Our Heavenly Father is eagerly anticipating the day when He creates something new for the children who love Him. Our finite human minds cannot comprehend the size, form, features, and the beauty of the new earth. One thing we do know: it will be infinitely more beautiful and wonderful than the original old earth in its original perfect state.

And God shall wipe away all tears from their eyes; and there shall be no more death, neither sorrow, nor crying, neither shall there be any more pain: for the former things are passed away. And he that sat upon the throne said, Behold, I make all things new. And he said unto me, Write: for these words are true and faithful. (Revelation 21:4-5)

Imagine the first day after the final day! It will be joy unspeakable and full of glory!

The Second Coming of Jesus on the Final Day shall be:

- Singular
- Sudden and unexpected
- Atmospheric
- Visible
- Noisy
- Disruptive
- Fiery
- Glorious
- Judgmental
- Final

EPILOGUE

FRIGHTENING YOU ABOUT THE end of the world was not my motive in writing Final Day. Our focus must always remain fixed on the first day after the final day. It will be joy unspeakable and full of glory!

None of us know if we will be alive on earth when Jesus returns. Multitudes of Christians since the Resurrection hoped they would be among the blessed generation that would be caught up into the air to meet our Lord. They entered their blissful repose without seeing the manifestation of the promise. Like Abraham, they were looking for "a city which hath foundations, whose builder and maker is God." These saints died without receiving the promises of God. Having seen them far away, and convinced the promises were true, they told everybody they were only pilgrims passing through a foreign country on their way home.

These all died in faith, not having received the promises, but having seen them afar off, and were persuaded of them, and embraced them, and confessed that they were strangers and

pilgrims on the earth. For they that say such things declare plainly that they seek a country. And truly, if they had been mindful of that country from whence they came out, they might have had opportunity to have returned. But now they desire a better country, that is, an heavenly: wherefore God is not ashamed to be called their God: for he hath prepared for them a city. (Hebrews 11:13-16)

If we die before the Final Day, we can rest peacefully in the assurance that Jesus Christ will raise us up on the last day. Indeed, we shall see Jesus return to earth because He will bring our bodies out of the graves to witness the glorious appearing of our blessed hope. When we see Jesus, our bodies will be changed to be like Him. The resurrection is the hope of humanity.

The Bible tells the true story of a young man named Lazarus. His sisters were Martha and Mary, the same Mary who anointed Jesus with ointment and wiped His feet with her hair. Lazarus became very sick, and his sisters sent word to Jesus to come quickly to heal him. Jesus, however, waited two days. Afterward, He told his disciples that Lazarus was sleeping. They perceived He meant that Lazarus was resting. Jesus spoke plainly to them: Lazarus is dead.

By the time Jesus approached the outskirts of Bethany, Lazarus had been in his grave for four days. Many neighbors and relatives tried to comfort the grieving sisters. When Jesus finally approached the town's outskirts, Martha left her house to meet him. Mary, however, sat quietly in her home. Upon meeting Jesus, Martha wasted no time letting him know what she thought about his tardiness in responding to their late brother's health crisis. She told Jesus her brother would be alive if the Lord had come to Bethany days earlier. In other words, Martha said, "Thanks a lot Jesus! Our brother is dead because you are late. We believed you could heal him, but you took your time getting here and now he's dead."

To her credit, Martha made an abrupt U-turn and corrected her speech. She wisely said, "But I know, that even now, whatsoever you will ask of God, God will give it to you."

Jesus lovingly replied to His dear friend's grieving sister, "Your brother will rise again."

Martha was a Jew who believed in the resurrection of the dead. She correctly answered Jesus, "I know that he shall rise again in the resurrection at the last day." Martha believed in the Final Day!

Jesus answered by speaking the greatest words of all time! He proclaimed, "I am the resurrection, and the life: he who believes in me, though he were dead, yet shall he live; and whosoever lives and believes in me shall never die."

He asked Martha, "Do you believe this?"

Martha answered, "Yes, Lord. I believe that you are the Christ, the Son of God, which should come into the world."

Immediately, Martha went to tell Mary the good news that Jesus was calling her to meet Him. Mary bolted from the house to follow Martha. Her relatives and friends assumed Mary was going to the grave to mourn for her brother, and so they accompanied her. Instead, she traveled to the place outside of town where Martha encountered Jesus.

Upon seeing Jesus, Mary fell at his feet and said, "Lord, if you had been here, my brother would had not died." Jesus was moved with compassion as He saw Mary and the Jews weeping. Jesus wept too. Mary's friends realized how much Jesus loved Lazareth. Some of the Jews, however, mockingly said Jesus could have healed Lazareth since He opened the eyes of blind men.

In emotional agony, Jesus groaned as He walked toward the grave. Lazarus had been placed in a cave, and a stone covered it. Jesus instructed the people to remove the stone. Martha exclaimed, "Jesus, my brother has been dead four days! His body stinks."

Jesus replied, "Did I not tell you that if you believed, you would see the glory of God?"

The people removed the stone from the cave. Jesus looked up to Heaven and prayed, "Father, I thank You that You have heard Me. I know that You always hear Me. But because of the people standing around, I said this, that they may believe that You sent Me."

When he finished his prayer, Jesus cried out with a loud voice, "Lazarus, come forth!"

The Bible says that the dead man came out! His hands and feet were wrapped in grave clothes, and his face was wrapped with a cloth.

Jesus said to them, "Unbind him, and let him go."

What does it mean for us on the Final Day?

Jesus loved Lazarus as a dear friend. He truly cared about him. He wept at his grave. Yes, Jesus pitied Mary, Martha, and Lazarus' friends and relatives. More importantly, Jesus felt pity for all of mankind that was in bondage to death and Hades because of sin. He wept because His Father's wonderful creation was marred and scarred by Satan's revenge against God. Humans suffered sickness, pain, and death because of Satan, the devil.

As Jesus - the Son of God - befriended a human man named Lazarus, so too has Jesus befriended every man, woman, and child who believed on His name to save their souls from damnation. The King of Kings does not call Christians his "servants." He calls us his friends.

As Jesus prepared his disciples for his crucifixion, he told them: **I no longer call you servants, for a servant does not know what his master does. But I have called you friends, for everything that I have heard from My Father have I made known to you. (John 15:15)**

If you are a born again, baptized saint in Christ's holy church, you are Jesus' friend. He loves you as He loved Lazarus.

Almighty God never intended for people, animals, and plants to die. Originally, there was no death in the Garden of Eden. There was only life. Death was the result of Adam and Eve's disobedience to God and sin entered them. None of us can understand the sadness that God experiences every time an unsaved person dies and enters their grave. Without Jesus Christ as their savior, death has won another victory. Creation was never supposed to be this way. Satan introduced sin to humans, and everybody has paid the price - even animals and plants. Sin's salary is paid with the currency of death.

In the beginning of this marvelous story, Martha expressed to Jesus her religious belief in the resurrection of the dead. She had hope that the righteous would live again after going into their graves and descending to Hades. Martha is the one who fretted about preparing dinner for a full house of visitors when Jesus came to visit. Her sister Mary sat at Jesus' feet listening to him teach while Martha labored in the kitchen making a meal to satisfy everybody. Yet, this same Martha had hope! She believed in the resurrection of the dead.

In response, Jesus told Martha, "I am the resurrection, and the life: he that believeth in me, though he were dead, yet shall he live..."

Jesus did not say, "Martha, I believe in the resurrection too." He proclaimed that He *is* the resurrection!

If you repent of your sins, believe on the name of Jesus Christ to save your soul, and are baptized into His holy church, your dead body will be resurrected on the Final Day.

No man can come to me, except the Father which hath sent me draw him: and I will raise him up at the last day. (John 6:44)

You can be assured of it because Jesus is the resurrection. Believing on His name as Savior and believing in the resurrection are synonymous. Faith on the name of Jesus means you believe in the resurrection. Jesus is the resurrection. Faith in the promise of the resurrection requires belief on the name of Jesus to save your soul from eternal damnation. The glorious resurrection of Jesus Christ is our lively hope that we too shall be resurrected on the Final Day.

You are a valuable member of Jesus' inheritance which He purchased with His precious pure blood. He went to the Cross for you! You are His friend. And He will raise you up on the Final Day! He will not lose one soul given to Him by His Heavenly Father. Each person who heard the word of truth, the gospel of their salvation, and believed on the name of Jesus, and baptized into His church is sealed with the promised Holy Spirit unto the day of redemption. They have no reason to fear the sudden arrival of the Final Day. Jesus will raise them up on that day. This is why Christians participate in the precious rite of Holy Communion, also known as the Lord's Supper and the Eucharist (thanksgiving). In the holy meal, we eat His flesh and drink His blood to nourish our souls until the Final Day arrives. He promised to raise us up on the Final Day!

No man can come to me, except the Father which hath sent me draw him: and I will raise him up at the last day. (John 6:44)

Whoso eateth my flesh, and drinketh my blood, hath eternal life; and I will raise him up at the last day. (John 6:54)

THE SIN AMNESTY

I N THIS BOOK'S INTRODUCTION, I shared with you the true story of how the Holy Spirit inspired me to write a book in 1998 titled *Judgment Day*. As explained in the Introduction, I erred by adding the year 2000 to the title and in assuming the vision I received in 1998 was about anticipated chaos on December 31, 1999, caused by the Y2K computer rollover failure. There is something else I must tell you, however, before you close the covers of this book and put it on a shelf to collect dust.

When I finished writing the last chapter of Judgment Day 2000 in August 1998, the Holy Spirit whispered in my heart, "There is something I want you to say."

I asked Him to reveal it to me. The Holy Spirit instructed me, "Tell the people that I have declared a sin amnesty."

Puzzled by the unfamiliar term, I replied, "Lord, I have never heard of a sin amnesty. What is it?" He answered my question with a question. The Lord asked me, "Son, what is an amnesty?"

I said, "Lord, that's when a government announces that it will pardon lawbreakers who voluntarily turn themselves in to law enforcement and admit their guilt."

The Merriam-Webster Dictionary defines "amnesty" as, "the act of an authority (such as a government) by which pardon is granted to a large group of individuals."

And what is a pardon? According to the Merriam-Webster Dictionary, a pardon is "the excusing of an offense without exacting a penalty; a release from the legal penalties of an offense."

A synonym of pardon is remission. When something is remitted, it means that the offending party has been released from the guilt or penalty of their criminal acts.

And almost all things are by the law purged with blood; and without shedding of blood is no remission. (Hebrews 9:22)

This is the covenant that I will make with them after those days, saith the Lord, I will put my laws into their hearts, and in their minds will I write them; and their sins and iniquities will I remember no more. Now where remission of these is, there is no more offering for sin. (Hebrews 10:16-18)

All humans are lawbreakers. God gave Moses the Ten Commandments engraved by His finger on stone tablets. The commandments were not new information to Moses and the Hebrews. They had been known to mankind for a long time. God personally wrote them in stone for the benefit of the Hebrews. Abraham lived centuries before Moses was born, but Abraham kept the commandments! It verifies Enoch's claim that Pre-Flood men and women heard the Gospel. The Good News is that Jesus Christ paid the penalty of our sins of breaking God's commandments.

...because that Abraham obeyed my voice, and kept my charge, my commandments, my statutes, and my laws. (Genesis 26:5)

For whosoever shall keep the whole law, and yet offend in one point, he is guilty of all. (James 2:10)

Jesus Christ - the Son of God and the Last Adam - shed His holy blood on Calvary's cross for the remission of our sins. We commemorate His sacrifice every time we eat His flesh and drink His blood in the sacrament of the Lord's Supper, the Eucharist, our great thanksgiving feast.

And he took the cup, and gave thanks, and gave it to them, saying, Drink ye all of it; for this is my blood of the new testament, which is shed for many for the remission of sins. (Matthew 26:27-28)

What must we do to receive God's promise of a sin amnesty? Repent, believe on the name of Jesus Christ, and be baptized! John the Baptist "came into all the country about Jordan, preaching the baptism of repentance for the remission of sins." In the Book of Acts, Apostle Peter proclaimed the Good News to Jerusalem's Jews. He "let all the house of Israel know assuredly, that God hath made that same Jesus, whom ye have crucified, both Lord and Christ." When the Jews heard Peter's words, their hearts were pricked with conviction. They asked Peter and the other apostles, "Men and brethren, what shall we do?" Then Peter said unto them:

...Repent, and be baptized every one of you in the name of Jesus Christ for the remission of sins, and ye shall receive the gift of the Holy Ghost. For the promise is unto you, and to your children, and to all that are afar off, even as many as the Lord our God shall call. And with many other words did he testify and exhort, saying, Save yourselves from this untoward generation. (Acts 2:38-40)

Almighty God loves you so much that He sacrificed His only begotten Son on a cross for the remission of your sins against Him. It was when Jesus was nailed to the cross that God proclaimed a worldwide sin amnesty for mankind. Almighty God threw open His loving arms to receive all who come to Him for forgiveness. He amended the qualifications for membership in His race of chosen people. He enlarged the population of Israel by accepting more than Jews. Now Israel's membership is open to all races, tribes, and ethnic groups. This is truly Good News!

All Christians are obligated to share the Good News with other sinners who have not yet heard or accepted God's sin amnesty. The Great Commission obligates us to inform all sinners in every nation that God has offered to forgive their sins, pardon them from their just punishment, and even expunge their criminal records in Heaven's court. The sin amnesty is available to every man, woman, and child in every nation and among all races of mankind. All are chosen to be God's people! The terms are simple: Repent of your sins, believe on the name of Jesus Christ to save your soul, and be baptized into Christ's church in the name of the Father, and the Son, and the Holy Spirit. Any lawbreaker who turns in himself or herself and admits his or her guilt will be forgiven, pardoned, and their criminal records will be expunged in Heaven's court. Your file folder of sins will be empty on the Final Day when Jesus Christ sits upon His great white throne of judgment.

There is, however, a deadline to accept the terms of God's sin amnesty. You must surrender and turn yourself in to Him before you die or the arrival of the Final Day – whichever comes first. Individually, the sin amnesty abruptly ends the moment we take our last breath on earth. Corporately, the sin amnesty ends before the last trump and Jesus shouts that He has arrived in the atmosphere on clouds of great glory. If anybody foolishly ignores God's gracious sin amnesty, their punishment shall be doubly harsh on the Final Day. They had the opportunity to be forgiven, but rejected or ignored it. Woe unto them on the Day of Judgment.

You just finished reading my book about the Final Day of mankind. If you have never confessed to Almighty God that you are a lawbreaker who deserves eternal punishment, I beseech you to cry out to your Maker now and ask for forgiveness of your sins. Tell the wonderful Creator of all life that you believe on the name of Jesus Christ to save your soul. Ask Him to write your name in the Book of Life. Find a devout Christian pastor and ask him to baptize you in water in the name of the Father, and the Son, and the Holy Spirit. Confess with your mouth to other people that Jesus Christ is your Lord and Savior. Turn from your wicked ways and live! Ask God to fill you with his Holy Spirit. With the Holy Spirit's help, you can live a holy and righteous life until you die or the Final Day arrives - whichever comes first.

Your Maker does not desire that you spend eternity in the Lake of Fire. God earnestly desires that every man, woman, and child be saved through faith in Jesus Christ.

The Lord is not slack concerning his promise, as some men count slackness; but is longsuffering to us-ward, not willing that any should perish, but that all should come to repentance. (2 Peter 3:9)

Perhaps you are a confessing Christian, but are secretly trapped in sinful behavior. It could be sexual immorality such as fornication (sex between two unmarried people), adultery (sex between one or two married people), homosexuality (sex between two people of the same gender), or an addiction to pornography. Any sexual activity outside of marriage between one man and one woman is sin. You may be addicted to alcohol, illegal drugs, pain killers, antidepressants, gambling, or other destructive behavior. You may have a physically or emotionally abusive temper that explodes on other people and damages them. Or, you may be involved in financial crimes in your business or place of employment. Sin comes in a wide variety of shapes, colors, and sizes. Regardless, sin's salary is paid with death.

Whatever is outside the commandments of God is sin, and you must repent and turn from it. Don't let your pride prevent you from admitting you have problems and need help. All of us were born into a sinful world. We are flawed creatures living in sin-prone human bodies. I tell people, "God made us with dirt and water. We are mud pies with eyes!"

The Good News is that God's grace is greater than our sins. Father knows that we dwell in mortal bodies of human flesh that are subject to temptation and sinful thoughts and actions. We desire to obey and please Him, yet we often fail in our daily lives to be the person we desire to be for God's glory. He is not looking for ways to condemn and reject us. He gave us a solution for our dilemma. He gave us a Savior. We need our Savior more than once. We need Jesus Christ every day no matter how long we have been a Christian. Yes, Jesus was there on the day you asked Him to save your soul. Without Him, we could not enter into salvation. His saving grace did not stop on the day you were saved. It flows abundantly every minute of each day of your life. I often say, "Grace is like gravy. It goes with everything." Whatever you did, said, or thought today, whatever problem is troubling your soul, whatever stress you are under, put a heaping helping of God's grace on it and watch how your Savior will get you through it.

Your Heavenly Father does not desire to punish you. He already knows the sins you've committed. He desires you to admit your guilt to Him and yourself. Stop denying the truth about your life. Don't allow your pride to prevent you from admitting you are a sinner who deserves to be punished in Hell. Admit that you've done many wrong things in your life. You have a Heavenly Father who dearly loves you and desires to forgive you. He has an even bigger surprise waiting for you. Every person whose name is written in the Book of Life will live forever with God in a new Garden of Eden. Do you desire to be there? Jesus Christ desires to call you His friend. He cannot call you His friend until you renounce your citizenship in Satan's kingdom of this world.

The sin amnesty is still in effect. It could expire any day. None of us know the hour the Final Day will arrive. Nor do we know the final second our heart will stop beating. The Bible says that our lives are like a wind that passes by and never returns. Therefore, nobody should foolishly dismiss or delay their acceptance of the sin amnesty. All who put their trust in Jesus Christ shall be preserved and saved on the Final Day. You will be marked by angels and protected. The angels will not have a problem with mistaken identities on the Final Day. Each human will have a mark: the mark of the beast or the mark of Jesus Christ. The angels are well trained and proficient in distinguishing who are the wheat and the tares.

I fulfilled the Lord's instruction, to the best of my human ability, to tell you about the Final Day. Likewise, I have now told you about the sin amnesty. The ball is in your court. It's up to you to make a move. Will you move toward God or keep running away from him?

Say this prayer aloud and mean it.

"Almighty God, I come to you as a sinner. I have violated all of your commandments. I deserve punishment because I am a lawbreaker. I read that you declared a sin amnesty to forgive and expunge from your court records all the wrong things I have done, said, and thought in my life. I desire to be forgiven. Today I confess that Jesus Christ is my Savior, Messiah, and Lord. I will obey and follow Him the rest of the days of my life. Please write my name in your Book of Life. Please preserve my soul from eternal damnation. Please fill me with your Holy Spirit. I promise to find a church pastor who will baptize me in water. And I promise to tell other sinners that I am now forgiven by faith in Jesus Christ. Thank you for forgiving my sins, and thank you for saving my soul. I pray these things in the name of Jesus Christ. Amen."

If you sincerely prayed this prayer, please tell me so I can rejoice with you. Contact me at FinalDay.com and enter your email to receive correspondence from me.

Your friend,

Richard Wiles

A wretched sinner saved by God's grace

ABOUT THE AUTHOR

Richard D. Wiles is a husband, father, and grandfather. He is also a business executive, entrepreneur, faith futurist, talk show host, news commentator, author, presbyter, and teaching elder. He married Susan Llewellyn on June 1, 1974. They have two children: Jeremy Wiles and Karissa Washburn. Presently, Richard and Susan have 10 grandchildren. Eight of the grandchildren were adopted from Russia, Ukraine, and Ecuador.

Mr. Wiles was born in Western Maryland. Most of Mr. Wiles' ancestors were members of the German Reformed Church who migrated from Europe to America in the 18th and 19th centuries. They were members of a church jointly established in 1747 by German Reformed and Lutheran settlers in Western Maryland. Mr. Wiles has relatives today who are members of the same Reformed church.

Richard D. Wiles' career in the communications media industry started at age 21 in 1975 as an advertising sales representative for a new FM radio station. In 1980, Mr. Wiles became one of the first sales professionals in the USA to sell cable television advertising. He was an early pioneer in the cable television advertising interconnect industry when he built and managed an advertising sales rep team that sold local and regional advertising in Mid-Atlantic states. In the mid-1980s, Mr. Wiles worked for the Christian Broadcasting Network as the national marketing manager for affiliate relations for the CBN Cable Network, which later became the Family Channel. He worked for Trinity Broadcasting Network in the 1990s as director of marketing.

Richard D. Wiles was the Republican nominee for the District 2B seat in the Maryland House of Delegates in 1994. His opponent was the former Democratic Majority Leader of the House of Delegates. Few people gave him any chance of defeating the powerful state legislator. It was the closest election in the State of Maryland in 1994. When Mr. Wiles went to bed on election night, he was trailing the incumbent by 10 votes. The election was decided by absentee votes and Mr. Wiles lost by 72 votes.

The calling of God to preach the gospel first came upon Mr. Wiles in the mid-1980s when he was living in Virginia Beach, VA, while working for CBN. He struggled many years trying to walk in the assignment to deliver an unpopular message to the American people to repent of their sins. The calling of God returned even stronger in April 1998 when he experienced a profound vision of a major city on fire. He resigned from TBN in September 1998 and traveled throughout the USA speaking to church congregations and Bible study groups, and appearing on local radio and television talk shows.

Mr. Wiles launched a radio talk show in Dallas/Ft. Worth, TX in May 1999. The show was originally broadcast on an AM radio station, but the station changed its format five months later. With no time slots available on other local radio stations, Mr. Wiles was compelled to find an alternative. He chose international shortwave radio and Internet streaming. Thus, he turned adversity into an opportunity by becoming a pioneer in 1999 in live Internet streaming and audio-on-demand media distribution. He has often quipped, "I was podcasting before there were pods."

The original name of the radio show was *America's Hope*. His message was "Jesus Christ is America's only hope." The weekday talk show was renamed *Trunews* in 2003.

Mr. Wiles recorded over 5,000 interviews between 1999 to 2016. His guests included members of the United States Senate and House, governors, former intelligence agents including the former chief of the Russian KGB, retired U.S. generals and admirals, best-selling authors, scientists, astronauts, solar scientists, economists, billionaires, investors, financial advisors, celebrities, famous athletes, pastors, evangelists, and Bible teachers.

In 2008, Richard Wiles sponsored a meeting of Christian pastors in Nairobi, Kenya. Five thousand pastors gathered in Nairobi's Kenyatta Convention Center to hear his message that "Jesus Christ is Kenya's only hope." His ministry was among the first organizations to respond to the mega-earthquake that struck Haiti on January 12, 2010. Days after the earthquake, Trunews airlifted tons of food, water, blankets, tents, and other goods to Port-au-Prince. Trunews also chartered a cargo plane in Jamaica that transported humanitarian aid to orphanages in Jacmel, Haiti. Trunews erected heavy-duty military-style tents to house children in numerous towns who had been orphaned by the earthquake. The ministry also kept the temporary orphanages well-stocked with food throughout 2010.

Trunews transitioned in 2017 to a roundtable discussion format distributed on the Internet as a video program. Presently, Mr. Wiles continues to appear on Trunews as a commentator, but his passion is devoted to building global digital platforms for Christian media content. His mission is to complete the project by 2030. He also desires to build a Biblical theme park and Bible college for children.

Contact Information
To Connect With
Richard D. Wiles

I would love to receive comments from you! Please communicate with me to:

- Write an online review of Final Day.
- Share comments about the Second Coming of Jesus.
- Tell me the impact that Final Day had on you.
- Let me know the "aha!" revelations you had while reading the book.
- Tell me your insights into the Second Coming of Jesus.
- Receive my newsletter.
- Join the Final Day social media community.
- Know where I will be appearing to speak about the Final Day.
- Receive invitations to participate with me in special online or in-person events.
- Be the first to know about my next book, video, conference, or any other project.

Sign up for my free newsletter!
FinalDay.com